No Small Dreams

No Small Dreams

J. ERIK JONSSON—TEXAS VISIONARY

Darwin Payne

DALLAS
DeGolyer Library
Southern Methodist University
2014

In memory of Kenneth Brent Jonsson

Contents

Introduction

John Erik Jonsson, the only child of hardworking Swedish immigrants, latched on early to the American dream of success. Defying his father's Old World notion that he take over the family's small cigar shop, he became a visionary industrialist who led then-unknown Texas Instruments to the top of the electronics revolution that transformed American life. Then, following the assassination of President Kennedy in his adopted city of Dallas, he guided the city in its darkest hour, becoming the greatest mayor in its history.

When he enrolled as a freshman in 1918 at Rensselaer Polytechnic Institute, Jonsson struggled to make up academic deficiencies while holding part-time jobs. He graduated on time, and then began a remarkable journey that led him to the National Business Hall of Fame.

As a wealthy industrialist, knowing full well that education had provided his entry point to success, he promoted the value of learning, especially the sciences and engineering, and he backed up his convictions with his philanthropy. Many institutions benefited immensely from his gifts. Eleven of them awarded him honorary doctorates.

Important as his philanthropy was, John Erik Jonsson is best remembered for more visible achievements elsewhere, especially at Texas Instruments. His leadership there led to his inclusion in the first class elected to the National Business Hall of Fame, one of only four living Americans chosen.

Such an irony that Dallas, a proud Texas city then noted for its insularity, looked to a Brooklyn native to lead it from its despair after the assassination of President Kennedy. In his seven years as mayor, Jonsson left an enduring legacy: an architectural gem in its marvelous new city hall, an airport that became one of the world's biggest and busiest,

a Goals for Dallas program that involved citizens of all walks of life, a
new central library, a coveted designation as an All-American City, and
a new sense of self-esteem for the city.

Leadership came naturally. His tall frame, deep voice, easy manner,
and commanding presence reinforced the fact. After being the guiding force in Texas Instruments' transformation from an oil-exploration
company into a worldwide modern electronics firm, civic responsibilities dominated his schedule.

His pattern of leadership was consistent. He envisioned long-term
goals, carefully recruited those who could carry them out, convinced
them of the worth of their assignment, and monitored their progress
regularly. In a large sense, he was an educator with a huge classroom.

Through his Goals for Dallas program, he enlisted thousands of
ordinary residents to define what they wanted Dallas to be. He played
the dominant role in building Dallas/Fort Worth International Airport,
then the world's biggest airport and the primary catalyst for the entire
region's development. Against significant opposition, he led the drive
for a new and dramatic city hall, now recognized as one of the nation's
most significant public buildings.

Municipal politics in Dallas was nonpartisan, a fact that Jonsson
carefully observed. However, he was a lifelong Republican, cut from the
traditional GOP cloth of the day. Always a pragmatist, he was a champion of reason and scientific inquiry and was especially committed to
research in all things.

Jonsson's longtime marriage to Margaret Fonde, his Tennessee belle,
produced three children who became accomplished adults in their own
rights. By his own acknowledgment, though, his family life took a back
seat to his many business and civic obligations. Although he had told
his long-suffering wife that he would retire early so they could travel
the world and enjoy the comforts that hard work made possible, that
moment never came.

It is impossible to truly calculate the impact of a man like J. Erik
Jonsson. The ripple effects of his work and philanthropy go on and
on and on in numerous areas: the technology of the information age,
higher education, medical research, D/FW Airport, social agencies,
Dallas's monumental city hall, and eager youngsters and researchers at
the J. Erik Jonsson Central Public Library.

What is certain is that Jonsson well understood the longtime payoff inherent in such work. These things would make a difference in the quality of American life. Always he was motivated by the lines from a favorite childhood poem, "Ulysses," by Alfred, Lord Tennyson. It became his personal credo in life: "to strive, to seek, to find, and not to yield."

Acknowledgements

J ohn Erik Jonsson kept a meticulous record of his activities beginning with his childhood. It grew in size and complexity as his life became increasingly noteworthy and varied. Almost all of these documents are now in 170 containers constituting the J. Erik Jonsson Papers at Southern Methodist University's DeGolyer Library. I am especially indebted to Russell L. Martin III, DeGolyer's librarian and director, for the many courtesies and assistance he provided as I made my way through these papers. Indeed, as head of SMU's DeGolyer Library he is the publisher of the book, and a most distinguished one indeed. Joan Gosnell, the university archivist, was an always cheerful helpmate who assisted me in countless ways. Ada Negraru was especially helpful with photographs, as was Carla Mendiola. Others on the staff who have made my days at DeGolyer so pleasant include Pamalla Anderson, Cynthia Franco, Terre Heydari, Anne E. Peterson, Betty Friedrich, Ben Huseman, and Kathy Rome.

I happily spent most of my working life as an SMU professor before retirement, and even after "retirement" it provided provided financial resources that led to the publication of this biography.

Members of Jonsson's family were unfailingly helpful during the rather long process between inception and publication. They provided details that gave me a better understanding of the man they knew as father and grandfather, and without exception made no effort to influence the final product. It would be natural, though, for some of them to disagree with my emphasis or failure to emphasize certain aspects of Jonsson's life, but I hope they find this work to be a fair representation of the man they so much admired.

Of the family members I think first of a grandson, the late Kenneth Brent Jonsson, who initially encouraged me to undertake this biography of the grandfather he resembled so much. Tragically, before this book could be completed, Kenny died from a malignant brain tumor, leaving his wife Holly and two young twin sons, Will and Oliver. Margaret Ellen Jonsson Rogers, Erik Jonsson's daughter, gave me full access to family documents in her possession that are not duplicated in the Jonsson papers at DeGolyer. In our pleasant interviews she also enhanced my understanding of her father as only a daughter can do. Erik Jonsson's eldest son, Philip (Kenny's father), was especially gracious in interviews and various communications throughout my work, and I am indebted to him and to his wife Diane for their support. Steven Ward Jonsson (Kenny's brother and Philip's son), gave me access to a number of documents he had collected, including a fine tape recording interview he and his father made with Erik and Margaret Jonsson. I appreciated especially the support of Philip's daughters, Christina Ann Jonsson, Suzanne Elizabeth Jonsson and Eileen Margaret (Petie).

The second of Erik Jonsson's sons, Kenneth Alan, now deceased, lived in California. His contributions are reflected in excellent interviews conducted by Richard Tuck.

I am especially indebted to Richard Tuck for his careful research on Erik Jonsson, which he completed prior to my own work. Richard, a former TI employee, electrical engineer, and later a technical consultant, graciously turned over his research files, transcripts of interviews, and photographs of Jonsson's early homes in Brooklyn and New Jersey and his places of employment. Many thanks to you, Richard, for your kindness and your excellent work.

A constant sounding board and source of information about the workings of Texas Instruments and of Jonsson himself was the late Bryan F. Smith, a retired company officer and board member who not only became a friend but who gave me access to his own unpublished work concerning Texas Instruments. He read early drafts of the manuscript, and I profited greatly from his keen eye, his knowledge, his perspectives, and his companionship.

Carl J. (Tommy) Thomsen, another early and long-time TI executive and board member, now deceased, was another knowledgeable source who submitted to interviews and made comments about pertinent portions of the manuscript. Rolf Haberecht another former TI official, read the manuscript and made valuable suggestions. Another interviewee who helped was the late Bryghte Godbold, who not only worked with Jonsson at TI but who also headed up the Goals for Dallas program.

John W. Wilson and Phil Bogan, both of Texas Instruments, read and commented on certain portions of the manuscript, and they provided me with their own authorized historical work on the company.

I am thankful to former Dallas mayor Wes Wise, who served on the city council while Jonsson was mayor and then succeeded him in that office. Wise read and made comments on sections of the manuscript, gave me interesting insights from his unique vantage point, and along with the late Bob Porter of the Sixth Floor Museum at Dealey Plaza conducted lengthy oral histories with Jonsson.

Other interviews—some by telephone to check specific points and others in person—were important. These included William E. Cothrum, the late Charles G. Cullum, Dick Davis, Gifford K. Johnson, W. Scott McDonald, Peter O'Donnell Jr., Ross Perot, George Schrader, John Schoellkopf, Carl Sewell, and Sid Stahl.

Dan Foster and the late Charles C. Sprague helped me recapture the contribution Jonsson made to the Southwestern Medical School to retain its future Nobel Prize winners, Michael Brown and Joseph Goldstein. I am indebted to Drs. Brown and Goldstein for permitting me to use an e-mail message they sent to Dr. Foster, and especially to Dr. Brown for recapturing that moment for me.

Michael V. Hazel was as usual a source of helpful information on many aspects. Jerome Sims, photo librarian at the *Dallas Morning News*; and Lindsey Richardson, Megan Bryant, and Gary Mack at the Sixth Floor Museum at Dealey Plaza; and Kerry Adams at the Old Red Museum of Dallas County History and Culture, helped with certain photographs that seemed essential to have. I especially thank Diane Bumpas, board member at the Old Red and guiding light for its J. Erik Jonsson exhibit for her encouragement, and also Zac Harmon, executive director and CFO. My thanks to Whitney C. Harris for helping me solve a technical problem regarding the manuscript.

Surely any author is thankful for the careful and often inspiring work of his or her copyeditor. I was particularly fortunate to have Kip Keller of Austin perform that work, noting more errors and inconsistencies in the manuscript than I would like to admit, and also sharpening my prose with his careful eye.

As always, I am lucky to be encouraged by my wife, Phyllis Schmitz

Payne, a sounding board for this book and for so many of the things we share together. Thanks to my sons and their wives and children, Mark and Kristin Payne and their son (and my grandson) Parker; Scott and Brandy Payne and their son (and my grandson) Grant; my daughter Sarah and her husband Bryan Kennedy; and my daughter Hannah Payne. My sister June Payne Marco, who lives in Dallas, was and is unfailing in her encouragement, and my other sister, Sally Ann Payne Estes, always lends her support from her home in Slaton, Texas, as does her husband Robert James Estes III.

A Boy in Brooklyn

In the early twentieth century, children of hardworking immigrants in Brooklyn's Bedford-Stuyvesant neighborhood busied themselves on the streets with all sorts of improvised activities—playing one ole cat with sawed-off broom handles, pitching rings at nails on a board, scrambling about in all kinds of things. Sometimes that new marvel, a horseless carriage, sputtered noisily across their territory. "Get a horse!" they often shouted.

One who remembered uttering that cry with his friends was John Erik Jonsson, only child of an immigrant Swedish couple.[1] Little could he realize that noisy automobiles, the electric lights replacing kerosene in dark walk-up flats, and the single-engine airplanes he saw rounding the Statue of Liberty in races marked a revolution that was changing the world faster than ever in history.

Henry Ford's automobiles would make the horse-drawn carriage disappear. Airplanes would carry passengers from coast to coast. Already, the hum of the electric motor was replacing steam-engine noise. The miracle of moving pictures was attracting curious crowds, and Edison's phonograph was presaging a new home entertainment industry. By the time Jonsson and his Brooklyn pals became adults, commercial radio would be the first true medium of mass communications. By their middle age, television would be common. How much further could it go?

Much, much further. An even-more sophisticated revolution stemming from breakthroughs in solid-state physics would create an unimaginable new age in the last decades of the century. The transistor, the integrated circuit, and the microprocessor would affect everything from the kitchen to space exploration. Millions of pieces of data could

be summoned in microseconds on a home computer or even on a laptop and stored for recall in an instant. Jonsson, the kid known as the
"big Swede," would immerse himself in all these changes—from the
automobile to the microprocessor.

It started for him with the motorcycle. Just as the automobile
became the favored vehicle for a Sunday-afternoon drive, the motorcycle (or "half-baked" automobile) was the choice of the "speed bug" who
moved down the streets with wide-open throttle. It captured teenager
Erik's heart. *Overland Monthly* described the motorcycle as a godsend
for "the man with ambition . . . who desires to have a business of his
own, who feels that he will be able to be more than a hired man." Such
a man Erik Jonsson became.[2]

His Swedish parents had immigrated separately to the United States.
His father, Johan Peter Jonsson, was born January 23, 1854, into a farming family. Since farming then was in decline in Sweden, Johan began
selling fine linens. At the age of thirty-two, he departed with thousands
of Swedes for the land of opportunity—the United States of America.[3]

Arriving in Philadelphia in 1886, he found a job in a textile mill.
That he was independent, stubborn, hardworking, and honest seems
certain. What was most striking at first sight, though, was his size. He
stood five feet two inches tall and weighed in maturity as much as 250
pounds. Erik thought he looked "like a sawed-off Santa Claus without
the beard."[4] By 1890, Johan was a department store salesman, and was
living in Brooklyn a year later.

An ornate document celebrates his marriage in 1893 to Ellen Char-
lotta Palmquist, who also had emigrated from Sweden.[5] She was one of
fourteen children. Later, Erik recalled that her father operated a delica-
tessen. In 1880 at the age of eleven, Ellen wrote to her brother from her
boarding school and declared (in Swedish) that the classes were "very
easy," adding, "I know I will be the best," showing early the confidence
that marked her entire life.[6]

She arrived in Boston in 1891 at the age of twenty-two, working at
first as a "servant girl."[7] Two of her brothers were already in the United
States. Joe worked as one of the last captains of the commercial sailing
vessels plying the Atlantic and then became a bank custodian in Larch-
mont, New York. Fred, a conductor on the Pennsylvania Railroad, lived
in Rahway, New Jersey.[8]

As Erik grew up, he was closer to his mother than to his father. His
strong business sense came from his father, and his mother, he be-

lieved, "had the quality" and made him appreciate a broader perspective on life.[9]

Ellen made her way to the New York City area, where she met her future husband at a dinner party for Swedish immigrants.[10] Johan Peter was fourteen years older and a half-foot shorter, but his experience as a settled, solid man must have appealed to Ellen. Their wedding took place at "Three 21 St. John's Place" in Brooklyn before three witnesses.[11]

By 1900, "John" Peter Jonsson (he then preferred "John" to "Johan") owned a "cigar shop" at 144 Fifth Avenue in Brooklyn at a stop for the elevated railroad to Manhattan. The shop offered far more than tobacco. One could buy newspapers, candy, notions, a low-alcohol beer known as *svag* (*svagdricka*, "weak drink" in Swedish), and other goods. John and Ellen lived above on the second floor.[12]

Later, Erik's father sometimes wished he had acted on his impulse to buy shares in the American Tobacco Company when James B. Duke organized it in the 1890s. Had he done so, he thought he could have made a substantial amount of money. Instead, he invested his savings in a cigar shop. For the rest of his working days, he was tied to its demanding daily routine. From as early as young Erik could remember, his father, determined to make up for his missed opportunity, sought to make a killing on Wall Street. He never succeeded.[13]

The 1900 U.S. Census indicates that in the early years of John and Ellen's marriage, a baby was born and died. In the space for the number of deceased children of Ellen Palmquist Jonsson, there appears the single digit "1." Erik seems never to have known this. But the 1910 Census fails to list a deceased child. The "1" listed in 1900 might have been an error, or the couple might have preferred to erase memories of their loss.[14]

If the Jonssons did lose their first child, the birth on September 6, 1901, of John Erik Jonsson gave them even more occasion to be thankful. Erik grew up as the adored only child of a mother who was thirty-two or thirty-three and a father who was forty-seven when he was born.

On the day of his birth, a self-proclaimed anarchist fired two pistol shots and fatally wounded President William McKinley in Buffalo, New York. The apprehended shooter, Leon Czolgosz, confessed. Speculation arose that he must have been part of a conspiracy. Within two months, he was convicted and executed.

Another presidential assassination would not occur until shortly after Erik Jonsson had personally greeted President John F. Kennedy at the Dallas airport in 1963. Within the hour, he had to tell an awaiting crowd that the president had been shot. As in the case of Czolgosz, millions of people refused to believe that Lee Harvey Oswald acted alone.

Bedford Avenue, a wide asphalt-paved street, was the main thoroughfare in the Jonssons' Brooklyn neighborhood. Its residents, not long removed from Europe, worked hard to achieve the American Dream. Erik was so familiar with their accents that he believed he could determine whether they were from eastern or western Europe or from a particular country. He remembered his neighbors as being unusually egalitarian, accepting the variety of those around them without prejudice.[15]

By the time of Erik's earliest memories, his father had relocated his cigar shop to Bergen Street, near a barn where trolley cars were parked. Conductors and motormen bought cigarettes or got change at the cigar shop for games of craps outside. After the gamblers departed each day, little Erik sorted through the dust and occasionally found a coin.[16]

Erik saw work defining his father's life. John Peter opened at six or six thirty in the morning to catch early commuters, not closing until ten thirty or eleven. Every afternoon, Ellen minded the shop while he napped on a plank stretched between two wooden shipping containers and used a roll of newspapers as his pillow. How a roly-poly figure could manage to sleep like that amazed young Erik.[17]

John Peter liked order and promptness. He spent money only when absolutely necessary, often dismaying Ellen, who worked almost as hard in the shop as her husband, along with the additional responsibilities of housekeeping and supervising Erik. John Peter spanked his son just once. "I never broke his rule of law after that," Erik recalled, for it was "a very thorough going over."[18]

During Erik's first twelve years, the family lived in four different places in Brooklyn. Inevitably, their apartment would be in a walk-up above or not far from the store, no higher than the second floor. In Erik's memory, these apartments seemed roomy and pleasant, but he later realized that they were "small, dark and mean," their chief recommendation being cheap rent. Each time the Jonssons moved, it was with the idea of gaining more light from the outside. In Erik's preschool years, the only light the family had besides sunshine was from kerosene lamps.[19]

It was apparent that in size Erik would take after his mother. At an early age he was nicknamed the "big Swede." Confusion reigned at the end of his first day in kindergarten. When Ellen arrived for him, the teachers did not know of an "Erik." He had used his first name, John, somehow thinking he could escape the nickname "Swede," which made him feel foreign. "I wanted to be as American as they [the other children] were," he recalled.[20]

Despite his robust appearance, Erik frequently was ill. "Until I was seven years old, I was sick abed with one childhood disease or another," he would recall. When he was four, a cyst in his right ear led to a mastoid operation that left him with half an eardrum and a deep cut behind his ear. The doctor had presented his parents with a dire possibility: "Your boy will either come off dead or he probably will have lost a good deal of reasoning power." The result was neither—he lost only a small part of his hearing.[21]

Erik later had a strong memory of his mother as "a steadfast, solicitous person for whom no chore was too great if it could add to the comfort or welfare of an ailing child." When he was three, she played recordings for him by Jenny Lind, the "Swedish Nightingale," on the phonograph, invented by Thomas Edison, whose laboratory was on the other side of Manhattan in Orange, New Jersey.[22]

She usually read to her son at bedtime. Later, as he began reading himself, Horatio Alger Jr. books became particular favorites. (As an adult, Erik would be cited as a poster child for the Alger stories.) He later favored Mark Twain too, and when old enough he began swapping with neighborhood boys, holding Tom Sawyer's example in mind.[23]

Ellen made certain that her son experienced cultural activities as well the business lessons his hard-nosed father gave him. She sometimes escorted him and his friends to Manhattan to visit museums and theaters. Unlike her husband, Ellen was very proficient in English. Her only difficulty was in pronouncing the letter *j*. In the midst of a conversation, she might occasionally startle a listener by saying something like "a yar of yelly."[24]

In contrast, John Peter Jonsson never lost his heavy accent. Yet Erik's parents rarely spoke Swedish in his presence. They wanted to make certain that their son was thoroughly Americanized. Erik learned only a few phrases in Swedish, a fact he later regretted.[25]

When Erik was about six, he saw President Theodore Roosevelt in a carriage on Bedford Avenue. "My father was a Republican, and so naturally he [Roosevelt] was my idol."[26] The adult Erik Jonsson also was a Republican.

At nine, Erik witnessed another memorable sight—a flying competition in which aviators turned around the Statute of Liberty. The famous "birdman" John B. Moisant, soon afterward to die in a fall from his airplane, won that competition. Erik saw other races, too, in which aviators often used the Statue of Liberty as a turn marker. His memories reemerged more than a half century later when he became the key figure in building the world's largest airport.[27]

Erik joined neighborhood games as soon as he was big enough. Boys often took to the apartment rooftops, which were covered with tarpaper and pebbles. Inevitably, the urge arose to toss pebbles at passersby below and then jump from one roof to the next to escape detection. Sometimes a miscreant would travel an entire block by rooftop before descending and walking jauntily past his target, whistling innocently.[28]

Halloween was far rougher. Gang fights sometimes broke out. Boys would fill their stockings (which they wore with short pants until they were about twelve) with flour and flail their opponents with them. Some tougher gangs went further, putting pebbles or rocks in the stockings.[29]

When Jonsson was about six or seven, a neighborhood bully began picking on him. A fight ensued, and Erik suffered a black eye and a loose tooth. It was the only fight he ever had, and he was "prouder" of his black eye than anything.[30]

At the first opportunity, he learned to ride a borrowed bicycle. When he got one of his own, he used it to deliver cigars to his father's customers. He played on neighborhood baseball and football teams, and became a formidable collector of baseball cards. Erik had a head start because the Sweet Caporal cigarettes his father sold contained the cards.[31]

The forerunners of the Brooklyn Dodgers—the "Superbas"—played at Washington Park, a few blocks away. Sometimes Erik paid for a seat in the bleachers, but more often he and others peered in from the outside. He saw players who became legends—including Christy Mathewson; the infield trio of Joe Tinker, Johnny Evers, and Frank Chance; and the popular outfielder Casey Stengel.[32]

Among Ellen Jonsson's friends was Mrs. Anderson, a dressmaker who lived on Staten Island with her husband and their two sons. Erik and his mother frequently visited them, riding the ferry to get there. The Andersons had ducks, chickens, and a cow, and Ellen thought this was a healthy contrast to Brooklyn. For several summers, she boarded her son with the Andersons. Those days later took on an idyllic cast for Erik. He remembered sweet Concord grapes growing on the Anderson fence, wildflowers and berries, the trees loaded with apples.[33]

Early report cards show Erik as a student who was perhaps better than average but not by much. They indicate frequent illnesses—nineteen absences in a five-month period in the fourth grade. By the sixth grade, his attendance had improved, and Erik was making straight As for "effort" and straight B-pluses in "proficiency."[34]

John Peter Jonsson, assuming that one day he would pass on his shop to Erik, was determined to imbue him with a strong business sense. At the age of nine, Erik started his own business, the Jonsson Stamp and Coin Co. Soon he concentrated on stamps, buying supplies with his twenty-five-cent weekly allowance. He made solitary forays into lower Manhattan to visit such dealers as Scott's to buy unsorted packages, sorted them, repackaged them, and sold them to friends for a small profit. A special thrill came one day when he found a stamp valued at $12. He even distributed "approval sheets," for which his customers paid only for the stamps they kept. Erik arranged with superintendents of apartment houses in Manhattan to obtain discarded envelopes bearing canceled stamps. Many years later in retirement, Jonsson, who still had a part of his old stamp collection, said that if he needed money and could not sell himself in any other way, he would go into the stamp and coin business.[35]

Business tutoring from his father began at an early age. "Now, my boy," John Peter once told him, "vhen you grow up, you vill no doubt go in business and if you go in business vit a Swede, you can trust him. If you go in business with a Norvegian, watch him, and if you are tinking of going in business with a Dane, do not go in business." Jonsson later suspected that some Dane must have given his father a "good trimming." Jonsson later related his father's advice to the Danish ambassador to the United States, who did not find it funny.[36]

Although profit margins were small for John Peter's business, he managed to open a second shop on Bergen Street (evidently after closing the first one), then another on Utica, and finally a third store on Sterling Place near Albany Avenue. Each was operated by a single person—John Peter, Ellen, and a hired hand named Johansen.[37]

Erik remembered especially the store on Utica, which the family lived above. Renting a room from them was Johansen, a meticulous dresser with a Vandyke beard. On a freezing night in early January 1908, a fire broke out. Erik heard his mother yelling to his father and to Johansen to hurry out as she frantically wrapped her son in a quilt and carried him down the stairs amid "angry tongues of flame." John Peter escaped in his nightgown and a stocking cap, clutching a bath mat he had grabbed for extra warmth. But where was Johansen? The stairway was taking on the appearance of a small inferno when at last he appeared, walking through the doorway with great dignity, "a perfect picture, perfectly dressed, with not a single hair seeming to be out of place." The next morning, Erik helped his father sift through the ruins to see what could be found. Erik spotted a few silver coins in the ashes, but the paper money had been incinerated. Almost nothing of value remained. John Peter closed the store.[38]

⌒

When Erik was about ten, he began accompanying his father across the Brooklyn Bridge to Wall Street. John Peter would have $200–$300 with which to speculate in the market. Father and son would watch the ticker tape for a couple of hours before returning home. It was a great experience for Erik, but not a profitable one for his dad. "Papa did nothing but lose money," his son recalled.[39]

John Peter had a special distaste for Democrats. When Erik was in high school, his father implored him "as soon as possible" to join a "good Republican Young Men's Club." The adult Erik, a lifelong Republican, believed his father would have been shocked to know that on some occasions he had voted for a Democrat.[40]

John Peter's hardheadedness, especially concerning money, often brought him into sharp conflict with Ellen. Sometimes she resorted to subterfuge. Erik began taking piano lessons from a neighborhood woman, paying extra to practice on her piano. Soon it became apparent that he needed his own piano. John Peter would not have approved, so Ellen secretly purchased one on installments from her household allowance. Rather than experiencing John Peter's certain ire, she kept the piano at the teacher's house. The time came when the secret had to be revealed because the Jonssons were moving across Manhattan to Montclair, New Jersey, where John Peter was opening a new cigar shop. "The scene was stormy," Erik recalled, but "finally my father became accustomed to the idea that from then on we were to have a piano around the house."[41]

The move to Montclair took place in 1913, when Erik was entering the seventh grade. He was twelve years old. A different life awaited him, but the Brooklyn years always remained vivid. In later years, he spoke in great detail about his childhood there. "It was pretty thin living, but it really wasn't bad," he recalled.[42]

Becoming a Workaholic

The Jonssons moved to New Jersey so their son could experience country air and a better environment. Montclair was a prosperous town half a dozen miles north of Newark, worlds removed from Brooklyn. Erik saw it as "a rich man's town." Many of its workingmen commuted to lower Manhattan's financial district. "All the kids around me lived in fine houses," Erik later said. "I wasn't an untouchable but I wasn't a member of the club either. I was a minority."[1] He could hear people discussing the future and ways to shape it—not how to put the next meal on the table. (Later, he would guess that this was where his Goals for Dallas program began.)[2]

Despite Erik's feelings of being "a little bit alone," there is no evidence of any sense of inferiority on his part as he entered seventh grade at Watchung Elementary. He was confident and outgoing, big for his age.[3]

As usual, the family lived above John Peter's shop, located at Montclair's principal business intersection, Park and Watchung Streets, across from the Erie Railroad's Lackawanna station. Commercial neighbors included a grocery store, a market, and a barbershop. Jonsson's corner location offered two sides for signs: "Ice Cream & Soda Water" and "All Kinds of Imported & Domestic Cigars."[4] As in Brooklyn, his shop carried tobacco products, sporting goods, stationery, ice cream, candy, and other items. Few men rivaled John Peter's ability to identify the best cigar. Even Erik became expert at it, although his special assignment was to tend to the soda fountain.[5]

In the three-room apartment, Erik slept on a wire cot with a thin mattress doubled over for comfort. When a friend spent the night, the mattress unfolded to accommodate both boys. Ellen Jonsson worked even longer hours than before, and the family was able to afford an African American woman, "Annie," as their cook.[6]

Erik joined the Watchung baseball team, which was well uniformed in contrast to his Brooklyn team. A team photograph shows the adult manager in a black suit and tie. There is even a batboy. Erik appears surprisingly poised, nearly grown up in his new environment. He still maintained one advantage—access to baseballs, bats and gloves at his father's shop.[7]

An early Montclair friend was Arthur Sylvester, later a reporter for the *Newark Evening News* and assistant secretary of defense for public affairs under Presidents John F. Kennedy and Lyndon B. Johnson. When a teacher offered extra credit for reading books, Jonsson and Sylvester competed fiercely with each other. One of Erik's favorite authors was Burt L. Standish (a pen name of Gilbert Patten), who wrote the popular Frank Merriwell novels for young people about a Yale college athlete.[8]

In keeping with Old World customs, John Peter was molding his son to take over the family business. As Erik neared the end of the eighth grade, his father decided that elementary school graduation should mark the time when his son could work full-time at the shop. Such an idea was not unusual at the time. Many boys began working after the eighth grade rather than go on to high school. Erik, though, had different ideas. "This was one of the things about which we had a very fundamental difference that hurt," he recalled. He and his mother enlisted the support of teachers, who began stopping by the shop and innocently proclaiming what a good student Erik was. Finally, Erik's grade school and high school principals directly implored John Peter to let his son stay in school. Erik added an ultimatum: "I told him I'd run away and he wouldn't find me if I couldn't go to high school." His father, who had envisioned Erik taking over the shop and becoming an independent businessman who could make a good and honest living, acquiesced.[9]

Erik had made his first important business decision. He saw that his father's shop required too many transactions just to make a dollar. As he put it later, "I made up my mind before I was ten. . . . I wasn't a candidate for the store business ever."[10]

Erik and his teachers had good reason to insist that he continue his education. He was curious, he had an excellent attitude, and his grades had showed steady improvement. Ironically, his only Cs in the eighth grade were in a subject that was appealing more and more to him— writing.[11]

In high school his grades further improved. The principal, H. M. Dutch, wrote to Mr. and Mrs. Jonsson that because of their son's "exceptional scholarly work," he was on the honor roll.[12] Toward the end of Erik's second year, Mr. Dutch sent his parents another glowing report: "I feel sure that you will not regret the course that he is taking, and will some day not only be proud of him but will be amply repaid for the sacrifices that you are now making."[13] The words contained a subtle hint. If John Peter would permit his son to continue his education even further, one day Erik would earn more money and perhaps devote some of it to the family's well-being.

John Peter insisted that Erik keep working part-time in the family shop and elsewhere too. Erik never minded working hard, but he had already determined to continue his education beyond high school, which more young people of average means were doing in those days.

Erik's interests had taken a literary bent, and he was writing short stories and poems beyond class assignments. In the first story, written when he was thirteen, the subject revolved around one that seemed like an eternal problem in the Jonsson household—money. Erik described a young, hard-up apprentice farmer who avoids the temptation to steal from his employer. Other stories had remote settings and punchy moral conclusions. There is even the beginning of a novel. Erik's interest in writing inspired him to save enough money to buy a used typewriter.[14]

His English teacher, Mary Caroline Smith, especially encouraged him. "She was tough; she marked me lower than I had been used to, and she forced me to try to do better because I'd made up my mind that I would make her give me some good marks," Jonsson later recalled.[15]

His immediate goal was publication in the high school literary magazine, the *Bulletin*. In April 1917 he received a typewritten note that thrilled him: "My dear Erik Jonsson: The Committee in charge of THE BULLETIN wishes to inform you that you have won the position of assistant editor-in-chief on the Board. It trusts that you will put all possible energy into this new task and thus render a real service to your school."[16] This achievement meant that he would be in line to be editor in chief during his senior year. But he knew he would not have a senior year. Before his father could change his mind and pull him from school, Erik, with the help of Mr. Dutch, had doubled up on course work so that he could graduate a year early. He had "six subjects to prepare each night, plus the chores that came [his] way, plus the need to hold down some jobs in order to make the money that would make college possible."[17]

He wanted to start out as a journalist and afterward become a novelist. He supposed later that he made this decision based on "reading about the romantic life of reporters." His friend Art Sylvester must have made the same decision at about the same time. To prepare himself and to "get a leg up on the average reporter," Erik took courses in shorthand and typewriting as well as doing yeoman work for his English teacher and working on the *Bulletin*.[18]

Knowing that early graduation would prevent him from becoming editor of the *Bulletin*, Erik organized, edited, and published a single edition of his own magazine, entitled the *Junior Banner*. He could recruit only one friend to submit a story, so he wrote the other stories and poems himself and printed them under pseudonyms. He sold advertising to cover printing costs. The *Junior Banner* was well designed, well edited, and surprisingly literate, a worthy rival to the *Bulletin*. Erik's story under his own name, entitled "The Crook," tells of a softhearted thief who stole goods at Christmastime to give to an impoverished family.[19]

Erik's duties at the shop continued to expand. Besides working at the soda fountain, he scuttled coal from the basement to the shop and family apartment. He made deliveries to customers by bicycle.

One customer, Everette Lee DeGolyer, was a wealthy young oilman who within a few years would become a key figure in Erik's life. Though Erik did not know it, DeGolyer already was one of the world's leading petroleum geologists, and the ruddy-faced, stocky young man who tipped Erik a quarter for each delivery intrigued him. DeGolyer had recently organized the Amerada Petroleum Corporation, with its headquarters in New York City, which prompted his move to Montclair in 1916. He would later be recognized as a pioneer in applying scientific approaches to oil exploration, as a collector of one of the world's best libraries on the history of science, and as a successful businessman.[20]

Mrs. DeGolyer occasionally stopped at the shop to make small purchases. She became friendly with Ellen Jonsson. As Ellen's health declined and she sometimes was bedridden, Mrs. DeGolyer frequently visited her in the apartment upstairs.[21]

Becoming more important than Erik's work in the family shop were his outside jobs. During the summer of his fourteenth year, looking older because he was already six feet tall, Erik worked ten hours a day at a lathe in a munitions factory, making fuses. He arose daily at five in the morning and commuted by riding on a series of trolley cars.[22]

He returned to the job the following summer. Erik recognized that the lathe and other laborsaving devices made dramatic differences in productivity. Workers' pay depended on how many fuses they completed, and since it was essential to have a productive machine, Erik took special care of his. One day a temporary foreman ordered Erik to move to an inferior machine so that a friend of the foreman could take over the one Erik had carefully nurtured. Erik refused, and he was fired. He was proud of his stance, and he learned a lesson he would not forget: employees must be treated fairly. For the rest of the summer, he worked in an aircraft factory where DH-4 airplanes, sometimes derided as "flaming caskets," were assembled.[23]

Entirely different was his work as a magazine salesman. He was evidently the best boy in Montclair at selling the *Saturday Evening Post*, then approaching the peak of its unparalleled dominance in the magazine world. The publisher, Curtis Publishing Company, named Erik president of the local "Ten Club," which was intended to prepare Curtis's young salesmen for full-time positions. "We regard your boy as the leader among his fellows and our District Agent's right hand man," Curtis's vocational manager wrote to Mr. and Mrs. Jonsson in 1915.[24]

Erik's lifelong characteristic as a workaholic had taken form. He worked weekends as a janitor's helper at a church. He delivered maple syrup on his bicycle for $0.25 a can. For a while he worked in a drugstore on weekends from about eight in the morning to seven at night, and after school on weekdays until about six. A single pay envelope survives for an unidentified job when he was fourteen. It notes the payment of $14.93 for fifty-four hours of work, along with the notation "Bonus Added."[25]

The part-time work that influenced him the most happened at two garages. He began by pumping gas and then assisted with repairs. He had a talent for mechanical work, and in an age when defective parts were repaired rather than replaced, he became a competent mechanic. "The mechanics . . . taught me how to take an engine apart and put it back together down to the last nut and bolt," he later recalled. His abilities improved greatly when he found himself alone and forced to deal with repairs. Towing disabled cars became routine for him. He drove his first car at thirteen.[26] During this period he became better acquainted with DeGolyer, who stored his Buick at one of the garages. Erik enjoyed brief conversations with him when he came by for his car.[27]

In those days, garages frequently leased cars for short-term rentals. Many customers could not drive, so Erik began driving for them. He soon offered lessons, earning, to his astonishment, a dollar an hour. Sometimes he could squeeze in two or three lessons on a Saturday. Before long, he had experience with driving practically every make of vehicle on the road.[28]

He realized that a person with imagination might earn more by making deals than by working for hourly wages. He understood that this kind of entrepreneurial activity required a willingness to accept risks. In an early deal, he bought a dilapidated Maxwell automobile, sold its tires, and disposed of the remainder to a junk dealer, making a profit of twenty-five dollars.[29]

Erik opened a savings account at a local bank, making weekly deposits ranging from a quarter to a couple of dollars with the same teller, a "grouch" who glared wordlessly at the young whippersnapper. One day Jonsson slipped a five-dollar bill under the teller's window, bringing his balance to one hundred dollars. The teller, who had never spoken to him, "stopped dead in his tracks and said, 'Good morning,'" and he continued to do so on every subsequent visit. Jonsson never forgot the change in behavior. "It tells you a lot," was his later comment.[30]

At the age of fifteen, defying his father's wishes, Erik bought a used two-cylinder Indian motorcycle. He argued that he could use it to make faster deliveries for the shop. It afforded him a sense of freedom he had found nowhere else. His life began to revolve around his motorcycle. His literary interests became secondary to such things as tinkering with the carburetor to get maximum performance. Erik's best friend, Malcolm Bedell, acquired a Harley-Davidson motorcycle. The two became fiercely partisan about the relative merits of the Indian and Harley-Davidson. They joined a handful of others in cruising through Montclair and on surrounding roads.[31]

Inevitably, they raced one another. "If one fellow won, then by the next time the other fellow had tuned his engine a little bit to get that extra mile out of it," Erik recalled. One stunt was to lean over and pick up a handkerchief from the ground at a high speed. When making turns, the riders tilted their motorcycles over as far as possible, touching their footboards to the ground. The most daring riders were recognized by the amount scraped off their footboards. Erik was particularly adept at this maneuver, his well-worn footboard marking him as the "dean" of the Montclair riders. But because of his lanky frame, he was never able to reach down to snatch the handkerchief.[32]

"I did some completely foolish things on motorcycles," Jonsson later recalled, referring especially to a Sunday morning when he arose early to ride alone down a redbrick highway with a powerful image in mind. He had seen a magazine photograph of a rider standing straight up on his motorcycle saddle with both arms extended horizontally, speeding down the road. He told himself that if he wanted to be a man, he had to duplicate that act. In this act of bravado, unseen by anyone else on a lonely brick highway, he succeeded. But he never tried it again.[33]

Eventually, before he was out of high school, he graduated to a more powerful motorcycle, a Henderson. Years later, in oral histories, he returned again and again to his fondness for motorcycles, especially the Henderson. One could not earn a living from such a passion, though, and Erik's decision to become a journalist remained.

After three accelerated years of high school, Erik graduated on June 20, 1918, one of 138 students, the largest graduating class in Montclair history. He won a $100 scholarship for "general merit and excellent scholarship," the only such scholarship given. This fact loomed large in Erik's imagination as well as in his immigrant parents'. It boosted his college savings to $440.[34]

Several factors persuaded John Peter to agree to Erik's college plans. He was especially pleased that Erik had finished high school early. His new attitude was affected as well by the expectation that his son eventually would earn plenty of money to help with the family's finances. "I don't blame him. His life was hard indeed," Erik later said. On another occasion, he cited a visit to his father by his principal, Mr. Dutch, as a convincing factor.[35]

Erik believed that his high school courses and work on the *Bulletin* had prepared him for Columbia University's School of Journalism, convenient to Montclair because of its upper Manhattan location. But Columbia informed him that he needed another year of high school. Erik, having worked so hard to graduate early, considered other options.[36]

As he deliberated, a catalogue from Rensselaer Polytechnic Institute (RPI) in Troy, New York, arrived. His background for its engineering studies was woefully inadequate. RPI was as different from journalism school as one could imagine. It emphasized exclusively engineering and sciences. He had not taken solid geometry, trigonometry, chemistry, or physics, but Erik saw that he might gain conditional admission and make up his deficiencies as a mechanical engineering student. With the skills he had developed at the garages and through his extensive tinkering with motorcycles, he saw that mechanical engineering could be a logical course of study. If he could get into Rensselaer, he later might transfer to Columbia.[37]

But RPI, too, advised him to return to high school for his fourth year. The director (president) of RPI, Palmer C. Ricketts, sent a letter to Mr. Dutch, asking his opinion. Dutch urged Ricketts to accept Erik right away, and he told Erik not to return to high school. "I have faith in you, and I *know* that you will make good."[38] RPI, encouraged no doubt by Mr. Dutch's recommendation, agreed to accept him on condition. Erik feared, too, that a year's delay might mean he would never get to college.

There was another option. One of the garage owners, John Svenson, also owned the first regularly scheduled bus line in Montclair, but was too busy to oversee it. Svenson, a native of Sweden, told Erik that if he would stay in Montclair, he would "give" him the bus line. "No, John," Erik replied, "I have to go to college."[39]

⌐

In the fall of 1918, barely seventeen, John Erik Jonsson gathered his essential belongings, boarded the night boat in New York City, and sailed up the Hudson for more than 150 miles, stopping just past Albany. He stepped off at Troy, population about 70,000, then trudged uphill to the campus, luggage in hand.[40]

Rensselaer was an attractive place with redbrick buildings on a twenty-three-acre hillside site. Established in 1824 to educate students for farm and factory work, it began to concentrate on serving industry by teaching engineering and science. It was the first college in the nation successfully devoted to these purposes. Its engineering program provided a model for other institutions that established separate schools for engineering and science.

RPI fraternity men greeted Erik and other freshmen as they arrived and invited them to their houses. "Don't be in too big a hurry to put on a pledge pin," RPI's handbook advised. Yet RPI encouraged students to make friends as fast as they could and to "speak to everyone on the 'Hill,' whether you know them or not."[41]

On his second day, freshmen elected class officers. Erik gathered his courage and nominated for president a fellow Montclair graduate, Hanson Dodd, who returned the favor by nominating Erik. Neither was elected. Erik received only one vote—Dodd's. He later took stock of himself: he was not well dressed and his hair was not well combed. He recalled, "I made a most unprepossessing figure."[42]

On the first Saturday, he participated in a bizarre annual mass ritual for several hundred totally naked freshmen and sophomores. The "Grease Rush" took place on an abandoned baseball field on Green Island in the middle of the Hudson. Freshmen and sophomores, all male, covered themselves with grease, and then—prodded by upperclassmen bearing leather straps—charged to the middle of the field to see which class could get the most hands on a thirty-inch cane. Erik documented the event with his camera, and he posed for a picture with a discreetly positioned towel.[43]

He settled into his dormitory room at Hunt Hall with $170, and no idea how long it would last. The understanding was that his father would help him with about half his expenses; Erik would earn the rest. When he quickly spent about $50 for books and instruments, the situation darkened. A short week later, with his bank account beginning to "look sick," he told his parents that he would send his laundry home in order to save money.[44]

To alleviate his stress, he found the first of what would be a wide assortment of part-time jobs, in a bookstore. The possibility of greater assistance loomed through a campus program, the Students Army Training Corps, which trained students for military service in Europe, since the United States had entered the world war the previous April. Trainees received free room and board and uniforms. Erik began drilling in the afternoons with others who intended to sign up. He advised his parents not to buy any clothes for him because the army would provide uniforms. He learned, however, that eighteen was the minimum age, and he was barely seventeen. It was a bitter blow, and on October 1 he could only watch while 650 eligible students signed up for the program.[45] His financial situation would improve the next year, he assured his parents, because he would be old enough to join the corps and get clothes, room and board, and tuition. But, he added, "If the war doesn't last I guess I'll have to get out and hustle for a year or so." A month later the war was over.[46]

Despite the rigor of studies and his part-time jobs, Erik found time to begin working out with the football team. At seventeen, he was younger than most players and, despite the fact that he was approaching six feet one, he weighed only about 150 pounds. He made the team his first two years, but "absorbed nothing but splinters on the bench."[47]

Erik implored his parents to write longer letters, but the thing he truly missed, he wrote, was the Henderson motorcycle he had sold. "If I could only afford to have one of those joy busses here now I think I'd be completely happy and would get about 100% on all my studies every day," he said.[48]

He found one, "dirt cheap." He could restore it and sell it for a profit of $50 to $100. He asked his father to advance him the money, offering to repay him at 6 percent interest and urging him to rush his reply before "some other stone headed boob" got the bargain.[49] John Peter declined. Erik took the refusal in stride. "Don't think I'm sore about the Henderson," he wrote. "I'm only sorry I couldn't get it because it was such a bargain."[50]

In October, the Indian motorcycle dealer in Troy offered him a commission for selling motorcycles, but Erik accepted a more reliable job as driver and mechanic for Mr. Allen, the bookstore owner. Allen had an automobile, but he couldn't drive it. Erik began earning about eight dollars a week from Allen for something that was more fun than work. "You ought to see how straight and proud I sit up in that little Maxwell," Erik wrote home. After being away from a garage for a month and a half, the smell of gasoline was "great."[51]

When Allen tried to raise Erik's pay to ten dollars a week, he refused to take it. To earn more than forty cents an hour would be a crime, he declared. He kept the job until April 1919, near the end of his freshman year, when class work began to be too heavy.[52]

Or perhaps the reason he quit was the reemergence of a motorcycle. Erik obtained a "business loan" of $175 from his father to buy a Henderson. Allen had offered to lend him the money, but Erik told his father he preferred to get the money from home. His parents sent him items for restoration work—a can of blue Henderson paint, goggles, a sparkplug, some chain links, a can of tire patches, and other tools. Erik upgraded the Henderson without spending a penny. By April, when all the repairs were made, he placed an ad in the newspaper to sell it for a profit, intending to repeat the process by buying another one right away.[53]

Erik had learned his father's lessons well. During his four years at Rensselaer, he added to his résumé a rich variety of moneymaking ventures: washing dishes, hawking peanuts at sporting events, and waiting on tables. But there was more. With his father's access to supplies, he sold fellow students such disparate items as binders, skates, and cameras. And he also sold cigarettes forwarded to him by his father.[54]

He worked out an arrangement with Allen in which he called on students and sold them necessities for classes. Arriving freshmen could expect a visit from Erik, who offered drawing supplies, T-squares, drawing boards, paper, and instruments, with delivery the next day. Sometimes he earned twenty-five dollars on a single sale, and he might make three or four sales in an evening. "I was getting rich," he later told his son and grandsons.[55]

Erik expanded his offerings by buying tanned kidskins and having them fashioned into soft pillowcases with special lettering—"Rensselaer" or fraternity symbols or class years. Each kidskin cost him from five to six dollars, and he sold them for fifteen dollars apiece. He arranged also for the production of various pennants and "oddments," which he sold at "outrageously high prices."[56]

Years later, Jonsson treasured the lessons he had learned as a young entrepreneur. At Texas Instruments, he sought to identify prospective employees with his same penchant for entrepreneurship, but found the trait difficult to identify.[57]

Erik's most ambitious adventure stemmed from his love of motorcycles and his friendship with his Montclair pal Malcolm Bedell, who had enlisted in the navy before graduating from high school. Jonsson urged Bedell to join him at RPI when he got out. Early in the fall of 1919, the newly discharged Bedell arrived on campus. The two pals found a room together in a private house.[58]

Erik went to Director Ricketts to plead for Bedell's admission, touting him as a mechanical genius who had left school prematurely. Ricketts refused. Disappointed but determined to stay together, the two turned to their passion—motorcycles. An Indian franchise was available in Mechanicville, twelve miles north of Troy, requiring an investment of $1,000. Persuading his father of its promise, Erik borrowed $500 from him, and Bedell chipped in the other $500. The two set up a business selling new and used motorcycles and bicycles and making repairs.[59]

It was a daunting challenge for two young men with little money, little experience, and—certainly in Erik's case—little time. Bedell handled the business during the week, and Erik joined him on weekends. The Indian factory in Springfield, Massachusetts, about a hundred miles away, provided new motorcycles. To bring them one at a time to Mechanicville, Erik and Mal rode there double so that one could return on the new machine.[60]

The entrepreneurs earned their first two dollars for a bicycle repair. They sold a new Indian motorcycle the next month, prompting a celebration with a "real meal."[61] The business ensured that Jonsson would have a motorcycle to ride. "You can't imagine what a comfort it is," he wrote home. "No use talking, a motorcycle is about half of my life."[62]

As an inducement for more business, Jonsson helped organize the Troy Motorcycle Club in early 1920. He was elected treasurer. The club, with thirty-two charter members, announced plans for hill climbs, reliability runs, tours, races, and other forms of competition as well as social outings.[63]

In his letters home, Erik detailed the agonizing struggles involved in keeping the franchise afloat. The difficulties became almost unbearable when Bedell went to Montclair for about six weeks because of a throat ailment requiring surgery (perhaps a tonsillectomy). "Of course he can't help that, poor chap," Erik wrote home, "but meantime our little gold mine [Erik] is going to waste." Erik was frantically juggling his classes with work and riding his motorcycle to and from Mechanicville virtually every day.[64]

He was "so confoundedly" busy that he could hardly take time to breathe. Yet when Erik asked his father to increase his monthly allowance, John Peter responded by pressuring him to work even more. Erik replied that perhaps he could work a few more hours, but it would only earn him three or four dollars. And if he didn't, he could devote more hours to extracurricular activities and become "one of the big men" on campus.[65]

Erik's occasional requests for more money from "the account" suggest that his father's loan of $500 was an investment with an expected return. "I wonder if you can let me have that last $50 to square up with the firm, as we are playing pretty close now and need every cent we can get," Erik wrote in April 1920. "Have a date to meet a chap next Saturday in Mechanicville, and am quite sure I will sell him a bike. If we can only sell some of our second hand busses [motorcycles] now we'll be quite well fixed, though a little low on capital. Guess we can pull through all right, though." In another letter, Erik alerted his parents that he might want to borrow "a little more money" to buy more bicycles and a motorcycle. Evidently, they agreed, for Erik next reported that he was going to

Springfield to pick up a new motorcycle. The concern for profits made Erik's studies seem secondary. "If I were only finished with school, we could make some money all right," Erik wrote home.[66]

By the summer of 1920, the struggle was ending. The two partners began seeking a buyer for their business. They had started at an unfortunate time. The brief economic boom after World War I was followed by a depression in 1920–21. They also were victims of their own inexperience, a lack of capital, and—in Erik's case—not enough time.[67]

On July 26, 1920, Erik reported that they had sold the shop on credit to a man in Troy. Erik paid a lawyer to draw up papers with a monthly payment schedule. "So we're pretty well protected," he naively wrote home.[68] As it turned out, after they were given two hundred dollars, the payments ceased. Efforts to collect failed. Bedell returned to Montclair.[69]

Erik kept a Henderson motorcycle for himself. In late summer, he took a cross-country trip through upper New York and New England with his Montclair friend Bob Garrabrant, a Cornell student, who rode in the sidecar. They visited friends and camped out in a pup tent.[70]

Erik's studies, astonishingly, suffered only slightly during his vexing sophomore year. In February 1920, five months before selling the franchise, he reported having passed solid analytical geometry and a stiff course in electricity. But he failed differential calculus. He was not concerned; he would make it up. And he did.[71]

How Erik Jonsson found time for anything but classes, studying, and running a new business during his sophomore year is almost impossible to imagine. But, as he had told his father, he had no intention of forsaking extracurricular college activities. In the same year that he and Malcolm started their business, Erik joined Alpha Tau Omega, a social fraternity.[72]

At his initiation, fraternity men ordered him to lie down in a graveyard for two hours and left him there. They next blindfolded him for a run of about five miles through woods and over fences "and Lord knows what." He crawled through mud puddles on his hands and knees, and finally, around a bonfire, they shampooed his hair with Limburger, cornstarch, castor oil, and "other dainties." Afterward, the initiates had to eat from the same mixture.[73]

The next year, Erik became an energetic hazer himself. On one occasion he and a fraternity brother blindfolded an initiate named

Robert Sherman, ran him around for four hours, left him blindfolded in a deserted shack, and warned him to speak to no one. A woman who thought a robbery had occurred called the police. Officers arrived, and one of them pointed a revolver at Erik. Finally, he convinced them that no crime had occurred. Sherman later became Erik's roommate and a close friend.[74]

Despite his constant need for money, Erik enjoyed the activities of a stereotypical college student in the early years of the Roaring Twenties. These included formal dances that required a tuxedo. (Erik owned one.) He even kept a goldfish in his room (no report of anyone swallowing it), and he played the banjo. In letters home, he often mentioned girls he had dated.[75]

There were no female students at Rensselaer, but a large number of single women worked in Troy's shirt and collar factories. RPI's fraternity men did not worry too much about finding dates.[76]

As 1921 arrived, Erik began keeping a diary. His entries lasted only thirteen days, but they provide a snapshot of his personal life during the holiday season. On New Year's Eve, he attended the finest party he had ever seen, at a house on 89th Street in New York City. He became enchanted with one of the girls who let him kiss her: "She's so beautiful. I can't think very straight when I'm with her." Back on campus, he boxed two rounds with a friend, with painful results. He vowed to get in better shape. The next day he went to the RPI gym, won four games of handball, and ran eight laps. At that point, with classes beginning, his diary entries end.[77]

When Erik moved into his fraternity's rambling frame house on Pawling Avenue, his first roommate was a senior named Roland Beers, one of the "top men" in the fraternity. One day Beers showed up wearing the sorority pin of an attractive young lady who had captivated Erik. Hard feelings developed, and Beers moved out. Robert Sherman, the former pledge whom Jonsson had initiated, moved in.[78]

That winter, a fire destroyed the fraternity house. "Everything went, house furniture and toothbrushes," Erik told his parents. Erik lost some clothing and a few textbooks that he no longer used. His minor losses turned into a windfall. Erik's father had taken out a $500 fire insurance policy on his son's possessions. The insurance company paid Erik $425, the largest unencumbered amount of money he had ever possessed. He immediately purchased two suits.[79]

For a while, Erik became house manager of the new fraternity house, saving about $35 a month in rent. Then, following a serious argument with his father, after which he briefly spurned further assistance from him, he became the dishwasher too, a job that included free meals. The argument followed a series of mishaps during a vacation period that caused Erik to return home one night at about three in the morning. Although details are missing, Erik had become briefly engaged to a New York City woman (perhaps the one he had kissed at the party). He arranged a double date for her sister with Malcolm Bedell. Afterward, returning to Montclair by train, he and Bedell tried a shorter route via Hoboken. They arrived there too late to catch a train to Montclair and had to return to New York City to do so. John Peter refused to accept Erik's explanation. He accused him of having been with "ladies of the evening," a charge that infuriated Erik.[80]

The next morning, Erik packed his belongings and said he would henceforth live without his father's assistance. He returned to campus in anger. The rift between father and son ended none too soon after Erik was "politicked" out of his dishwashing job. He soon took on another job—sweeping up and running errands at a jewelry shop.[81]

At the end of two years, Erik, quite unbelievably, could claim a good record of extracurricular activities: two years on the football team, two years on the class track team, two years as a reporter for the school news-paper, a term as treasurer of the Scholarship Club, and membership in the Mandolin Club. He was later elected treasurer of the junior class, and he became president of a new group called the Triangle Club.[82]

But he still wasn't through with motorcycle sales. He began earning a 5 percent commission on each motorcycle sold for the Troy dealer. He concentrated on classes in the morning and motorcycle sales in the afternoons. Still another possibility loomed: "Am trying to write words for a song that one of our fellows has composed. If I can do it, and it's accepted their's [sic] bound to be some money in it."[83]

⌇

During these years, Erik developed an interest in a subject that would encompass a significant part of his adult life—aviation. With the war over, many army-trained aviators, reluctant to give up their new skills, began barnstorming, selling rides, and offering flying lessons. Erik paid one such aviator fifteen dollars for his first ride, sitting in the front "angel's chair." The aviator took off from a recently harvested cornfield, and as he climbed upward, Erik, noticing that the gas indicator was on empty, pointed to it. "Oh, that damn thing never did work," the aviator responded. Erik swallowed hard and enjoyed the ride.[84]

He and his friend Bob Garrabrant briefly discussed enlisting in the service for aviation training at the end of Erik's freshman year. But as Erik later recalled, John Peter Jonsson had other ideas: "My father told me in no uncertain terms that if I did, he would get me yanked back out." Still, Erik's interest continued. He took a three-week course in aeronautical engineering the first time RPI offered it. Later, he hoped to design a complete airplane.[85]

In his final summer before graduation, Erik tried to get a job at an airplane manufacturing plant. He was hired, but his experience with automobiles placed him in the garage. At lunchtime he watched workers put together the de Havilland DH-4 and the Handley-Paige, the first two-engine bomber ever built in the United States.[86]

During his senior year he bolted down a four-cylinder motorcycle engine used on the Henderson, ran it wide open, and measured the horsepower, torque, and other aspects with RPI's special equipment. He reached 5,025 revolutions per minute, about twice as many as other engines were capable of at the time, and reported his findings in his senior thesis, "Determination of the Performance Characteristics of an Ace Motorcycle Engine." Part of the requirement was to read his thesis aloud. He was one of a 168 graduates who read their theses in a ritual requiring seven days.[87]

Before graduation, one of Erik's favorite professors, Arthur M. Greene, gave him advice. "They will be handing you a sheepskin which declares that you are a mechanical engineer," he said. "You and I know that you won't be. But outside they won't. Therefore, if somebody asks you if you can do something in engineering, if after due consideration you think that it can be done then say yes and go ahead and do it."[88] Erik would remember this advice and use it as a working proposition in the years ahead.

He was one of thirty-two students awarded the ME (mechanical engineering) degree. He scribbled a note on his graduation program—his parents were not there, because "they had a store to keep."[89]

The graduates' educations, except for English and French classes, had been entirely scientific, mathematical, and technical. In four years, Erik took only one elective course. The humanities were virtually nonexistent in the RPI curriculum.[90]

He had no clear picture of the future, but he recognized an advantage that he had over many classmates—a "fair degree of confidence" because he had paid so many of his own expenses. This, he realized later, was one of the real advantages of "coming up the hard way." In fact, it was truly the "easy way" because he had learned to take in stride the inevitable bumps in life.[91]

Rensselaer gave much to Jonsson, and he did not forget it. And if Rensselaer quickly lost track of this nondescript graduate, which it did, a few decades later it resumed a relationship with Jonsson with great profit. In 1990, RPI's board of trustees declared that no person in the institution's history had had a greater impact on RPI than Erik Jonsson.[92]

His difficult journey to such a declaration now began.

Lessons in Business

If Erik Jonsson had had his choice, he would have started as an engineer at an automobile or aeronautical manufacturing company. His
love of automobiles was long-standing, and his course in aeronautical design had whetted his fascination with airplanes. No such offers
surfaced, but two others did, a fact that puffed him up because most
graduates had no more than one job possibility, and some none. His
first possibility came from an industrial equipment manufacturer
whose interviewer asked whether he was married. No, he replied, but
he asked why. At your salary you can't afford to be, the man responded.
"I weeded that job right away," Jonsson said.[1]

Professor Greene recommended him to the Aluminum Company of
America, or Alcoa, whose interviewer told him he could start at $125 a
month, with a raise to $150 after six months. Thereafter, raises would
depend upon performance. Jonsson accepted immediately.[2]

Wall Street analysts were touting Alcoa because of its dominant
position in the United States and its wide foreign interests. An important new use for aluminum was in the bodywork of automobiles and
airplanes. It was light but strong, highly workable, an excellent conductor of electricity, and resistant to corrosion.

The young college graduate reported to Pittsburgh for orientation
on July 1, then worked for a few days at a plant in nearby New Kensington. Afterward, he had three choices: return to New Kensington, go to
Edgewater, New Jersey, or begin in eastern Tennessee. Edgewater was
close to Montclair and his parents, but living expenses would be high.
Jonsson had never been to Tennessee, and its cost of living was half as
much as New Kensington's. He chose Tennessee.[3]

He traveled by train to Maryville, in the foothills of the Great Smoky Mountains, where the Alcoa complex resembled a college campus.[4] Taking temporary lodgings at Maryville's Eureka Hotel, Jonsson strolled down the main street and was pleased at what he saw in this southern town. The people seemed friendly, and he was optimistic. He rented a room in the county sheriff's house.[5]

Mindful of obligations that he believed he owed his parents, Jonsson invited his parents to join him. His mother's arthritis had worsened. John Peter had sold his shop, and they had about $12,000 put away for their retirement. Just how long their savings might last was uncertain because Ellen's health made higher medical bills inevitable.[6]

John Peter, now sixty-eight, entertained the idea of opening a shop in Maryville, but Erik advised him that the town was too small. If they came, he wrote, he could rent a lovely cottage for the three of them for $18 a month. If his dad wanted to speculate on Wall Street, he could commute to Knoxville by train and make transactions there. Finally, the Jonssons declined to come.[7]

Erik's job at Alcoa was as promised. He learned operations at the rolling mill—said to be the world's largest when it opened in 1920—from the ground up, doing the same physical work as any beginner. Being a college graduate made no difference, he told his parents: "I keep my mouth strictly shut about R.P.I. unless someone asks questions." His nickname resurfaced. His boss's assistant called him "Swede."[8-]

Although he kept quiet about college, his knowledge paid off. He liked one employee, a thin, tobacco-chewing "drink of water" named McKinney who had never been to school but could kill cockroaches with a spit of tobacco juice. Mac, complaining that he had forgotten his specs, often would ask Jonsson to figure out whether an aluminum sheet would "roll out to the right size." Erik did this easily, and he soon realized that Mac had difficulty doing the arithmetic. Erik devised a two-piece circular slide rule, mounted it on Mac's desk, and showed him how it worked. Mac stopped forgetting his specs. When the superintendent saw it, he asked, "What the hell is that?" Erik overheard Mac reply triumphantly, "Sir, that is a slide rule," and demonstrated it. Several years later, Erik visited and found his slide rule still being used.[9]

Erik was even prouder of a one-handed circle shearer he made with the blacksmith shop's help. Unlike the two-handed shearer in use, it left a hand free for getting the next piece ready. Erik believed his shearer increased production by 25 percent. As he explained, he was a disciple of the time-and-motion studies of Frank and Lillian Gilbreth and Frederick Taylor. (Years later, he endowed a chair in engineering at RPI in honor of the Gilbreths.)[10]

Invariably, southern people intrigued him. The workers wore blue cotton shirts, overalls, shoes, and sometimes no socks. "They're a good natured, simple, big hearted bunch of people. I like them," he wrote to an RPI pal.[11]

After four months, though, Erik began discussing with his parents a possible return to New Jersey, perhaps to the Edgewater plant. His reason had nothing to do with the locals: "Still my work here is nice, and every one is good to me and willing to help me learn, so I've no kick coming."[12] He had not informed his parents of an important personal development: at a Halloween party, he met a tall, attractive young woman who worked in the cost department. Both were wearing masks, but Erik knew who she was. He kept asking her to dance, and, she later said, "I was glad."[13] He persuaded her to go with him for a ride the next afternoon in his secondhand Model T Ford. Margaret later joked that she went because his mask prevented her from knowing what he looked like.[14]

Jonsson found something charmingly different about Margaret Fonde. He was instantly smitten with her. On their ride into the mountains, they stopped at a place with a beautiful view. Jonsson suddenly asked her to marry him. His boldness irritated her. "The trouble with you damn Yankees," she said, "is that you come down into a small country town and think that you can kid all of the country girls." Jonsson assured her that he was serious. But the day's magic vanished. They returned to town without much conversation.[15]

They continued to date, though. He learned that Margaret was a daredevil herself. Erik had once stood up on a moving motorcycle, and she could stand up on a moving horse. They often drove into the mountains, enjoying the wildflowers and clear streams. "To have this in profusion, it's hard to describe," Jonsson said half a century later.[16]

Margaret began to share Erik's feelings, and on a Thursday afternoon, February 6, 1923, having stopped at another place with a pretty mountain view, Jonsson again asked her to marry him. This time he had a date in mind—that weekend. She agreed. They had several rationalizations for eloping. One was Margaret's father, who would object to her marrying a "damyankee." Another was her mother. When Margaret's older sister married, her mother burst into loud tears, and Mar-

garet vowed never to let that happen at her own wedding. A third reason was Jonsson's parents. They would not approve of his marrying a
woman they had never met.[17]

The couple obtained a marriage license in Knoxville. Jonsson handed
the clerk a $10 bill for the $3.50 fee, and when he returned too much
change, Erik gave it back with a request—"How about keeping this out
of the paper for a few days?" The clerk seemed amenable.[18]

They intended to marry at noon on Saturday, February 8, in Knoxville, then notify Margaret's parents and take a weekend honeymoon.
But the clerk had not kept the marriage license out of the paper. Friends
of the Fondes saw it listed in Saturday morning's newspaper, and the
couple found themselves called on the carpet at the Fonde household,
explaining themselves. Protests or not, Erik and Margaret were determined to go through with it. They married at five that afternoon at a
place called Minister House. Jonsson was twenty-one; his bride, twenty.
There were no witnesses and no wedding ring.[19]

The newlyweds checked into the Farragut Hotel and went to a movie.
The next morning, they boarded a boxcar for Calderwood Lake, where
Alcoa generated hydroelectric power. Jonsson wanted to see the dam,
powerhouse, and lake that Margaret's father had helped build. They
returned to Maryville and moved into a room at the home of Jonsson's
Alcoa supervisor, Bill Gardner.[20]

The Fondes recovered from their shock, accepted their son-in-law,
and four months afterward presented the couple with deeds for two lots
in Mobile County, Alabama, which had been inherited by Margaret's
mother. The property was not a significant asset, nor much of a hin-
drance. Nor, if such was the intention, did it ever give Erik and Margaret reason to settle in Alabama.[21] (Margaret's parents, Hiram Cornelius
Fonde and Carrie Watkins Fonde, had moved from Mobile to Maryville
a few years earlier with their five children. After the Calderwood Dam
was completed, Fonde stayed there as a builder and contractor.[22])

Erik's parents were just as surprised at the marriage as the Fondes,
and perhaps less pleased. They had counted on their son's support in
their old age, but now he had married a southern woman they did not
know.[23] Erik assured them that he would seek a transfer to Edgewater
to be near them, and he enclosed a check to lessen their pain. Ellen
responded pleasantly, graciously using Margaret's name first in the sal-
utation ("Dear Margaret & Erik"), but returned his check.[24]

Jonsson's request to transfer to Edgewater soon was granted. Margaret agreed to the move, but it must have been painful to leave her parents. As Jonsson realized, "She was a good soldier."[25]

His last contribution at Alcoa's Tennessee plant was an elaborate description of the manufacturing processes he had learned. He thought it would help the next apprentice as well as others. The seventy-page typewritten manuscript resembled a graduate thesis without footnotes. He completed it on May 15, 1923, and then departed with Margaret for New Jersey.[26]

The trip was exhausting. Jonsson's Model T broke down frequently, and in Washington, D.C., it finally stopped for good. The couple abandoned it and boarded a train.[27] In New Jersey, they rented a "cracker-box house" in Coytesville for $50 a month. The contrast between this house at 2454 Second Street and a "lovely cottage" that would cost $18 a month in Tennessee disheartened them. The young bride was surely further distressed when her husband's parents moved in with them.[28]

The Edgewater plant, across the Hudson River from Manhattan, was smaller than the one in Tennessee. Jonsson's assignment, paying $175 a month, was for an Alcoa subsidiary, Aluminum Index Co., that made and sold aluminum items, principally guides for filing cabinets.[29]

Jonsson, as factory manager, handled correspondence, wrote material for salesmen, and taught them about the products. Later, he uncharitably declared the job "useless." Yet his duties placed him in a role that later would become familiar—a generalist with overall responsibilities rather than specific engineering assignments.[30]

But his ingenuity in the manufacturing end of business soon paid off. Concerned that costs were too high, he wandered around machine shops in Connecticut for a week to find some tooling that would be more efficient and economical. He found a man could build a progressive die for $550, which would reduce the costs of making the company's most expensive product by about 50 percent.[31]

At home, the Jonssons' tiny house was almost impossible to keep warm. The heating bill equaled the $50 monthly rent. Existing on Jonsson's $175 monthly salary was impossible.[32] Margaret began work as a bookkeeper, but not for long. She was pregnant. On November 1, 1924, their first son, Philip Raymond, was born in an Englewood hospital.

Desperate for more money, Jonsson took advantage of a new phenomenon: radio. Following the first commercial broadcasts in 1919, stations began broadcasting sporting events, news, music, and weather reports. Since manufacturers were unable to keep up with the demand, amateurs were building their own radios.

Jonsson was well qualified for that. He began purchasing components from General Instrument Corporation on Broadway, staying up as late as two in the morning to assemble the radios, and then selling them to friends and neighbors, earning a profit of $35–$40 on each one. The extra money kept his family going.[33]

There was enough money to take Margaret and Philip, not yet a year old, on an airplane ride over New York City in an enclosed Dutch model. The engine started sputtering over Central Park, but they returned safely. The incident frightened Margaret, but not her husband.[34]

By 1926, Jonsson's late hours were taking a heavy toll. Circles appeared under his eyes, and his boss asked him why he was killing himself with nighttime work. "I can't eat if I don't do this," Jonsson replied. The result was a raise of $35 a month (to $210) if he would give up his radio work. He agreed.[35]

But another possibility soon interested him. He saw an advertisement in the *Saturday Evening Post* for a new automobile model, the Pontiac. "That automobile is going to sell," he told himself. A nearby dealer gave him a weekend job selling Pontiacs. He began making more money selling cars than working at Alcoa.[36]

Buying a car had become easier than previously with the introduction of time payments. Concrete and asphalt roads were enhancing the possibility of people making longer trips by car. The Federal Highway Act of 1921 had allotted money to states to encourage the construction of a national network of highways. A transportation revolution was well under way.

The Pontiac was offered through General Motors' long-suffering Oakland automobile division. Priced from $700 to $900, the new product cost more than the Chevrolet and less than the Oakland. It introduced a new concept—many of its parts were interchangeable with those of the Chevrolet.

Another salesman, John A. Jochim, approached Jonsson: if he had $500 to match his $500, they could acquire a franchise. "It did not look possible," Jonsson said, "but he showed me that it was. And it was." Jonsson borrowed $500 from "a friend and another fellow," and with Jochim, a "real super salesman," obtained a franchise for the New Jersey town of Dumont, north of Montclair. They would have to sell Oaklands as well as Pontiacs.[37]

They incorporated as the Bergen Oakland Company, Inc. Jonsson, Jochim, and their wives were the officers and sole shareholders. Each man had 300 shares; each wife, 100. Jochim was president, and Jonsson treasurer.[38] Jonsson, optimistic but cautious, kept his regular job at Alcoa and devoted evenings and weekends to the car company.

The co-owners signed a five-year lease for property at 137 Washington Avenue in Dumont at $90 a month, borrowed money to buy a nearby property for servicing and storage, acquired a selection of Pontiacs and Oaklands, accumulated a few used cars, and opened for business at a time when closed cars were replacing open-top ones. Several weeks later, the Oakland Motor Car Company informed them that they could not use "Oakland" as part of their company name. They chose Jochim-Jonsson, Inc., as their new name.[39] The tongue-twisting name Jochim-Jonsson often caused legal instruments to be marred by misspellings, leading to problems. After nine months, the name was changed again, this time to the Dumont Motor Car Company.[40]

Jonsson's instincts about the Pontiac were right. Pontiac's anticipated production of 65,000 vehicles for 1926 climbed to 77,000. In the last half of the year, Jochim-Jonsson's six salesmen sold $45,581 worth of Pontiacs and Oaklands. This put the aluminum business in the shade, Jonsson told himself.[41]

A fully equipped Pontiac coupe with a spare tire, tube, tire cover, front snubbers (shock absorbers), stop light, and front and rear bumpers cost $925. These items, even the bumpers, were extra on lower-priced models. A one-third down payment was required, and payments could extend for twelve months.[42]

Business seemed promising enough that Jonsson borrowed $2,500 from Margaret's father to buy a two-story house at 443 Conrad Road in Englewood. Jochim also bought a house, a seemingly innocent event that would prove significant to Jonsson.[43]

The year 1927 was when potbellied Babe Ruth hit sixty home runs and the lanky aviator Charles Lindbergh flew solo across the Atlantic. The stock market was booming. But two weeks after Jochim-Jonsson's name change to Dumont, a bank officer called Jonsson with surprising news: the company was overdrawn. Jonsson, as treasurer, was shocked. How could this be? A quick investigation showed that Jochim had used company funds to buy his house. There was a confrontation. Jochim admitted his impropriety. To settle the matter, he simply gave his half of the company to Jonsson. Suddenly, Jonsson was the sole proprietor of the Dumont Motor Car Co. He quit Alcoa, effective May 31, 1927, carefully explaining why and winning an assurance that he could return if things did not work out.[44]

Jonsson's responsibilities included the array of duties required to operate a car dealership: keeping a manageable inventory, generating sales, hiring and training salesmen, creating an advertising program, servicing automobiles, making repairs, selling parts, handling complaints, taking trade-ins, keeping accounts, giving driving lessons to buyers of new cars, and, of course, generating profit. There was endless correspondence with Oakland officials in Pontiac, Michigan, and to the district office in New York City. He was twenty-six years old.

It was not easy. Even new cars sometimes arrived with problems. One batch of Pontiacs had "decidedly rough motors." Heavy, thumping knocks could be heard. Jonsson tore down the engines and examined the parts, but could find nothing wrong.[45]

Pontiac sales across the nation were great, but the Oakland continued to struggle. "We are so badly over-sold on Pontiacs that we hardly know which way to turn," the district manager wrote. "What we most desire at this time is increased sales activity in the delivery of Oakland Cars ... and we would appreciate your co-operation."[46] But Jonsson was selling twice as many Pontiacs as Oaklands, which was on its last legs and destined to end production in 1931. To boost sales, he contracted with radio station WODA in Paterson, New Jersey, to broadcast twenty-four 100-word commercials.[47]

Overdue and unpaid bills continued to arrive. He begged his creditors for more time. "We've just gone through a reorganization and housecleaning that took a solid three months," he explained to one. The Oakland office, noting his delinquent parts account, told him that it would ship future orders by COD only. An auto supply company placed its $207.85 claim with a collection agency. A repair shop turned over its $56.50 claim to a law firm that threatened to sue if payment was not received within five days. The New York Central Railroad Company refused to accept further checks; transportation charges for cars had to be paid in advance.[48]

Jonsson's parents' difficulties added to his problems. Sometime earlier, they had rented a house. But things had not worked out, and the stay ended disastrously when John Peter falsely accused their landlord of embezzling a $50 check he had given her to purchase a wheelchair for Ellen.[49] Jonsson sent them what little money he could, but he was so busy that he relied heavily on Margaret to help them.

In 1928, Jonsson renegotiated the mortgage on the Conrad Road house so that its principal of $5,000 plus interest would not be due until 1931, when they would lease it for income. He managed to buy another house for the couple's residence. It was valued at $7,000, and located at 264 Hillside Avenue in Palisades Park, New Jersey.[50]

Problems at Dumont Motor Car marched relentlessly on. Letter after letter demanded payments, expressed disappointment about broken promises, and sometimes threatened legal action.

Jonsson's disillusionment was reflected in a complaint to the district manager. The factory had sent him a Pontiac Sport Roadster, which he "*did not order*" and would have trouble selling. "We have an exceptionally poor market here for roadsters, and we think the one which we now have in stock is enough—in fact, we wouldn't keep that if it weren't required by our contract," Jonsson wrote. "If," he emphasized, "in direct contradiction to all that has been said to us by your representatives . . . we are to be forced to take merchandise that we don't want, that franchise has lost its most attractive feature." But he took the unwanted cars. He feared he might otherwise lose the franchise.[51] Jonsson later elaborated this way: "In the Spring when we wanted Sport Roadsters . . . they would suddenly [send] what they call Lando Sedans with mohair upholstery for the worst winter. If you wanted them painted green, you got them painted red. . . . They would send you six greens with no variety. They would be on the siding with a bill of C.O.D. You rushed to the bank to borrow the money and unload the car and take them or else. So it was kind of rough. And I could not see any end to it."[52]

To make matters worse, he had difficulty in making payments on the Conrad Road house. In January 1929, the mortgage company threatened foreclosure unless he sent a check by return mail. When he stopped paying on his fire insurance policy, the mortgage company ordered him to resume making premium payments or else it would handle the matter and add the charges to his loan.[53]

Letters to the dealership demanding payment for overdue accounts became even more insistent. A few creditors accepted postdated checks. Some threatened to sue. When his *Bergen Evening Record* account became overdue, the newspaper discontinued his advertising.[54] To

"Robbie," Jonsson explained his debt this way: "I know you're sore as the devil with me and are thinking all kinds of things about me, but I just can't help it." A letter he wrote to John, to whom, two years earlier, he had promised (but failed) to deliver monthly payments of $100, showed some humor: "My naturally cheerful disposition working in conjunction with my exceedingly fine profile will undoubtedly bring in enough business from the ladies to keep us afloat. (Well put, I calls that.) Well, son, keep your chin up, among other things, and some day you'll be a successful business man like me."[55]

In early 1929, Jonsson sold Malcolm Bedell a share of the dealership for $800. But Bedell's capital, his help in the front office, and his emotional support could not turn the tide.[56]

To compound problems, Jonsson had his own problems in collecting from his customers. While the General Motors Acceptance Corporation (GMAC) financed automobile purchases, Jonsson carried notes for extra accessories such as bumpers, spare tires, trunks, and convertible tops. Suppliers of these products were trying to collect from Jonsson while he attempted to collect from his customers.

By May 1929, he had made the inevitable decision to shut down the business. Before he could close, Wall Street suffered its shocking Black Thursday collapse on October 24, 1929, a day followed by further declines that marked the end of the Roaring Twenties and the beginning of the Great Depression.

In December 1929, Jonsson sold his remaining cars in a job lot. He owed GMAC $983.50. He surrendered two of his three business properties for indebtedness as well as his house on Hillside, losing $6,000 in equity to settle a note of about $2,500. He and Margaret moved with Philip into an apartment. Jonsson owned a used Studebaker worth $125. He had no money and no job. He took out a $326 loan on his life insurance policy.[57]

Margaret's father was not surprised. He returned a $1,000 note Erik had signed two years earlier, which, with interest, had reached $1,150. Since it was a personal loan, Fonde doubted that Erik would "get it in," evidently a reference to the possibility of reclaiming a portion of it in bankruptcy proceedings. "Sorry the business has gone bad," he wrote. He added a postscript: "Would be glad to have you or Margaret write us about your future plans when you have any."[58]

More bad news came on April 28, 1930. Jonsson's mother, Ellen, died at the age of sixty-two. As she lapsed in and out of a coma-like state, she twice called loudly for her son by name.[59] A Montclair funeral home, Van Tassell & Roy, Inc., handled arrangements and presented the $497 bill to Erik. He could pay only $50. Half a year later he paid an additional $50. The funeral home said it "would be forced to take steps in the way of forced collection of this account." The debt lingered for years. Another invoice came from the convalescent home where his parents had been living. Erik was deemed responsible for the $190 bill. "Mr. Jonsson please try and pay something on this bill," the home pleaded with him a year after it was first due.[60]

The financial obligations were overpowering. Bankruptcy lay ahead. And so did something else—another risk-taking decision, but one that would pay off.

A Calculated Risk

Four and a half million Americans were unemployed. J. E. Jonsson, or John E. Jonsson, as he alternately referred to himself, was out of work and mired in debt. He and Margaret and their son shared a two-bedroom apartment with another couple. Much of their furniture was stored in a warehouse.[1]

Margaret envied a neighbor who daily set out milk for her cat when there was so little for Philip. In fact, Philip's lack of nutrition brought on rickets. Jonsson, somehow, remained confident that better times lay ahead.[2]

Looking for work at Western Electric's New Jersey plant, he saw employees producing telephone parts "no bigger than your little fingernail." The sight depressed him. "I had not starved quite enough," he said later, rejecting the possibility of a job.[3] (Years later, ironically, he would make a fortune by manufacturing tiny electronic parts.)

In desperation, he returned to Alcoa's Aluminum Index Co., signing on as a sales engineer at the office in Newark for $250 a month, $25 less than before, but supplemented with commissions on sales, primarily aluminum chairs and aluminum roofing. After six weeks, his commission was only $46.56.[4]

His first sale was for the roof on a fifteen-story apartment house under construction in Orange. Jonsson rode with the architect to the top in the construction elevator, climbed a ladder over space with nothing below, and walked on wooden planks fifteen stories high. "I didn't want to do it, but I did, which shows you that in dire financial straits you'll do what you have to do," he later said. He made the sale, the first aluminum roof the company sold to anyone. "Boy, was I ever proud of that," he recalled. He soon made other sales, including gutters for a development of 3,000 houses, which he never collected because the builder went broke.[5]

⌒

The encounter on which his fortunes turned forever occurred on a blustery day in March 1930. The switchboard operator informed him that he had two visitors.

He knew one of them, John Clarence Karcher, who was married to Margaret's cousin Lydia Kilburn. The two men did not have a close relationship, but the Jonssons had exchanged visits at Christmas with the Karchers, who were living in New Jersey. Jonsson considered Karcher, half a dozen years older and with a PhD, to be a brilliant scientist, which he was. Karcher already had done the work that would lead to his acclaim as father of the reflection seismograph, a sophisticated sound-wave device for discovering underground formations likely to yield oil. The other visitor was Eugene McDermott, two years older than Jonsson, born and reared in Brooklyn, the son of a New York City assistant postmaster.

They seemed rather bedraggled, shabbily dressed in old clothes and wearing casual workmen's caps. Jonsson later said they looked just a bit better than the out-of-work apple sellers on the streets of New York. The two men had formed a new company, which was soon to be converted into a corporation to be known as Geophysical Service Inc. Karcher explained that earlier they had placed an order for aluminum castings and needed faster delivery. Remembering Jonsson's position there, Karcher thought he possibly could expedite the order. Jonsson agreed to try.[6]

The two men also wanted to establish credit for future orders. Jonsson assured them that there would be no problem. They had another concern. Did Jonsson have a relationship with a bank? Jonsson did, and he escorted them across the street to the National Newark and Essex Banking Company, where he had his own small account, and Alcoa a much larger one. The men opened a surprisingly large account, which immediately elevated Jonsson's status at the bank.[7]

Their unkempt appearance was explained by hard work and long hours. Karcher and McDermott were working and sleeping in a two-room hotel suite while they built Karcher's new seismic equipment to record underground sound waves generated by dynamite blasts and thereby identify formations that were likely sites for oil reservoirs. They had hired several draftsmen, and in the interests of secrecy, they were subcontracting the manufacturing of components to different shops in New Jersey. Karcher already had signed four contracts to search for oil in the Texas-Oklahoma region. Crews were assembling in Texas.

Jonsson did not imagine that he might play an important role himself in their endeavor. Nor did he know that their dominant partner was none other than the oilman Everette Lee DeGolyer, to whom he had delivered cigars as a boy. DeGolyer had put up $100,000 to start the company, giving him 50 percent of the stock. Karcher, with 30 percent, was president. McDermott, with 15 percent, was vice president. The remaining 5 percent was for staff members. The company's primary offices were to be established in Dallas, Texas, convenient to oilfields in that part of the country. They were working in New Jersey because it offered more manufacturing facilities than Texas did and was far from the prying eyes of competitors. Both men knew the area, too.[8]

↜

The circuitous route that led Karcher and McDermott to Jonsson's Alcoa office in Newark represents an interesting segment in the history of the American petroleum industry as well as a turning point in Jonsson's life. It also planted the seed that led to the formation of the company that eventually became Texas Instruments.

Karcher's graduate studies on sound waves, including experiments during World War I to locate enemy artillery by calculating the distance traveled by their air and seismic waves, had failed to be useful, but he was using the same technique to discover likely underground oil sources with his reflection seismograph method. This consisted of recording on moving paper the sound waves transmitted through the earth by dynamite blasts.

For help, Karcher had brought in McDermott, who had impressed him when he previously worked under him at Western Electric for a summer. McDermott gave up his doctoral studies in physics at Columbia in return for this "damn interesting" proposition. He and McDermott were in a rush to do further design work, have components made, and assemble the parts for the crews.[9]

Incorporation of Geophysical Service Inc. took place in Dallas on May 16, 1930, just as Karcher had told Jonsson it would. GSI offered a turnkey, scientific approach to identifying potential pools of oil. Seven additional contracts were added to the four in hand. New crew members were being hired in Dallas, and Jonsson already knew one of them. It was his onetime RPI roommate, fraternity brother, and rival in love—Roland Beers.[10]

Another new hire was H. Bates Peacock, a thirty-two-year-old PhD from the University of Iowa who would work out of Houston as a party chief. Peacock operated the company's first field-size reflection seismograph crew.

By July 1930, GSI's Newark shop was located above a Ford dealership at 185 Clinton Avenue. A handful of employees were assembling seismographic instruments there. Eugene McDermott's brother, William, was running the shop temporarily, and as Karcher and McDermott pondered his permanent successor, they thought of Jonsson. Should they ask him to leave Alcoa for their new company? They agreed to leave that decision to him. On July 12, 1930, "out of the clear blue sky," Jonsson received at his Alcoa office a telegram from Karcher in Oklahoma City, addressed to "Eric Johnson": "SEEKING COMPETENT MAN TO TAKE CHARGE OUR NEWARK OFFICE STOP WOULD YOU BE INTERESTED STOP TELEGRAPH ME WELLS ROBERTS HOTEL HERE AND SEND YOUR HOME ADDRESS." Twenty minutes later Karcher sent a telegram to Jonsson's home address with further details: "DESIRE YOU TAKE CHARGE OUR NEWARK OFFICE STOP YOU WILL HAVE CHARGE MANUFACTURE OF OUR INSTRUMENTS STOP YOU WILL BE EXPECTED TO MAKE OCCASIONAL FIELD TRIPS STOP CAN OFFER YOU FIVE THOUSAND PER YEAR STOP EXPECT TO BE AT WELLS ROBERTS HOTEL HERE FOR NEXT FEW DAYS."[11]

Jonsson knew nothing about geophysical instruments, but the proposed $5,000 salary dwarfed his $3,000 base pay at Alcoa. Philip was six years old, and Jonsson had just learned that Margaret was pregnant again. He was twenty-eight, with monumental debts. His job at Alcoa was, as he put it, "as safe as being in church." He could stay there for a lifetime. If he left Alcoa again, he surely could not return a third time. Karcher, McDermott, and the others might become millionaires, but he needed security in his life.[12]

But he recognized that Karcher and McDermott, both brilliant, were taking risks. Maybe, if they succeeded, he could advance with them instead of being mired in a big corporation. Karcher had told Jonsson that he had lost $75,000 in the stock market, and yet he seemed unperturbed. Here indeed was a bold adventurer.[13]

After agonizing for three days, Jonsson paid for a long-distance telephone call to Oklahoma City. Karcher assured him that he could handle the job. He suggested that Jonsson visit the shop and talk to William McDermott. "If he can do it, you know darn well that you can." After more agonizing, Jonsson accepted the offer. His Alcoa job was "plain vanilla," and he preferred a richer flavor.[14]

On July 26, 1930, Karcher, writing from Dallas, welcomed "Eric Johnson" to the company: "We are mighty glad to have you join our staff and help us push our work. There is considerable apparatus under construction at Newark now and we will wish to start more shortly." He wanted Jonsson to visit Texas soon to acquaint himself with GSI's fieldwork and possibly equip a small repair shop there.[15]

In early September 1930, Jonsson went by train to Texas for a ten-day visit. He would never forget his overwhelming sense of cleanliness when he reached Dallas, a feeling shared by others from the East, where buildings were discolored by soot from coal. Dallas's important energy source, natural gas, left no visible marks on its buildings. "But most of all," he said, "I was impressed by the cheerful demeanor of the people . . . . Just going into a store and having a clerk greet you with a bright smile and say, "what can I do for you?" . . . instead of "what do you want?" . . . and then saying "thank you, hurry back" at the end of the transaction . . . this was something new to me!"[16]

He spent a day or so in Dallas, a week in the oil fields of East Texas and Oklahoma, and another couple of days in Dallas, where he met more people and watched trucks being equipped with instruments that he had assembled in Newark.[17] Back in New Jersey, he told Margaret that he had seen where they should be living and that one day, perhaps, they would. Margaret replied that anywhere south of the Mason-Dixon line would suit her. For the next four years, though, they would remain in Newark.[18]

Working with Jonsson at the "laboratory" were Alfred Morel (draftsman), Henry Stoll (toolmaker), and Tony Case (electrical assembler).[19] Sometimes, when Karcher was there, Everette DeGolyer would come, although Jonsson had no idea why. On those occasions, Jonsson reacquainted himself with his former cigar customer, who sometimes sat next to his desk to chat. Two years passed before Jonsson discovered that DeGolyer was GSI's primary owner.[20]

As Karcher and McDermott spent time in New Jersey, Jonsson realized that he preferred dealing with McDermott. Karcher seemed egotistical and distant, a perception shared by others. McDermott, friendlier, appreciated Jonsson's practical side. In late 1930, Karcher promised Jonsson a much-needed raise in early 1931. This was sensational news for the economically strapped shop manager, but to his growing distress, no raise would come for another five painful years.[21]

In October 1930, on the enthusiastic endorsement of Roland Beers, McDermott hired an electrical engineer named Cecil H. Green as a field-crew chief. When a child, Green had departed his native England with his parents for Canada; they then relocated to San Francisco just before the great 1906 earthquake. This frightening event prompted their return to Canada, where Green grew up, developing a lifelong interest in music and becoming an accomplished violinist. He earned undergraduate and master's degrees at the Massachusetts Institute of Technology and then worked with firms such as General Electric and Raytheon, and finally with Charles V. Litton in California.[22]

Green's wife, Ida, upset with her husband's long hours with Litton, began venting her frustrations by mail to Roland Beers and his wife, whom she and her husband had met at Raytheon. Beers described the appealing adventures he was experiencing with GSI in the Southwest. Both Greens, who loved adventure, were intrigued. In 1927, when such a drive was a daring act, they made a thirty-three-day cross-country automobile trip to the West Coast, traveling 4,388 miles. A year later they returned to the East Coast, and a year after that they made their third transcontinental automobile trip.[23]

When GSI hired him, Green and his wife were in the New York City area, so they stopped by Jonsson's house to get acquainted. Green immediately impressed Jonsson. Their long friendship and association thus began.[24] The two appreciated the fact that they had much in common: both had immigrant parents; both had a fascination for automobiles; both had learned much about cars through jobs as mechanics; both had been hired as chauffeurs by men who owned cars but could not drive them; and both had been fascinated by wireless receivers. Jonsson had built them and Green, as a student at the University of British Columbia before transferring to MIT, had helped organize a wireless club.[25]

⌒

Karcher and McDermott regularly forwarded new sketches to Jonsson. He, nearly 2,000 miles away, dealt with the practicalities of implementing their designs. To ensure secrecy, Jonsson and his employees continued to take separate sections of the designs to different shops and then assembled the parts into a whole instrument.[26]

Uncertainties plagued him. Hearing no more about his promised raise, he feared that GSI might be in trouble. Yet every three months or so, he received something else to fabricate. Intent upon economizing, he urged Karcher and McDermott to reduce the size of the shop. Stop worrying, they told him. He had no idea that GSI was making fine profits.[27]

His confidence in his own abilities grew as he successfully refined the seismometer. Karcher and McDermott both had better skills as designers than he did, but Jonsson realized that he could improve their designs and make the equipment faster, cheaper, smaller, lighter, and more usable. The initial thirty-four-pound instrument was cumbersome, and Jonsson remembered an airplane designer's motto: "Simplify and make it lighter." Following that principle, he substituted aluminum and magnesium for heavy brass and steel parts, which also lowered costs by about 25 percent. Another benefit was faster production.[28]

Karcher and McDermott wore coat and tie when wooing new customers, shirtsleeves while at the drafting board, and work clothes in the field. One day Karcher, sweaty and mud covered, was handling one end of a two-man auger to drill shot holes for dynamite. The second man, a new employee, was pressed into service as a drill hand. He did not know Karcher, and he was none too happy about manual labor. "I'm a field observer," he complained, "and I hired out to be a field observer when I came to GSI. I didn't hire out to dig any holes."

"Neither did I," Karcher grunted.

"What did you hire out to be?" the new employee asked.

"Well," said Karcher, "I'm president. So, I guess I hired out to be president."[29]

McDermott likewise worked as a jack-of-all-trades. He spent much time circulating among clients to keep them happy, and he visited GSI's twelve crews as they worked in Oklahoma, Texas, and, by 1931, Mexico.

Party chiefs such as Green earned $600–$700 a month, considerably more than Jonsson. To find them and other skilled employees—surveyors, computers, and observers—colleges were scoured for engineers who could appreciate the technology and work in harsh environments. Employees had to be adaptable. In a single year, Cecil and Ida Green moved thirteen times.[30] This unusual lifestyle constituted the heart of GSI's operations.

⌐

Jonsson's own work was nothing like this. The failure to get his pay raise was a major disappointment, but he reminded himself that at least he had a job. His unpaid debts remained crushing, though, and he was making little headway in paying them off. Money was so tight that the Jonssons moved in for a while with Malcolm Bedell, who was married with two small children.[31]

On January 5, 1931, Jonsson's financial obligations assumed larger dimensions when his second son, Kenneth Alan, was born. Nine days later, one of Jonsson's remaining automobile dealership properties, at 59 East Madison Avenue, was foreclosed on and sold at a sheriff's auction.[32] "It will take a session over the friendly cups to spill our hero's autobiography," Jonsson wrote shortly afterward to an RPI friend, Stewart McFarlane. "Suffice to note our acquisition of a most suitable spouse and two sons, Skippy aged six and Kenneth aged six weeks. Further progress along this line may be reported when the depression lifts—quien sabe—as we used to say in dear old Stockholm."[33]

The purchase of a home at 1144 Magie Street in Elizabeth, New Jersey, accomplished with the help of Margaret's father, temporarily buoyed the family's spirits. But by May 1931 an important decision had been made. Jonsson could see no way to pay his debts. His promised raise was nowhere in sight. He was falling further behind.

He chose what seemed to be his only option: bankruptcy. His new house would be protected. On July 23, 1931, George W. W. Porter, referee in bankruptcy for the U.S. District Court in New Jersey, declared John E. Jonsson bankrupt. A printed schedule listed Jonsson's liabilities at more than $12,000, including $2,760 owed to his father-in-law. He had assets of just $80 ($50 in clothing, $10 in golf clubs and fishing tackle, and $20 in books). Two months afterward, on August 21, 1931, creditors began proving their claims. Almost a year later, on August 1, 1932, the court declared Jonsson discharged from bankruptcy.[34]

Jonsson's father, John Peter, took what Erik cynically called "his usual cheerful perspective." He declared gloomily that his son would never recover. He was ruined. Erik, not agreeing, laughed, which enraged his father. "He thought I was making fun of him," Erik recalled.[35]

Margaret's father felt "partly responsible" for Erik's "unfortunate investments" because of his loans to the couple. To help a little, Hiram Fonde reduced a note he held against Erik and Margaret from $2,750 to $1,500. As a further gesture, he enclosed in his December letter a $4 money order so they could "buy something for Christmas for those two fine boys."[36]

Perhaps a new dog would cheer things up. Philip, or Skippy, as his parents called him, was now seven years old. Jonsson tried to win a *Newark Ledger* contest for a free dog for the best-written request. "How we came to let him get this far along in his life and experience without a dog, I can't explain," Jonsson wrote. "But one thing is certain—since we read about your contest in the Ledger, it's going to be pretty tough on Daddy if we don't win."[37]

He sent a more fanciful letter to the radio broadcaster Lowell Thomas for "The Tall Story Club." He had been persuaded, he wrote, through Thomas's sponsor, Sun Oil Company, to fill his car with its gasoline and its "mercury process oil." The ride afterward had been so smooth and hypnotizing that he had driven right past his New Jersey house to the World's Fair in Chicago. (The Century of Progress International Exposition was held in Chicago from May 1933 to October 1934.) Returning very quickly for an appointment the next morning, he later heard that tornadoes had been spotted along the highway. "That tornado," Jonsson explained, "was nothing but the Big Wind following my car, and the whole thing wouldn't have happened if you and Jimmy hadn't persuaded me to change my brand of gas and oil." In a postscript, Jonsson added that he also had tried a few drops of Sunoco household oil on an old grandfather clock that had been idle for five years. The clock not only started running, he wrote, it "went so fast that it made up those past five years and was now eight years fast."[38]

Perhaps such humor helped conceal stress. Margaret's father had lent them another $1,750 at 6 percent interest, and they had been unable to repay him. On May 5, 1933, Hiram C. Fonde filed suit—undoubtedly a friendly one—against his son-in-law and daughter in the circuit court at Elizabeth, New Jersey. Fonde evidently knew that they were planning bankruptcy for Margaret, and he was establishing priority for payment upon liquidation of her assets. Margaret's few assets had been untouched by her husband's bankruptcy, and she now filed for bankruptcy in her own name. On June 16, 1933, George W. W. Porter, the same referee who had declared her husband bankrupt, made that declaration for Margaret Jonsson.[39]

Philip, now nine, was sent to summer camp in Maine so that he would not see the family furniture auctioned off. Before he returned home, though, his parents had managed to buy back the furniture. Thus, the unsuspecting Philip found the house and furniture just as he had left it.[40]

Throughout the Jonssons' financial difficulties, Fonde, aside from his small loans, believed it best to stand aside. A few years later, Mrs. Fonde told her daughter that she worried "dreadfully" as her husband merely watched during these hard times. Based on Margaret and Erik's own experiences with Fonde, she said, they would never believe how good he could be to people in need. Perhaps, though, she surmised, he had been "right in the long run" by declining to come to their assistance.[41]

⌒

Reconciling his own problems with GSI's prosperity must have been difficult for Jonsson. GSI's reflection seismograph method, the *Oil and Gas Journal* reported, was "in particular vogue." By the end of 1933, GSI crews were operating in twelve states from New York to Montana to Louisiana, in three Canadian provinces, and at three locations in Mexico. In 1934 they reached Venezuela.[42]

So busy were Karcher and McDermott that they again turned to Jonsson. At dinner in New York City, Karcher told him that administrative details were overburdening them in Dallas because they were so often in the field. With some two hundred scattered employees, affairs were increasingly complex. The rationale for the shop in distant New Jersey had faded. Karcher wanted Jonsson to close it down, ship the equipment to Dallas, and move there himself to oversee the shop and help in the office.[43]

Jonsson had been unhappy with Karcher. For four years he had been waiting for the promised raise. Nevertheless, he had known since visiting Dallas in 1930 that he wanted to live there. So his response was immediate. Would Monday be too early?[44]

In April 1934, Jonsson sent the equipment and his household goods to Dallas by rail. Two other Newark employees, Al Morel and a man remembered only as Otto, joined the Jonsson family in a two-car caravan for Texas, letting out Margaret and the two boys in Tennessee for a visit. Jonsson's fraternity brother Roland Beers had already established himself in Dallas, but since he usually was out of town, he let Jonsson stay in his house until he found his own place.[45]

Within days, Jonsson found a "perfectly wonderful duplex" at 4424 Westway Avenue in Highland Park, an island town within Dallas. The duplex, rented for $75 a month, had only two bedrooms, but it was large and beautifully done. There were even servants' quarters over the garage. Jonsson's transfer did not bring the long-delayed pay raise, but Dallas's lower cost of living helped considerably.[46]

Dallas's unremarkable location on the flatlands of North Texas had prompted Jonsson's traveling companion, Otto, to make a telling remark as they approached it and saw skyscrapers: "Now yust vhy vould dey build a city so far out in de country?"[47] Dallas's population, swollen to some 300,000 by arrivals from surrounding farms, was a city in which leading businessmen dominated civic affairs. As GSI's decision to locate there indicated, a number of oil fields, especially the East Texas field, were transforming its economic base from agriculture and cotton to petroleum. Dallas's Republic National and First National banks were prospering because of their willingness to make loans based on oil reserves beneath the earth's surface. Rising above the skyline was the twenty-nine-story Magnolia Petroleum Building, topped that year by a new and distinctive, double-sided flying red horse, Pegasus.

When Margaret and the boys arrived, Jonsson drove them around town in his 1932 Pontiac, pointing especially to the large homes along Armstrong Parkway in the affluent Highland Park area. Philip, ten years old, remembered later how his father went on and on about Dallasites' "can-do" spirit. Dallas forever would be home for them, Jonsson told his family. Margaret was just happy to be nearer her southern roots.[48]

Their social life immediately improved. On their first Christmas in Texas, they entertained the Karchers and the Greens at their duplex. A week later, the Jonssons and Greens spent a late New Year's Eve at the Karcher house—the Greens didn't get home until three thirty in the morning. A few hours later on New Year's Day, both families returned to the Karcher residence. This time, Ida Green noted in her diary, there were "no drinks served."[49]

The relationship between the Jonssons and Greens grew close. Jonsson and Beers supported Green's formal application for citizenship. Jonsson's expertise with automobile mechanics led him to alert Green to possible problems with the rod bearings in his Buick. Sure enough, Green found five of eight bearings "shot" and had them replaced.[50]

A curious John Peter Jonsson asked his son to send him a map of "Dallas City" and some newspapers. John Peter, now living alone, was intrigued at the possibility of moving there, but if Erik thought Texas summers would be too hot, he would stay in New Jersey. (Much later he would move to Dallas.) Jonsson was sending his dad small monthly stipends as well as $10 payments to Bedell's mother, "Granny Bedell," on an old loan.[51]

What Karcher and McDermott needed from Jonsson was someone who could tend to the office while they were away. They had contracts with Magnolia, Sinclair, American Liberty, Sun, Gulf, Shell, and other oil companies. Although brilliant, they could not be administrators from the field.

Jonsson reassembled his shop at the corner of Browder and Canton Streets at the edge of downtown, but almost immediately he began spending most of his time at a desk between those of the usually absent Karcher and McDermott. Dozens of details needed attention. As he handled them, his responsibilities soon encompassed purchasing, personnel, insurance, and advertising. He gave orientations to employees hired by Karcher or McDermott who came to Dallas to fill out the paperwork. When GSI field crews needed supplies, they asked Jonsson to order them. Financial matters fell into his lap. He sometimes handled bank accounts for employees in the field, and he became the point man for the company's accounts at Republic National and First National. Before long, he was negotiating loans.[52]

Writing letters and other documents posed no problem. His all-around capabilities, combined with a fine temperament, were undeniable. As weeks and months passed, Jonsson became immersed in all the company's administrative aspects. He even began to ponder long-term company objectives. He was becoming indispensable.[53]

Sometimes he would not see either of his bosses for ten days or more. When he discussed problems with them on the telephone, they told him to do whatever he had to. Jonsson handled pressures very well—he was accustomed to them. "It was, shall we say, my dish," he later said.[54]

He found an entirely different business environment in Dallas from the one in New Jersey, where purchase orders were "pretty close" to being legal contracts. In Dallas, he made verbal agreements, "eyeball to eyeball" or over the telephone, writing up the order later. "This was a new world for me, and I liked every bit of that," he said years later. He was so confident about staying in Dallas that after about a month he purchased cemetery lots.[55]

Before his first year in Dallas ended, Jonsson was elected secretary of the corporation. The title of treasurer was not far away.

His relationship with the hard-driving Karcher was not as smooth as he would have liked, though. One Friday afternoon, he was sketching an idea about improving the seismometer when Karcher asked what he was doing. "Oh, I just had an idea I thought I would pursue and see if it was any good," Jonsson responded. "You could do better to keep your job caught up all the time," Karcher replied. Furious, Jonsson went home. On Monday he returned with a letter of resignation, which he placed in his desk, vowing that if Karcher reproached him again, he would hand it to him. But from then on, he left the engineering to Karcher and McDermott.[56]

Actually, both Karcher and McDermott were pleased at Jonsson's performance in the office. Years later, Philip Jonsson asked his father to explain how he rose from shop foreman to chairman of the board and chief executive officer of one of the world's largest and most innovative technology corporations. Jonsson said he had simply watched his bosses to find things they didn't want to do and then did those things for them.[57]

Jonsson had found a niche that particularly suited him. He was an organization man. He did not enjoy working alone. Being a manager was what he liked best.[58]

His sense of humor was an asset, and some of his practical jokes became legendary in company lore. He played golf with the warehouse superintendent, E. J. (Jim) Toomey, and a third man, who usually won. Jonsson and Toomey injected a golf ball with mercury and secretly substituted it before their friend putted. The putt veered wildly as planned, but somehow found its way into the hole, leaving all three in tears from laughter. On another occasion, two GSI employees, returning from a South American assignment on a weekend when the banks were closed, used Jonsson as their reference when they attempted to write checks at the hotel's front desk. Jonsson, contacted by the hotel, expressed amazement that these two "were out already." Any check they wrote up to $2 or $3 would probably be all right, he said. Only after a lengthy explanation was the air cleared.[59]

On February 26, 1935, at long last, Karcher authorized Jonsson's pay raise, in a strangely redundant letter to "Mr. J. E. Jonsson." He wrote: "You are hereby authorized to increase the salary of J. E. Jonsson from $416.67 to 500.00 per month effective as of March 1st nearest."[60]

A reminder of Jonsson's lingering financial difficulties came two months later. George O. Van Tassell, who had handled funeral arrangements for Jonsson's mother, threatened to sue him to reclaim the old balance of $497. Jonsson responded that bankruptcy cleared his debt in 1931. "What little remained to us after my own bankruptcy was swept away when my wife also had to go through bankruptcy in 1933," he said.

"At that time we had to borrow money to buy back our households goods and pay legal expenses, and we are just now finishing payment."[61] At any rate, Jonsson eventually paid Van Tassell, who sent him a notarized "General Release." Years later, Jonsson told his daughter Margaret Ellen that he had repaid everyone.[62]

↜

Some family difficulties occurred in adjusting to Dallas. Philip, a fourth grader, perceived some hostility because he was a "Yankee." A school counselor told the Jonssons that an outside interest would help. Philip, encouraged by a friend, began making both crystal and tube radio sets. Jonsson was supportive in this, but he did not reveal the many late hours he had spent building radios himself. Oftentimes, Jonsson took his son to school. Already, though, his duties at GSI were taking much of his time. Six-day workweeks were normal.[63]

Margaret Jonsson's initial difficulties were mitigated by her friendship with Lydia Karcher. Margaret became active in the Parent-Teacher Association at Philip's elementary school. Often, when he went through the school lunch line, he was served by his own mother. Margaret's spirits were buoyed in late 1934 when her mother visited and instantly adored the city. "People there have money and spend it," she said.[64]

↜

The more Geophysical Service expanded, the more work fell to Jonsson. Final decisions on contractual matters belonged to the owners, but Jonsson assumed authority over them. Contracts required careful attention to detail because of the wildly different fields of operations, especially as international operations grew. Would the crew work in a jungle or desert? Would vehicles or mules work best for transporting equipment? Would four-wheel drive be required? Dealing with such details gave him an invaluable overview of operations.[65]

When the company needed to borrow money, Jonsson made the arrangements, usually from Republic Bank, in whose building GSI offices were located. In these negotiations Jonsson dealt with the bank's president, Fred Florence, one of Dallas's most influential behind-the-scenes leaders. GSI's profitability permitted quick repayment, and Jonsson was able to negotiate loans from Florence with a minimum of red tape.

In 1936, GSI crews were sent to Colombia. A year later they were in Saudi Arabia, Java, Sumatra, and Ecuador. Their increasing numbers called for more and more equipment, and the machine shop was moved to a two-story building at 2114 North Harwood Street. It had an upstairs machine shop and a ground-floor garage big enough to hold eight or nine specially outfitted exploration trucks. Because of tough oil field conditions, the vehicles had to be overhauled every couple of years.[66]

In remote locations such as Colombia, conditions were so primitive that mule trains were used. Sending supplies to crews in faraway places was a major task requiring imagination and nerve, and Jonsson was ultimately responsible for it.[67] Accordingly, in 1935 he applied for and received membership in the Society of Petroleum Geophysicists.[68]

His work as purchasing agent, which he had done since joining GSI in 1930, now occurred on a bigger scale. He joined the Dallas Purchasing Agents Association, and a year later was on its board of directors. In April 1937 he was elected vice president. His photograph, appearing in the statewide *Southwestern Purchaser*, revealed a tall man with a slightly bemused expression and thinning hair parted in the middle. This affiliation marked his first experience in stepping outside GSI and becoming involved in professional affairs.[69]

A year later he became the association's president, earning a glowing word portrait in the *Southwestern Purchaser*: "[He] has made himself one of the most popular newcomers to Dallas business circles in many years. He combines both seriousness of purpose and good fellowship into one nature and his wit and love of fun has enlivened many meetings. It is certain that under his leadership the Association will reach a new high in both accomplishment and social activities."[70]

Jonsson now entered another new phase of his life—speech making. His humor and his ability to view his work in perspective were evident. A purchasing agent, Jonsson said, was "a chap just like you and me—someone alive and warm with the same hopes and desires, the same fears, the same ambitions." He was something like a salesman, but without the expense account. Purchasing, Jonsson said, was both a science and art, and the purchasing agent had to be a master of both.[71]

In 1940 he was one of several featured speakers in Fort Worth at the annual conference of the Southwestern Sales Managers. He entitled his talk "A Few Facts about Purchasing Agents and What They Do and Do Not Like about Salesmen."[72]

⌒

On August 7, 1938, the birth of a daughter, Margaret Ellen, completed the family. The caesarean birth was difficult for the mother, and Jonsson later would say, "We almost lost her when the baby came." The children, each seven years apart, were born at wildly different periods in their father's fortunes. Philip arrived in 1924 when his father's future seemed boundless; Kenneth came in 1931 amidst the Depression and failure; and Margaret Ellen began life as the daughter of a middle-management executive who was looking to the future with great anticipation.[73]

Another Turning Point

Geophysical Service was setting new standards in science-based oil exploration. Oil companies contracted with GSI to find deposits all over the world: Canada, Venezuela, Colombia, Saudi Arabia, Java, Sumatra, and Ecuador.

A GSI crew found the first oil in Saudi Arabia, a country synonymous ever after with the world's richest deposits. Crew members there lived in brush huts before eventually enjoying the relative luxury of tents. The desert heat forced them to arise before dawn to begin work. Tanks of water for bathing sometimes became too hot.[1]

In Sumatra, the only way to move equipment and supplies into flooded jungle sites was on the backs of workers, who maneuvered across the water and through the undergrowth on fallen tree trunks. To function in such an environment, a GSI crew of twenty required the support of at least seven hundred workers. Tigers and elephants occasionally were onlookers.[2]

Eugene McDermott observed that GSI's real work "was out in the fields where the crews were, not in the office."[3] Erik Jonsson identified with these experiences only from his desk, but his seat was good. No matter where GSI employees worked, their contact at headquarters was that man behind the desk. That man wrote and signed the letters stating their terms of employment; that man arranged for the equipment they needed in the field; that man made certain their salaries were deposited in a bank while they were away; and that man often was the only GSI officer present when they visited headquarters in the Republic Bank Building. It was also Jonsson, not Karcher or McDermott, who arranged GSI's loans for the company's expanding activities. So if, as

McDermott said, GSI's "real work" was in the fields, the glue that held the company together was Jonsson.

Ford Motor Company bought a full-page magazine advertisement in 1938 to tout its trucks' toughness. Three GSI trucks were shown. The featured letter documenting GSI's satisfaction with Ford trucks bore J.E. Jonsson's signature. "In some foreign countries the trucks have been operating in localities where there were no roads at all for as much as six months at a time," he wrote. For this reason, Jonsson said, all of GSI's trucks were Fords.[4]

Karcher and McDermott recognized his value. When Roland Beers left to form a competing company, Karcher feared that Jonsson might follow his former roommate. When he did not, Karcher rewarded him in April 1936 with another pay raise and a block of shares in a new GSI subsidiary, Coronado Exploration Company. The four-page contract guaranteed Jonsson's services for the next two years. The 444 shares of Coronado stock were to be awarded at intervals during the period of the contract.[5]

Karcher's and McDermott's establishment of Coronado as a subsidiary represented a new aspect of operations. When contracts with oil companies expired, GSI crews often found themselves at a remote site with nothing to do. The temptation to keep them busy in that area instead of laying them off was impossible to resist, for otherwise they might take their skills to a competitor rather than await GSI's next call. Retaining their expertise was important. Crews in this situation would now continue to look for oil, but for GSI itself. Their discoveries for GSI, and the oil subsequently produced by the fields, began to bring in more money than their work for other companies. The tail was beginning to wag the dog. Some clients were uncomfortable about this situation, and forming Coronado as a subsidiary was a thin disguise for GSI's own pursuits.

A reorganization in late 1938 reversed the relationship of GSI and Coronado. Wildly profitable Coronado became the parent company, and GSI the subsidiary. Coronado had the express purpose of producing oil; GSI would confine its activities to exploration in behalf of customers. Karcher became president of Coronado and established separate offices in downtown Dallas.[6]

The newly constituted GSI, chartered in Delaware and capitalized at $575,000, had McDermott as president, H. Bates Peacock in Houston as vice president, and Jonsson as secretary-treasurer. Headquarters remained in the Republic Bank Building. McDermott, preferring research, left administrative details to Jonsson, whose annual salary reached $8,400.[7]

The Jonsson family now could afford more comfortable surroundings. Margaret Ellen's birth in 1938 called for a bigger house. A two-story house that Jonsson purchased in 1939 at 4305 Belclaire for $15,750 was just a few doors from Armstrong Parkway, where Jonsson had driven his family in 1934 to show them Dallas's big houses. The house had eight rooms and servants' quarters. The move made Philip realize for the first time that the family's situation had significantly improved. A new Chickering grand piano seemed to confirm that fact.[8]

Inclined always to be a joiner, Jonsson began dipping his toe into civic waters. His luncheon club, the Loyal Knights of the Round Table, met weekly. His picture appeared in the *Dallas Morning News* as commissioner of the Boy Scouts of America division that was leading the local finance drive. Besides belonging to the Glen Lakes Country Club, where he frequently played golf on weekends, he joined the downtown Dallas Athletic Club, where businessmen took midday swims, workouts, or lunch. He and Margaret occasionally played tennis on the public courts along Turtle Creek Boulevard. On free evenings they liked to read and listen to the radio—Jack Benny, George Burns, and Gracie Allen. Once or twice a month they saw a movie. Margaret enjoyed gardening, knitting, crocheting, and reading, and she continued her friendship with Lydia Karcher. Cecil and Ida Green were frequent visitors, and the McDermotts came too, but less often than before. After Margaret Ellen's birth, the family got part-time help, but Margaret prepared most of the meals. Sometimes after dinner the family drove to an ice cream shop or a root beer stand.[9]

Philip, a teenager, went downtown on Saturday mornings with his father to the office, where, duplicating his dad's experience in Montclair, he sold copies of the *Saturday Evening Post*. Afterward, he peddled extra copies on the street from his shoulder bag.[10] Jonsson refused to let Philip take up his own youthful preoccupation with motorcycles. "Absolutely not," he said. "I know how dangerous they are."[11]

Someone told Philip that because of his interest in radios, he must be intending to attend the Massachusetts Institute of Technology. Philip asked his dad what it was. "It's the best technical school in the country,"

Jonsson replied. "But you don't need to worry about it because with your grades you won't have a chance." The words stung. Philip began studying harder and his grades improved. Upon graduating from high school, he applied for admission to MIT. He was advised first to go to another college for a semester. If he did well, he would be admitted to MIT. Philip enrolled at the University of Texas at Austin, made four As and one B, and transferred to MIT.[12]

Young Ken began caddying for his dad on the golf course when he was eight years old. When he was nine, in 1940, he spent part of a summer at the LZ Ranch in the Texas Panhandle. It was a "life summer training boys' camp" where he rode horseback, helped round up cattle, milked cows, and was imbued with training for "the responsibility of home life and citizenship."[13]

Margaret Ellen was the picture of health. Before too many more years passed, she would take up ice-skating and become a fierce competitor with great ambitions.

On the family's first significant vacation, they drove to Yellowstone National Park, stopping en route at the Broadmoor Hotel in Colorado Springs. The Broadmoor became a Jonsson favorite. Occasionally, Margaret took the children via train to visit her parents in Tennessee. Sometimes the Fondes, impressed by their son-in-law's rise in fortune, came to Dallas.[14]

John Peter Jonsson, feeble and able to walk only at a snail's pace, was eighty-six in 1940. He continued to buy and sell small amounts of stock, still trying to find gold at the end of the rainbow. A letter from his broker in September 1939 suggested the nature of his luck. "Baldwin Locomotive, which you bought on outside advice, not ours, cost you $43.70. It is quoted currently on the stock Exchange at 19 ½."[15]

His personal needs were being taken care of by a woman in a private home; Erik paid the expenses. The Montclair garage owner John Svenson was watching John Peter's condition carefully and keeping Erik informed. Discussions about a possible move to Texas had been going on since 1934, and now seemed more likely to be acted on.[16]

Sometime in 1940 or 1941, Jonsson brought his father to Dallas to live out his remaining years. John Peter Jonsson, a remote figure to his grandchildren, died in a nursing home at eighty-eight on Saturday, September 26, 1942, with his only child at his bedside. In his last days, John Peter told Erik that he had "added the whole show up" and was satisfied.

Cause of death was "arteriosclerosis and senility." He was buried at the Hillcrest Mausoleum in North Dallas. His obituary was limited to a few lines in the classified advertising section of the *Dallas Morning News*.[17]

"My father was a gruff person but he had a couple of traits I admired," Jonsson said in an understatement. "He had unbelievable persistence in the face of difficulty and he never made a great deal of money but he kept his credit unbelievably shiny."[18]

‿

Since GSI thrived on international exploration, the worldwide war that began in 1939 had a profound impact on its operations. Green was so discouraged that he announced his intention to quit the company, settle in California, and enter the aircraft industry.[19]

But in June 1941 startling news surfaced. Green mentioned it in his June 12, 1941, diary entry following a meeting with McDermott in Los Angeles. Karcher was selling Coronado to Stanolind (the exploration and production arm of Standard Oil of Indiana). There might be a chance, he had told McDermott, for key employees to buy GSI rather than include it in the sale.[20]

Karcher advised Jonsson that if a group of GSI principals could raise $300,000, they could buy GSI's 10,000 outstanding shares.[21] Jonsson called McDermott in California for direction. "Well, you are there," McDermott said. "Figure out a group of people that can do this and make some arrangements and call me back sometime during the week and tell me what you've done."[22]

Here, perhaps, Jonsson calculated, was the chance of a lifetime for a handful of compatible men. First would be McDermott, of course. Peacock in Houston and Green in California, both of whom knew field operations intimately, had to be included. Someone would have to run the company from headquarters, and Jonsson logically saw himself in that position. So these were the four critical men. McDermott, wealthy through the ownership of oil properties, could handle a one-fourth stake with no problem. Peacock, a scientist who had been paid well by GSI for a decade, similarly had ample resources. Jonsson by now had 444 shares of Coronado, and they were available as partial collateral for a loan, but he would need help. Green, too, was without sufficient resources. He might need even more help.[23]

On June 14, Green received an early-morning telephone call from Jonsson. The other three potential buyers needed his assurance. Would he join them? The answer was a tentative yes. In August, the four men met in Dallas and concluded that they would try to buy the company.[24]

Green changed his mind when he returned to California and heard Ida's strong desire to stay there. He wrote to say that he was resigning from GSI. When Jonsson read the letter, he picked up the telephone and told Green that his resignation would not be accepted until he returned for further discussions.[25]

Green knew, as did the others, that the departure of Coronado's moneymaking abilities would significantly reduce GSI's earning potential. By late 1941, only half a dozen crews were working. Domestic work had almost withered away in favor of international operations. Survival was uncertain. The company faced possible losses of as much as $10,000 a month.[26]

Nevertheless, here was an opportunity to buy at book value a company recognized as an innovator. In its short existence, GSI had discovered more than 150 oil fields. Many jobs would be lost if Stanolind sought to integrate GSI's geophysical services into its own geophysical unit.[27]

Green, responding to Jonsson's call, arrived in Dallas with Ida, each separately driving a Buick, a sign that they expected to stay. Peacock came from Houston, and on Monday, October 27, the four began discussions, frequently continuing over lunch at the Petroleum Club, that continued into the next week.[28]

Green sought outside advice from a man named Jack McClure, who knew the situation. "He said lots to encourage me—with particular reference to Erik Jonsson," Green wrote in his diary. Concerned that "radical" salary raises might be given foolishly, Green "tackled" McDermott and won assurance that this would not happen. Green also wanted there to be an agreement to sell the company if the Depression worsened. All agreed that if at least two of the four wanted to sell, it would be done. These assurances won over Green.[29]

On November 10, 1941, McDermott confirmed Stanolind's purchase of Coronado. Two brief stories appeared in the afternoon newspaper: "Karcher Sells Oil Company" and "Four Texans Buy Geophysical Firm Capital Stock." Actually, the "Texans"—two of them Brooklyn-born and another born in England—had not yet consummated their loans.[30]

Stanolind bought Coronado for $700 a share, or $7 million. DeGolyer, with 5,000 shares, grossed $3,500,000, having invested just $100,000 in 1930 to start the company. Karcher, with 2,995 shares, also earned a handsome profit.[31]

While preliminary arrangements had been agreed upon, the $300,000 loan was not completed. Jonsson later described a ten-day deadline to finish the transaction by Monday, December 8. He made arrangements, and on Friday, December 5, the four men, accompanied by the attorney Tom Knight of the Dallas law firm Thompson & Knight, went downstairs to Fred Florence's bank office and signed the documents.

The agreement acknowledged that Jonsson and Green lacked sufficient collateral for their $75,000 portions. To help them, GSI purchased half of their 1,250 shares for $37,500 to hold until the two could buy them back and reequalize the partnership. (They did within two years.)[32]

After signing the documents, the new owners and their wives celebrated. The next morning, Cecil and Ida Green drove to the Jonssons' house, where, as Green noted in his diary, it was necessary for Erik to apologize to Ida for "carrying on at [the] Petroleum Club late last night as result of drinking too much."[33]

"I felt good," Jonsson later said. "I owed more money than I had ever owed before and I had put up everything I had, but I was in business with three partners. While we weren't making money at that time, I thought I knew how to turn the red ink into blue."[34]

The GSI management structure continued, with McDermott as president, Peacock and Green as vice presidents, and Jonsson as secretary and treasurer. Peacock would stay in Houston, and Green would move to Dallas as operations manager. Each man would own 2,500 shares of the 10,000 shares of common stock.[35] Except for a favorable cash position and six functioning crews, GSI had not much to offer. "But we took our chances on this because we did know how to run the business, we had been running it pretty much autonomously, and we didn't see any reason why we couldn't bring it back by hard work," Jonsson said.[36]

⌒

On Sunday, December 7, 1941, two days after the transaction, Jonsson left his house after lunch to play golf at Glen Lakes Country Club. En route, he turned on his car radio. The Japanese had attacked and virtually destroyed the U.S. naval fleet at Pearl Harbor. "A million worries crossed my mind," Jonsson said, "not the least of which was that I probably had lost a lot of money I really didn't have. So maybe I was broke again; I didn't know. Maybe Cecil was broke again; I didn't know. Peacock and Mac—I knew they could stand it."[37] War would mean no more international exploration, shortages of critical geophysical supplies, and difficulty in fulfilling personnel needs. It might mean bankruptcy.

In the first few months after the United States entered the war, the temptation to lighten the owners' financial risks was great. Three weeks after Pearl Harbor, Bates Peacock wanted to broaden ownership by selling stock to employees. Green noted in his diary, "Erik balked at the idea." Peacock's proposal thus failed.[38]

Five months later, Green wanted to sell GSI to "the highest bidder, if any," because the four owners were being squeezed by taxes and employee wages. Green, McDermott, and Jonsson went round and round with the idea. McDermott agreed with Green, but Jonsson was adamantly opposed. Two days later, Peacock drove up from Houston for further discussions. McDermott, Green, and Peacock all favored selling GSI. Jonsson alone balked, and he held his ground despite the earlier agreement that if two of the four wanted to sell the company, they would.[39]

Jonsson agreed, however, that merging with a high-grade outfit such as Hoover United Geophysical, owned by Herbert Hoover Jr., might help. Hoover came to Dallas, and Jonsson visited Hoover's operations in San Francisco. In July 1942, Hoover made a merger offer on a 60–40 basis that would leave him controlling all the stock. All four GSI men agreed to reject his offer.[40]

Green confided to Jonsson his belief that leadership—referring evidently to McDermott and Peacock—had been lacking during these critical moments.[41] Actually, the period represented a turning point. In successfully resisting his partners, Jonsson had asserted his own strength. In years ahead he would provide the leadership to show that he had been right.

↶

As it turned out, the war did not ruin GSI. Thanks largely to Jonsson, the company prospered through government contracts. Even exploration recovered and eventually increased. GSI's six operating crews in 1941 had expanded to sixteen by 1945.

Earlier fears about survival were amply justified, though. The federal government did not consider oil exploration essential to the war effort. During the first year of war, military conscription of GSI personnel threatened to effectively shut down the business. Jonsson saw a solution. "Let's get into something that can be considered important as a sideline," he told his partners. Jonsson's idea, Green said, was to find a service essential to the military that GSI could provide.[42]

In May 1942, Jonsson took the first of many trips to the nation's capital to see what might be done. "I became a salesman part time, traveling to Washington," Jonsson later said. By the time the war was over, he had flown so many times on cramped passenger airplanes that for the first time flying became an ordeal instead of a pleasure.[43]

In 1942 he assumed a new title—vice president and treasurer. The added cachet helped as he searched for government contracts.

The first and most significant wartime contract that he secured was to build a magnetic airborne detector (MAD) for detecting enemy submarines. McDermott had been alerted by a friend at Columbia University that the navy needed manufacturers for such a product, and Jonsson went to Washington and won a contract.[44]

MADs were originally used to locate subterranean geological basins that might contain oil. Towed by aircraft with a 200-foot cable, the detector outlined sedimentary basins. Its ability to identify changes in the earth's magnetic field gave the navy's Bureau of Aeronautics the idea that it might also be able to detect German submarines.[45]

GSI began work in secrecy. A young engineer named Darwin Renner designed a prototype. Tests indicated that it worked. A bright ensign in Washington, D.C., Patrick E. Haggerty, had the job of assessing possible MAD contractors and awarding final contracts to two of them. GSI won a contract. Jonsson and Haggerty began what became a lasting working relationship.[46]

To do the work, GSI established a second machine shop in Dallas. A *Southwestern Purchaser* article referred to the project in cloaked terms for security reasons. The writer identified it only as "something that defies description," and he confidently declared that it held "the future of Texas industry."[47]

Fulfilling the contract was another matter. With many qualified men in military service, workers were scarce. Many of those capable of helping were earning excellent wages at munition plants. E. J. Toomey recalled how difficult it was to retain employees at $0.80 an hour when they could make $1.80 an hour at North American Aviation. Toomey, himself offered twice his GSI salary by North American, declined because he reasoned that a North American job would disappear at war's end. There was another factor too. "I had known Erik and Mc-

Dermott through the years and could not desert them," Toomey said.[48]

A second problem was in locating raw material. Jonsson turned to Malcolm Bedell, who combed East Coast junkyards for usable scrap metal. One of his discoveries was a heap of discarded metal billboards, which GSI converted into usable metal cases.[49]

In 1943 the MADs played a significant role in the Atlantic and Mediterranean in the struggle against German U-boats. Most notably, a navy squadron of Catalina flying boats nicknamed "Madcats" because of their use of MADs patrolled the Bay of Biscay in 1943 and triumphed in the "big Bay slaughter" of July 28–August 2, in which nine German U-boats were sunk.[50]

By this time it was clear that a modern war could not be won without abundant oil. Secretary of the Interior Harold Ickes established the Petroleum Administration for War (PAW) and appointed DeGolyer and Ralph Davis of Standard Oil of California as administrators. The two successfully lobbied for further exploration and against the indiscriminate drafting of geophysical personnel. GSI's exploration activities began to expand.[51]

Equipping new crews was difficult. Specially outfitted small trucks were essential to most field operations, but they were unavailable, since the automobile industry was producing only military vehicles. GSI bought discarded trucks, reduced them to their frames, rebuilt them, and painted them with GSI's standard silver and dark green. Often, parts retrieved from three junked trucks were required to create a single rebuilt one. The Harwood Street shop virtually became a small-truck assembly line.[52]

By war's end, GSI had done about $1 million worth of government business, earning a net profit of 10 percent. This was enough to pay off the loans from Republic Bank and enough to give the four owners— each with 2,500 shares—handsome dividends of $6.67 a share in 1942 and 1943 and $7 in 1944. In the last year, the value of the capital stock rose to $40 a share.[53]

Largely under Jonsson's guidance, internal operations were being transformed into those of a sophisticated company with excellent benefits for its employees. A profit-sharing trust for employees was inaugurated 1942 with $30,000, augmented by $40,000 the next year. A formula was established for further contributions. Employees earned shares proportionate to their earnings and years on the job.[54]

Green created a company newsletter. He encouraged employees and their families to send chatty, personal contributions to the publication, *GSI Grapevine*. Typical was this passage: "Al Storm's party in Canada expects to stay through the winter. Brrr. Well, Ray Wright's party is in Miles City, Montana, and they expect to tarry a while yet. Fred Agnich's party, late of Miles City, went South for the winter—to Laramie, Wyoming."[55]

During visits to Washington, Jonsson dealt notably with Haggerty, the ensign (soon lieutenant) who had chosen GSI to produce MADs. The scope of Haggerty's responsibilities was not suggested by his insignificant desk in a temporary wooden structure. His confident demeanor in a beehive of activity impressed Jonsson, and he noted the deference with which higher-ranking officers treated him. Haggerty, likewise, was impressed by this confident visitor named Jonsson who came from a small company whose one million dollars in military contracts was minuscule in comparison with others he awarded. A mutual admiration society developed. "It was easy for me to work with Pat," Jonsson later said. "He was clear, crisp and fair in whatever he proposed. It was also obvious that he was possessed of a high order of intelligence and extraordinary drive to get things done."[56] Whenever Jonsson visited Washington, the two would have a meal or a drink together. Jonsson met Haggerty's wife and three small children at their home in Arlington. The relationship paid further dividends when Haggerty began tipping off Jonsson to other wartime products the company could make.[57]

"I have run into a lieutenant up there in Washington that can make admirals jump right through the hoop when he wants to," Jonsson told R. C. (Bob) Dunlap, a field supervisor. "I haven't said anything to him and won't so long as this war is going on. But we've talked about starting something that can kind of back up GSI and kind of cushion some of these rises and falls. That's the guy going to do it. He doesn't know it yet but he's sure going to do it."[58] Hiring Haggerty amounted to one of Jonsson's finest contributions to the company that within a few years would be transformed, by a special boost from Haggerty, into Texas Instruments.

At the outbreak of war, Erik Jonsson—or John E. Jonsson as he continued to refer to himself—was a few months past forty. He was tall (six feet one and a half), big boned, and slightly balding, with a deep voice and commanding presence. His rise at GSI from machine shop supervisor to first among equals in a four-man partnership had reinvigorated a sense of self-worth that had been jeopardized in New Jersey. Even in his past distresses, though, he had held on to a conviction that his troubles were temporary. That confidence, it now was apparent, had been well placed.

⌒

The only Jonsson child to be affected by the war was Philip, who was in the army in California awaiting a ship-out date to the Pacific when the war ended. Philip returned to MIT in 1946 to receive degrees in physics and in business and industrial administration.[59]

GSI's wartime success meant there was money for luxury items. Jonsson's salary for 1942 was $14,599; stock dividends amounted to an additional $11,005. In 1943, his income jumped to $16,999, plus dividends of $19,941. Philip playfully called him "the big exec."[60]

With Karcher's sponsorship, Jonsson joined the Dallas Country Club, the city's most prestigious. He belonged to the Petroleum Club, the Civic Music Association, and the Dallas Museum of Fine Arts. He and Margaret purchased an expensive ($1,700) Persian rug for the living room, and he bought a $650 ermine coat for her at Neiman-Marcus. He donated $25 to the Republican Party just before the 1944 presidential election. In a community and state dominated by Democrats and practically devoid of Republicans, Jonsson was a Republican.[61]

He enjoyed fellowship at the Loyal Knights of the Round Table, a club he joined in the late 1930s, at Friday lunches at the Adolphus Hotel. Its members were "an oddly assorted group of madcaps" who were heads of businesses or "alarmingly staid and stolid company treasurers or vice presidents." In this club, Jonsson met some of his best friends, especially Hugo Koch, owner of Southwest Blueprint Company, and Walter Graham of Southwestern Life Insurance Company. Jonsson was the club's president in 1942–43, and from 1945 to 1948 he represented the Southern Division as one of four vice presidents of the international Loyal Knights of the Round Table.[62]

One of the wildest entertainments occurred in 1943 at a "woman-less wedding." Jonsson, president, dressed up as the bride. A wig with golden tresses covered his head, and a lock of hair hung down over one eye in the manner of the movie star Veronica Lake. The "ceremony" was interrupted when Margaret Jonsson stormed onto the scene carrying a realistic doll, shrieking that she hadn't been done right by the groom.[63]

Jonsson attended the organization's international convention in 1948 in Washington, D.C. For perhaps the first time in print, he was identified as J. Erik Jonsson.[64]

〜

As a GSI owner, Jonsson knew he would spend long hours away from his family. When the opportunity to buy in arose, he summoned Margaret and the children. A good outcome would mean more opportunity for all of them, he said, but if he pursued this course, they would not be seeing as much of him as they might prefer. "If you tell me you'd rather I become a family man and perhaps less successful, then that's what I'll do," he told them. "But if you tell me to have at it, I'll do that. What do you say?" They agreed that he should go ahead.[65]

What he told his family became accurate on every count. Wealth would bring luxuries for the Jonssons, their children, and succeeding generations. Erik and Margaret would donate millions of dollars to worthy causes. Equally true was his prediction about his hours and days away from home.

He and his partners would achieve success to a degree they never could have imagined. Through their generosity, their riches would be shared throughout American society as they donated millions of dollars to higher education, medical research, and other worthwhile causes.

Foreseeing the Future

Later, Erik Jonsson stated, "The whole history of Texas Instruments really began during the war." Other companies might return to peacetime pursuits afterward, but he thought GSI should intensify its efforts to win military contracts. As treasurer, he was mindful of the need for a steadier flow of income to provide ballast against the vicissitudes of the seismic exploration business and resources for a sustained research program. As an engineer and the executive who oversaw GSI's laboratory, he knew the company's capabilities. As the one who negotiated wartime contracts and was familiar with governmental bureaucracies, he was confident that further contracts would be available.[1]

He had discussed these ideas with Pat Haggerty, twelve years his junior but prescient about such matters. Both men anticipated a postwar arms race with the Soviet Union. Both saw a continuing need for MADs and other electronic products. Both believed that GSI should establish itself in the electronics business as a government contractor.[2] There was some irony. At Rensselaer, Jonsson had taken some electrical engineering courses but had "cordially hated" them.[3]

Jonsson wanted to hire Haggerty. A few days after Japan's surrender, Jonsson was in Washington, ostensibly to discuss the cancelation of MAD contracts, but primarily to hire Haggerty. He could not tell him just what GSI would be doing in military or government electronics, and Haggerty's background did not particularly fit GSI's normal business requirements.[4] But, Haggerty said, if Jonsson could establish a unit for electronic engineering and manufacturing, then he was "damned interested." Jonsson talked over these possibilities with his partners. McDermott and Green approved; Peacock, committed to the oil business, acquiesced reluctantly.[5]

Haggerty visited Dallas and was favorably impressed. He found the GSI owners to be "unusual human beings" surrounded by "an awful lot of other nice people." Before his return flight to Washington, he and Jonsson discussed the visit over drinks. In a remark that later would have embarrassed him, Jonsson leaned over in his avuncular way and said, "Well, Pat, old Erik hasn't done so bad for himself. Must be worth a quarter of a million already!"[6]

Haggerty's friendship with Jonsson was an important factor in Haggerty's taking the job. He saw in Jonsson a fundamental honesty and morality. He also had a high opinion of Dallas and Texas, for he and his wife, Beatrice, had driven through the city and much of the state in 1938 en route to Mexico for their honeymoon. They liked its "flavor."[7]

Wartime experience had taught Haggerty that two kinds of companies did well with government contracts. First were the big ones such as Western Electric, blessed with magnificent manufacturing plants, well-trained engineers, and deep financial pockets. Such companies were good but "slower than hell." It seemed to Haggerty that a moderately sized company could handle a complex job as well as a big one if it were so closely knit that it could move with the speed of a small one.[8]

Jonsson had several Bureau of Aeronautics men in mind to hire as well. First, he asked Haggerty to help recruit Robert W. Olson, with whom Haggerty had fantasized about forming a company "that would let us take a flight into electronics, to see where we could go." Now was their chance. Haggerty reported in October 1946 that Olson would come, too.[9]

"I am 'champing at the bit and raring to go'!" Haggerty wrote to Jonsson. Anticipating his release from the navy on about November 1, Haggerty said he planned to be on the train for Dallas the very next day. Olson and two other Bureau of Aeronautics colleagues who also soon would join GSI, Carl J. (Tommy) Thomsen, and Walter (Wally) Joyce, drove him to the train station. Olson arrived in Dallas two weeks later.[10] The GSI Grapevine breezily reported their arrival: "We have lifted a couple of technical men from BuAer and have put them to work on GSI problems.... You'll be hearing more of these gents after they've had a chance to get their feet on the ground."[11]

Haggerty took charge of a new unit reporting to Jonsson, the Laboratory and Manufacturing Division. Its name was presumptuous, given that the division, as Jonsson said, amounted to "just a little one-time garage space with a few guys sitting around wondering why we had them there." Rather than leapfrog Haggerty over several senior employees, Jonsson delayed announcing that intention. "I put him in there and let the people find out in six months that he was better than any of them," he said. When he named Haggerty general manager, there was no dissension. Haggerty's starting salary of $600 a month was jumped to $1,000 with his promotion. Only the four GSI owners earned more. Haggerty was thirty-two.[12]

Olson assumed responsibility for the technical aspects of several military contracts. In common with Jonsson, Haggerty, and many scientists and engineers of the day, Olson had had an early fascination with radios, building his first one when he was ten years old. He grew up in Minnesota, worked his way through the University of Minnesota, and had worked for a while in Dallas for the Magnolia Petroleum Company.[13]

⤙

In 1946, Haggerty's first full year at GSI, with business largely confined to oil exploration, sales were approximately $2.25 million, with net earnings of $147,000. Less than two decades later, with highly diversified products and services, sales reached about $1.5 billion. "Pat Haggerty, in my opinion," said Jonsson, "was the principal driving force in getting the company into the big time." But it was Jonsson who had had the concept, vision, and motivation to bring Haggerty on board to achieve that goal. McDermott, Green, and Peacock concentrated on geophysical exploration; Jonsson supervised manufacturing. As McDermott later acknowledged, Jonsson forever changed the company: "We were just prospectors until Erik set out to make us a manufacturing business."[14]

While growing up in remote Harvey, North Dakota, Patrick Eugene Haggerty, the son of a railroad man, was president of his high school class, first in his graduating class, winner of the city tennis tournament, and a member of the American Legion baseball team. His interest in radios led him to a degree in electrical engineering from Marquette University, where he was praised as one of its brightest students ever to receive an engineering degree. Haggerty's younger brother, also a straight-A student, followed him to Marquette. But the contrast between him and Patrick was so sharp that his peers began calling the honor roll student the "dumb Haggerty."[15]

After graduating in 1936, Haggerty became assistant production manager at Badger Carton Company, a folding-carton business. He became convinced that sound business management could be a science.

He systematized production for Badger Carton and revolutionized its operations. With the onset of war, he obtained a navy reserve commission in hopes of being sent to sea. His degree in electronics, however, led him to the Bureau of Aeronautics, where his efficiency and work ethic made him the leader of his group.[16]

As Jonsson and Haggerty envisioned it, GSI's Laboratory and Manufacturing Division would build and refine the geophysical equipment that had been the heart of the company, reenter the field of government electronics, and develop nonmilitary markets. Eighty-five of GSI's approximately 600 employees, including seventeen engineers, transferred from geophysical operations to work under Haggerty.[17]

While Jonsson, Green, and McDermott had offices in the Republic Bank Building, Haggerty worked principally at the Harwood Street shop. A few months after Haggerty's arrival, Jonsson began planning a new facility. He negotiated a $325,000 loan from Travelers Insurance and built a 38,000-square-foot building, big enough to bring all of GSI's operations under a single roof. "Jon$$on's Dream Castle," as the *Grapevine* in described the new building at 6000 Lemmon Avenue, was completed in 1947. Space was more than ample for offices, manufacturing, machine shops, laboratories, a warehouse, and a snack bar.[18]

Jonsson's office was peculiar for a vice president and treasurer. Not far from the machine shop, it had a concrete floor, like the work areas. He preferred this, for— he wanted all workers to feel a sense of kinship. Other top officials' offices were also austere, attracting the attention of visiting financial analysts. The workers' areas had paintings and prints on the walls.[19]

The new building was significant enough to be written up in *Architectural Forum*, which described it as "one of the most striking industrial facades erected since the war." Construction had been accompanied by groans of anguish over escalating costs, which soared from $200,000 to just over $400,000.[20]

The facility lifted morale. "We sure had the feeling we were taking off," said E. J. Toomey, who had been with the company since 1933. "Everybody I knew felt that 'this was good. We were on solid ground now.'"[21]

Interested in what he was hearing, another former Bureau of Aeronautics officer whom Jonsson and Haggerty wanted to hire, Carl J. Thomsen, visited in August 1946. Thomsen accepted a position as controller of the Laboratory and Manufacturing Division. Thomsen, like

Jonsson, was a Rensselaer graduate, having earned his degree in 1938 in industrial engineering. His accounting experience in Washington and at Westinghouse enhanced his value. Within a few years, he would become a member of the board of directors and remain a principal officer of GSI and Texas Instruments for the rest of his career.[22]

Walter Joyce, who had been with Haggerty at Marquette University, Badger Carton, and the Bureau of Aeronautics, at first declined to join the others at GSI, but in 1948 he was at loose ends. Haggerty visited him at his home near Oyster Bay, New York, and urged him to take charge of the manufacturing division. Joyce agreed, and moved his family to Dallas the next year.[23]

Yet another Navy man closely associated with Haggerty and the Bureau of Aeronautics, S. T. (Buddy) Harris, joined GSI in 1949. Harris had been involved in arranging the installation of radar in military aircraft. After the war, he took another job, but when he visited Texas in 1949, he had dinner with Olson, who took him to the Lemmon Avenue plant to meet Jonsson. "Erik told me all about the operation, plans for future, gave me the real snow job and I was sold," Harris said about accepting a job offer. Like the others from the Bureau of Aeronautics, he became an invaluable and longtime employee. He had a hard-driving approach to sales and marketing and an ability to win military contracts. His enthusiasm and mercurial personality were unmatched.[24]

These former navy engineers—Haggerty, Olson, Thomsen, Joyce, and Harris—now formed an important nucleus of GSI. Jonsson was proud of them. "I knew they would clobber somebody someday," he later said. Their presence unsettled some GSI employees who were more accustomed to the freewheeling days of the oil patch.[25]

As these new employees, joined by some old-timers, debated proposed projects, sessions often became stormy. On one occasion, Haggerty kicked a wastebasket across the room. Before the next meeting, Thomsen placed the wastebasket in the center of the room, as if setting it up for a kickoff. "This sort of thing eased the tensions that were bound to come when a group of such individuals were pulling together with diverse ideas, all aimed at a mutual goal," Wally Joyce recalled.[26]

⤸

Haggerty's intimate knowledge of the Bureau of Aeronautics brought in a number of small contracts, as did GSI's acceptance of an 8 percent profit margin rather than the conventional 10 percent. Before long, more space was needed. Jonsson, or Jon$$on, as the *Grapevine* was now regularly labeling him, arranged financing for expansion through Republic Bank. In 1949, as three shifts were rotating at the plant, an additional 22,000 square feet was added. In 1952 the building was enlarged by another 90,000 square feet.[27]

As envisioned, military electronics was becoming one of the company's primary activities. Seismic exploration continued to be the main source of income, but it was being relegated to secondary status. The biggest postwar military contract with the Bureau of Aeronautics involved an antisubmarine airborne radar instrument known as the APS-31. GSI's ability to handle such a project was boosted by the addition of Buddy Harris, whose wartime involvement with radar was invaluable. Winning the contract could mean millions of dollars, but competition was tough, especially from the electronics giant Philco, the sole antisubmarine radar supplier during the war. After intensive study, GSI submitted a bid that turned out to be lower than Philco's. Despite GSI's good record with MADs, the Bureau of Aeronautics was skeptical. Could GSI deliver? Did it have enough start-up money?[28]

Haggerty told Jonsson that GSI would need a $400,000 line of credit. John Dufford, who was responsible for pricing estimates for GSI's contract proposals, remembered Jonsson's reaction. "Okay," he said, and he "jumped into his black Cadillac, went downtown, and an hour later came back and said, 'Okay, you've got your money.'" Jonsson had visited Fred Florence at Republic Bank, who assured the bureau that GSI would have that line of credit.[29]

GSI risked much on the APS-31 project. Some speculated that the company might fail if it did not deliver. Within eight months, GSI engineers had to develop, test, and produce a successful unit. Six- and sometimes seven-day workweeks became the norm. To the relief of all, the units were successful. GSI's young engineers began to see themselves as energetic hotshots who could perform miracles under pressure.[30]

⌐

By the end of 1948, business was good and the future looked even brighter. With capital stock valued at $100 a share, GSI's owners approved a 25-for-1 stock split. The four owners now had 48,750 shares each. Despite the promise of electronics manufacturing, geophysical services in 1949 accounted for $4.9 million of GSI's $6.4 million in sales. By 1950, Haggerty, the highest-paid employee, was earning close to $50,000 annually in addition to stock awards and large cash bonuses.[31]

When the Korean conflict began in June 1950, the United States again found itself in combat in a distant land. The military desperately needed radar and other electronic products. Large electronic firms that had fulfilled these needs in World War II were preoccupied with the postwar consumer boom in radio and television. They were not inclined to abandon these markets for a war of possibly short duration. GSI, on the other hand, was eager to step into the breach. By the time the Korean conflict ended in 1953, GSI's annual sales had reached $27 million, with $1.3 million in profits. Electronics manufacturing had become dominant.[32]

Bates Peacock failed to share in the manufacturing enthusiasm. In an effort to ease his concerns, his fellow partners had made him president in 1948, bringing him to Dallas. McDermott became chairman. Jonsson continued as vice president and treasurer, maintaining control over the Laboratory and Manufacturing (L&M) Division. Green, as vice president, headed the geophysical division. McDermott, Peacock, and Green continued to spend most of their time on geophysical operations, leaving manufacturing to Jonsson and Haggerty.[33]

Designating Peacock as president failed to bring harmony. He alone had opposed borrowing money to build the Lemmon Avenue plant, and he continued to resist new initiatives. While McDermott as president had been content to leave administrative details to Jonsson, Peacock was not. Less sociable than his three partners, he found himself more and more alone. McDermott, Green, and Jonsson regularly outvoted Peacock as they moved the company in new directions.

Jonsson's quarterback, Haggerty, wholeheartedly supported by McDermott and Green, had become the primary architect as well as general manager of L&M. As Haggerty outlined new strategies, Jonsson looked over his shoulder with approval, lent advice, and provided him the backing he needed.[34]

Haggerty, as general manager of L&M, and with Jonsson's encouragement, issued a new challenge in 1949: annual sales of some $200 million, a thirty-five-fold increase, with profit after taxes of $10 million. The figures were so ambitious that they were shocking. And so was the projected date for this goal—only a decade away.[35]

The goal could be achieved only with electronic products for civilian consumers, the consumer market. Since the company's Texas charter did not authorize the building of civilian products (military products were exempted from the charter's restriction), a new charter had to be obtained. The result was a transformation similar to the reorganization that saw GSI and Coronado reverse roles. GSI became a subsidiary; manufacturing became primary. This reversal required a name change.

Finding a suitable name was a problem. Dozens were tried. Finally, General Instruments, Inc. was selected as representative of what the company was—a corporation producing a general line of instruments. The name came only after heated debate. Peacock wanted a name that reflected the company's original purpose. Haggerty, some speculated, liked the similarity of General Instruments to General Electric.[36]

The announcement declared that the company would "assume all research, development and manufacturing operations heretofore performed by the Laboratory and Manufacturing Division of Geophysical Service Inc." GSI, its subsidiary, would continue to offer seismic services to worldwide clients "as the pioneer contractor in geophysical exploration for oil."[37]

General Instruments' chairman of the board was Eugene McDermott. Jonsson became president and treasurer; Haggerty, executive vice president; Cecil H. Green, vice president; and C. J. Thomsen, secretary. Two of the company's five officers (Haggerty and Thomsen) were former Bureau of Aeronautics engineers recruited by Jonsson. Green, who knew the seismology business so well, became president of GSI as well as a vice president of General Instruments. Peacock, still out of sorts with the others, took the title of chairman of GSI's board.[38]

A few months later, Jonsson received a surprising telephone call from the president of a New York company already known as General Instruments, which had registered the name in several states. How could Jonsson have forgotten? As a needy young father, he had purchased parts from General Instruments to build his radios.

Another name had to be selected. Voices again were raised. "I won't work for a company with a name like that!" Jonsson proclaimed at one suggestion. When there was a movement at one point to break up a meeting and postpone the selection, Haggerty blocked the door. "Now, goddammit, nobody is leaving this room until this company has a name!" No one left. Finally, the name Texas Instruments Incorporated was chosen. It would have no comma.[39] The name pleased Jonsson: "I thought the name 'Texas' and the name 'Instruments' said more than General Instruments did. It said we were makers of something that you could call instruments and that we came from Texas. . . . A little later when we came to be listed on the exchange the name proved to be magic." It became effective in January 1952.[40]

A booklet, written in folksy language, explained the name change: "As a matter of fact, we started out only a few months ago as a plain G.I. (General Instruments) from Dallas. But sure as shootin (even before the printin on our visitin cards got good and dry) just about everybody started calling us 'Tex'. Well, podnuh, we'll do just about anything to get another chance to brag about Texas so we're changing our brand from 'General Instruments Inc.' to '*Texas*' Instruments Incorporated'— and from now on we're gonna relax and enjoy it!" In keeping with that introduction, company advertising featured for a while a cartoon cowboy named Tex. The initials "TI" were simpler to say than "Texas Instruments," and so the company became popularly known as TI. [41]

⌐

Before too long, the name would be familiar the world over. The origin of this breakthrough came in mid-1948 when Bell Telephone Laboratories (Bell Labs) announced a new invention. "We have called it the Transistor," said the spokesman, "because it is a resistor or semiconductor device which can amplify electrical signals as they are transferred through it." The transistor (Bell's capitalization of the word soon was dropped) could accomplish the same feats as the vacuum tube, but with far less power, far less heat, and far less space. (Three Bell scientists, William Shockley, John Bardeen, and Walter Brattain, won the Nobel Prize in Physics in 1956 for their work on developing the transistor.)[42]

Early reports noted the tiny device's possibilities. "Tubeless Radios" was the *Science Digest* headline. The vacuum tube, used by virtually every electrical circuit at the time, had limitations. It wore out quickly; it was cumbersome; it required a warm-up period; and it generated heat that could become excessive. When first developed, thirty-five years earlier, the vacuum tube provided an important basis for the communications revolution brought about by radio in the 1920s and television in the 1940s.[43] It was useful for the world's first programmable computer, the ENIAC, unveiled in 1946 and powered by 17,000 heat-generating vacuum tubes.[44]

In contrast, the transistor was amazingly simple, working on a principle discovered by Bell Labs. Its principal parts were two hair-thin tungsten wires separated by two-thousandths of an inch or so and touching a pinhead made of solid semiconducting material—germanium crystal—soldered to a metal base. Bell scientists had found a way to improve the conductivity of germanium to the point that signals could be sent in ten-millionths of a second. Enclosed in a simple metal cylinder not much larger than the tip of a shoelace, a hundred or so transistors could be held in the palm of a hand. The transistor promised electronic instruments stability and long life.[45]

News of its possibilities did not escape eager minds in Dallas. Haggerty and Olson were especially intrigued, and so was McDermott. In 1949 they obtained a few transistors and experimented with them. Perhaps this was the moment the company had been waiting for. Haggerty saw it this way: "If we are to be a giant and compete with the giants, where are we better fitted to take on a giant than in a field where the giant is also just starting?" The big companies—General Electric, Westinghouse, RCA, Philco, Admiral, and others—had assets tied to the vacuum tube and were inclined to see the transistor as a sideline.[46]

"It was by no means obvious in 1948 and 1949 and 1950 that the transistor would be the kind of fundamental contribution it has become," Haggerty later recalled. "But slowly, during 1949 and 1950, a portion of it at best became clear to me." The future of electronics, he realized, would be profoundly influenced. By early 1951, Haggerty began to formalize a strategy aimed at developing, manufacturing, and marketing transistors or semiconductor devices.[47] American Telephone and Telegraph soon would offer licenses for transistor production to selected manufacturers through its Western Electric entity.

Such a license, Haggerty told Jonsson, was a window into the future for Texas Instruments. Would the company make the commitment? Jonsson assembled the board—McDermott, Green, Peacock, and himself—to hear Haggerty's presentation. With only Peacock opposed, TI decided to seek a license to build transistors.[48]

Obtaining it was not easy, though. After months of pestering Western Electric by mail and telephone, Jonsson, Haggerty, and Olson went to New York in late 1951 to make a personal plea. Western Electric had anticipated issuing licenses to giants such as General Electric and Raytheon, not a newly organized company in Texas. The license fee, $25,000, was substantial, too.

Western Electric appeared reluctant to sell the license to the Texans. "They were both amazed and amused that our little company would have the effrontery to think we could make transistors," Haggerty said.[49] Jonsson insisted. "Listen," Jonsson said he told them, "You have no right to refuse me because you have an opinion that isn't based on facts that we can't do it. I want the license. I have the money and I'm ready."[50] Without any conviction that Texas Instruments could succeed, Western Electric granted the license. TI indeed seemed to be an improbable licensee.[51]

A history written later absurdly described the TI contingent as lanky cowboy types wearing blue jeans and ten-gallon hats. "Robert Olson, Erik Jonsson and I were those who first discussed the possibility of transistor patents with Western Electric," an exasperated Haggerty later exclaimed. "None of us are native Texans, wear blue jeans or Stetsons, and only Erik could be described as lean!"[52]

Haggerty announced the news to his senior management group in words that Bob Dunlap would never forget: "There is a time when things are right and if you act at that time, you are all right. You can be either too early or too late. Three years ago, we couldn't possibly afford this sort of thing. Three years from now, it's going to be too late to do it." Big companies like GE and RCA would not push it the way TI would, Haggerty said, because they had less reason to do so.[53]

For the twenty-six companies that obtained licenses (including General Electric, IBM, and other giants), Bell Labs conducted a ten-day symposium in April 1952 on building transistors. More than a hundred engineers and scientists attended. Success would go to those licensees who could master the difficult production problems.

TI's Haggerty, Olson, Boyd Cornelison, and a young engineer named Mark Shepherd Jr. attended the symposium. On their return, Haggerty and Olson turned over the project to Shepherd. He and his team would be assisted by the symposium proceedings, published in two volumes entitled *Transistor Technology*, known in the burgeoning transistor industry as "Mother Bell's Cookbook."[54]

Shepherd, born in 1923, was a native Dallasite and a navy veteran whose childhood was difficult after his policeman father was immobilized by a stroke. The family moved to a small town in East Texas where a mother, an ailing father, and an only child could live more cheaply. Shepherd held part-time jobs as a boy, built radios as a hobby, and graduated from high school at fourteen. He earned a bachelor of science degree in electrical engineering from Southern Methodist University and, specializing in radar and electronic maintenance, served on a navy cruiser. After earning a master's degree from the University of

Illinois, he worked for Milo Farnsworth, the television pioneer, in Fort Wayne, Indiana. Shepherd returned to Dallas in 1948 for his father's funeral. While there, he visited a former SMU classmate, Lawrence Congden, at GSI. Shepherd looked around the factory without much thought and returned to Fort Wayne.[55]

Not long afterward, one of his superiors stopped at his desk. "What about this GSI in Dallas?" he asked. Shepherd told the supervisor all he knew based on his brief time there, but wondered why he was so interested. "Well, they just took one of our more lucrative government contracts, the APA5 [radar]," he said. Shepherd returned to Dallas, visited Haggerty, and promptly was hired. Only twenty-five years old, tall and lanky, Shepherd greatly impressed Haggerty with his work. Haggerty placed fifteen engineers under him in the new Semiconductor Design Research Department.[56]

Peacock continued frowning. He disliked taking out loans when the company still owed money; he disapproved of the manner in which military contracts were bid; he was not enthusiastic about buying a license for transistor production.[57] His contributions had been important, though. GSI's stature as perhaps the leading geophysical services company had been maintained even as Jonsson and Haggerty devoted substantial resources to electronics manufacturing. But his discomfort was unsettling to others.[58]

The situation was resolved on September 16, 1952, when he sold his 46,325 shares back to the company for about $1 million and resigned. Jonsson, McDermott, and Green took about 30 percent of those shares. Twenty-seven employees who already owned shares were allowed to buy more, and the remaining shares were offered to other key employees. The number of employees owning TI shares grew from thirty to forty-nine. Pat Haggerty led that list, with 16,000 shares. Showing up for the first time as a shareholder in November 1952 was Malcolm Bedell, now a TI employee, with 100 shares. No outsiders owned any TI stock.[59]

Peacock missed the huge fortunes to be made just ahead. But according to those who knew him, he never expressed regret. His service as a founder was largely overlooked in future years.[60]

᠆

One of Jonsson's particular interests was Oriental rugs. Shortly after he and Margaret married, they splurged and paid about $20 for a Baluchistan mat. Twenty-five years later, they were still using it. Now they began acquiring far more expensive Oriental rugs. Similarly, Jonsson's

childhood fascination with postage stamps continued, but now he purchased mint sheets.[61]

Jonsson had become a familiar figure in circles where important
people were seen. At the Petroleum Club, he rubbed shoulders with
the city's wealthiest oilmen. In January 1949 he was elected the club's
president. He played golf at the Dallas Country Club, the city's oldest
and most exclusive, and he took his family there for meals several times
a month.[62]

He enjoyed weekly lunches with the Knights of the Round Table,
declining an offer in 1949 to be a candidate for president of the national
organization. He belonged to the Nomads, a club for traveling salesmen; the Dallas Sales Executives Club; the Dallas Purchasing Agents
Association; the Society of Exploration Geophysicists; and the Dallas
Symphony Society. Upon the recommendation of Everette L. DeGolyer
and George Waverly Briggs, he accepted membership in the Newcomen
Society, an organization devoted to an appreciation of the rise of material civilization. Despite his new station in life, in a "personal history
statement" filled out in 1948, he listed in the space for nicknames one
that long had been forgotten: "Swede."[63] He invested $1,000 as an angel
to take to Broadway Tennessee Williams's *Summer and Smoke*, recently
debuted in Dallas under the direction of Margo Jones. He turned over
this minor investment to his son Philip.[64]

He became active in the Dallas Figure Skating Club because of Margaret Ellen's devotion to the sport. He served as general chairman of
the "Ice Parade of 1950," an elaborate two-day event at which Margaret
Ellen was a solo skater, as she was in other years.[65]

Ice-skating was a passion that lasted throughout her youth. In October 1951, determined to get the best training, her mother took her to
Colorado Springs, where they lived at the Broadmoor for about a year
and a half. Margaret Ellen underwent a rigorous practice regimen
there under the renowned coach Edward (Edi) Scholdan.[66] Finally,
she decided that a good education would be more beneficial than the
uncertainty of an ice-skating career. She graduated from high school at
the private all-girls school Hockaday.

Kenneth Jonsson, a student at Highland Park High School, worked
summers in the Harwood Street machine shop. After the new Lemmon Avenue facility opened in 1946, he was hired there as a turret lathe
operator. Inspired by Philip, in the fall of 1948 Kenneth entered MIT,
majoring in mechanical engineering and graduating in 1952.[67]

Philip became a field engineer with J. C. Karcher's new oil company, Comanche Corporation. When Karcher's son Paul started the Big Horn Corporation, he hired Philip as president. Philip moved to Midland, where the company was headquartered and where he came to know two future presidents, George H. W. Bush, soon to start his own exploration company, and Bush's young son George W.[68]

Margaret Jonsson stayed busy with family affairs, gardening, and the Dallas Woman's Club. Although she preferred being out of the limelight, she occasionally took center stage for social events. When the Karchers' daughter, Colleen, became engaged in 1944, Margaret hosted a tea for some two hundred guests at the Dallas Country Club. Helping her were Mrs. Everette L. DeGolyer, Mrs. Eugene McDermott, and Lydia Karcher.[69]

⌒

As mentioned, one of the Jonssons' favorite vacation sites was the Broadmoor Hotel in Colorado Springs, and in October 1952 it was the site of TI's first formal planning conference. The company had grown nearly tenfold since 1946, and the planning conference was remembered as a turning point. Its influence, Pat Haggerty thought, contributed significantly to TI's success over the following years. Strategies were devised that in the next decade would enable TI to be among the nation's two hundred largest corporate entities—the good big company it desired to be.[70]

The conference ended with a joke on Cecil Green. Throughout the three days, several participants signed their tabs with his name. At checkout time, they hid in the lobby to see his reaction. "Jesus Christ!" Green shouted as he looked at his bill. "I've only been here three days and have a $1,700 bill?" After a moment he caught on to the joke and then paid the tab in full.[71]

A New Day

In 1961, *Fortune* declared Texas Instruments to be "one of the most sensational growth companies in the U.S." During the decade before that pronouncement, little-known TI was at the heart of a technological revolution.[1]

A reorganization dramatically showed how much former Bureau of Aeronautics veterans assumed leadership roles. Four new divisions were led by vice presidents who came from the bureau or had been closely aligned with it, in addition to Pat Haggerty. Buddy Harris was over sales; Robert Olson headed engineering; Wally Joyce supervised manufacturing; and Carl J. Thomsen was vice president for control and finance. He also had succeeded Peacock on the board of directors.

Erik Jonsson continued to handle the company's increasingly complicated financial affairs. Eugene McDermott, chairman of the TI board, and Cecil Green, chairman of GSI, concentrated on the geophysical side of the business.

TI needed several things in order to realize its ambitions—more money, consumer products, and mergers. All would be achieved. For money, the resources of the investing public were needed. A New York Stock Exchange (NYSE) listing was essential. Rigid standards would have to be met to fulfill Securities and Exchange Commission (SEC) requirements. TI had no one sufficiently knowledgeable in these areas.

In early 1951, during the brief period when the company was known as General Instruments, Jonsson went to New York City to interview a prospect for the firm's in-house counsel, someone knowledgeable about corporate law. The interviewee was Bryan F. Smith, a New Jersey native with four years' experience in a New York City law firm. Smith had attended MIT, graduated from Harvard, and earned a law degree from Columbia, but he was interested in a change of location. He had sent a résumé to MIT's placement office, where it was matched with a query from a "small, privately owned company"—General Instruments—whose help-wanted advertisements in Dallas had generated no interest. Jonsson met Smith over lunch at the Harvard Club of New York, decided that he was the right man, and asked him to come to Dallas. Smith preferred to wait until his pregnant wife gave birth to their first child. Jonsson insisted that he come right away. "Young man," he admonished, "if you are interested in this job I suggest you get on an airplane." Thus prompted, Smith boarded the airplane, accepted the offer, returned in time for the birth, and came back to Dallas on June 1, 1951, to begin a long career with Texas Instruments.[2]

He soon was named company secretary, a position requiring his attendance at board meetings. (The board, at this point, consisted only of the founders and Haggerty.) Smith's ultimate goal was to establish the procedures required of publicly held corporations, including the filing of annual reports.[3]

The first annual report, written in a conversational tone by Carl J. Thomsen for internal use only, was issued in March 1952 on two folded-over letter-size sheets. He reported assets of $6,788,375 and liabilities of $4,228,088. In 1953, his four-page annual report listed nearly $18 million in sales for the previous year and profits after taxes of almost $677,000. Further growth would depend in part on "success in obtaining satisfactory long term financing."[4]

This responsibility lay primarily in Jonsson's hands as treasurer and president. First, he made tentative arrangements with a Midwestern insurance company for a $1 million loan to pay off the Lemmon Avenue property debt, leaving some funds for working capital. While Jonsson was gone, Smith was visited by one of his former MIT instructors, Robert Legg, a specialist in matching corporate lenders and borrowers, who offered advice: Texas Instruments should have sought a lender with far more resources for future loans. This insurance company's loan to TI would be the big biggest on its books.[5]

Upon request, Legg recommended instead the world's third-largest insurance company, Equitable Life Assurance Society of the United States. Jonsson saw the wisdom of this, and with new resolve but many doubts about whether he could succeed, he asked for a much larger, $2.5 million loan. To his surprise, Equitable granted it. A close relationship developed over the next years as Jonsson obtained more loans from Equitable. Five years after the first loan, Equitable asked him to be on its distinguished board. He accepted and served for many years.[6]

The Equitable loan gave TI financial breathing room and offered verification of its soundness. After all, a prominent institution had examined it carefully and recognized TI's worth. The vote of confidence gave TI new respectability in the business world.

⌐

TI turned now to the possibility of mergers. In February 1953, the first one took place with the acquisition of Engineering Supply Co. (ESCO), based in Dallas; McDermott, Jonsson, and Haggerty already owned shares in the company. ESCO and its affiliate distributed geophysical and electronic supplies in the Southwest.[7]

In December 1953, TI acquired Houston Technical Laboratories, whose thirty-five employees manufactured the Worden gravity meter and other sophisticated geophysical instruments. The meter, less expensive than seismographs, identified underground geological structures capable of bearing oil. TI transferred its own seismic operations to Houston, and three years later Jonsson dedicated there a new 40,000-square-foot plant for the combined operations. Three more small corporations with seismographic crews, two of them with ocean-going equipment for offshore oil explorations, were also acquired. These additions considerably beefed up GSI's geophysical operations.[8]

Still needed, though, was a listing on the NYSE. One possibility was to merge with a corporation already represented on the Big Board. Finding such a company became a priority.

Legg identified a company called Intercontinental Rubber Co., which had $1.3 million in liquid assets and some 1,700 stockholders. Its earlier heyday as a rubber producer had declined after the introduction of synthetic rubber. The company was operating at a loss by 1953 and seeking a partner with whom it could put its cash to work.[9]

None of TI's principals wanted to engage in rubber manufacturing. They simply desired Intercontinental's NYSE listing.[10] Finally, after hard negotiations, a deal was made through an exchange of shares. TI retained its name; Intercontinental's name would disappear. Three of its members joined TI's board.[11]

Whether TI now could assume Intercontinental's place on the exchange was uncertain, but Jonsson's expanding contacts paid dividends. At a regional meeting in Bandera in the Texas Hill Country of the Conference Board, a nonprofit business and research organization, he had struck up a friendship with Keith Funston, the new president of the NYSE. Jonsson discussed the merger with Funston and convinced him of its merits.[12]

Thus, on October 1, 1953, the day after the merger, Texas Instruments was listed on the NYSE with the symbol TXN. Jonsson, McDermott, Haggerty, and Buddy Harris watched the ringing of the opening bell at ten and saw TI appear first that day on the ticker tape: "New York Stock Exchange . . . October 1, 1953 . . . Market Open . . . TXN 5¼." The group, joined by other TI officials in the gallery, cheered and applauded. Jonsson bought the first publicly offered TI shares, one hundred of them issued as Certificate No. 1.[13]

As a wide-eyed boy, Jonsson had frequently visited Wall Street with his father to watch the Big Board. The twosome—a gangling boy towering over his short, stocky father—must have made a comical sight. Jonsson surely felt a twinge of regret that his father could not be with him on this day.

The price of TI stock closed that day at its opening price, 5¼. Within a year, it would almost triple to $14. Demand for shares became so high that exchange representatives at one point asked Jonsson, McDermott, and Green to sell some of their stock in order to maintain an orderly market. They happily complied.[14]

Except to the principals, Texas Instruments' appearance on the NYSE was a matter of little note. Bigger news that day was a World Series game in which the New York Yankees, behind Mickey Mantle, defeated Jonsson's favorite childhood team, the Brooklyn Dodgers. Earl Warren accepted President Eisenhower's offer to be nominated as chief justice of the Supreme Court. *The Robe*, the first CinemaScope movie, was showing around the nation. A Philco television set with a twenty-one-inch screen cost $299.

America's investing resources now were available for TI, but the loss of anonymity also brought unwelcome changes. No longer would TI be a sleeper among bidders for contracts. Thousands of shareholders—owners themselves—had to be considered before making decisions that risked company assets. SEC regulations had to be met. Jonsson, McDermott, and Green continued to hold more than 50 percent of TI's outstanding stock, but shareholders had to be apprised of company activities.

The next summer, TI offered $4.5 million in preferred stock. The choice of an underwriter was important. Jonsson's good friend E. O.

(Orville) Cartwright, Merrill Lynch's representative in Dallas, had been wining and dining Jonsson and other TI officials for such an eventuality. But new board member Ewen C. MacVeagh, from Intercontinental, preferred Morgan Stanley because of its deeper Wall Street connections. Morgan Stanley won the assignment.[15]

Choosing Morgan Stanley symbolized TI's emergence as a company that was outgrowing local banking and legal institutions. Republic National Bank, so important from the beginning, and Thompson & Knight, which had handled much of TI's legal affairs, continued to be part of TI's family, but they often lacked the depth of resources the company now needed. TI began using larger institutions in New York City; Jonsson took more trips to Manhattan.[16]

Before the merger, TI's directors consisted of half a dozen insiders: McDermott, Jonsson, Green, Haggerty, Thomsen, and the veteran Fred Agnich. Major decisions were easily made. Now, three additional members from Intercontinental were on the board—MacVeagh, Anton D. Bestebreurtje, and Emory G. Ackerman—and they were sophisticated in affairs of business.

Only now did some of Jonsson's old New Jersey friends discover that the big Swede had become hugely successful. A brief flurry of letters, filled with nostalgia for old times, ensued.

↩

"We want to make semiconductors. It's your problem." With these words, spoken on an airplane while returning from Western Electric's transistor symposium in 1952, Haggerty had given that assignment to Mark Shepherd. Shepherd and a dozen or so men at first worked in the back of the 6000 Lemmon Avenue facility, a former bowling alley. It was challenging to start only with the knowledge gained from Bell's symposium and the bible presented to licensees. Frustrations often exploded. At one point Shepherd told Haggerty the job was impossible; he could not do it. Haggerty roared: "Goddammit! You can!" Work continued.[17]

Haggerty was right. In July 1952, assisted especially by impromptu sketches that Boyd Cornelison had made at the Bell symposium, Shepherd's team managed to build a germanium crystal puller for "growing" crystals, a complicated process in which a single crystal is pulled from a melt of germanium. Crystals were the essential element for fabricating point-contact transistors. Cornelison's sketches, so important, earned him praise as "the first hero of the company's semiconductor effort."[18]

Only seven other American companies were manufacturing transis-

tors when TI made its first sale of ten germanium point-contact transistors in December 1952 to the Gruen Watch Co.[19] Three months later,
a lengthy *Fortune* article entitled "The Year of the Transistor" failed to
mention Texas Instruments. In a couple of years, it stated, the principal
transistor makers would be RCA, GE, Raytheon, and Sylvania.[20] What
the article failed to recognize was that these well-known manufacturers' commitments to vacuum tube technology hindered their efforts at
developing transistors. For Texas Instruments, however, the new technology was a top priority.

Buddy Harris's aggressive TI sales force called on manufacturers
of paging equipment, electric organs, small home appliances, hearing aids, and anything that might use solid-state amplifiers. The first
large order came from Sonotone, a hearing aid manufacturer. Harris
and Thomsen, recognizing the sale's importance, personally packed the
transistors for shipping. By the end of 1953, TI had sold 9,998 transistor
units for $82,486. Shepherd's group, numbering about sixty employees
now, was upgraded to division status.[21]

In January 1954, the company launched a nationwide advertising
campaign. "Keep An Eye on TI" headlined the half-page *Fortune* advertisement. TI described itself as a pioneer in developing and manufacturing precision seismic equipment and semiconductors. Full-scale
production of these semiconductors, or transistors, was said to be
making many existing electrical products smaller and better, and they
promised to make possible new electrical products. Precisely what these
products might be was left to the readers' imaginations.[22]

⌐

Producing the germanium transistors was agonizingly difficult. In
the midst of its struggles, and realizing it needed help, the company
placed a "blind" advertisement in the *New York Times* for an electronics
researcher. The advertisement caught the attention of a native Texan,
Gordon Teal, a researcher at Bell Labs who had been significantly
involved in developing the transistor but who felt unappreciated. Teal,
a graduate of Baylor University, held a doctorate in chemistry from
Brown University. He had worked at Bell Labs since 1930 with a special interest on the chemical and electrical properties of germanium.
In 1942 he made Bell's first germanium rectifier and provided Shock-
ley, Bardeen, and Brattain with the grown single-crystal germanium
materials so critical to their experimental work. Later, he sometimes

expressed resentment that he had not been named a Nobel Prize recipient with them.[23]

The idea of doing pioneering electronics research in Texas was appealing to him and to his wife, who yearned to return to her home state. Teal had been one of the instructors at the Bell transistor-technology symposium in 1952.[24] Haggerty offered him a position as research director for semiconductors. Teal could select his own projects and staff. With this appealing prospect, he accepted the offer. "Any scientist worth his salt has his own ideas of what he wants to work on," he later said. What most interested him was further experimentation with silicon as a transistor. Bell had not encouraged that line of research, even though Teal already had grown the first silicon single crystal with PN junctions—that is, positive and negative junctions for controlling a current. In December 1952, Teal moved to Dallas to begin work.[25]

Although silicon was abundant in nature (found in sand as silicon dioxide), it was quirky. Researchers recognized, however, that if tamed, it would have qualities superior to those of germanium, particularly the ability to withstand far greater heat. Germanium transistors lost their effectiveness at about 150°F; a silicon transistor could operate at 300°. This quality made silicon far more suitable for military or industrial purposes.

In forming his staff, Teal hired two PhD physicists, Willis Adcock, of Brown University, and Morton Jones, of California Tech. Using Cornelison's germanium machine as a model, an instrument for pulling silicon crystals was constructed. Pure silicon was in short supply, but Teal, because of his reputation and experience at Bell, was able to buy the expensive substance from the nation's sole supplier, E. I. DuPont de Nemours and Co., at $500 a pound.[26]

Work progressed far faster than anyone had expected. In April 1954, Haggerty received a telephone call from an excited Teal. Come across the street to the "bowling alley," Teal told him and see the first grown-junction silicon transistor, six months ahead of schedule. A jubilant Haggerty authorized immediate production.[27]

This breakthrough would be sensational news in the electronics industry, but Teal proposed delaying it for a month until he presented a paper at the National Conference on Airborne Electronics in Dayton, Ohio.[28] There, Teal, who was next to last on the program, heard several speakers mention the promise of silicon transistors but say that production was years away. With a handful of silicon transistors in his pockets, Teal saved his announcement until the end of his talk. Contrary to opinions already expressed, he said, TI had the silicon transistor in production. The future would "begin immediately." The audience stirred. Did he say that TI already was producing them? Yes, Teal said, pulling three from his pocket to demonstrate. First, he set up a record player amplified by a germanium transistor and then dunked the germanium transistor into hot oil; the music ceased. Next, he switched to a silicon transistor, resumed the music, and dunked the silicon transistor into the same hot oil. The music continued without pause or distortion. Astonished audience members dashed to grab copies of Teal's talk. A representative from one of the electronic giants rushed to a telephone and was heard to shout: "They got the silicon transistor down in Texas."[29]

A month later, TI advertisements extolled the breakthrough. "Silicon transistors now in *production!*" appeared in big block letters in advertisements in three electronics trade publications. "Silicon transistors— long awaited by the electronics industry—are finally out of the laboratory and on the market . . . brought to you *first* by Texas Instruments." A life-sized image of the silicon transistor, smaller than a fingernail, was displayed.[30]

It was another important turning point. The silicon transistor gave TI a remarkable lead over competitors and let it capture the military and industrial market. As *Fortune* magazine summarized in an extensive two-part profile, TI "was suddenly in the big leagues."[31]

Not until 1958 did TI face competition for silicon transistors. The big companies, Jonsson later observed, had become "fat and lazy" because they were covered with orders for television sets. The president of one of those companies told Jonsson: "Don't get too egotistical about it, Jonsson; we'll take you on a little bit later when we have more time." When that moment eventually came, it was too late to recover the lost ground.[32]

The silicon transistor was particularly useful for the military because of its resistance to heat, a great advantage in aircraft and missiles. The nation's first satellite, the *Explorer*, which was launched in 1958, used TI's silicon transistors as well as other TI components. So did the Jupiter-C rocket that carried the *Explorer* aloft. TI would reap huge profits from its new military and government contracts.[33]

TI publicity pointed especially to the silicon transistor's potential in computers. The first electronic computer, the ENIAC (Electronic Numerical Integrator and Computer), developed in 1946, was so large and heat sensitive that it had to be placed in its own air-cooled room. That now would change. As the first TI news release stated, "Electronic 'brains' approaching the human brain in scope and reliability came much closer to reality today. By using silicon instead of germanium, the initial commercial silicon transistor immediately raises power outputs and doubles operating temperatures!" Unstated was the fact that substituting transistors for vacuum tubes made possible a dramatic reduction in size. The laptop computer and other endless electronic wonders were on their way.[34]

Before 1954 ended, TI had mastered the process of creating its own silicon. In December 1956, the company opened a silicon plant and began selling high-purity silicon. A few years later, TI was the world's leading producer of high-purity silicon, which sold for $980 a pound. DuPont, unable to match TI's prices, stopped selling the material.[35]

TI led the industry in producing germanium and silicon transistors, but far greater profits would result if an imaginative consumer product could be developed. Haggerty conceived of a striking example: a portable radio small enough to fit into a shirt pocket. He told RCA and other established radio manufacturers that TI would develop and supply the essentials if they would assemble and market the radio. They declined, staying with the vacuum tube.[36]

Undeterred, Haggerty made arrangements to team up with a small company, the Regency Division of Industrial Development Engineering Associates, Inc., an Indianapolis electronics manufacturer. TI began a crash program to have the pocket radio ready for 1954 Christmas sales.[37]

Haggerty's stipulation that it had to be small enough to fit into a shirt pocket was complicated by the arbitrary decision that its retail price be no more than $50. A germanium transistor alone cost $16. To reach the $50 retail price target, TI concluded that it had to bring down the cost of a single germanium transistor to $2.50. Regency could buy four transistors for each radio for $10, put the rest of the parts together for less than $20, sell the radio at retail for $50, and enjoy a profit. After anguished trial and error under Mark Shepherd's leadership, a satisfactory radio was announced on October 18, 1954.

Besides four germanium transistors to amplify its sound, the radio contained a 2.5-inch speaker and a single battery. The Regency TR1, as it was dubbed, weighed less than twelve ounces and sold for $49.95. The nation's first transistor radio, comparatively tiny but producing a great volume of sound, seemed nothing short of a miracle.[38] Many compared it to Dick Tracy's imaginary wristwatch radio. A photograph of it beside a teacup adorned the cover of a national magazine. Magazine advertisements and billboard announcements proclaimed its uniqueness.[39] A TI press release suggested that the radio had introduced a new era. Company officials believed that the transistor radio accelerated the introduction of other transistor applications by some twelve or eighteen months.[40]

Sensational though public reception was, the radio appeared on the market too late to capitalize fully on the 1954 Christmas season. Regency had been able to ship only 1,500 of them. Wherever available, though, it quickly sold out. The companies realized that demand would have justified a far higher price tag.[41]

While TI used the radio to introduce the transistor to the consumer, it had decided not to manufacture its own radios. Later, Haggerty lamented this decision. Meanwhile, TI became the principal supplier of transistors to the major manufacturers of radios, who were forced to enter this new market—Admiral, Motorola, Zenith, Magnavox, Westinghouse, and GE. A tremendous rush of orders ensued. Those few manufacturers who attempted to build their own transistors usually gave it up as too difficult. By 1956, TI was supplying almost two million transistors a year to these major customers.[42]

In Tokyo, a company named Tokyo Tsushin Kogyo Ltd. (soon to be known as the Sony Corporation) jumped into the market. Its transistor radio captivated the imaginations of the Japanese, and the Sony brand reached America. Other Japanese firms would gain a worldwide reputation for manufacturing and exporting transistorized products. When Sony began manufacturing television sets with transistors in the 1960s, U.S. leadership in consumer electronics began a descent.[43]

The transistor radio and the silicon transistor, both headline-making breakthroughs, made TI's name familiar across the nation. Sales in Shepherd's Semiconductor Products division jumped from less than $83,000 in 1953 to $3.4 million in 1954. By the end of 1955, the division, which had started with a dozen workers, had 429 employees and was doing almost $5 million in business. TI was the nation's leading semiconductor manufacturer. Between 1952 and 1955 the company spent $1.25 million on research and development for transistors, and committed assets of $3 million to the project. The investment was large for a company of its size, but it paid off in spectacular fashion. A few years later, the research would pay off in yet another achievement—the integrated circuit.[44]

Ironically, overall TI sales for 1954 declined from the previous year. The end of hostilities in Korea brought a dramatic decline in military needs, and sales dropped from 1953's record $27 million to $24.3 million. Considering the circumstances, this lower figure was viewed as outstanding.[45]

IBM led the nation in producing computers. Because of their size and expense, buying one was a major capital investment, often requiring a company's board of directors' approval. Thomas Watson Jr., who had succeeded his father as IBM's chairman, was especially interested in developing a transistorized computer, but his company was having "a dreadful time" with it.[46]

Watson summoned more than a dozen of his top executives and handed a Regency transistor radio to each. Not one of these radios contains a vacuum tube, he pointed out. "Does that tell you something? I want you to go back and I want you to figure out a way to transistorize the IBM computers." If a little outfit in Texas could achieve such a thing, he said, so could IBM.[47]

Two years later, forced to give up, Watson turned to TI. In 1957 he signed an agreement for the company to deliver 600,000 transistors to IBM. TI became IBM's sole source for millions of transistors. This extraordinary volume permitted TI to sell transistors to IBM for less than the cost of the high-grade vacuum tubes IBM had been using. All of IBM's products, Watson decided, including the popular punch-card machines, had to be transistorized. But punch-card designers resisted. For months, every design they sent to IBM headquarters still had vacuum tubes. Finally, Watson issued a memorandum over his signature: "After October 1, 1956, we will design no more machines using vacuum tubes." Watson carried Regency radios with him so that every time he heard an engineer say the transistors were undependable, he would challenge him to wear it out. Soon, the engineers were convinced. TI and IBM became virtual partners in this new era.[48]

A dramatic development in 1955 occurred after the Bank of America commissioned the Stanford Research Institute to design a machine that could process checks simply by reading magnetic characters at the bottom. Once a prototypical electronic recording machine was completed, Bank of America would sell the design rights and guarantee to purchase thirty-six of them. The successful result, the ERMA (electronic recording machine), could read and process hundreds of checks every minute. The problem was that ERMA weighed several tons, contained more than ten thousand vacuum tubes, and required tons of cooling apparatus. Twenty-six prospective manufacturers, including RCA, GE, IBM, Sperry, and Honeywell, sent teams to San Francisco to examine the model.[49]

Among them was Texas Instruments. TI had no vacuum tubes, but it had something better—the silicon transistor. TI thus proposed using transistors for ERMA instead of vacuum tubes. Doing so would dramatically reduce its size and bring other advantages. The Stanford Research Institute agreed. With that decision made, Texas Instruments and GE became the two final bidders for the contract. GE submitted the lower bid and won it, but TI claimed a major victory in demonstrating the superiority of the transistor and in seeing it incorporated into ERMA's design.

Mammoth computers once powered by thousands of vacuum tubes became dinosaurs. Not far away was the desktop computer, the laptop, a computer that could be held in the palm of the hand, and other marvels.[50]

TI's business was so good that it opened a leased facility in Bedford, England. Operations began in 1957. Semiconductor products were assembled and tested in Dallas, then flown to the new plant for distribution to European customers. Four years later, an entirely new plant containing 132,000 square feet was built just north of Bedford. By then, TI also had a physical presence on the Continent through a leased 22,000-square-foot property on a scenic hilltop outside Nice. At the insistence of French authorities, huge trees were planted to camouflage the plant's presence.[51]

TI was growing so fast that its Dallas headquarters were unfolding like a fast-moving blossom. In 1947, the Lemmon Avenue plant contained 35,000 square feet; by the end of 1956, it had been expanded to 218,000 air-conditioned square feet, with an additional 25,000 square feet under construction.

In 1955, a 296-acre site was purchased in far north Dallas on North Central Expressway. There, a new semiconductor plant was built to accommodate IBM's orders for transistors and related products such as diodes and rectifiers. It opened as the world's largest plant dedicated to such products. The site was destined to become TI's headquarters as well as a manufacturing center, and it would expand further in the years ahead.

When Jonsson and his partners gained control of GSI in 1941, the company had a payroll of 175. By the end of the war, that number was 508. In 1950 the total was 1,206. At the end of 1955, TI had 2,663 employees, and by the end of 1956, employment had reached 4,280. New hires now were being added at the rate of 108 a month. The number of seismic crews operating around the world had climbed by the mid-1950s to 64.[52]

Texas Instruments plowed back all its earnings into long-range-growth projects, paying no dividends. The board member A. D. Bestebreurtje mildly complained on shareholders' behalf after Haggerty, looking to increase working capital and make additions to facilities, proposed no dividend payouts for several years. The board did not agree with Bestebreurtje. Not until 1962 would TI pay its first dividend, 48 cents per share.[53]

With all their accomplishments, many TIers felt justified in seeing themselves in a flattering light. "The chance to work hard and be successful and be surrounded with equally stimulated kinds of people was just a fantastic experience," recalled Cecil Dotson, a boyhood pal of Shepherd's who had instituted important work-simplification processes at TI before taking over operations in England. He added: "We set tough goals for ourselves and we had tremendous success. We were all a young bunch of guys who were excessively cocky in terms of what we had accomplished, and we were revolutionizing the world."[54]

Frivolity sometimes relieved their hard work. Company sales conferences involved contests, skits, props, and sometimes cheerleaders. At one such event, Dotson pretended great dissatisfaction with sales of a particular item. He rushed into the audience, grabbed the offending manager, Zee Pique, pulled him outside, and bound him to a stake ready for firing. Just as Dotson was ready to light the pyre, a fire truck roared up. From it emerged none other than Miss Texas, wearing a glamorous gown with a sash designating her high office. Her pleas to save Pique's life worked. Dotson agreed to give him another chance and set him free.[55]

TI's dramatic accomplishments did not escape the business press.

Jonsson gained by far the most attention of the founders. At the end of 1956, *Business Week* carried his portrait on its cover with the caption: "Jonsson of Texas Instruments paves the road to production with Ph.Ds." The theme of the accompanying story was how TI had surged to a leadership position by encouraging scientists and technicians to work together on everything from basic research to the assembly line. In addition to Jonsson, Haggerty, Shepherd, and Teal were portrayed in some detail.[56]

Growth continued unabated. Net sales jumped from $28.6 million in 1955 to $45.7 million in 1956, then to $67 million in 1957. Jonsson told shareholders that he expected net sales of $80 million in 1958. He was wrong; they were greater—$92 million. In 1959 that figure more than doubled, reaching a whopping $193 million.

At about the same time the *Business Week* article appeared, Jonsson spoke optimistically to the New York Society of Security Analysts about prospective markets for semiconductor products. The death knell was being sounded, he said, for all plug-in radios. By 1959, Jonsson predicted, all car radios would be using only transistors. Next would come television sets. Transistors, along with semiconductor diodes and rectifiers, would make many processes feasible for automation that previously had been hindered by the space requirements and other limitations of vacuum tubes.[57]

By the mid-1950s, Jonsson owned more TI shares than either McDermott or Green. His 516,204 shares represented 17 percent of the outstanding voting shares. McDermott had 465,123 shares, and Green 430,614. Jonsson's shares were worth nearly $8 million. Haggerty had done well himself. With just under 150,000 shares, he was TI's fourth-largest shareholder. By 1959, when TI shares sold for as much as 73⅝, Jonsson's holdings were worth more than $35 million. Two years later, shares prices reached a high of $256, earning TI recognition as "one of the most sensational growth companies in the U.S."[58]

In March 1958, *Texas Parade* singled out Jonsson, a man with a "ready smile and an amazing capacity for getting things done," as TI's key force. In a characterization that became familiar, he was portrayed in Horatio Alger terms as a man who rose from humble Brooklyn beginnings to the presidency of one of America's biggest electronics manufacturers.[59]

"Now that TI is a success, I'm supposed to be an oracle," Jonsson wryly observed during this publicity blitz. He ruefully noted that he had the same brains he had had when nobody was listening.[60]

As TI's most visible executive, he was in demand as a speaker from coast to coast. He carefully prepared his remarks, but delivered them easily and conversationally. "You are without question one of the most articulate businessmen I have ever had the pleasure of listening to," the vice president for financial affairs of the University of Southern California wrote to him.[61]

In 1955 all his speaking engagements were in Dallas, but from 1956 to 1959 he spoke in San Francisco, New York, Atlanta, Houston, Boston, Chicago, Miami, Atlantic City, Minneapolis, and other cities. This busy schedule would pale in comparison to the one he kept in 1960s. Most of his talks were to professional groups, but he also spoke at educational institutions such as Harvard, Southern Methodist University, and Texas A&M.[62]

As he developed his speeches, Jonsson began to reflect on how a man such as himself could reach the heights of business and industry. All his life he had been working hard to grab the golden ring. Now that he had it, he was ready to share his secrets. In a panel discussion for the American Marketing Association, he elaborated. Money, he said, ceased to be a significant factor when there was enough. More important was the challenge: "Can I do this thing? . . . You ask yourself if you've got the guts to do it. You set the most difficult goals that you think are possible of achievement—not unrealistic goals, but *tough* goals. Then you sit back and say to yourself, 'Well, boy, you have announced to everyone what you intend to do. Now let's see if you've got what it takes to go out there and do it.'"[63]

Secondary but still important, he said, was one's relationship with colleagues: "You discover that there is just damn little you wouldn't do for this gang that has helped you so many times when you've been on the spot." Another factor, he said, came at a certain age. One begins wondering how many years are remaining to make a contribution, and so begins to press to see how much more can be accomplished.[64]

↜

Outside activities were taking almost as much of his time these days as TI. Haggerty, as executive vice president, had assumed many of Jonsson's previous duties. One of Jonsson's favorite professional activities was his commitment to the American Management Association conferences, which were attended by top executives from across the nation. Through the AMA, Jonsson came to know many of the nation's leading businessmen, including Peter F. Drucker, who, as it happened, lived in

Montclair, New Jersey, and was becoming probably the nation's leading theorist on business management.[65]

Jonsson's involvement in the AMA reached a height in January 1955, when he made a presentation at the General Management Conference in Los Angeles. His talk about Texas Instruments, "Controls for Growth," was published in the AMA's General Management Series. He outlined key practices that he believed had been essential, that had become part of the company's culture, and that might serve as a model for others. First were annual planning periods ending in a weeklong conference. At these conferences, TI's company or division heads presented their projections for sales, capital expenditures, and operations for the succeeding year. At proper intervals during the year, these heads met with top TI officials to discuss their progress. Since each division head acted like the owner of an individual business, a degree of competition was involved. Rewards were earned in almost direct proportion to successful performances.[66]

Jonsson became a member of the AMA General Management Division's East Coast Planning Council, and in 1956 the AMA executive committee elected him vice president in charge of the General Management Division. Jonsson thus presided over both the East Coast and West Coast planning councils.[67]

The contacts that Jonsson was making through the AMA reached a peak in May 1958 when he chaired the national Economic Mobilization Conference and became acquainted with some of the nation's leading figures, including President Dwight D. Eisenhower and Vice President Richard M. Nixon. (Nixon was just back from his goodwill tour to South America, during which he was stoned and spat upon.) The conferences, held at the Hotel Astor in New York City, garnered major headlines and live broadcast coverage as business leaders explained how they were mobilizing their own companies' resources to meet the economic recession then affecting the nation. At the dinner at which Eisenhower spoke, attended by 2,600 leading business leaders, Jonsson sat at the head table between Nelson A. Rockefeller and Norman Vincent Peale.[68]

In its coverage of the event, *Finance* magazine commented that in the midst of concerns about the recession, "one fellow even had the guts to admit that his business has never been better." That fellow was identified as J. Erik Jonsson, president of Texas Instruments.[69]

Agent of Change

In some ways, American life during the 1950s picked up where it had left off in 1929. The nation was back on track after the upheavals of the Great Depression, World War II, and the Korean War. Business was booming. Life was good. The future looked better.

Erik Jonsson, who had contributed $100 to Dwight Eisenhower's election campaign in 1952, had made a fortune. So had his partners. His counsel was sought and cherished. He was recognized in national business circles, and he was a popular leader in Dallas civic circles.

Pat Haggerty assumed TI's presidency in early 1958, and Jonsson became chairman of the board. Eugene McDermott, chairman since 1949, took a new title: chairman of the executive committee. The changes for Jonsson and Haggerty were in name only, for Haggerty's former position as executive vice president was not filled.

Jonsson, with Bryan F. Smith as point man, oversaw TI's relationship with Wall Street as well as the company's banking and financial matters; Haggerty oversaw virtually everything else. Through his leadership and hard work—more than seventy hours a week—Haggerty became a legendary figure at TI. Only he could have described a workaholic like Jonsson as "a lovable guy but he procrastinates."[1] Just as Jonsson identified Haggerty as his successor, Haggerty became the chief mentor of Mark Shepherd, a future TI president and chief executive officer.

Jonsson continued to be TI's ambassador to the larger business community and especially to his adopted city, Dallas. He still enjoyed trips to New York City, where he talked so expansively on Wall Street that some TI executives feared he revealed too much. Instead of calling on stamp dealers in Lower Manhattan, he visited art galleries and looked for paintings with price tags as high as $20,000.[2]

༄

Two months after he took the chairmanship and ten years after the transistor launched the semiconductor industry, a new TI plant on North Central Expressway opened with a three-day ceremony, June 22–24, 1958. The signal that cut the ribbon was beamed from space by the *Vanguard* satellite, which was powered by Texas Instruments transistors.

The three-level building, enclosing 310,000 square feet, was not particularly attractive, but it was eminently functional. Its keynote was flexibility. *Architectural Forum* declared it "one of the most significant industrial plants of the last decade." Its lightness of form and close architectural adaptation to function represented a "new order of light industry" that might be the technical prototype of a new order.[3]

Hundreds of trees, mostly native, were planted on the 296-acre campus, which was big enough to require a long-range master plan. O'Neil Ford, a San Antonio architect noted for his attention to the Texas landscape; Richard Colley, a city planner; Arch B. Swank Jr. of Dallas, a former partner of Ford's; and Sam Zisman, a land planner, joined as architects under the name Associated Architects and Land Planners.

Executive offices remained stark. One reason for this was that TI executives shifted locations as needs developed. The bare-bones offices were outfitted generally with gray metal desks, a sofa, a couple of chairs, and little else. This reflected a philosophy shared by Jonsson and Haggerty—the main business of TI was in manufacturing.[4] By 1963, the campus had added five more major structures, and by 1965 the original building had more than doubled in size. A headquarters building was envisioned.

༄

A month after the new building opened and most TI employees had departed for their traditional two-week July vacation, Jack St. Clair Kilby, a lanky Kansas-reared engineer who had joined the company two months earlier, stayed behind. Kilby, who held a bachelor's degree from the University of Illinois and a master's degree in engineering from the University of Wisconsin, had been hired to try to further miniaturize the transistor, a special interest of his.

The semiconductor at this point was a device consisting of a transistor, a diode, and a rectifier or capacitor that had to be wired to other components. Every soldered joint was a potential trouble spot. The goal of the micromodule program, for which Kilby worked, was to make all components uniform in size and shape. With most TI engineers away, he addressed the problem in a relatively deserted laboratory. He believed that resistors and capacitors, passive devices, could be made from the same material as the active devices—the transistors. If all devices could be made from a single crystal or chip of semiconductor material, a complete circuit could be formed without the cumbersome interconnections. His work continued after the vacation period ended. On September 12, 1958, using a sliver, or "chip," of germanium, he succeeded in the effort he had begun in July, and he demonstrated his accomplishment for TI executives. In March 1959, the first "solid circuit," about the size of a pencil point, was demonstrated publicly. As TI's annual report summarized, the industry's stunned reaction was similar to that occasioned by the introduction of the silicon transistor in 1954. The integrated circuit leapfrogged over all other advanced concepts aimed at miniaturization.[5]

Kilby, not yet thirty-five, had invented the integrated circuit.[6] A new foundation for the modern microelectronics industry was laid. Society would be transformed by an explosion of consumer electronics products that seemed almost impossible to imagine.

In 1961, the first commercially available integrated circuits went on the market, and TI delivered its first integrated-circuit computer to the U.S. Air Force. In the following year, TI's integrated circuits were used in the Minuteman missile.

Haggerty, mindful of the breakthrough that had been achieved with the pocket-sized radio, urged Kilby to produce a "demonstration project" to showcase the circuit's nonmilitary potentials. He suggested a pocket-sized calculator that would be as powerful as desktop models. Kilby and his colleagues succeeded, and in 1967 the handheld TI calculator was introduced.

Integrated circuits, or microchips, began to replace individual transistors and their accompanying parts. The integrated circuit became the heart of all electronic equipment—computers, watches, calculators, word processors, navigational systems, sound systems, smartphones, and many more. It was the first great invention capable of storing and processing information. It made possible the navigation systems of spacecrafts, and it led to diagnostic aids in medicine, remote controls for household electrical appliances, video games, dolls that "talk," and the storing and retrieval of massive amounts of information in tiny spaces. In the year 2000, an integrated circuit smaller than a penny could hold 125 million transistors![7]

Worldwide sales of integrated circuits would reach $177 billion by the year 2000 and nearly $300 billion by 2012. Kilby, whose high school grades had been too average for him to be admitted to his first college choice, MIT, won the National Medal of Science in 1970 and the Nobel Prize in Physics in 2000.[8]

∽

Jonsson especially believed that TI had an important obligation to its community. He sought to fulfill that obligation, in large part, by affiliating with Dallas organizations. Comfortable in groups of like-minded men, able to conceive of and articulate distant goals, blessed with wit, and at ease on the speaker's podium, he assumed leadership roles naturally.

Republic National Bank of Dallas, the state's largest bank, elected Jonsson to its board in March 1955. His service there reunited him with J. C. Karcher, still president of Coronado Petroleum. Especially through the closeness of their wives, the two men had maintained a social relationship over the years. In 1958, Jonsson joined the board of Dallas Power & Light. In the same year he became a board member of the Equitable Life Assurance Society, serving alongside such men as David Rockefeller (Chase Manhattan Bank), Augustus C. Long (Texaco), and Sterling Morton (Morton Salt).

Texas Instruments was viewed in Dallas as an interesting newcomer. For decades, executives of banks, department stores, utilities, and daily newspapers had dominated civic affairs. Those downtown executives, often native Dallasites, retained a tinge of suspicion of those who spoke with anything other than Texas accents. Cotton and then oil had dominated the Dallas economy, and now, through TI, electronics was moving to the fore. Texas Instruments' primary offices were located in far North Dallas rather than downtown; its business was worldwide, not local. Nevertheless, the TI newcomers, especially Jonsson, had gained other leaders' respect and admiration. The fact that TI was now the city's largest employer was no small factor in contributing to that esteem.

Few civic organizations were as important to businessmen as the Dallas Chamber of Commerce. Jonsson had joined that organization soon after coming to Dallas; in 1954 he became a director. In 1957, he was elected president, signaling his arrival as a major civic leader. His service brought him wide visibility, an almost endless round of public and social engagements, and regular photographic appearances in the city's two daily newspapers.

At the end of his first year, he was able to list a huge number of initiatives and accomplishments—efforts to attract new industry, a campaign to build the city's retail and wholesale markets, the expansion of transportation facilities, the opening of a new municipal auditorium and two major downtown hotels, and a record-breaking drive for new members.[9]

He never could be certain just what promotional appearances his civic office might entail. When an international chess tournament was played in Dallas in 1957, he made the ceremonial first move for Samuel Reshevsky of the United States. He recalled the time he played chess against a friend and found himself in a desperate bind. Seeing that he soon would be checkmated, he said: "I wish I was playing your side of the board and you mine." The friend promptly turned the board around and went on to beat Jonsson in six moves.[10]

At the end of his second term as Chamber of Commerce president, which had followed naturally because of his success, the organization had more than eight thousand members and was said to be the largest of its kind in the world. Years later, his service would be memorialized by the J. Erik Jonsson Award, given to those displaying the highest ideals of citizen leadership.[11]

Besides his work with the chamber, Jonsson became an influential leader of the Dallas Citizens Council, a powerful organization founded in 1937 whose membership was limited to chief executive officers. After President Kennedy's assassination, the group would become known as the oligarchy that ruled Dallas from behind the scenes.

Jonsson's civic service brought him recognition as Dallas's salesman of the year for 1958. There was talk that he might run for mayor. He ended speculation when, in March 1958, he told the *Dallas Morning News* that he had no political aspirations.[12]

‿

Life was good. Every year Jonsson traded his Cadillac in for a new one. He kept a thirty-five-foot Chris-Craft speedboat on nearby Lake Dallas. He usually played in the Petroleum Club's annual golf tournament. Weekday lunches at the club were followed inevitably by gin rummy, especially with the stockbroker Orville Cartwright and Jonsson's friends Morris G. Spencer and Roy Guffey. He enjoyed the club's gin rummy tournaments, and several times won the championship.[13]

One of his gin rummy opponents, the oilman H. L. Hunt, beat him consistently. Jonsson told Hunt he couldn't understand why. Hunt had him shuffle a deck of cards and place them faceup on the table. Hunt studied the cards for a few minutes and then secured them in the same order with a rubber band. "Now take these cards home and call me tonight," Hunt said. When Jonsson called him, Hunt named the cards in their exact order.[14]

The Jonssons moved in 1951 into a twelve-room house at 4831 Shadywood Lane in the wooded Bluffview area of Dallas. The three-level Colonial Revival house, constructed in 1947, was on a secluded 1.5-acre tract with a creek in front and back. The property provided an inspiring setting for Margaret's interest in landscaping.[15]

Margaret Ellen enrolled at Skidmore College in Saratoga Springs, New York. Philip, in his early thirties, was still in the oil business in Midland, married to the former JoAnn Gamble of Pittsburgh, Pennsylvania. They were the parents of four children: Christina Ann, Steven Ward, Eileen Margaret (Petie), and Suzanne Elizabeth. A fifth child, Kenneth Brent, would arrive on December 31, 1963. Kenneth Alan, who, like his older brother, graduated from MIT, had begun working at TI as a sales engineer after his marriage in June 1952 to Diana Elizabeth Gordon, a Wellesley College graduate from Pittsburgh. After a few years in Dallas, the couple moved to Brentwood, California. They would become the parents of four children: Michael, Mark, Erik, and Anne.

↬

In November 1952 Jonsson, Margaret, and Margaret Ellen, now fourteen, had embarked with Cecil and Ida Green on a grand tour of Europe. Besides pleasure, the trip provided an opportunity to conduct some routine TI business matters. Years later, Margaret Ellen remembered this trip to Europe with "Uncle Cecil" and "Aunt Ida" with great pleasure. It was thrilling to see so many new things, but also a shock to see the lingering effects of the war. In Germany, they saw bombed-out towns that had not yet been rebuilt. Margaret Jonsson fell ill during the trip. A doctor in London recommended special nourishment—an egg a day. Because of the continuing food rationing in Britain, the doctor wrote a prescription for the egg. Jonsson each day went to the pharmacy and obtained a single egg for the hotel kitchen to prepare for his wife.[16]

The Jonsson family regularly visited Hawaii and Lake Tahoe. The Hawaii trips began in the mid-1950s, usually aboard the SS *Lurline*. Lake Tahoe had been recommended by Kenneth Alan. A weekend visit to Henry J. Kaiser Jr.'s magnificent Lake Tahoe summer home in June 1960 reinforced Jonsson's positive thoughts about Tahoe. "It is a spot as beautiful as any I have ever seen," he wrote in a thank-you note.[17]

In 1961 the Jonssons bought a large property on the California side of the lake. The house was built of logs during the 1920s. The grounds had tennis and croquet courts, and a boat was maintained. It would remain a favorite family gathering place for many years. Later, Jonsson sold it to Kenneth Alan.[18]

In the spring of 1954, Jonsson, traveling alone in Europe, visited his parents' ancestral Sweden. He hoped to locate in Stockholm long-lost relatives from his mother's family. Remembering the address of his mother's sister, he found it, a four-story walk-up apartment house. No one there knew of her.

He next tried to find some trace of his uncle, the Reverend Hugo Palmquist. A neighborhood church official knew about Hugo, but, surprisingly, only as a poet. He directed Jonsson to a distant cousin, living with her artist husband in an apartment cluttered with his paintings. The couple spoke English, but the meeting was awkward. The cousin unburdened herself, telling this rich cousin from America of financial difficulties. Jonsson politely asked whether he could help her in any way, but she said no.[19]

Six months later, though, she sent a letter to her newfound cousin. She had reconsidered his offer. Perhaps, she hoped, he could help arrange a showing of her husband's paintings in America. It would "cost a good deal of money," she noted.[20] Jonsson declined, and he did not maintain further contact with his long-lost cousin.

Never again did Jonsson seriously inquire into his Swedish heritage. But he enjoyed reminiscing. He became especially concerned about his mother's unmarked grave in Montclair. At Jonsson's request, Malcolm Bedell in 1958 located her grave site and arranged for a marker.[21]

⤳

From boyhood on, Erik Jonsson was remarkably prescient in understanding the long-term payoffs of education. He kept his college textbooks in his office.[22] He insisted that his own children be educated in fine institutions. By the time he reached his forties, Jonsson decided that when he retired, he would concentrate on advancing education.[23]

He was not alone in his commitment, for McDermott and Green shared these intense feelings. All three recognized that TI could not have made its contributions without the advanced training of its prize employees. The founders would become honored and widely recognized for their generosity in donating millions of dollars to educational institutions across the continent. The same was true for Pat Haggerty.

One of Jonsson's early educational interests was the all-girls Hockaday School, which Margaret Ellen attended and which attracted students from across the nation and world. In 1952, Jonsson was elected a Hockaday trustee. As Margaret Ellen progressed through the grades, Jonsson also advanced, becoming chairman of the trustees in 1956 and holding this office through spring 1964. Each spring he handed out diplomas to the graduates. Hockaday was, as Cecil Green said in late 1957, Jonsson's "pet project."[24]

Since 1919 the school had been located on a crowded 9.5-acre site on Greenville Avenue in East Dallas. Jonsson initiated a plan to build a new campus elsewhere. Karl Hoblitzelle, a former chairman of the Hockaday trustees and a Republic Bank executive, agreed to donate a 100-acre site on gently rolling terrain at a prime North Dallas location if sufficient funds to construct new facilities could be raised. Jonsson took on that task and raised $946,500.[25] Classes began in 1961 in an ultramodern, $2.5 million facility that included a two-story classroom building with a connecting wing for administration, two three-story dormitories, a gymnasium, and an auditorium. In honor of Jonsson's "unique leadership . . . and the generosity of his family," the main classroom building was named Jonsson Hall.[26]

⌒

Texas Instruments hired many scientists and engineers with doctorates. They usually came from the Northeast, where strong graduate programs existed at such institutions as Harvard, MIT, Brown, Columbia, and Cornell. Comparable institutions did not exist in the Southwest. Individuals who left Texas for graduate studies seldom returned. In 1957–58, only 5 percent of doctorates awarded in the United States came from institutions in the Southwest. While many companies were moving to the Dallas area, certain high-tech ones declined to do so because of the lack of scientific support. What was desperately needed, Jonsson, McDermott, and Green saw, was a first-rate graduate institution with research capabilities similar to those in the Northeast or on the West Coast. Boston had Harvard and MIT; San Francisco had Stanford, the

University of California, Berkeley, and Lawrence Livermore Laboratory. These areas were becoming famous as centers of high technology; Dallas, even with a head start from Texas Instruments, was not.[27]

The same growing need for graduate education was recognized at Southern Methodist University, where officials proposed the creation of an organization to be known as the Graduate Research Center, which would coordinate efforts by area universities to offer graduate degrees in science and technology. For help, they contacted the Dallas Chamber of Commerce and its president, Erik Jonsson.

Jonsson discussed the proposal in a board meeting during his first term as chamber president. He had been perturbed after an electronics firm employing some 6,000 workers declined to move to Dallas because of the scarcity of PhD graduates and the absence of major research labs. TI and the aircraft manufacturers Temco and Chance Vought, as the area's biggest employers of engineers and scientists, were especially concerned.[28]

At a special meeting of some twenty business and industrial leaders in October 1957, Jonsson, Green, and McDermott announced their willingness to be chief sponsors of a nonprofit entity known as the Graduate Research Center (GRC) to generate basic scientific and engineering research. Jonsson would be chairman of the GRC board. The GRC would be headquartered on the SMU campus. Together, SMU and the GRC would work "toward advancement of knowledge in the pure and applied sciences, and in the training of graduate students."[29]

SMU, which until then had not awarded doctoral degrees, would offer PhDs in select areas of the pure and applied sciences. Other area universities would be involved. Less than three weeks later, Remington Rand installed, rent free, its million-dollar Univac 1103 computer at SMU, the first ever at a U.S. university. The arrangements had been made by the Dallas Chamber of Commerce. The computer was placed in a special building constructed at a cost of $125,000. Jonsson noted that only a few people were aware of the Univac's importance. "The implications are social and intellectual and they reach into industry and business," he said.[30]

The Univac could compute in less than an hour what a skilled mathematician could do in about seventy-five years. Its first message, which Jonsson saved as a personal souvenir, emerged on yellow perforated tape: "SMU Computing Center Heralds Great Future for Engineering and Research in the Southwest."[31]

In March 1959, Jonsson, McDermott, and Green presented gifts totaling $750,000 to pay for a science research library as the GRC's centerpiece.[32] Its resources would be available via electronic means to area researchers. Additional GRC buildings eventually would be constructed on a separate 600–700-acre site "easily accessible to SMU." SMU's president, Willis M. Tate, said the GRC campus would ultimately be as large as the SMU campus. "I think very soon the Graduate Research Center in Dallas will rank with any such center in this nation or the world," he predicted.[33]

On November 4, 1960, Erik and Margaret Jonsson and Eugene and Margaret McDermott were honored guests at the groundbreaking for the research library, known as the Science Information Center. A month later, Jonsson announced the appointment of the GRC's first president, Lloyd V. Berkner, recognized as the intellectual father of the International Geophysical Year and a champion of American space exploration. Berkner instantly became a prominent presence on the SMU campus. The university's alumni magazine called him "one of the most distinguished men to have graced the University campus."[34]

In the same month that Berkner arrived, SMU's new chairman of the board, the banker Eugene McElvaney, introduced Jonsson as the speaker at the Park Cities Rotary Club, describing his "compelling and inspired leadership, and civic responsibility." History would record, McElvaney said, that Jonsson's greatest contribution was the Graduate Research Center—destined, in McElvaney's opinion, to become "one of the great research centers of our modern world."[35]

But in February 1961, in keeping with Berkner's concept of establishing an even-broader umbrella organization in which SMU would be but one of a number of participating institutions rather than an equal partner, a new organization with a similar name, the Graduate Research Center of the Southwest (GRCSW) was formed. The Jonssons, McDermotts, and Greens each donated 20,000 shares of TI stock for initial funding. For the moment, the GRCSW's headquarters would remain on the SMU campus with the GRC. Jonsson would be chairman of both organizations, but his primary focus would be on the new one. The three TI couples also pledged to give the GRCSW an additional $1 million—$333,333 each—in TI shares as soon as public funds equal to that amount were raised.[36] An initial endowment of $20 million was sought to cover expenses for the first five years and for constructing the first buildings. An annual budget of $11.3 million was forecast.[37]

Berkner's plan was published in the May 1961 issue of the newly entitled *Journal of the Graduate Research Center*.[38] He wrote a lengthy cover
story for the *Saturday Review* (June 3, 1961) entitled "Renaissance in the
Southwest." Community leaders and university educators were mobilizing through the GRCSW, he wrote, to increase the 400 doctorates
awarded each year in the Southwest to 2,000 annually within fifteen
years. An accompanying article, titled "Engineer of the Intellect: John
Erik Jonsson," profiled the man acknowledged as most responsible for
founding the GRCSW. "He Designs Moneybags for the Superior Feed-
ing of Brains," was the offbeat subtitle. He was said to have found his
calling not so much in established technology ("the record of contem-
porary engineering lists no major contributions opposite Jonsson's
name"), but in financial planning tuned to the explosive expansion of
modern science.[39]

Interested as SMU was in these ambitious goals, it had needs in
other areas too, such as the fine arts. When SMU announced a $4.5 mil-
lion fund-raising drive for an arts school building and for renovation
of its aging McFarlin Auditorium, Texas Instruments' trilogy of donors
dutifully stepped forward. They jointly contributed $500,000 toward
the $4.5 million goal, and Jonsson served on the committee that raised
the rest of the money.[40]

In November 1961, he spoke at the dedication of the Science Information Center. The words that seemed especially meaningful came
from Eugene McElvaney, chairman of SMU's trustees. "There has been
no more important event in the 50-year history of SMU," he declared.
Entrance to the three-story building was enhanced by a bronze bust of
Everette Lee DeGolyer.[41]

By then, however, SMU was having second thoughts. Evidently, it
had been these thoughts that had prompted the establishment of the
GRCSW. Doctoral programs, especially in the sciences and engineering, were extraordinarily expensive. SMU, owned by the South Central
Jurisdiction of the United Methodist Church, was not well endowed.
The graduate dean, Claude Albritton, issued a doleful report frankly
explaining how the university could not afford expensive new graduate
programs. The minimal cost for adding a program of advanced studies in pure and applied sciences would be approximately $4.72 million;
yet the university had no more funds than the interest earned annually
on an available $1.5 million. While the university would not insist that
all expenses of a PhD program be ensured by an endowment, neither

should it "tempt fate" by setting forth on such a path with just a little maintenance money. As Albritton put it, "Our position is simply that of a gambler who knows something about the mathematics of probability and a lot about the history of higher education in the South and Southwest."[42]

SMU president Willis M. Tate sent the report to Jonsson, adding, "I hope you will find the time to study this report before the next meeting of the Trustees of the Graduate Research Center." He asked for his personal reaction.[43] There is no direct record of Jonsson's response, but SMU's new attitude disappointed—perhaps infuriated—him. Years later, Jonsson was candid in his recollections. "We built a building for them (the Science Information Center) and we put a man out there (Berkner) to handle it for them, and in less than a year he came to me and said, 'I hate to tell you but I think it's a waste of money and pretty hopeless.'"[44]

In 1963, SMU issued a master plan that did not include graduate programs in engineering and the sciences as priorities. The goal of SMU was to educate the whole human being through a liberal education. "Our capital funds are pathetically insufficient, even for our present programs," it declared.[45]

Over the next years, at its own pace, SMU enhanced its science and engineering offerings through new graduate and doctoral programs. But some twenty-five years after the split between SMU and the GRCSW, the Dallas magazine *D* opined, perhaps unfairly, that "it was Tate who cost SMU the most important deal in its history."[46]

In years to come, Jonsson would number college presidents and other academics among his best friends; he would donate millions of dollars to institutions of higher education across the nation. But he was always critical of the academic world's pace: "The only thing that alarms an academic is the sound of snails whizzing past him."[47]

Jonsson, McDermott, and Green found 1,400 undeveloped acres in northwest Richardson, eighteen miles north of downtown Dallas and a dozen miles from SMU, for the new campus. In September 1962, Berkner announced that this would be the location for the Southwest Center for Advanced Studies (SCAS), to be administered by the GRCSW. A "research park" with space-age industries would surround the campus.[48]

In September 1964, the Founders Building, named in honor of Jonsson, McDermott, and Green, opened. At the October 29, 1964, dedication, Jonsson took his customary role as master of ceremonies; Texas governor John Connally was the main speaker; and President Lyndon B. Johnson spoke via long distance. Two months later, the center hosted an international symposium on gravitational collapse that attracted more than three hundred leading scientists from around the world. News coverage of the symposium introduced to the public the word "quasar."[49]

Unfortunately, Lloyd V. Berkner suffered a severe heart attack in June 1964 while in New York City. After spending almost two months in a hospital, he recuperated in Florida before returning for the opening of the Founders Building. He had suffered residual heart damage, however, and he resigned in 1965.[50]

In June 1964, the same year that the Founders Building opened, SMU awarded Jonsson an honorary doctor of laws degree. He was proclaimed an "educational statesman whose philanthropy and leadership have benefited institutions of learning and research over this nation" and whose "humane values and integrity have brought wisdom to the many problems of society, business, and education in an age of explosive technological growth."[51]

Such words did not salve Jonsson's ire. He relayed his thoughts to Tate, complaining that SMU should have been forthcoming earlier about its inability to expand its graduate programs. Jonsson expressed special disappointment in his dealings with SMU board chairman McElvaney, whose praise for Jonsson a few years earlier had been unrestrained. In the future, Jonsson said, he would deal only with Tate, not McElvaney.[52]

Tate, in a four-page handwritten response, sought to soothe Jonsson. There indeed should have been more frankness, he said, but the university had been operating at a deficit for the past two years. McElvaney, Tate said, was a banker who saw things from that viewpoint and who, as chairman of SMU's board, had personal accountability for financial risks. Tate hoped that in the future he and Jonsson could discuss things "eyeball to eyeball." "I make many mistakes but I will always level with you, and you will never have to wonder where I stand," he said.[53]

By 1968, SCAS had established itself as one of the leading institutions in space radiation research. The head of its Geosciences Division, Anton L. Hales, was selected to conduct the principal investigation of rocks brought back from the moon. SCAS did not yet grant degrees, but its fifty-eight professors had an enviable professor-student ratio—there were just forty-two students. Thirty-five of the fifty-eight faculty members were listed in *American Men of Science*.[54]

SCAS continued to be financed largely through the beneficence of its original founders—Jonsson, McDermott, and Green—but there seemed to be no end to the funds required for continued growth. Gifford K. Johnson, who replaced Berkner as president, proposed to Jonsson that SCAS be merged with a first-class state institution. Jonsson agreed.[55]

In 1969, SCAS became a part of the University of Texas system, taking a new name, the University of Texas at Dallas (UTD). In 1975, Jonsson, as president of the board of trustees of the Excellence in Education Foundation—successor body to the SCAS board of trustees—announced the donation of an additional 500 acres of land north of the campus, worth about $12 million. Many additional substantial gifts would follow.[56]

෴

Creating and nurturing the institution that became UTD was an incredibly time-consuming endeavor for Jonsson, but two other colleges, Rensselaer and Skidmore, also benefited especially from his philanthropy. His involvement as a Rensselaer alumnus began modestly in 1948 with a $50 contribution to RPI's 125th Anniversary Fund. In August 1958, he spoke at the Alpha Tau Omega Congress in Houston, where he enjoyed getting to know four RPI representatives.[57] In the following summer, Rensselaer awarded Jonsson, its now-famous alumnus, an honorary doctorate for "building one of America's great new companies serving the engineering profession."[58]

Six months later, he and Margaret pledged $1 million toward RPI's new $9.5 million Science Center. It was one of the largest amounts given in years to RPI, enough to pay for one of the center's four projected buildings. The gift was a "shot in the arm to all," wrote the grateful chairman of RPI's board of trustees. Jonsson also made two $5,000 contributions to establish endowments for separate prizes to be awarded annually, the Erik Jonsson Prize and the Arthur M. Greene Prize (named for his favorite professor).[59]

In November 1960, he began a four-year term as trustee of RPI and was asked to oversee the southern region's efforts in the continuing fund-raising drive for the Science Center. In October 1961, Erik and Margaret Jonsson attended the opening of the Jonsson Laboratory at the Science Center. In the summer of 1963, Rensselaer named Jonsson a life trustee. He continued to give to and to be closely involved with his alma mater for the rest of his life. A tally made by RPI in December 1979 showed that up to that point he and Margaret had donated $10,143,282 in various gifts to the institution.[60] "Never before in the history of Rensselaer" was there an individual who had made a greater impact on RPI than Jonsson, RPI trustees declared in 1990.[61]

⌐

Perhaps more dramatic was Jonsson's unlikely involvement with Skidmore College, the all-female institution that Margaret Ellen attended as a freshman. Skidmore was in Saratoga Springs, New York, about thirty miles north of Rensselaer, on thirty-five acres interspersed among privately owned parcels of land. Margaret Jonsson told her husband that among his many activities he should not neglect their daughter's college. In the fall of 1957, Margaret Ellen's sophomore year, Jonsson visited the campus, met the president, Val H. Wilson, and gave 425 TI shares to the college, the first of many such gifts.[62]

That same fall, Margaret Ellen withdrew from Skidmore and returned to Dallas to make her social debut. It appeared that Jonsson's relationship with the college would end. But he had become interested in the school, and he was enjoying a fine relationship with Wilson.[63] He reassured Skidmore's president: "[I have] neither lost nor lessened my interest in your fine institution which I shall be anxious to help in any way I can."[64]

With its fiftieth anniversary approaching, Skidmore was planning its largest fund-raising drive in history. Wilson arranged for a college official to brief Jonsson in New York City.[65] Jonsson, typically, worried about the adequacy of the plan for the future. Despite the advance work on a master plan, Jonsson wanted to scrap the plan and relocate the campus. He and Margaret flew to Saratoga Springs in late June 1960 with a unique offer. If Skidmore agreed, they would pay for the new property.[66]

The property Jonsson had in mind was a historic 1,000-acre site known as Woodlawn Park, about two miles from the existing campus. In earlier days, Woodlawn Park was a showplace for magnificent homes, but over the years they had been left vacant, damaged by vandals, and destroyed by fire. The land, though, was beautiful, full of forests, pastures, slopes steep enough for skiing, and miles of roadways.[67]

A special meeting of Skidmore's board of directors heard Jonsson, accompanied by O'Neil Ford, the proposed architect for the new campus. Ford later recalled that Jonsson cautiously and modestly told the board what he thought should be done. His "devastating sincerity" was so evident, Ford said, that it produced "a great calm—a powerful silence."[68] The directors, encouraged further by Jonsson's promise of $1 million in addition to the purchase of the land, accepted the offer enthusiastically. The announcement brought exclamations. "Texan Gives Skidmore Woodlawn Park" was the banner headline in the *Saratogian* newspaper.[69]

For Skidmore, the advantages were manifold. New buildings could be constructed for specific purposes; space would be available for future growth; excessive maintenance costs would be reduced; and the move would dramatize Skidmore's forward-looking spirit.[70]

George Davis, the chairman of Skidmore's general campaign, told Jonsson he could never imagine the gift's impact. It had provided inspiration and a much-needed lift to the institution's spirits. "What you have done for Val [Wilson] can't be described," he wrote.[71] Other congratulatory letters poured in from Skidmore trustees, alumni, and residents of Saratoga Springs.[72]

When, in November 1960, Jonsson sent the final check from the Jonsson Foundation to complete his pledge, he wrote: "Believe me, Val, sending you this check and the one that preceded it gave our family one of the greatest thrills it has ever experienced."[73] In February 1961, Jonsson became a Skidmore trustee, a position he would hold through 1977.

In 1963, Jonsson made good on his promise to give an additional $1 million, the largest such gift in Skidmore's history. Jonsson, now a trustee at both RPI and Skidmore, had given more than $2 million to these institutions, a fact duly noted in an area newspaper: "The example he has set . . . is one that leaders in business and industry throughout the nation can well emulate."[74]

In 1964, Skidmore bestowed an honorary master of letters degree on Margaret Jonsson. The Margaret Jonsson Tower, a high-rise, twelve-story dormitory that was the tallest building in Saratoga County, was constructed before the end of the decade as one of nineteen buildings on the new campus. By the end of the decade, investment in the campus had reached $22.3 million. In 1972, at another groundbreaking, Erik Jonsson was given an honorary doctor of laws degree.[75] By 1976, the college's plant assets had grown from $4 million in 1961 to more than $36 million. Student enrollment had doubled to more than 2,000, and thirty-eight new buildings had been completed, with others under way.

By 1980, the Jonssons could look back on gifts to Skidmore that totaled $3 million.[76]

The Jonsson family's affection for Skidmore continued, for in 1981 their granddaughter, Emily, the daughter of Margaret Ellen and her husband, George Charlton, enrolled as a freshman. By then, Skidmore, like so many all-female colleges, had become a coeducational institution.

⤳

While the Jonssons preferred always to give large amounts of money to institutions where its impact would be significant, exceptions occasionally were made. When a medical student wrote to the Dallas Woman's Club in 1960 requesting scholarship money, Margaret brought it to her husband's attention. He met with the student, Tommy Sparrow, and made a deal. He agreed to give Sparrow $500 under certain conditions: he would repay the principal five years from the date of the loan with the interest compounded semiannually at the rate of 3 percent. But if Sparrow maintained an average of B or better, Jonsson would forgive the interest. If his grades averaged B+ or better, one-half of the principal would be forgiven. And if he achieved all As, Jonsson would forgive the entire loan. Sparrow and Jonsson both seemed pleased. In 1961, Jonsson lent Sparrow another $800 for medical school expenses, and in 1962 another $500.[77]

Center Stage at a National Tragedy

Erik Jonsson was so intertwined with Dallas that it would have been almost impossible to realize his extensive involvements elsewhere. Few if any of the city's leaders, even old-timers, enjoyed a higher profile. His physician friend Martin S. Buehler expressed his admiration on a prescription pad note: "Dear Erik: I wish I knew how you manage to get '30 hrs' in a 24 hr. day."[1]

Local plaudits mounted. In recognition of his leadership, in 1961 Jonsson was awarded the city's most prestigious civic honor—the Linz Award. He was cited as a "great Christian, a great industrialist, a great civic leader and a great humanitarian," and, more specifically, was singled out for his work with five Dallas groups: the Graduate Research Center, the Dallas Pilot Institute for the Deaf (later the Callier Center), the Dallas Foundation, the Dallas Symphony, and the Hockaday School. He had served in the previous year as board chairman of each of those organizations and had worked on fifteen national and state boards or committees.[2]

On the same day he received the Linz Award, Jonsson accepted another important civic assignment: presidency of the Dallas County United Fund. He led its critical first year of operation in bringing together all charitable fund-raising efforts in Dallas. After a successful effort in which more than $2.9 million was raised, he was reelected president for 1962. The 1962 goal of $4.6 million also was surpassed, and Jonsson further enlarged his duties by becoming a member of the nationwide United Fund Advisory Council. Years later, in 1978, the Dallas County organization, known by then as the United Way, recognized his successes by establishing an award in his honor, the J. Erik Jonsson Award for Voluntarism.[3]

One organization to which Jonsson accepted an invitation to join in 1960 was not so time-consuming, but it was prestigious. This was the Critic Club, a group founded in 1908 by leading men of Dallas—mostly businessmen—known for their intellects. The sixteen members rotated in hosting and giving talks on widely varying topics at monthly meetings, always preceded by "pre-prandial" drinks. Many of the talks were scholarly, but Jonsson's talk in 1962 was entitled "What Am I Doing Here?"[4]

Margaret tolerated her husband's schedule, waiting for that promised retirement so they could enjoy time together. He had made a fortune as he approached his sixtieth birthday. Because of that success, they could travel and experience good things, as he had told her. Meanwhile, Margaret dutifully accompanied her husband to events when her presence seemed important. On arrival, he would instantly be the center of attention, laughing and bantering easily while she melted into the background. She would have been just as happy—or perhaps happier, she sometimes said—if she had married a farmer. She preferred spending time with their children's families, which included eleven grandchildren, and overseeing their large home.[5]

Her major role, she told a reporter, was to let her husband know that she was behind him and to realize that his schedule was more important than hers.[6] Sometimes Jonsson pushed her into the spotlight. In 1961, as chairman of the Dallas Committee for Prosperity, he stressed the theme "Buy What You Need Now—The Time Is Right." A salesman called to see whether he practiced what he preached. Would he buy a new Cadillac from him? Jonsson did, and he sent Margaret to get it. A newspaper photographer was present, and Margaret posed at the car as she accepted the keys.[7]

Sometimes Margaret's picture appeared in the newspapers because of her own activities, especially at the Dallas Woman's Club, which she had joined in 1935. In 1958 she began a five-year term on the board of governors, culminating in her presidency in 1961–62. As president, she provided the leadership in building a new facility designed by O'Neil Ford.

Another favorite activity that brought her some attention was gardening. She served as president of the Dallas Garden Center from 1964 to 1966, and she worked closely with a landscape architect on the 1.5-acre grounds of the Jonsson home. The charming plot featured terraces and slopes, native trees of various sizes and shapes, a stone bridge over a creek, wide swaths of ivy ground cover, an irregularly shaped pond, and flowers that burst into color every new season.

⌇

Jonsson, McDermott, and Green continued to have a close relationship. McDermott and Green had been content for Jonsson to take the lead in transforming TI, and given its nearly unparalleled success, they had no reason to complain. McDermott, quieter, did not share Jonsson's eagerness for high-visibility endeavors. Green enjoyed the limelight, but he accepted Jonsson's higher profile.

The cordiality was never more confirmed than by the 1961 decision to unite in a venture unrelated to Texas Instruments. The three, joined by Haggerty, purchased as equal partners a controlling interest in Braniff Airways from interim U.S. senator William A. Blakley, who owned Exchange Park, where TI's executive offices were located. They paid $13.5 million for 1,006,000 shares, about one-third of the outstanding common stock, at $13.50 a share, giving them a 34 percent interest. Braniff, founded in Oklahoma as a small regional airline, had become one of the nation's largest carriers. Jonsson explained that the "sole reason" for the purchase was that the men considered it to be "a good personal investment."[8]

More than his partners, Jonsson had a special interest in aviation. Consequently, Jonsson alone joined Braniff's board and executive committee. In 1964, McDermott, Green, and Haggerty took handsome profits by selling their shares for $25 each, nearly twice what they had paid. Jonsson held on to his investment.[9]

Under a new president and chief executive officer, Harding Lawrence, Braniff's stock was climbing in value. In August 1965, Jonsson sold his shares for $62 each, more than four times what he had paid, turning his original $3.4 million investment into a profit of about $12 million. (Under Lawrence's flamboyant leadership, Braniff made headlines as it expanded routes and decorated its aircraft in bright colors. Finally, the airline encountered turbulence—in the form of high fuel prices and airline deregulation—and declared bankruptcy in 1982.)[10]

⌇

The primary organization for Dallas' business leaders was the Dallas Citizens Council. From its beginning, the DCC was more influential than the elected city council. Jonsson became president of this powerful group in January 1963. Little could he or anyone know that he would therefore find himself at the center of one of the most dramatic episodes of modern American history—the assassination of President John F. Kennedy.

President Kennedy was not popular in conservative Dallas. The state's Democratic Party was split between conservatives and liberals or loyalists, and conservatives held the upper hand. Kennedy carried Texas by a slim margin, but Dallas went for Richard M. Nixon. Led by the *Dallas Morning News*, the city tilted far to the right after World War II, fearful of federal interference in local affairs and wary of perceived accommodations with the Soviet Union.

In the fall of 1963, President Kennedy made plans to shore up support and raise money in Texas for his 1964 campaign. Texas governor John B. Connally, a former secretary of the navy under Kennedy, had become increasingly conservative, but the White House designated him as the logical host for the Texas visit. Connally, later to become a Republican, declared that Kennedy's Texas trip would include "political" and "nonpolitical" visits. Dallas, Fort Worth, and San Antonio would be nonpolitical stops; Houston and Austin would be political.[11]

Before flying to Washington, D.C., for a strategy session, Connally stopped in Dallas to confer with the city's business leadership—namely, the top rung of the DCC. Besides Jonsson, this group included Robert B. Cullum, president of the Dallas Chamber of Commerce; Robert L. Thornton; Joe Dealey of the *Dallas Morning News*; and Albert Jackson of the *Dallas Times Herald*.[12]

In the private session, Connally bluntly said that Kennedy's visit was going to be awkward for him. He viewed the president as a political liability, but he could hardly ask him not to come. Still, he had no intention of being the president's errand boy. "I don't intend to default to the liberals," Connally said. "I've got to have a nonpolitical body to represent Dallas, and you gentlemen are it by your associations." For Connally, it was an opportunity to strike a blow against his enemies in the Democratic Party—the liberals. President Kennedy's Dallas visit would be in the hands of the DCC. As president of this organization, Erik Jonsson, a Republican, would be the primary host.[13]

Less than a month before the president's arrival, a frightening event put the issue of his security at the forefront. United Nations ambassador Adlai Stevenson, speaking in Dallas on October 26, was subjected to a torrent of abuse from an audience packed with right-wing extremists. Police had to remove the founder of one extremist group who interrupted Stevenson with a bullhorn. Repeated disturbances continued throughout the ambassador's talk. Afterward, a jeering mob confronted him as he left. He was hit on the head with a picket sign and spat upon, and members of the crowd rocked his car. Television captured the nasty scene for national audiences. Bold headlines appeared in newspapers across the land. Fears for the president's safety in Dallas were raised immediately.

Time magazine declared Dallas "a city disgraced." The *Christian Century* blamed the incident on the civic leaders' refusal to respond to previous irrational behavior. The ABC radio commentator Edward P. Morgan said that "Big D now stands for disgrace."[14]

Dallas, which had become a gathering place for activist, publicity-minded ultraconservatives who generally followed the theories of the John Birch Society, was in crisis. When Major General Edwin A. Walker resigned from the U.S. Army under pressure because of his "pro-blue" political indoctrination of troops, he settled in Dallas. H. L. Hunt was writing and publishing conservative tracts with titles such as *We Must Abolish the United Nations* and *Hitler Was a Liberal.* Frank McGehee, who had interrupted Stevenson's talk with his bullhorn, had founded in Dallas the National Indignation Convention (later Conference), which had chapters across the nation. The local chapter of the John Birch Society had a membership that included some of the city's oil-rich. The *Dallas Morning News* publisher, E. M. (Ted) Dealey, had carried his anti-Kennedy diatribes straight to the White House when at a presidential luncheon he urged Kennedy to get off his daughter Caroline's tricycle and lead the nation like a man on horseback. Headlines such as "Birch Leader Says He Doubts Ike Red" appeared in Dealey's newspaper. The Birch official said he was "not convinced that Dwight David Eisenhower is a dedicated conscious agent of the Communist conspiracy," a statement hinting strongly that such a possibility might be true.[15]

Dallas's reputation as a citadel of ultraconservatives had become notorious, but neither Jonsson nor any of the principal civic leaders approved of their behavior. Neither, however, had they discouraged it. Now, with the president arriving within a month, they were alarmed. Another unseemly episode would bring lasting harm to the city's reputation. A number of people, including Stanley Marcus and U.S. Attorney Barefoot Sanders, both eyewitnesses to the Stevenson incident, urged the president to stay away from Dallas.

In this atmosphere, the DCC's sponsorship of the presidential visit was announced. James R. Killian Jr., President Kennedy's scientific adviser, called Jonsson to see whether additional sponsors might be obtained. Jonsson added two organizations with which he was intimately familiar—the Graduate Research Center of the Southwest (to which, in the text of his speech, Kennedy paid generous compliments) and the Dallas Assembly. The latter was a "junior" DCC composed of leaders younger than forty.[16]

The presidential luncheon was billed as a special meeting of the DCC at the Trade Mart, owned by prominent member John Stemmons. Jonsson would preside and sit next to the president. One might have expected the mayor or the head of the county's Democratic Party to have that role in a presidential visit, but as Governor Connally had planned, this was a "nonpolitical" visit. Jonsson had thirty-six of the closely held tickets, many of which he gave to TI executives.[17]

Of course, arranging for a presidential visit was not a matter left entirely to Jonsson and the DCC. A multitude of entities were represented at early planning sessions: the White House, FBI, Secret Service, Texas Department of Public Safety, Dallas County Sheriff's Department, Dallas Police Department, and others. The decision as to the luncheon's location rested primarily with the White House's Jerry Bruno, advance man for the Democratic National Committee. Several sites were considered and rejected. Dallas's Memorial Auditorium, with a seating capacity of 11,000, was too large. The Women's Building at Fair Park had a ceiling that was too low. Market Hall was already booked. That left the Trade Mart, which seated about 2,600. Stemmons offered it free of charge, and his generosity was accepted.[18]

Jonsson believed the choice to be "particularly bad" for security reasons: it had too many entrances and different levels. Still, he had no fears for the president's safety. "As far as I was concerned as representative of the Citizens Council, anything I could do to make the visit a pleasant and courteous reception would be done." Jonsson would preside at the luncheon.[19]

As the day approached, Margaret Jonsson, fretting about her own role, privately recorded her frustrations: "The first I knew of his [Kennedy's] planned visit to Dallas was when I read it in the newspaper. The second information that Erik my own husband was to be the host I also read in the newspaper." She naturally wondered what she might have to do. The answer her husband gave was, "I don't know." Finally, "after much thought," she called Robert B. Cullum, chairman of the arrangements committee, who explained that she, of course, would be the "hostess." He suggested proper clothing, and he informed her that she would be seated at the head table on the other side of the president.[20]

Kennedy's first Texas stops, in San Antonio, Houston, and Fort Worth, were uneventful except for the excitement generated by any presidential visit. After breakfast in Fort Worth on the morning of November 22, the presidential party flew to Dallas via *Air Force One*, a short hop of some thirty miles. Here the situation was not welcoming.

Crude handbills accusing the president of treason had been spread about downtown Dallas. An associate of Edwin A. Walker's had arranged for their printing. On the morning of Kennedy's arrival, the *Dallas Morning News* carried a shocking full-page advertisement, surrounded by a funereal black border, addressing twelve accusatory questions to the president. On seeing it, Kennedy turned to his wife, Jacqueline, and said, "We're really in 'nut country' now."[21]

At 11:40 a.m., *Air Force One* landed at Love Field, followed by a second aircraft bearing Vice President Lyndon B. Johnson, Lady Bird, and their own entourage. Margaret and Erik Jonsson stood in a receiving line that included Mayor Earle Cabell and his wife, Dearie, with whom the Jonssons had ridden to the airport, and Governor Connally and his wife, Nell. Dearie Cabell presented red roses to Mrs. Kennedy.

The Jonssons skipped the motorcade, driving directly to the Trade Mart in order to be there before the president's arrival. The motorcade passed directly in front of the Texas Instruments plant on Lemmon Avenue. Here and all along the way exuberant crowds cheered and waved to the president and his wife.

By the time the Jonssons arrived at the Trade Mart, awaiting guests, monitoring the progress of the motorcade via pocket-sized transistor radios, were alarmed. News bulletins were announcing that as the motorcade reached Dealey Plaza, three shots rang out. The president's limousine had raced immediately to nearby Parkland Hospital.

Not knowing more, Jonsson desperately sought information. Motorcade buses carrying the press soon arrived and discharged their frantic passengers, uncertain themselves about what had happened. Jonsson, Stemmons, and a few others sought information by telephone, but they could reach nobody. "I think every telephone line in Dallas was busy," Jonsson said, "and time was going on."[22]

Finally, at 1:01 p.m., thirty-one minutes after the shots had been fired, Jonsson spoke with understated words from the podium: "There has been a delay in the arrival of the motorcade. There has been a mishap. We do not know the extent of it or the exact nature. We believe from our report we have just received that it is not serious. We hope you will keep your seats. As soon as we have something to tell you, believe me, we'll do it."[23]

Nine minutes later, Jonsson, far more shaken because of the new information he had learned, told the audience that he felt a "little bit like the fella on Pearl Harbor day." President Kennedy and Governor Connally, he confirmed, had been shot. "We do not know how seriously. Our reports are scant, they are difficult to get. We shall tell you as much as we know as soon as we know anything."[24]

Jonsson had made his words as "plain vanilla as possible." Anything else, he feared, might cause pandemonium. He had been born, after all, on the day McKinley was assassinated; he had "read a lot" about presidential assassinations. He knew he had to be careful.[25]

The shock, though, was overpowering. It was assumed instantly that right-wing zealots had carried their protests to the ultimate. Someone shouted, "Those damn fanatics, why do we have to have them in Dallas?" The Reverend Luther Holcomb, executive director of the Greater Dallas Council of Churches, offered a prayer, which was followed shortly by one from the Reverend William H. Dickinson Jr., the Jonssons' family pastor at Highland Park Methodist Church. Finally, with the audience in disarray, Jonsson advised them to go home but to avoid downtown because of the chaos.[26]

Margaret Jonsson found her way home alone. Her husband stayed at the Trade Mart with a few others, especially fellow DCC leaders, watching television accounts revealing the president's death and the governor's serious wounds. Sandwiches were sent for; the sumptuous luncheon meals were barely touched. Jonsson, as he said later, knew the tragedy meant "deep trouble" for the city.[27]

Jonsson and the other officials who were to have welcomed the president composed a statement. The original draft, which he saved, shows incomplete sentences, strikeouts, and inserts reflecting tortured deliberations over the proper wording. The final statement read: "Our hearts are filled with sorrow, as are those of every citizen of the United States, at the tragic and untimely death of President John F. Kennedy and the serious wound suffered by the Governor of our State. We are deeply distressed and grieved that the respectful and enthusiastic welcome in progress for our President was terminated by an act of lunacy." Edited out of the original draft was a statement that soon became a persistent theme as city leaders sought to deflect criticism—the assassination could have occurred anywhere.[28]

Jonsson, W. Dawson Sterling of the Dallas Assembly, Lloyd V. Berkner of the GRCSW, and Robert B. Cullum also signed individual telegrams to Jacqueline Kennedy. Jonsson's was typical: "Desolate and helpless is our grief for you, your children and our country. We pray most humbly for you, yours, and a nation grieved beyond expression."[29]

The day became more complicated when Dallas police officer J. D. Tippit was shot to death in Oak Cliff by Lee Harvey Oswald. With Oswald's arrest, attention turned to the Dallas Police Department, which identified him as the primary suspect in the assassination.

Jonsson got home at about eight o'clock, but the day was far from over. DCC leaders arrived, and the Jonsson house became a command center. Charles G. Cullum, Robert Cullum's brother, remembered terrifying conversations: "What was Dallas going to do to deal with the situation?" Those present sought to coordinate responses to an angry world. The Jonsson phone was "ringing off the hook," as it would be for several days. Everybody in town, it seemed, had a suggestion about what should be done.[30]

Nelle Johnston, Jonsson's personal secretary at Texas Instruments, arrived to manage the calls, remaining for three days as ashen-faced civic leaders continued to make the house their headquarters. Holland McCombs of *Life* magazine showed up. Stanley Marcus called from New York to discuss a memorial. Pat Haggerty arrived to support his boss. A mysterious car spotted outside the house and the appearance of uninvited persons raised fears. Jonsson hired a security guard.[31]

⌒

On Sunday, two days after the assassination, yet another unimaginable event occurred that gave further reason to hold Dallas in contempt. As police escorted Oswald to a car in the department's basement for transfer to the Dallas County jail, the nightclub owner Jack Ruby stepped out of a crowd of detectives, uniformed officers, and newsmen and fired a fatal pistol shot into Oswald's abdomen. The primary suspect in the assassination, who had been handcuffed to a detective as a security measure, died without uttering more than a moan, taking his secrets to the grave.

Stanley Marcus called again to recommend a sunrise service at the Cotton Bowl. "We'll not have any meetings of any size anywhere if we can help it," Jonsson responded, fearing further calamities. Marcus described the rapid and growing anger against Dallas that he was sensing in New York. That very day, two days after the assassination, New York sports fans were calling the Cowboys the "assassins."[32]

When Jonsson heard that permission had been granted for a parade of mourning, he took steps to stop it. Threats already had been made against the mayor's life. Learning that local Catholic churches had requested the parade, he turned to Haggerty, a prominent Catholic, to implore church officials to cancel the parade. Police chief Jesse Curry advised Jonsson that he had no authority to stop a legally sanctioned parade. Finally, Dallas city attorney Henry Kucera told Jonsson that the mayor possessed that authority. When Jonsson reached Cabell and expressed his concerns, the mayor agreed with him and canceled the permit.[33]

With Oswald's murder, wrath towards the city redoubled. Not only had Dallas permitted the president to be slain, its police had allowed a disreputable nightclub owner to be present in the police station and to shoot and kill the only suspect. Erroneous reports that Dallas schoolchildren cheered upon hearing news of the president's death added fuel to the fire. The intense suffering experienced by the nation and the world could be seen in the emotionally wrought letters, telegrams, and telephone calls flooding city hall. Some were supportive, but most reflected intense animosity. Reports of verbal abuse directed at Dallasites who happened to be visiting other cities surfaced immediately. Dallas was the "city of hate." Its big businessmen, and especially the DCC, were vilified as an oligarchy that controlled the city with an iron fist.

Jonsson later observed that in no other instance was an entire city blamed for such an event—not Washington, where both Lincoln and Garfield had been assassinated, nor Buffalo, where McKinley had been fatally shot. It was clear that this would not hold true for Dallas.[34]

Jonsson and the other DCC leaders, exercising their acknowledged proprietary interest in the city's welfare, were desperate to respond appropriately. The three or four days at the Jonsson house following the assassination were for Margaret "a nightmare." Her house was filled with men "hungry & thirsty and holding secret meeting[s] in every corner. I never worked so hard in my life."[35]

Even the question of where Oswald should be buried came to their attention. A distinct feeling emerged that he should not be buried in Dallas. The Reverend Holcomb advised Jonsson of speculation that someone might dig up Oswald's body if he were buried in Dallas. Deciding on a burial location was not normally the type of question reserved for a group of civic leaders, but in this case they exerted themselves. Suggestions came "from all over town" that Oswald should be buried in Fort Worth, where his mother, Marguerite, lived and where he had spent time as a child. Jonsson agreed. Somehow Jonsson managed to talk by telephone to Oswald's Russian-born widow, Marina, about it. Fort Worth Police Department officials gave assurances that a guard would be placed over Oswald's grave site if the burial took place there. Finally, the suspected assassin was buried in Fort Worth at Rose Hill Cemetery.[36]

One of the earliest decisions Jonsson and the others made was that Dallas's civic leadership had to be conspicuously present at the Kennedy funeral on Monday in Washington. Jonsson, Cabell, Holcomb, and Sterling would attend with Marcus, who was already on the East Coast. As Jonsson later said, "[We would] be sure that we were seen at the time of the parade . . . and that the news carried the news that we were there."[37]

They planned to depart at midafternoon on Sunday, November 24, but a bomb scare—presumably directed at the mayor—caused the flight to be delayed. As the men waited at the Jonsson house, Eddie Barker, who was the most prominent television broadcaster in Dallas as news director of KRLD-TV, the local CBS affiliate, realized that everyone he wanted to interview seemed to be at the Jonsson house. Jonsson told Barker that interviews were impossible; they were leaving for the airport within the hour. Barker urged him to delay their flight because television stations around the nation would be asking to borrow his film of their comments, and if he did not have it, those stations would instead interview people whose statements would likely be unpredictable. "We'll stay," Jonsson said. The interviews were conducted, and Jonsson and his party caught a plane at 11:30 p.m., arriving very late in Washington. The foursome went to the Texas Instruments apartment in Washington, where they got no more than an hour's sleep before daylight on the day of the funeral.[38]

They viewed the funeral procession from the roof of the Mayflower Hotel. The Dallas Chamber of Commerce's lobbyist, Dub Miller, alerted the news media of their presence. They spent the rest of the day talking with the media. "We did everything we could to inform [them] that we were there, that we'd do everything we could when we got back to Dallas to see that things were handled in a proper manner," Jonsson said.[39]

But the avalanche of national and world bitterness toward Dallas was unrelenting. A torrent of hate mail, long-distance telephone calls, and telegrams continued to pour into the mayor's office and police station. Typical was this one: "The unbelievable incompetence of your police is only surpassed by the apparent underlying bigotry, ignorance and lawlessness of the people of Dallas that encouraged these dreadful events. Your city and Texas are disgraced in the minds of men everywhere."[40]

No one in Dallas publicly uttered the thought, but a great feeling of relief had arisen when it was learned that Oswald was not a right-winger. Even more solace was found in an unwarranted rationalization that Oswald had been an outsider with no ties to Dallas. Conveniently forgotten was the fact that he had lived in both Dallas and Fort Worth.

A Dallas minister asked from the pulpit, "In the name of God, what kind of city have we become?" Robert L. Thornton, the aging civic leader now near the end of his life, said, "All I could do was pray." A *Dallas Times Herald* editorial stated that the city was "undergoing the dark night of the soul."[41]

On his return from Washington, Jonsson hurried home, having hardly slept since the assassination. He learned that Eddie Barker had interviewed two local African American ministers who were critical of Dallas. Barker, Jonsson believed, had "cut us to pieces" with these interviews. He called the newscaster to "tell him what I thought of him, and it wasn't a merry conversation."[42]

Jonsson saw something else. "The town itself looked dead and behaved dead," he said. "Everybody was in mourning." Journalists from around the country and across the globe, in Dallas to probe the city's soul, had filled the hotels. One of the things they discovered was the powerful influence of the DCC, whose members were sought out for in-depth stories.[43]

Jonsson spent the next days at city hall, where the visiting press's attention was centered. He began to play a leading role in responding to reporters' questions, and appeared frequently on national news shows. As DCC president, he was bombarded with suggestions about what Dallas should do to mitigate the harm to its reputation. Suggestions included a memorial to Kennedy, razing the Texas School Book Depository, placing an eternal flame at the assassination site, and implementing an ambitious public relations program.[44]

Less than three weeks later, a national public relations newsletter, *PR Reporter*, excoriated the city for its failure to do the last: "Once proud

Dallas bows her head in shame today, her image self-scarred and ugly for all the world to see, her spirit subdued, her voice mute. . . . But Dallas does nothing, and America waits for moral reassurance with diminishing hope and rising resentment."[45]

When the potential crisis over school integration had confronted the city in 1961, the DCC initiated a successful public relations program to ensure peaceful compliance. Now, however, Jonsson did not believe a public relations campaign would be appropriate. The city had to redeem itself through good works, not words.

O'Neil Ford described the depth of the problem in an emotional handwritten letter to Jonsson three days after the assassination. Dallas, he said, would share in history the same stigma associated with places where other tragedies had occurred—Sarajevo, Waterloo, Auschwitz. "It isn't fair—and it doesn't make sense—but yet it is deadly certain it will never be erased."[46]

The idea of a Kennedy memorial took hold. Toward that purpose, Mayor Cabell and county judge W. L. (Lew) Sterrett announced a list of twenty men representing different organizations to serve on a committee under the temporary chairmanship of John Stemmons. Jonsson was named an ex-officio member. After considerable effort, a memorial designed by the architect Philip Johnson was built years later on county property two blocks from the assassination site.[47]

In his hours at city hall, Jonsson heard that Mayor Cabell intended to resign in order to run for Congress as a Democrat against the Republican incumbent, Bruce Alger. He called Cabell, who confirmed it. "The day I announce it, I have to resign," he told Jonsson.[48]

Congressman Alger, a symbol of right-wing extremism, had become a liability for the city. Many leaders now believed he should be replaced by someone with more moderate views. In a roundabout way, sending a Democrat to Congress would seem to affirm that no matter what the rest of the nation thought, Dallas had not hated Kennedy. The election of Cabell, a conservative Democrat who had become more centrist as mayor, would help. Cabell thus could expect to gain widespread support from most establishment leaders.[49]

Jonsson asked Cabell who his successor as mayor would be. The answer, specified by the city charter, was the mayor pro tem, Carie Welch, a respected businessman from Oak Cliff. Jonsson and DCC directors believed Welch's credentials were inadequate for what Dallas then required. The city needed a mayor who could command national respect, who was accustomed to dealing with the press, who knew about long-range planning, who was comfortable in managing huge numbers of employees, and who was familiar overseeing budgets in the hundreds of millions of dollars.[50]

By early January 1964, rumors had surfaced that Jonsson would replace Cabell as mayor. He did not deny them. He was a logical choice because of his growing national visibility, his DCC presidency, his experience as a leader in so many civic endeavors, his obvious administrative capabilities, his popularity, and his oft-expressed love for Dallas.

Installing Jonsson as mayor rather than Welch would have to be carefully arranged. John Stemmons, Jonsson's successor as DCC president, and six Dallas city council members—all Citizens Charter Association members (the nonpartisan, probusiness political group that dominated at city hall and was unofficially linked with the DCC)—called on him at his home and asked his consent to accept a draft. The six council members, constituting a majority of the nine-member council, would have the authority to elect the new mayor rather than accept Welch's automatic succession in formal session. Mayor Cabell was not himself present at Jonsson's house, and excluded on purpose were the two independent council members, Elizabeth Blessing and Joe C. Moody.[51]

Years later, in a 1992 oral history, Jonsson spoke disingenuously about his decision to accept. "I don't think anybody was more surprised than I was when they came and asked me if I would take that job," he said. He had promised his wife, he told them, at least two trips around the world, and he could not break his promise. "So, you get somebody else." Their response was that this was an emergency. He would have to take the job. "You go ask Momma if she'll let me be the mayor," Jonsson recalled telling them. "And my God, they went."[52]

In words that sounded more like his than hers, Jonsson paraphrased his wife's comments afterwards:

> I've seen these crazy guys and they say they want you for mayor. They don't have anybody on the council that they'll stand hitch for, and it's not possible to have another election and not break this town into pieces. . . . You've lived here long enough, so that every nickel you've made . . . and you've made a few . . . has been because you've had lots of friends, and when you asked for help, you got it. When you asked for

cooperation of any kind, you got it. This is Dallas, Texas. This is a people town, you remember, and they're calling you a people person like they did at TI. So, I don't see how you could do anything else but take it.[53]

In 1976, Margaret Jonsson said that she knew that her husband would like the job and that it would mean something to him. "And I knew that Dallas needed a good leader. When they asked me, I said, 'You needn't talk to me; I've already been sold.'"[54]

In a 1971 television interview, Jonsson acknowledged that his selection made sense. Few if any mayors of Dallas had ever been in charge of a big business, but they should have been, he said. With the city's annual budget of $150 million or so, it seemed "rather ridiculous to put that much money for careful management into the hands of a layman who has never succeeded in running a shoe shine parlor, say, or some very modest business establishment." In his view, his own experience gave him "a certain know-how" that could be gained in no other way.[55]

Francis Raffetto, a city hall reporter for the *Dallas Morning News*, wrote a page-one story affirming unequivocally that Jonsson had consented to become mayor if Cabell resigned to run for Congress.[56] The afternoon paper, the *Dallas Times Herald*, included an interesting sentence that turned out to be untrue: "It was understood that Mr. Jonsson would serve only the remaining portion of Mayor Cabell's term and would not seek re-election in 1965."[57]

The two independent city council members who had not been invited to the meeting, Moody and Blessing, expressed their displeasure. Moody contended that selecting Jonsson would violate the city charter. "The charter reads that the whole Council will elect the person to fill the vacancy, then the nine members will choose the mayor from among themselves," he said. "Anyone with any brains at all can see that this is a CCA choice handed to CCA members, to like it or lump it. Why did the CCA council members all just happen to end up at Mr. Jonsson's house?" Mrs. Blessing agreed that the CCA was abusing the city charter. "We have resorted to government by the few, and they exercise tremendous power over us all. In this instance, this action subjects Dallas to valid criticism that we have government, not of laws, but of men," she said.[58] Aside from these public criticisms, the news prompted a torrent of supportive mail for Jonsson from friends.[59]

Municipal politics in Dallas, by long tradition, was nonpartisan. Jonsson earlier had agreed to appear with Republican congressman

nly son Erik Jonsson towers above his Swedish immigrant parents, Johan and Ellen Jonsson, as they pose in this
ark in Montclair, New Jersey, where they had moved from Brooklyn when Erik was twelve so he could experience
me fresh country air. Photo courtesy of Jonsson Papers, DeGolyer Library, SMU.

s a high school student in Montclair Jonsson played all sports, including track (indicated here by the spikes on
oes). Jonsson is third from left on the back row, the tallest boy on the team. Photo courtesy of Jonsson Papers,
eGolyer Library, SMU.

A favorite pastime as well as money-maker for Erik as a young man was to drive cars for owners who didn't know how. He also worked as a mechanic on cars. Here he poses happily in front of the strip of retail shops in Montclair that included his father's cigar shop. Photo courtesy of Jonsson Papers, DeGolyer Library, SMU.

Rejected as a journalism student at Columbia University, Jonsson turned to the engineering school, Rensselaer Polytechnic, where he majored in mechanical engineering despite his lack of sufficient academic preparation for the program. Photo courtesy of Jonsson Papers, DeGolyer Library, SMU.

At Alcoa in Tennessee, where Jonsson took his first full-time job, he met his future wife, Margaret Fonde. They took frequent rides into the nearby Great Smoky Mountains. She rejected Jonsson's marriage proposal on their first date, but she soon accepted him. Photo courtesy of Jonsson Papers, DeGolyer Library, SMU.

J. C. (Doc) Karcher hired Jonsson in Newark, New Jersey, to help make instruments needed for his reflection seismic instruments in finding underground oil deposits. Everette Lee DeGolyer was a silent partner in the company, Geophysical Service, Inc. Photo courtesy of Texas Instruments Records, DeGolyer Library, SMU.

Eugene McDermott was another principal in GSI when Jonsson began working for the company. McDermott, like Jonsson, was a native of Brooklyn. He would be a longtime partner with Jonsson and Cecil Green at Texas Instruments. Photo courtesy of Texas Instruments Records, DeGolyer Library, SMU.

Cecil H. Green, a native of England who came to the United States with his parents, joined GSI not long after Jonsson. The two became close friends as well as business associates. Green is seen here in the 1930s in his working clothes as he tours an oil field in Oklahoma. Photo courtesy of Texas Instruments Records, DeGolyer Library, SMU.

Green became one of the four GSI officials who purchased the company rather than see it merge into Stanolind in 1941. Photo courtesy of Texas Instruments Records, DeGolyer Library, SMU.

ese four GSI officials ponder the future of their company after they took it over in 1941. Left to right, Jonsson, cDermott, Green, and H. Bates Peacock. Peacock would relinquish his ownership when GSI began concentrat-g on electronics manufacturing. Photo courtesy of Jonsson Papers, DeGolyer Library, SMU.

When Jonsson began visiting Washington, D.C., during World War II to win government manufacturing contracts, he encountered the brilliant Patrick E. Haggerty, who became a close associate at GSI and then Texas Instruments as he led its ascent into electronics. Photo courtesy of Texas Instruments Records, De-Golyer Library, SMU.

Haggerty was Jonsson's protégé when he came to Dallas to join the GSI owners and took charge of its manufacturing division. The two hard-working men also became close friends. Photo courtesy of Jonsson Papers, DeGolyer Library, SMU.

The Lemmon Avenue plant won plaudits for its design and efficiency when it opened in 1947 as GSI's headquarters. The company had not yet taken on the name of Texas Instruments. Jonsson is standing with an employee as they hold elements for the Falcon missile nose cone. Photo courtesy of Texas Instruments Records, DeGolyer Library, SMU.

Gordon Teal, disappointed for being overlooked at Bell Laboratories for his essential role in developing the transistor, went to work for Texas Instruments and spearheaded its surprising leadership in manufacturing the superior silicon transistor. Photo courtesy of Texas Instruments Records, DeGolyer Library, SMU.

:k Kilby displays micro-
ips and the first hand-held
lculator, all products of
xas Instruments. The
nazing microchip trans-
rmed the industry and
ade Kilby a winner of the
obel Prize. Photo cour-
sy of Texas Instruments
cords, DeGolyer Library,
1U.

Pat Haggerty gave Mark
Shepherd, Jr. (left) later
Texas Instruments presi-
dent and chief execu-
tive officer, the difficult
assignment of making the
company's first transis-
tors or semi-conductors.
Photo courtesy of Texas
Instruments Records,
DeGolyer Library, SMU.

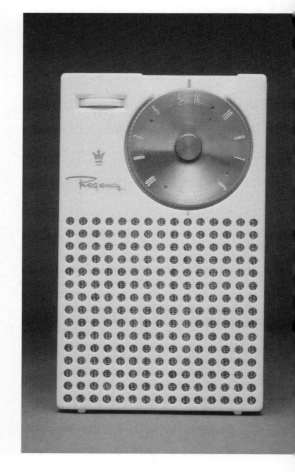

This tiny radio, small enough to fit into a
shirt pocket, was produced by Regency upon
assignment by Texas Instruments. It was revolutionary for its compactness and high quality
of sound, and became a national sensation.
Photo courtesy of Texas Instruments Records,
DeGolyer Library, SMU.

TEXAS INSTRUMENTS
INCORPORATED

new plant

PROFILE

pattern for a dynamic future

Dedicated: June 23, 1958

xas Instruments' new headquarters in North Dallas on N. Central Expressway was acclaimed for its function-
ty. When it opened in 1958 the signal that cut the ribbon came from the Vanguard satellite in space and was
wered by Texas Instruments transistors. Photo courtesy of Jonsson Papers, DeGolyer Library, SMU.

Jonsson once had declined a possibility to go to work at Western Electric because he saw employees producing telephone parts "no bigger than your little fingernail." Little did he know what the future had in store for him. Photo courtesy of Jonsson Papers, DeGolyer Library, SMU.

As Texas Instruments prospered Jonsson began to spend much of his time as a participant and the leader in various civic activities. Here, as president of the Dallas Chamber of Commerce, he posed with SMU football quarterback Don Meredith. Photo courtesy of Jonsson Papers, DeGolyer Library, SMU.

nsson paid special attention in his philanthropy to Rensselaer Polytechnic. Here, with RPI official Ed Fitzgerald the 1960s, he relives his youthful fascination with the motorcycle, about which he once said: "No use talking, a otorcycle is about half of my life." Photo courtesy of Jonsson Papers, DeGolyer Library, SMU.

As president of the Dallas Citizens Council, host of President Kennedy's visit to Dallas in 1963, it fell upon Jonsson to announce to the waiting crowd that the president had been shot en route to the Trade Mart. Courtesy of Sixth Floor Museum at Dealey Plaza.

MAYOR of DALLAS
2-1714

TEXAS INSTRUMENTS
INCORPORATED

Jonsson was recruited to become mayor of Dallas in 1964 following the assassination of President Kennedy. He would hold the office for seven years. Photo courtesy of Texas Instruments Records, DeGolyer Library, SMU.

One of Jonsson's greatest achievements as mayor was instituting the Goals for Dallas program. Here he whips into action four leaders for the initial Salado conference. Left to right: William H. Dickinson, Charles LeMaistre, Stanley Marcus, and Donald Cowan. Photo courtesy of Jonsson Papers, DeGolyer Library, SMU.

1965 Jonsson s elected for his st regular term as ayor. With him fellow council mbers, left to ht, J.W. (Sandy) nderson, Frank A. ke, W.H. (Bill) berts, William E. thrum, Jonsson, arles Cullum, yl Hamilton, R.B. rpenter Jr., and Joe Golman. Photo urtesy of Jonsson pers, DeGolyer rary, SMU.

Family members helped Jonsson celebrate at his 1965 election. At center is his wife Margaret, his daughter Margaret, and his son Kenneth. Photo courtesy of Jonsson Papers, DeGolyer Library, SMU.

At the Goals for Dallas planni[ng] session in Salado, Jonsson is seen leading a panel discussion. The lady looking up in h[is] direction is Lillian Bradshaw, director of the Dallas Public L[i]brary. Photo courtesy of Jonss[on] Papers, DeGolyer Library, SM[U]

mayor, Jonsson presided regularly over important events. Here he speaks at the opening of a Dallas Housing thority project on Tioga Street. Seated on the front row are Dr. Milton Curry (center) of Bishop College and allas City Councilman George Allen (right). Photo courtesy of Jonsson Papers, DeGolyer Library, SMU.

Many branch public libraries opened during Jonsson's seven years as mayor. Here he signs autographs for children at the Northlake Library opening. Photo courtesy of Texas Instruments Records, DeGolyer Library, SMU.

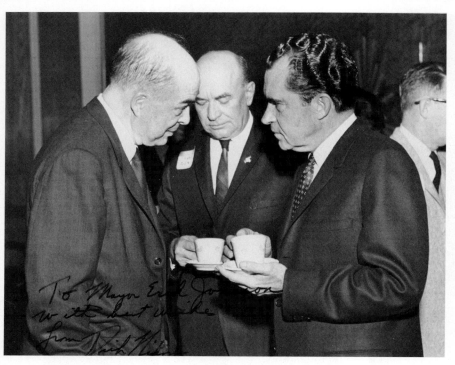

Jonsson led the drive to unite Dallas and Fort Worth in the mid-cities airport that became Greater Dallas/Fort Worth International Airport. Jonsson here is signing documents with a Delta official to move its flights from Love Field to D/FW upon its opening. Photo courtesy of Jonsson Papers, DeGolyer Library, SMU.

r twelve years Jonsson was chairman of D/FW Airport. He speaks here at the dedication of the airport. Behind
n is Gov. John Connally, and just behind Connally is his wife Nellie. Photo courtesy of Jonsson Papers, De-
olyer Library, SMU.

allas' new city hall, designed by I.M. Pei, was a special Jonsson achievement, for without his determined push it
rely would never have been built. Photo courtesy of Jonsson Papers, DeGolyer Library, SMU.

Texas Governor John Connally and Jonsson were associates in many ventures. Their friendship seems evident here. Photo courtesy of Jonsson Papers, DeGolyer Library, SMU.

A special admirer of Jonsson's achievements was Dallas entrepreneur Ross Perot, seen here with his wife Margot visiting at the Jonsson table with the former mayor and his daughter Margaret at an event honoring trustees of the Excellence in Education Foundation. Photo courtesy of Jonsson Papers, DeGolyer Library, SMU.

Jonsson's first-born son, Philip, left, stands alongside his parents. Photo courtesy of Jonsson Papers, DeGolyer Library, SMU.

The Texas Instruments trio of leaders with their wives in 1973 at a University of Texas at Dallas event. Left to right: Ida and Cecil Green, Margaret and Erik Jonsson, and Margaret and Eugene McDermott. Photo courtesy of Jonsson Papers, DeGolyer Library, SMU.

One of Jonsson's achievements was leading the drive to raise money for a new central Dallas Public Library. It was named for him in October 1986. Courtesy of Dallas Municipal Archives.

The Jonsson grandchildren at their grandparents' fiftieth wedding anniversary (all with Jonsson surnames unless otherwise noted). Back row: Steve, Mark, Anne, Kenny, Erik Charlton, and Michael. Immediately and just above Jonsson's left is Chris; to his right is Suzanne. The four in front are Laura Charlton, Petie, Erik, and Emily. Photo courtesy of Petie Jonsson Lewis.

Bruce Alger on a thirty-minute television program. Concerned about showing partisanship, Jonsson canceled his participation.[60]

⤳

On Monday, February 3, 1964, at the regular city council meeting, Cabell resigned. As the next order of business, council members unanimously appointed Jonsson to fill the vacant council seat. When Jonsson next was nominated to be mayor, Blessing offered a substitute motion. She nominated the mayor pro tem, Welch. Moody, the other independent council member, remained silent. Blessing's motion died. With hers as the only dissent, council members elected Jonsson as their new mayor.

He took the oath of office immediately and became, for the first time, a public officeholder. His wife and daughter watched from the audience. The outspoken Mrs. Blessing wryly observed, "This may be a benevolent oligarchy—but it isn't representative government." Jonsson's election, she said accurately, was a "power structure decision."[61]

Few in Dallas criticized his selection. One who did was Lawrence Kelly, executive director of the Dallas Civic Opera, of which Erik and Margaret Jonsson were significant supporters. He was quoted as saying Dallas probably was "the only city in the world" where such an election could have happened. "Any other place there'd be a thousand pickets down there protesting it. Somebody, for some reason, has to be against him. But—not a peep in Dallas."[62]

Both daily newspapers hailed his selection. "We think J. Erik Jonsson, a dynamic industrialist and ceaseless toiler for the betterment of Dallas, is a natural for the task," editorialized the *Dallas Times Herald*.[63] That newspaper's popular, gossipy columnist Dick Hitt added another note: "Something you can look forward to under Mayor Erik Jonsson: excellent speeches, ad lib or otherwise. His New Honor is a splendid phrasemaker."[64]

For the rest of the week, Jonsson, often accompanied by Cabell, visited city hall offices. He also responded by mail to scores of congratulatory letters. (His files contain not a single negative letter concerning his election.) Three days after being sworn in, in his first public appearance, Jonsson spoke at a Greater Dallas Council of Churches prayer breakfast. He had accepted the job at a time, he said, when he had "hoped to give up some work rather than take on more." But the honor was too rare to turn down, and as he emphasized, he believed he should pay his dues to the city that had been so good to him.[65]

The challenge was unusually large, he said. "Since Nov. 22 our city has, through no fault of its own, suffered many verbal attacks which I can only judge to be irresponsible, immature and unthinking. In time the attacks will abate and the scars will heal." Meanwhile, he said, all residents must "with proper dignity, renewed dedication and reasoned judgment in our actions and our words," continue the business of building a fine city with a bright and promising future. And redemption was possible: "In the long run, performance, not words, will be the yardstick by which it will be measured."[66]

Among the flood of congratulatory letters was one from Cecil and Ida Green. "You just naturally make us both feel all the more pleased that we elected long ago to become citizens of this great city, so good luck and fond regards." Another letter came from the venerable banker Robert L. Thornton, who thought Jonsson was "exactly what Dallas needs." Less than two weeks later Thornton, who for some four decades had been identified by his exuberant boosterism of Dallas, was dead at the age of eighty-three.[67] Jonsson's gin rummy friend, the stockbroker Orville Cartwright, told Jonsson that he had long been his personal choice for mayor: "It never occurred to me, however, that you would get it the easy way—without making a single speech."[68]

Generally there was a presumption—as the *Times Herald* news story indicated—that Erik Jonsson stepped in only to fill the remainder of Cabell's term. Jonsson himself evidently thought the same. As he told W. M. Holland, Dallas's first native-born mayor, who served from 1911 through 1915, "I trust that during this interim appointment I shall merit your confidence."[69]

In the Public Arena

Mayor J. Erik Jonsson did not maintain a city hall office. Nor was he expected to. The mayor was not the city's chief operating officer. That was the city manager, a professional administrator who held office at the pleasure of the city council. This council-manager system had been devised in the Progressive era as an antidote to "big-city bosses." It held that the mayor and council members were civic leaders who took off a few hours a week from their regular jobs to serve as a municipal board of directors.

American mayors who had achieved historic status (such as Fiorello La Guardia of New York, Tom L. Johnson of Cleveland, and David L. Lawrence of Pittsburgh) had not labored under such limitations. Jonsson would chafe under the council-manager plan, but he would overcome its limitations by the force of his personality.

His salary was $20 for each council meeting. His nominal duties were to preside over weekly council meetings, establish with council members policies that the city manager would implement, and be the city's chief spokesperson. He had appointive power, but he did not set the budget; he did not hire and fire; and his contacts with municipal departments, by ordinance, went through the city manager. The city manager headed all city departments except for the offices of the city attorney, city secretary, auditor, and public utilities supervisor, all of whom reported directly to the city council.

The mayor and council members were elected every two years by citywide vote. Those elected inevitably reflected a conservative, pro-business bias because, with occasional exceptions, they were businessmen endorsed and funded by the Citizens Charter Association (CCA), which, although not officially connected with the Dallas Citizens Council, was identified with it. Council candidates ran in nonpartisan races, never as Democrats or Republicans. For an independent candidate to overcome the power of the CCA was rare. No one from an ethnic minority group had ever served on the council; no woman served until 1957. With the exception of two Depression-era terms, CCA candidates had maintained a lock grip on the council since the organization's founding in 1930.

Despite limited powers, the mayor's job in 1964 required far more hours than originally intended. Strict compliance with the council-manager plan had eroded, and serving as mayor had become virtually a full-time position. The hours Jonsson spent in office dominated his schedule from his first day. Jonsson prepared himself for Monday-afternoon council sessions by studying in advance—frequently over the weekend—endless documents that were part of the lengthy Monday agendas. These included materials related to zoning issues, the awarding of contracts, the approval of expenditures, consideration of new municipal ordinances, and other matters requiring council approval. The official meetings, preceded by a noon luncheon at which city staff members provided a private briefing, lasted from one thirty in the afternoon until as late as six. But every day was busy.

The new mayor had to maintain good relations with council members. He had to be patient when ordinary citizens took the microphone to advocate a particular cause or to describe a grievance in detail. He had to read and respond to letters from people throughout the city, nation, and world, many of them with special requests—a key to the city, a cowboy hat, an autograph, a proclamation, or a meeting.

As mayor, Jonsson was a member of the Dallas Public Transit Board, which was charged with overseeing city bus operations. He met regularly with the city manager for briefings. He was expected to appear at countless luncheons and dinners, always prepared to make a few remarks. He welcomed to the city many visiting groups. There were daily, largely impromptu interviews—by telephone or in person—with reporters from the two competing daily newspapers, whose editors had insatiable appetites for city hall news. Speeches, welcomes, and ribbon cutting became routine—after less than a year in office, Jonsson's secretary counted eighty-three such occasions.[1] All these functions were added to Jonsson's TI obligations, board meetings of organizations such as the Graduate Research Center of the Southwest, and many others.

He did not follow Cabell's popular routine of seeing citizens without appointments on Wednesday afternoons and Thursday mornings. He had neither the time nor inclination for that.

During his first three years as mayor, Jonsson worked from his TI office. Assisting him was Nelle Johnston, a forceful, unmarried native of a small West Texas town who, with the help of two others, had been serving Haggerty, McDermott, and Jonsson. Now, with Jonsson's added mayoral obligations, she devoted her time exclusively to him. She soon gained a measure of local fame as a stern gatekeeper who permitted only those with acceptable explanations to reach her boss. She opened and read Jonsson's incoming mail, frequently jotting down suggested responses. Sometimes she answered his letters herself. In this new, semipublic role, although on the TI payroll, Nelle Johnston became recognized as a powerful figure in her own right. When Jonsson, still mayor, moved his office from TI to the downtown Republic National Bank Building in 1967, Nelle Johnston went with him.[2]

Jonsson's challenges were in some ways more complex than those he had faced in business. Yet Dallas's $162 million annual budget was considerably smaller than the one at TI. Similarly, TI's 24,000 employees (worldwide) dwarfed the number of City of Dallas workers. Other mayors might feel overwhelmed by responsibilities, but not Jonsson.

He was different from traditional Dallas mayors, who so often came from the ranks of bankers, department store owners, or utility company officials. He was not a downtown businessman. His frames of reference were broader. He headed a huge business with worldwide interests, headquartered in far North Dallas, not downtown. He viewed problems and challenges from a regional, national, or even international point of view.

Business domination of Dallas's affairs was severely questioned after the assassination. As the national and world press dissected the city and learned about the power of the DCC, learned of the proprietary instincts of the business establishment over city affairs, learned of the exclusion of labor and teachers and many professional people from meaningful municipal participation, and revisited the ugly evidences of the extreme right in Dallas, the city faced a public relations crisis of major proportions. *Fortune* magazine published a critical eleven-page article entitled "How Business Failed Dallas."[3] Stanley Marcus, touring Europe in 1964, wrote to Jonsson that mention of Dallas was "sufficient to create raised eyebrows, sardonic smiles, and an interminable number of questions."[4]

Dallas was experiencing a crisis both internal and external—how the outside world was viewing it and, almost as important, how Dallas residents viewed their own city. In Europe especially, and also throughout the United States, wild conspiracy theories sometimes alleged Dallas Police Department involvement in the assassination.

Jonsson had to deal with this massive, nearly unmanageable public relations challenge. Instead of TI shareholders, he had to please a diverse population whose minority members were becoming restless about long-denied rights, city council members who had their own agendas, and city hall professionals who considered themselves the real experts rather than the council members, who rotated every few years or less.

What concerned the new mayor immediately was the need to restore Dallas's reputation and erase that phrase "city of hate." The facts, he believed, did not warrant such a view.[5] In emphasizing the city's virtues, he chose to forget the ugly demonstrations that had made Dallas fearful of what might happen when the president came. In fact, extremism had become unacceptable in Dallas' muted post-assassination atmosphere. Extremists who had been so visible disappeared from view as the city struggled to regain respectability.

After a few days as mayor, Jonsson realized that a handful of officials in city hall were "really running the town." He started meeting them. Foremost was the city manager, Elgin E. Crull, a former newspaper reporter who had assumed that office in 1952. He was smart and forceful in a low-key way. Second was the city attorney, Henry P. Kucera, soon to begin his fortieth year in the office. The third was E. Lynn Crossley, the city auditor. Jonsson told himself that he had to work closely with these men if he wanted to achieve anything.[6]

This prospect was not promising. He was an outsider. These officials were not the civic leaders or businessmen he was accustomed to dealing with. Their longtime grip on municipal government contrasted with the tenures of council members, who inevitably served two terms in office and then left.

At his first meeting with Crull, Jonsson asked him frankly what his job as mayor would entail. "Oh, some fellows have a ball in it, you know, do anything," the city manager responded. Mayors, he continued, were independent of city hall management, which continued from one administration to the next. The mayor actually did not have much to do, but, Crull acknowledged, if Jonsson wanted to work, he could. It was his choice.

Jonsson wanted to work. Crull handed him two short documents—the city charter and one from the Texas Municipal League. Jonsson read them overnight and returned next day to Crull's office. He wanted more information: "Now, Elgin, why don't you just loosen up and tell me what the job is, as I asked you yesterday." Crull said he had told him the truth. He could do whatever he wanted as mayor. "I never took a job with the idea of doing anything but the best I could," Jonsson replied, "and that's what I'll do here." Crull's response was noncommittal—"That's fine." Jonsson was not pleased. The mayor, with his expansive personality, had not found a happy match in the laconic city manager.[7]

In presiding over his first council meeting, four and a half hours long, Jonsson won praise for his patience. It was tacit recognition that the TI chairman was unaccustomed to putting up with average citizens concerned about garbage collection.[8]

Less than two weeks after Jonsson took office, four firemen died in a disastrous fire that made a shambles of one of his favorite downtown restaurants, the Golden Pheasant. A saddened Jonsson watched their bodies being carried out.[9]

On the same Sunday, funeral services were held for "Mr. Dallas," Robert L. Thornton, four-time mayor of the city. Jonsson was one of several prominent citizens who paid tribute to the onetime cotton picker who made his fortune in Dallas and became its most recognized citizen.

⤙

It did not take long for Jonsson to feel constrained by the council-manager form of government. He was troubled by inefficiencies he found but could do nothing about, and also by the city manager's broader authority. After less than two months in office, he questioned whether the council-manager plan had the flexibility to cope with the problems of a growing city. Zoning cases required an inordinate amount of the council's time. By the time they reached the council for a de novo hearing, the same details had been heard once or twice by the city planning commission. Nothing could be done about this, he was told. Many other problems—transit, traffic, law enforcement—reached into different municipal jurisdictions. Closer liaison between municipal governments and the county government certainly would be needed, but accomplishing it was not on the horizon.[10] He and council members were so busy handling small details they had little time to initiate important matters that might have long-term benefits. "We must not become a group bogged down with weekly procedures," Jonsson admonished.[11]

He was heartened five months after the assassination by a sense of diminished animosity towards Dallas. Those who had been wearing the "hair shirt" could take it off, he said, adding, "I've never felt we were guilty of anything as a community. I see no reason why I should change my mind." One of his techniques for measuring national sentiment may have been through stories in the *New York Times*. In March 1964 he took out a subscription for daily and Sunday home delivery. He subscribed as well to *Business Week, Fortune,* and *U.S. News and World Report*.[12]

෴

As always, planning for the future was an absolute Jonsson priority. After two months as mayor, he conceived of a way to recruit important civic leaders as allies in city planning. He revealed his idea at a luncheon to sixteen guests, including the publishers of both daily newspapers, developers, industrialists, oilmen, the city manager, and the Dallas parks director. He asked them to accompany him on a tour of Stockholm and Copenhagen, both exemplars of enlightened city planning and beautification, to gain ideas for Dallas. It was understood that on their return they would join him in mobilizing sentiment to implement positive changes for downtown Dallas.[13]

A semiofficial sanction for the group would add to its authority. This came from Jonsson's friend Robert B. Cullum, president of the Dallas Chamber of Commerce, who anointed all those who went—as it turned out, mostly prominent married couples but no public officials—as the chamber's Special Study Committee on City Planning. A local architect, Enslie (Bud) Oglesby, who had done graduate studies in Sweden, went as tour guide.[14]

When the delegation of about twenty landed at London's Heathrow Airport on a stopover, a contingent of thirty or so newsmen awaited. Jonsson, "quite unhappy" to see them, calmly answered their questions about the assassination and Dallas.[15]

In Copenhagen, the group was greeted at the airport by Lord Mayor Urban Hansen, who a few weeks earlier had visited Dallas. Once again, journalists were there with questions. Hansen took the Dallas visitors on a tour of Copenhagen, including beautiful Tivoli Gardens, the town hall, large apartment buildings, and the Nyhavn Canal, with its open markets. A pedestrian shopping street off-limits to automobiles particularly intrigued them.[16]

Of greater interest was Stockholm, the city of Jonsson's mother's childhood. Stockholm, about the same size as Dallas, also had shown tremendous recent growth. As in Copenhagen, the lord mayor and a large press contingent greeted the visitors. In addition to touring the city and seeing the downtown parks, subway stations, and underground and overground pedestrian walkways, the group heard briefings from city officials. They toured Stockholm's harbor, and Jonsson, accustomed to such, took the boat's wheel, with the pilot acting as his guide.[17]

Afterward, the Jonssons went to Nice, France, for a TI board meeting, the first one held outside the United States. They then returned to London for another TI meeting and an advance look at British Aircraft's One-Eleven jet airliners. Braniff had already placed an order for fourteen of the aircraft.

On this second London arrival, the lord mayor greeted the Jonssons in the full regalia of his office. Because of Dallas's "special circumstances," he made an exception to his normal rule of greeting only the mayors of capital cities in such attire. Jonsson had been advised by the lord mayor's office that if he had a "chain of office or other insignia" related to his own title, he might wear it. He did not have one. He dressed in a business suit and tie.[18]

Targeted again by ubiquitous Fleet Street journalists, Jonsson held a news conference at which he sought to correct the "injustice" of Dallas's image.[19] Their stories reflected surprise at the poise of this supposedly lawless city's mayor. The *Guardian* described him as "a quietly-spoken, conservative business man" who was an excellent choice for "regilding" the city's image.[20] The *Daily Herald*'s headline directly summarized the interview: "So We Are All Wrong about Big D." Instead of being a "city of boom and braggarts, millionaires and murders," it was, according to its mayor, a city of churchgoing, friendly, hardworking folk. When a reporter asked about "Big G," Jonsson was puzzled. He had never heard Dallas referred to as Big G. It stood for guns, gravy, gambling, and gasoline, the reporter said. Jonsson flared. "How far from the facts can you get! There has never been organized gambling or organized vice in Dallas." It was disturbing, he said, to have Dallas pictured as a place where everyone carries a revolver. "Do you carry a revolver?" a reporter asked.

"I have never carried one and I have never seen a policeman with a revolver drawn," Jonsson responded. He added that he did not even own a gun. (In this context, the *Daily Herald* reporter noted Dallas's "frightening murder rate," citing its 104 murders in 1963 compared with 143 murders in all of Britain.)[21]

Wire-service reporters sent many of Jonsson's comments as well as the delegation's earlier activities to Dallas for publication. Still, on Jonsson's return on May 29, a friendly local press was eager to hear more. Jonsson talked mostly about the urban developments that had been the purpose of the visit. He expressed admiration for the greenbelts woven into downtown and suburban developments. "Almost never did we go very far without seeing some kind of little park," he said.[22]

Although press reports failed to mention it, the mayor and others had been impressed with Stockholm's underground and aboveground pedestrian tunnels. Similarly impressed was another tour member, the developer W. T. Overton, who was planning a major downtown Dallas complex to be known as One Main Place. When Overton completed it in 1968, the impact of the Stockholm visit was evident. Overton's complex had a sunken plaza and underground pedestrian ways that provided the first major element for an extensive underground pedestrian tunnel system in downtown Dallas. Later, a system of skywalks connected many downtown Dallas buildings.[23]

In a talk at the City Club, Jonsson said he had seen "nothing in the cities of Europe that Dallas cannot equal and even surpass." Europe's mistaken ideas about Dallas could be changed "only through understanding and hard work—especially in the fields of beauty and culture."[24]

⤚

Dallas desperately needed a new city hall. The existing one, an ungainly add-on to the classic 1914 building taken over by the police department, was badly outgrown. Jonsson described it as a "henhouse added to a doghouse."[25]

A cramped office designated for his use, but never used, reminded him of the need for more space. He was in his office only briefly, before and after council meetings, with the press inevitably crowding in with cameras, lights, and recording devices. Reporters with their notebooks would be there, too. The space was too tight to move about in freely.[26]

Jonsson told city manager Crull that the city hall was "totally inadequate" for future needs. He wanted a new building. Crull saw no such need. "It's not too bad here," he said. "I never have been one to want an awful lot of space."[27]

A few days afterward, Jonsson saw Crull surrounded by a handful of council members. "Elgin was just telling us that we're gonna have to have a new city hall," one of them informed him. Jonsson was taken aback. He quietly stepped over to Crull and said, "You SOB. Did you tell them that you took my idea and worked on it and then you offered it as your idea?" No, Crull said, he now favored the concept. "In my mind," Jonsson said later in an oral history interview, "that was the end of my relationship with him."[28]

Crull proposed expanding city hall so that it eventually would take up an entire block with the exception of the Western Union Building on the east end. Jonsson suggested another approach—asking the DCC to conduct a study on whether the building should remain at its present location or be placed at a new site.[29] Evidently realizing the impropriety of placing such an important decision in the hands of a private organization, Jonsson instead appointed an ad hoc committee of citizens, approved by the council, to undertake that task.

Nevertheless, Jonsson packed his committee with colleagues: TI's Carl J. Thomsen; Sol Goodell, his personal attorney, who also had represented TI; James W. Aston of Republic National Bank; and other civic and business leaders including Mrs. Earl Cullum, whose husband was a Jonsson friend, prominent engineer and businessman, and civic leader. The mayor held an organizational meeting at Republic National Bank, advising members to envision a city hall beautiful enough to be displayed with pride and decrying the present building as essentially a "chicken coop." Crull, who was present, reminded committee members of their limited mandate. They were simply to recommend *where* the building should be located. Subcommittees were formed to examine possible locations, including expansion at the present site. Afterward, Jonsson stressed that he believed the question was far broader. He still wanted the committee to envision what Dallas would be like fifty years later.[30]

In December 1964, the subcommittees reported. The West End committee proposed a three-block site adjacent to the courthouse area, with the intent of fostering future cooperation between the city and the county. The East End committee recommended a three-block tract adjacent to the present city hall. The midtown committee suggested a twelve-block site between Harwood and Akard.[31] An overall selection subcommittee headed by Thomsen unanimously recommended the midtown site as the best choice. Jonsson agreed, and the city council officially agreed.[32]

Ironically, nearly twenty years earlier the same site had been earmarked for a civic center. Some land was even purchased toward that goal, but voters rejected the plan in a special bond election, and the property was sold back to private owners. Much of that property now would have to be bought back at several times its previous price.[33]

Little could Jonsson know it, but his mission to build a new city hall would preoccupy him for the next ten years, extending beyond his seven years as mayor and bringing great heartache before a triumphant success was achieved.

⌇

If a new city hall ultimately would be cited as one of Jonsson's greatest triumphs, so would the creation of what would be at the time the world's biggest airport, Dallas/Fort Worth International. Dallas had carefully nurtured Love Field since its 1918 origin as a military training center for army aviators. Through aviation, Dallas was able to escape limitations imposed by its inland location. M. J. Norrell, Dallas Chamber of Commerce manager, summarized the goal in 1931: "As an inland city, let the air be our ocean."[34]

Fort Worth, thirty miles away, competed fiercely for aviation supremacy. It had the advantage of being the site for the regional headquarters of both the Federal Aviation Administration and the Civil Aeronautics Board. While Dallas's airport dated from 1918, Fort Worth at the time already had three such facilities. (At one of those fields, an aviation cadet's worried mother sent him a letter: "Be careful, son. Do not be reckless. Fly very low and very slow.")[35]

Dallas, with its larger population and aggressive civic leadership, had grabbed the lead from Fort Worth. By 1950, it had almost twice as many passengers as larger Houston and eight times as many as Fort Worth.[36]

Airline stops at both Dallas and Fort Worth, convenient in earlier years, when much smaller airplanes were in operation, now were a nuisance. There had been talk for years of creating a single regional airport, midway between the two cities, but a preliminary agreement in 1941 ended in acrimony when Dallas concluded that the federally approved layout favored Fort Worth. After the war, Fort Worth plunged ahead and built its own modern airport on the midcities site, with much space for expansion. A number of airlines transferred flights to the new

Midway Airport (later Greater Southwest International Airport), and in 1948 the Civil Aeronautics Authority (sister agency to the Civil Aeronautics Board) recommended that it should be the primary airport for both cities.

Dallas, enraged, fought back. The CAA retreated and agreed to treat both airports equally. Dallas went ahead with expensive improvements to Love Field, including a new runway. The battle between the two cities raged over the next years through the courts and federal aviation authorities.

In 1962 the struggle intensified when Najeeb Halaby, the FAA's administrator, declared that Dallas exhibited "childish civic pride" in opposing a joint airport. The FAA, he warned, did not intend to spend another penny at Love Field because the federal government could not continue giving money for runways, taxiways, control towers, and navigational aids to two airports so close to each other.[37] In April 1964, two months after Jonsson became mayor, the CAB examiner Ross I. Newmann warned that Love Field's time was "running out."[38]

These comments were not lost on Jonsson, who virtually alone among top Dallas civic leaders seemed flexible. He believed that a "deliberate examination" was indicated. J. Lee Johnson III, president of Fort Worth's Chamber of Commerce and son-in-law of the late Amon Carter, warned that failure to act might permit Houston to take over as the state's aviation center.[39] Nevertheless, work continued at Love Field on a new runway, expected to cost more than $4 million. The need to buy surrounding property and tear down buildings made the project especially costly.[40]

In hearings before the CAB in Washington, Fort Worth claimed that the approaching jet age had doomed Love Field, that the congestion around the airport increased the possibility of a catastrophe, that surrounding residents were being subjected to one of the worst noise problems in the nation, and that failure to designate Fort Worth's Greater Southwest International as the regional airport would ultimately waste millions of tax dollars.[41]

On September 31, 1964, the CAB announced that Dallas and Fort Worth had to be served by a single regional airport. If the two cities could not select a site within 180 days, the CAB would "proceed promptly" to designate one for them.[42]

Love Field ranked eighth in the nation in enplaned passengers in 1963; its 2.1 million annual passengers dwarfed Greater Southwest's

46,000. A new terminal had opened in 1958 at a cost of $8.2 million; a new runway was under construction. "If there must be one airport, this well-established, well-equipped plant should be the one," said Robert B. Cullum. He saw nothing that would disqualify Love Field through the years. Cabell, campaigning for Congress, vowed to continue to fight for Love Field in the nation's capital.[43]

Jonsson expressed a bold conclusion that from a less respected Dallasite would have been heresy. In his opinion, a joint airport at a "mutually convenient location" probably should serve the two cities. Love Field "was already obsolete," doomed by its small size and lack of land for expansion. Having two competing airports was "a ridiculous thing." Now was the time, he thought, to build an airport of the future.[44]

Probably no one but Jonsson could have favored a joint airport without suffering severe criticism. And while no one publicly challenged him, neither were they ready to echo his sentiments. In emergency session, the Dallas Chamber of Commerce aviation committee emphasized its commitment to Love Field. Avery Mays, its chairman, said evidence overwhelmingly supported Love Field as a safe and convenient airport.[45]

Two days after the CAB ultimatum, Fort Worth officials, encouraged by Jonsson's comments, asked him to meet with them for "a final solution" to the matter. Jonsson agreed. On October 20, 1964, Jonsson, joined by Cullum and mayor pro tem Welch (appointed by the city council at his request), met with Fort Worth mayor Bayard Friedman, J. Lee Johnson III, and the banker H. B. Fuqua in Arlington.[46]

Their closed-door three-and-a-half-hour meeting went well. A second meeting by the same men the following week lasted four and a half hours. Jonsson reported that the Fort Worth men were "flexible and reasonable." For the first time, he said, Fort Worth and Dallas people were "listening to what the other fellows say and are believing what they hear."[47]

Previously strident comments about protecting Love Field at all costs were heard no more. There would be no court battle. Dallas and Fort Worth had decided to pick an airport site themselves rather than allow the CAB to do it for them.

Regular meetings, closed to the press, continued into December. Reports centered on progress and goodwill rather than details. Years later, the Fort Worth representatives Friedman and Johnson doubted that negotiations would have succeeded without the witty Cullum.

When tensions arose, Cullum would say to Fort Worth's Johnson, "Let's go out to the john. I've got something private to talk about." Inevitably, they would return in good spirits, and the talks would proceed productively.[48]

On the last day of December 1964, an announcement was made that addressed the question of administration. The negotiators recommended establishing a joint Dallas County–Tarrant County airport authority.[49] Civic leaders in both Dallas and Fort Worth heartily endorsed the proposal. Unofficial word from the CAB indicated that agency's approval, too. The deadline for selecting a site, March 17, 1965, was still two and a half months away.[50] While such a step pended future voter approval, Jonsson had other matters of concern.

⌒

A central difference Jonsson saw between Texas Instruments and the City of Dallas was TI's emphasis on long-range planning and the city's lack of it. At TI, long-range planning was carefully done, reviewed regularly, and adjusted as conditions changed. Little or none of this, Jonsson felt, took place at city hall. Pressing matters of the day seemed to prevent it. He realized that as mayor he was not applying basic business and management principles learned over a lifetime. "Don't you remember how to set goals, plan for their achievement, estimate costs, measure resources, set priorities and all the rest?" he asked himself.[51] Why not develop a set of goals?

Such a project would not only hold inherent advantages, but also demonstrate that Dallas was anything but a "city of hate." The work, Jonsson thought, should concentrate on "thinking up what kind of city we wanted to be."[52] He remembered President Eisenhower's similar project in appointing the Commission on National Goals, whose results were published as *Goals for America*. Jonsson had attended one of the seminars. Clifford Nelson, the president of American Assembly, the organization that had coordinated the program, encouraged Jonsson to move ahead.

He publicly revealed his idea in November 1964 at a luncheon speech to the downtown Rotary Club. Members of the city council, tipped off, also were present. What he wanted, Jonsson said, was to make Dallas the best city in nation. "I am totally unimpressed by the phenomenon of great size," he said. "But quality is something else again." He intended to recruit sixty to seventy-six of the "most knowledgeable, most experienced and most educated specialists" and hold a goal-setting conference. After goals were set, decisions would be made about priorities and affordability. Progress would be measured regularly in the months and years ahead.[53]

His proposal brought a standing ovation and front-page coverage in both newspapers. The *Dallas Morning News* called it a "magnificent vision." An editorial-page cartoon portrayed Jonsson holding a huge book, "The Goal Is Excellence," with his name as the author.[54]

With important support ensured, the mayor soon added further details. Those who set these goals, he said, would be volunteers. He would hire a director to oversee the program and "muster the intellectual resources of the city" for a series of essays that would address major concerns and represent a starting point.[55]

Next, a planning group, consisting of "the most knowledgeable, most experienced and most educated specialists," would gather at a "pleasant and remote spot" and work out initial goals. A mechanism would be established to review these goals and determine at intervals what progress was being made.[56]

The "Goals for Dallas" program intrigued the city from the beginning. The man who inspired it was widely acknowledged to be a visionary. One had only to look at TI to see that. It would not be an official City of Dallas project funded by tax dollars. How could Dallas not be better for it? Jonsson explained the excitement this way: "They needed something to do, to talk about, and to work with that was as far apart from the assassination and its grieving as possibly it could be made. . . . We were fortunate to hit on this, and we took full advantage of it."[57]

The seeds had been planted for a memorable project. Execution would follow some months later.

~

In November 1964, Earle Cabell easily defeated the Republican Bruce Alger and went to Washington to represent Dallas residents with a new voice. Dallas, the "city of hate," had sent a Democrat to Congress. Jonsson had a political decision of his own to make. Cabell's unfinished term, which he had taken over, was ending. In his few months as mayor, Jonsson had involved himself in important projects. Plans for a new city hall were under way. The possibility of a new airport held immense appeal for him. Opportunity awaited with his goals program. Should he leave office with so many projects unfinished?

As the Citizens Charter Association began considering a slate of candidates for the spring 1965 election, Jonsson remained coy. He spec-

IN THE PUBLIC ARENA

ulated that his role as chairman of the Graduate Research Center of the Southwest might be more important than being mayor. He would continue working on Goals for Dallas whether or not he was mayor.[58] Privately, though, he indicated that he would accept nomination for reelection.[59]

Meanwhile, he discovered that as mayor he was not immune to the zany tricks common to early TI days. One of his longtime friends there was Fred Agnich. When a citizen mistook Agnich for Jonsson, he asked him to take care of a traffic ticket. Agnich grabbed it, ripped it into shreds, and shook hands with the relieved citizen. Jonsson, told of the incident, grumbled good-naturedly, "That stunt alone cost me a hundred votes."[60]

Yes, he would run for a full term as mayor.

Master of City Hall,
Maker of the Airport

"I have never entered any competition to lose," Jonsson said, announcing his intention to campaign for a full term. He wanted a council composed entirely of CCA candidates. (Two of the nine council members were independents.) "Dissent and criticism are all right—if they are of the right kind," he stressed.[1]

The only organization challenging the CCA was the Dallas Charter League (DCL), which never posed a serious threat. Nevertheless, the CCA's president, Tom Unis, castigated this challenger: "We will fight any attempt to carry us backwards 35 years to the corruption of ward bosses and their bag men by a return to the ward system for the election of the City Council."[2]

The only two independent council members during Jonsson's tenure were Elizabeth Blessing and Joe Moody. Moody had turned unusually quiet. Blessing had single-handedly fought Jonsson, being especially critical of the "father knows best" attitude he seemed to reflect.

Blessing twice had defeated better-funded CCA candidates, and she had pondered running for Congress as a Democrat before declaring that she would campaign for mayor. No woman in Dallas had ever served as mayor or had even sought the job. Only a few had served on the city council.

Jonsson, she charged, had "fumbled through a year of inactivity and extremely low accomplishments." She opposed the status quo, closed meetings, and closed minds. If elected, she said, there would be changes in the administration—beginning with city manager Crull, whom she would try to replace.[3]

Forty-five years old, a mother of four, and the wife of a builder, Blessing enjoyed strong grassroots support. A favorite of newsmen, she was always good for a lively comment concerning matters about which others, including the mayor, preferred to keep quiet. Openness in government became her central campaign issue. She wanted to open all meetings to the public, including the private briefings held for the council before each session. She criticized, too, the secret airport meetings between Dallas and Fort Worth officials.

The best way to safeguard sensitive interests of Dallas, Jonsson countered, was to discuss them in private. "Boards of directors of businesses do not hold their meetings at Main and Akard," he argued.[4]

During the campaign, an invitation from the White House arrived for Jonsson, solidifying his credentials. He attended an all-day meeting with President Lyndon B. Johnson, his cabinet, and the National Industrial Conference Board to discuss national interests and the free-enterprise system throughout the world.[5]

In his campaign, Jonsson stressed his differences with Blessing. He was a successful businessman and industrialist; she was not. He had experience in commercial aviation and as an engineer; she did not. He made the contrast between them explicit: "I would ask my opponent if she has ever been in a radar tower and seen how it works." He was very familiar, he said, with that technology because Texas Instruments manufactured the radar that most airports were using. Where Blessing belonged, he said, was "back working on her kitchen stove."[6]

Assisted by a CCA-hired public relations firm, he spoke to civic groups, gave a speech on television, and broadcast political messages on radio. He stressed clean municipal government that kept taxes low and operated on sound business principles. He campaigned at African American churches, developing a good relationship with the ministers Caesar Clark and S. M. Wright as well as with the longtime civil rights advocates A. Maceo Smith and W. J. Durham, all of whom were capable of delivering large blocs of votes. He gained the endorsement of a Pleasant Grove hardware store owner named Max Goldblatt, who within a few years would become a popular grassroots councilman.[7]

His frequent theme was disparagement of the Dallas Charter League, which had endorsed Blessing and other independents. The league advocated something that two decades later would be mandated by a federal judge—election of council members by geographic districts. "We kicked the ward system out of Dallas politics more than thirty years ago and with good reason," Jonsson said. "Why should we now scrap our highly efficient council-manager system with its well balanced budget and tax picture and return to the expensive ward-heeling spoils system which is inevitable with ward elections?"[8]

In his speeches, though, he avoided bombast. He spoke softly, slowly, and understatedly. Only rarely did he refer to Blessing, mentioning instead his dislike of the hard knocks of politics.

Campaign money went directly to the CCA to promote its slate rather than to its individual candidates. Jonsson's fellow executives at TI were the largest contributors. Eugene McDermott gave $12,900; Cecil Green, $12,500; and Pat Haggerty, $6,000. Margaret Jonsson gave $6,700. TI executives also beat the drums for sizeable donations among their businessman friends.[9]

As the April 6 election approached, discourse got hotter. "I never knew that politics could be quite this way," Jonsson said, disingenuously. "I have been living a nice quiet life, well insulated from mud, rocks, and the like. But now it seems the insulation has worn a little thin."[10]

Several exchanges had prompted his comment. Blessing complained that Jonsson's Braniff ties tainted his airport negotiations. Tom Unis, the CCA president, charged that Blessing and her husband had been sued on seventeen occasions for failure to pay debts, and he displayed documents to prove it.[11]

Blessing countered with her own bombshell. She said she had been offered a bribe by a business leader not to run for mayor or even for reelection as a council member. The financial offer, she said, would have provided backing for her to go into real estate and get out of politics. "It is terrible when one can't raise his voice against the oligarchy in this city without having your feet cut out from under you," she said.[12] On the morning of the election, she placed a full-page advertisement in the newspaper decrying the CCA's tactics. Her ire was directed not at Jonsson, but at Unis, the "hatchet man" of the CCA.[13]

Blessing's spirited, headline-making campaign persuaded few voters. Jonsson, endorsed by both daily newspapers, claimed a landslide victory on April 6. He won by almost a 3–1 margin, 59,438 to 21,353, taking 142 of the city's 148 precincts and beating Blessing in her own precinct by a 6–1 margin.[14] He led the entire CCA ticket, winning nearly 8,000 more votes than the next most favored candidate, Charles G. Cullum. The CCA had spent $107,469 for its nine candidates, including Jonsson. Blessing spent $16,169. Except for the seat held by the independent

Moody (who claimed victory in a runoff two weeks later), Jonsson's fellow CCA candidates swept the field.[15]

That evening at CCA headquarters, celebrants loudly cheered their mayor, placed a paper crown on his bald head, and anointed him "King Erik." A front-page newspaper photograph showed the mayor; his wife, Margaret; his daughter, Margaret Ellen; and his son Ken from California around an ornate victory cake with an image of city hall on top.[16]

Jonsson vowed that from then on he would operate in sterner fashion. The last council had been "pretty free and easy," tending to talk too much and not pay enough attention to business. He wanted this council to keep "its nose to the grindstone."[17]

As it happened, the admittedly autocratic mayor would have far more time than this one full term to complete his major tasks and to launch others. He would fulfill this term and two more. Reelection would pose no problem. He had no opponent in 1967, and only a token one in 1969. By the time he completed his last term, in 1971, he had served as mayor for more than seven years, only one year less than Woodall Rodgers or Robert L. Thornton. While he was mayor, there would be talk of his running for governor of Texas and of receiving federal appointments, even becoming head of the National Aeronautics and Space Administration. These opportunities he would decline. He was too busy in Dallas.

～

The most daunting project—the one that would mean the most to the city, to North Texas, and to the aviation industry—was the midcities airport. The CAB's March 1965 deadline for selecting a site loomed. During his campaign, Jonsson had treated the subject gently, declaring that "the only reason" he was negotiating with Fort Worth was to protect Dallas's $53 million investment in Love Field and its bonded indebtedness of more than $29 million.[18]

Yet considerable progress had been made in the secret meetings. By early March 1965, negotiators had agreed that membership on the airport governing board would be based on population (thus giving Dallas larger representation); that the airport probably should be north of Greater Southwest International; that no less than 5,000, but probably not more than 10,000, acres would be required (greatly underestimating the more than 18,000 acres finally acquired); and that legislative approval needed to be gained to create the airport authority. There was one disagreement: Fort Worth would not accept Dallas's preference to let ten years lapse before ending flights at Love Field. Fort Worth insisted on seven years. This addressed the real issue—how soon could the airport be built?[19]

For a while, Jonsson, Cullum, and Welch privately agreed to consider Greater Southwest as a nucleus for the new airport, but when Fort Worth rejected the quid pro quo—that Love Field could continue operating for another ten years—that possibility ended. The two cities briefly resumed feuding.[20]

The CAB, presented with this impasse, issued a statement that emphasized progress and remanded the case to its examiner Ross I. Newmann, giving him "full authority."[21] Newmann led the parties to a decision to end Love Field flights in six to eight years, meaning that the new airport had to be completed between 1971 and 1973.[22]

Jonsson, Johnson, and Newmann, as a committee of three, hired as airport-planning consultants the New York City firm of Tippetts-Abbett-McCarthy-Stratton (TAMS). Walther Prokosch, a partner in the firm and the author of *Airport Planning*, became general consultant. Prokosch, other TAMS officials, and airport board members explored possible sites and chose an area immediately north of Greater Southwest, straddling the two counties' north-south boundary. It was an area of rolling farmland, largely free of valleys, creeks, floodplains, utility lines, industry, or residential developments.[23]

Almost overshadowed in this news was the creation of a temporary airport board, three persons from each city. Jonsson appointed himself, council member Frank A. Hoke, and the new Chamber of Commerce president, Hobart D. Turman, to represent Dallas. Cullum, whose contributions had been invaluable, was ineligible because he lived in Highland Park rather than Dallas. Jonsson predicted a new era of cooperation between the two cities.[24]

With the site identified, an outbreak of land speculation ensued. A farmer whose land had been appraised six months earlier at $750 an acre now was told that it was worth about $10,000 an acre. Jonsson warned speculators that they might be "badly burned" because the site was outlined only in a general way. "If the price of land gets completely out of hand," he said, "we could put the airport somewhere else."[25]

The amount of land to be acquired remained undetermined. Earlier estimates of 5,000 to 10,000 acres, considerably larger than Love Field or Greater Southwest, grew to 11,000 acres, and Jonsson began arguing for 25,000 acres. "They thought I was crazy," he said. "What they didn't know was that the jet would make the airplane business a whole new ballgame. I did know."[26]

Finally, the interim board approved the acquisition of as many as 18,220 acres, an immense size that astounded many. The property touched both counties and four municipalities. It encompassed Fort Worth's Greater Southwest, which would simply disappear, its runways becoming part of a highway.[27]

A revolution in travel was occurring. People of average means were flying. In 1960 the average number of passengers per plane in Dallas and Fort Worth was 21.2; in 1966 that figure doubled to 42.4. Even that number soon would be easily surpassed.[28] Jet airplanes were taking over for even short- and medium-range flights. Jumbo jets were expected to carry as many as 490 passengers and be roughly the length of a football field. Anticipated was something even more amazing—a hypersonic transport that would carry as many as 1,000 passengers, travel 6,000 miles an hour, climb to an altitude of about 100,000 feet (the edge of space), and go from New York to London in thirty-five minutes.[29]

The airport was designed to accommodate such developments. There would be four principal north-south runways and two north-west-southeast runways. The longer runways would have three miles of empty space before the property ended. The terminal was to be a single elongated building—about two miles long—in the center of the property.[30]

The airport would be "regional," representing all towns of both counties. Statewide voters routinely approved on November 8, 1966, a constitutional amendment authorizing the creation of an airport authority representing both counties. Dallas County and Tarrant County voters now would be asked for their approval.

Leaders throughout the area enthusiastically endorsed the authority. No significant opposition arose. Jonsson seemed confident. He gave radio and television interviews, recorded a telephone message for distribution, and then left town on election day, June 6, 1967, for Washington, D.C., before the outcome was known.[31]

The result was shocking. Dallas County voters rejected the authority, 26,385 to 24,125. Even City of Dallas voters opposed it, 17,104 to 16,014. Tarrant County voters overwhelmingly endorsed it, 25,160 to 8,747. Approval from both counties was required. The proposal was defeated.[32]

"Defeat Stuns Civic Chiefs" read a headline in the *Dallas Times Herald*. What had happened? Most Dallas voters simply had not seen how an airport so far from town could advance their own interests. Political parties, organizations, and personalities who were experienced at getting out the vote had not been involved. Labor leaders, denied assurance that an individual acceptable to them would have a place on the airport board, claimed credit for defeating the measure by sitting on their hands.[33]

One Dallas resident had another explanation: "People are growing tired of a 'managed town' where only a few make the decisions, often times behind closed doors. In our city elections we have only one slate of candidates to vote for, the slate, being selected by the 'Establishment.' Many people to whom we have talked would like to know to what extent conflict of interests enters into the building of the airport. In other words, how many of it's [*sic*] sponsors own airline stocks and to what extent."[34] The comments seemed directed at Jonsson.

Jonsson conferred with city attorney Alex Bickley, who discovered an escape clause. A 1947 state law authorized any two cities, presumably nearby ones, to build and operate an airport together. No further permission was required; the two city councils, which had already been acting independently of their county governments, could proceed.[35]

Jonsson assured the interim airport board that Dallas was ready to move ahead on a two-city venture. He suggested that Dallas and Fort Worth share costs on the basis of their relative populations and that the same proportions be used for board membership. Board members from Fort Worth agreed.[36] Dallas, with seven-elevenths of the combined population, would provide seven-elevenths of the financing and hold seven of eleven board seats. Each city council would appoint board members to four-year terms at staggered intervals. The cities would exercise the same taxing, land condemnation, and bond-issuing powers they already possessed.[37]

Dallas council members readily approved these specifics. So did the council in Fort Worth, although the city's new mayor, DeWitt McKinley, balked, saying that it "completely and forever" condemned Fort Worth to an inferior position.[38] Many years later, when he was ninety-two, Jonsson discussed the plan candidly. "I wanted absolute control of that board," he said. The Dallas majority of 7–4 on the board seemed to ensure that.[39]

He personally selected Dallas's board members, appointing himself and others with whom he knew he could work: C.J. Thomsen, his trusted TI colleague; former Dallas mayor pro tem Elgin B. Robertson; city council members George M. Underwood Jr. and Frank A. Hoke; the engineering consultant Earl Cullum; and his personal friend Morris Spencer. Fort Worth's board members were J. Lee Johnson III, Bayard Friedman, R. M. Stovall, and J. C. Pace Jr. Jonsson was the board's unanimous choice as chairman. Fort Worth's J. Lee Johnson III—said by Jonsson to be "deprived" because he had only one *s* in his name— became vice chairman.

The next step was to begin acquiring the property. By the time that task was completed, the total cost had reached $62 million, about three times the amount predicted. About $40 million of the total was Dallas's responsibility.[40]

An important decision was who to hire as executive director. Jonsson wanted the best man "from anywhere in the world" to build the world's finest airport. Thomas M. Sullivan, the man hired, was widely known. In Arthur Hailey's novel *Airport*, a reporter asked a prominent authority to identify "the most imaginative" airport executives, ones who could foresee the future. One of the four mentioned was Sullivan. A native Oklahoman, he had been chief of aviation planning for the Port Authority of New York, where he oversaw the building of Idlewild Airport (later John F. Kennedy International Airport). After Idlewild opened, Sullivan had been greeted with catcalls when he immediately urged the building of another New York airport. His advice was not taken. The result was airport congestion that caused passengers at New York City airports to sit at the end of the runways for one to two hours before takeoff.[41]

When Sullivan came to Dallas to negotiate his contract, he balked because some fringe benefits he had requested were omitted. Jonsson negotiated personally with him. "Go ahead and sign, Tom," he told him. "If they [the board] don't treat you right, I'll put you on my payroll." With this guarantee, Sullivan signed a five-year contract for $45,000 annually. Over the next years, Jonsson and Sullivan formed a formidable, hardworking partnership.[42]

↬

Amiable as he appeared, Jonsson could be impatient with those who failed to meet his expectations. Only those who would look far into the future and try to accommodate it won his admiration. An important Dallas city official whom he believed failed in this regard was the city manager, Elgin E. Crull, who had held that office for fourteen years, longer than any of his predecessors. Crull, a quiet man whose demeanor made one think of an accountant, was nonetheless effective and powerful. His innate conservatism was suggested by his modest lifestyle. Crull's early reluctance to agree on the need for a new city hall had rung alarm bells for Jonsson.[43] Similarly, Crull had been loath for Dallas to yield its position on Love Field, a stance that particularly irked Jonsson.[44]

Crull's closely guarded power hindered the broad plans that Jonsson believed were essential for the city. Their personalities did not mesh. Their differences were unknown to the general public, but city council members were aware of them.[45]

A majority vote of council members was required to fire the city manager. Jonsson quietly worked out a plan to achieve this coup. He approached a former city manager, James W. Aston, who, having hired Crull in 1939 as assistant city manager, now agreed that he would hire him again to oversee Republic Bank's properties. Jonsson quietly gained support from other council members, then presented Crull with an ultimatum—take the bank job with dignity or suffer a public firing. Crull resigned on June 6, 1966, and accepted the bank job. News stories contained no hint of conflict, and Crull was able to enjoy laudatory newspaper editorials about his services to the city.[46]

Crull's successor was his first assistant city manager, W. Scott McDonald, who had been with the city since 1942. McDonald's degree in engineering endeared him to Jonsson. "Scott, congratulations," Jonsson told him upon his election by the city council, "and you've now come into one of the toughest jobs in the world."[47] McDonald continued as city manager through Jonsson's tenure as mayor, retiring in 1972, the year after Jonsson left. His careful attention to detail earned Jonsson's admiration. McDonald began sending City of Dallas department heads and assistant department heads to Texas Instruments to attend special programs. Years later, he had only kind words to say about Jonsson: "I could not have asked for a better person to work with.[48]

An man who began working in the city manager's office six months before Crull's departure was George Schrader, who first met Jonsson through Goals for Dallas. Recognized as a man of promise, Schrader was hired as first assistant manager and heir apparent for the top position. (He succeeded McDonald in 1972 and become one of Dallas's most successful city managers.) McDonald assigned Schrader to work with Jonsson on the airport and the new city hall. The two men began a close relationship that would continue beyond Jonsson's time as mayor. It became McDonald's and Schrader's habit to meet Jonsson on Saturdays for long lunches at the Petroleum Club, where they would brief him on city hall affairs. Schrader continued these lunches with Jonsson through the 1970s and 1980s. To Schrader, Jonsson was a patriarchal figure who "radiated leadership and trustworthiness and distinction when he entered a room."[49]

Another entrenched city hall official was longtime city attorney Henry P. Kucera, the colorful, cigar-smoking son of a Czech immigrant who, to Jonssons relief, retired in 1965 at the age of sixty-eight. Alex Bickley, the first assistant city attorney, replaced him. It was said that Bickley, one of Jonsson's closest confidants at city hall, became "half-city manager." Bickley, a West Texas native, was destined to serve many years as city attorney and later as executive director of the DCC.[50]

↬

Jonsson now was surrounded by a city manager and a city attorney who viewed him not as an interloper but as a strong leader whom they viewed with a certain degree of awe. With a city council composed almost entirely of CCA members, Jonsson had no substantial opposition there. He had become a strong mayor in a weak-mayor system. Schrader observed that whenever the mayor passed through a city office and tried to exchange pleasantries, workers often were too frightened to respond.[51]

Jonsson's requests to the council concerning the airport and its needs were granted almost automatically. Even as costs skyrocketed, few questions were asked. As mentioned, the amount required for airport land tripled to $62 million. Construction costs ballooned. Jonsson remained unperturbed, even acknowledging a popular columnist's warning that airport costs might reach a billion dollars instead of the early estimate of just more than $200 million (by 1969 the estimate had reached $480 million). Yes, costs might reach a billion, Jonsson said. It was difficult for an average citizen to comprehend such a project. Some speculated that it was planned for so far in the future that it was impractical.[52]

Sullivan became dissatisfied with TAMS's plan for a single, two-mile long terminal. He believed it was a design for the past, incapable of accommodating the huge number of passengers who would be arriving in jumbo jets. An airplane crash or a fire would create havoc throughout the terminal. With Jonsson and the board's approval, two new firms were hired to develop a revolutionary alternative design—a series of freestanding, widely separated, semicircular terminals connected by a rapid transit "people mover." De-centralization would minimize congestion. The semicircles would provide enough perimeter to allow airplanes to come closer to each gate. They would represent a more "human" scale. And the new plan would cost about $30 million less than the old one.[53]

Walther Prokosch, who had designed the original terminal, was stunned. He had been working on his plan for three years. It had won approval from the airlines and the FAA. Jonsson met with Prokosch later at the Century Club in New York to soothe his wounded feelings.[54]

The newly hired firms, Hellmuth, Obata and Kassabaum of St. Louis and Brodsky, Hopf and Adler of New York City, completed their designs promptly. The separated terminals were "quicker to construct, cheaper, more flexible, more pleasant for the air traveler," Jonsson said. "We'll be getting more for less."[55]

Groundbreaking came on December 11, 1968, in tall weeds at the juncture of the Dallas County and Tarrant County boundary where Grapevine, Irving, and Euless came together. The master of ceremonies, George Haddaway, recognized it as the fiftieth anniversary of Jonsson's first flight, when a New York barnstormer took him aloft. Jonsson, along with Sullivan, J. Lee Johnson III, and U.S. Secretary of Transportation Alan S. Boyd, came on a helicopter, the first passengers to land by air. The men climbed aboard four separate bulldozers and broke ground before some 300 invited guests. After an exuberant, celebratory luncheon, Jonsson walked up to Fort Worth's Johnson. "You can kiss me now," he said playfully. "Erik," Johnson responded, "there are some things I just won't do for Fort Worth."[56]

The airport's name, chosen by board members, was the Dallas/Fort Worth Regional Airport (in 1987 its name was changed to Dallas/Fort Worth International Airport). Suggestions for something different included Trinity Field, Eisenhower Airport, Audie Murphy Regional Airport, Metro-Tex, and North Texas Airport. Later, Ross Perot would attempt to have it named for Jonsson, who absolutely refused.[57]

Construction activities remained mysterious to the average citizen. Bulldozers and earthmovers worked for a year and a half before concrete was poured. Few people could grasp the airport's size, eight and a half by nine miles. It would be three times larger than Kennedy, La Guardia, and Newark airports combined, and its air traffic would be equal to their combined volume. It would be bigger than the island of Manhattan. The amount of concrete laid, 600 million pounds, costing $57 million, was enough to build a four-lane highway between the airport and Oklahoma City, two hundred miles away.[58]

The matter of transferring airline operations from Love Field had to be arranged. At an impressive December 1969 public ceremony attended by top executives from the major airlines—American, Delta, Eastern, Braniff, Frontier, Ozark, and Texas International—Jonsson and board secretary Bayard Friedman signed agreements stipulating that they would move all their operations to the airport when it opened. They would abandon Love Field. (An important exception eventually developed. Southwest Airlines, founded at Love Field after the agreements had been signed and before the new airport opened, refused to leave and won a court battle allowing it to stay. Its close-in location, low-cost flights, and imaginative marketing brought a flood of customers, and Southwest grew into one of the nation's biggest and most profitable airlines.)[59]

As chairman of the airport board and its usual spokesperson, Jonsson was recognized as its dominant figure. He selected and appointed members for the necessary committees—construction, finance, and operations. He presided over the frequent board meetings, as many as twice a week during the long construction period. In the years ahead, many would recognize the airport as his greatest contribution to the Dallas–Fort Worth area.[60]

Goals, the Cowboys, and I. M. Pei

Although the Goals for Dallas program disappeared for a while from public view after its early announcement, Jonsson was still working on it: conferring quietly with Clifford Nelson of the American Assembly, determining which aspects needed to be included, lining up an institutional sponsor, and arranging for a full-time director.

Dallas's two master plans, devised in 1911 and 1943, along with later planning documents, had been handed to residents from the top down. Jonsson wanted something more representative of all residents, something more ambitious and more comprehensive than previous efforts. He wanted goals that looked beyond immediate needs and represented the highest wishes of everyday citizens. Expert help would guide the process, especially in the early stages, but he wanted the final product to reflect public consensus.

In December 1965, he called together for the first working session the twenty-three leading citizens who constituted his Goals for Dallas Planning Committee. Those attending the all-afternoon session at the Petroleum Club were told—no surprise—that the sponsoring institution would be the Graduate Research Center of the Southwest. One of its vice presidents, Bryghte D. Godbold, a retired U.S. Marine brigadier general, would be the full-time director. Jonsson would chair the overall committee. As far as was known, no city had before attempted such a project.[1]

Probably no one on the planning committee realized the magnitude of the job. One member finally asked Jonsson how long the project might last. Jonsson said he was thinking in terms of a decade, but it could be anywhere from five to fifty years. (It turned out to be twenty-six.) Godbold, who directed the program for the next eleven years, explained the basic schedule ahead: Writers and experts would prepare essays assessing the present situation. Based on these critiques, a select group of citizens would devise goals. In town hall meetings open to all, citizens would discuss and modify the goals. The next phase, implementation, then would begin.

The initial twenty-three-person planning committee represented an all-star cast of Dallas leaders, including C. A. Tatum, Robert B. Cullum, John M. Stemmons, E. O. Cartwright, and Stanley Marcus of the downtown business establishment; W. H. Dickinson Jr., pastor of Jonsson's church, Highland Park Methodist; Joe M. Dealey, publisher of the *Dallas Morning News;* James F. Chambers Jr., publisher of the *Dallas Times Herald;* and Pat Haggerty of Texas Instruments.

Jonsson appointed just one woman, Mrs. Stathakos Condos; one representative from labor, Allan L. Maley Jr.; and one African American, Milton K. Curry Jr., president of the all-black Bishop College. This reflected in a modest way his thought that all segments of Dallas should be represented.[2]

Goals for Dallas would be funded by private donations, especially Jonsson's, removing it from the vicissitudes of municipal politics. In late February 1966, Jonsson announced a campaign to raise some $100,000 to fund the program for the remainder of the year. He would handle any shortfalls.[3]

The completed essays outlined the present conditions of local government, the design of the city, health, welfare, transportation, public safety, elementary and secondary education, higher education, continuing education, cultural activities, recreation and entertainment, and the economy.[4] They were devoid of the self-promotion that traditionally marked local boosterism. Frank Langston wrote that minorities had little voice on the city council even though they dominated certain districts in population. The architect Pat Y. Spillman wrote that "for all its mercantile vigor and thrust," Dallas's central core lacked interest. The SMU English professor Marshall N. Terry wrote that "mediocrity is often the case" for Dallas culture, which falsely insisted on seeing itself as being in the "big leagues" of the arts.[5] Altogether, these essays undoubtedly provided the most complete and objective view of the city ever.

The group selected to set initial goals gathered at the historic Stagecoach Inn in Salado, about 150 miles southwest of Dallas. A sparkling stream gives the property an idyllic quality. Many of the conferees were prominent—bankers, lawyers, educational and religious leaders, business owners, and city and county officials—but many were not. One of those surprised to be invited was an African American physician, Dr. Emmett Conrad. "I assumed it was going to be another one of these white-washing 'we're a great city, and all is well and nothing is wrong' bits of business," he said. When he saw the essays, Conrad was surprised at the depth in which the city's shortcomings were explored. Still harboring some misgivings, Conrad agreed to attend the conference.[6]

A spokesperson who visited St. Mark's School (for boys) heard the young headmaster, Christopher Berrisford, complain that those in charge would hear what they wanted to hear, and that nobody there would be under forty-five. On the next day, Berrisford received a call from Jonsson, who told him, "I hear that you feel that the younger group isn't represented, and I'd like you to belong." Berrisford accepted the offer and became thoroughly involved.[7]

Lillian Bradshaw, the Dallas Public Library director, was incensed to see no one from the library on the list of conferees. She sent Jonsson a protest, thinking he would never respond. He called, admitted his mistake, and asked her to participate. She accepted, beginning a good working relationship between the two.[8]

Conrad, Berrisford, and Bradshaw were among eighty-seven conferees who arrived at the Stagecoach Inn in June 1966 for a four-day session that Jonsson intended to be a turning point in the city's history. Conrad was surprised at the variety of conferees: "They had laboring people, a shipping clerk from the gas company, an electrician. There were handicapped people there. I think there were twelve blacks, maybe fourteen. . . . We had a truck driver. We had a federal judge [U.S. district judge Sarah T. Hughes]. We had management people. We had lawyers. We had all sorts of diverse people—black and white."[9]

For Conrad, the discussions were eye opening. Previously, minorities had been excluded from meaningful participation in the city's affairs. The sessions represented the first time that he had had "a really frank discussion with a cross-section of Dallas." A year later, he would be the city's first African American school board member. (Four decades later a new high school in Dallas bore his name.)[10]

The most serious effort to modify the goals came on the last morning, when labor leader Gene Freeland sought to change the way that Dallas city council members were elected. Well aware of Jonsson's entrenched opposition, Freeland offered a motion to advocate electing six of the nine city councilmen by geographic districts rather than citywide. Judge Hughes, a longtime liberal, seconded his motion. Freeland's motion was defeated by approximately a 5–1 margin. Equal representation, clearly, was not a concern of the conferees.[11]

"Make no mistake about it," said Lillian Bradshaw, "there were no patsies there. It was a very articulate group—willing to dispute each other. Not just talk to each other, but dispute each other. And there were some wonderful arguments. But in the end, when we left Salado on Sunday at noon, we came out unified whether our favorite thought or project had been included or not."[12] Finally, Jonsson told the conferees: "We've put together something unique. . . . Whether it will come to anything is speculative."[13]

↫

The goals were printed in a thirty-seven-page booklet that included the mayor's ten-page introduction. They represented an ideal view of a humane city that would be beautiful, well functioning, and responsive to individual needs (including those of the poor); if all the goals were realized, Dallas would seemingly become a utopia among cities. How these goals—some lofty and general but others highly specific—could be achieved was another matter.

Only the last section addressed a subject typically acknowledged as Dallas's major concern—commercial growth. The others proposed a range of lofty aims: transforming the city into a place of beauty and functional fitness, one satisfying to the eye and mind; establishing one of the nation's great educational centers; reexamining the council-manager plan; providing the indigent with food, clothing, medical care, professional counseling, and housing; improving the city as a transportation and communications center; and establishing a heightened sense of the drama, beauty, and spiritual values of life. Following each general goal was a series of specific goals for achieving the general one. None of the specific goals were unrealistic, but they were so numerous and so varied that many years would be required to meet them.

In its first five years, Goals for Dallas involved more than a hundred thousand Dallas citizens. Highly attended town hall meetings were held, revisions were made (60 percent of the goals were modified, and twelve new ones added), priorities were set, strategies were planned on how to achieve the goals, and careful monitoring of the progress toward each goal was conducted. By 1970, a full-time staff of seven worked under Bryghte Godbold, and Jonsson reported that work was progressing on almost 90 percent of the goals. Some already had been achieved.[14]

Ten years after Goals for Dallas began, its annual expenses amounted to $1.7 million. About half of that sum came from individuals and corporations through a well-organized fund-raising drive in which Jonsson played a leading role. Jonsson donated the other half.[15]

Over the next years, as recommended, a community college system was established; kindergarten programs were initiated in the public school system; staff members were hired to assist city council members; and many other goals were met as the program became an integral though unofficial part of Dallas.

One of the few non-Dallas residents attending the Salado conference was one of the nation's most distinguished architects, I. M. Pei, a Chinese-born naturalized American who came to the United States at seventeen. "I was just listening. I contributed nothing. I didn't know much about Dallas," he later said.[16]

Pei was there because he had been selected to be the architect of the new city hall. Jonsson invited him so that he could begin to understand the city.[17] They had first met in 1964 at MIT when Pei's Earth Sciences Building, funded significantly by Cecil and Ida Green, was dedicated. Jonsson, impressed, casually said to Pei, "You know, maybe you can do something for us in Dallas one day."[18]

Pei, one of three finalists, had argued that the seven-acre tract for the new building was too small. He wanted to eliminate "a lot of honky-tonk stuff" on the "really rundown" street in front of the site. "I can't design a building like this and have no control over what is on the other side of the street," he told Jonsson. Some were shocked at this demand. "Jonsson was one that agreed with me—amazing," Pei said later. The extra acreage eventually acquired would provide space for a large plaza in front of the building and, eventually, a new library across the street.[19]

The committee's recommendation of Pei was accepted with enthusiasm. (Jonsson would say, probably accurately, that he personally chose Pei.) The project began a long relationship between the two men. Whenever they visited their respective cities (Pei lived in New York City) in the years ahead, they never failed to visit one another.[20]

Pei completed his plans in April 1967, and Jonsson called together some eight hundred business and civic leaders to a luncheon to unveil a stunning scale model. Nothing like the building existed in Dallas or in the nation, and probably not in the world.

Each floor was bigger than the one beneath on the building's front side, leaving an impression that it might tumble over. It would have nearly 800,000 square feet of office space with eight aboveground levels and three beneath. It was to be made of poured concrete with huge expanses of glass on the front that would allow workers to view a large plaza and downtown skyscrapers. The glass also would permit residents to see city employees at work. Its odd shape contrasted sharply with the skyscrapers it faced. Together, Pei explained, they would make a perfectly balanced whole.

The site was enlarged to the fourteen acres Pei wanted in order to accommodate a central plaza. A new cultural complex, including a concert hall, theater center, and library, was envisioned for the future. (Only the library would be built there; a concert hall and theater would be built years later in the Arts Center on the other side of town.) First-phase costs would be approximately $25 million for the building and $10 million for the land and underground parking. Completion might take ten years.[21]

Pei's compelling design won an enthusiastic reception, although some deemed its unusual shape impractical. In the next years, as projected costs climbed, critics gained strength. Controversy and delays were to be the building's hallmarks. Jonsson would expend large amounts of energy in confronting the naysayers.

Four months after the unveiling of the model, Dallas voters were asked to approve the largest bond election in their history, a $175 million "Crossroads" program inspired, in part, by Goals for Dallas.[22]

Jonsson campaigned hard for passage. Only two months earlier, voters had rejected the regional airport authority. A defeat for any of the propositions would jeopardize his good standing. Jonsson spoke, organized, encouraged others, and recorded a telephone message that went out automatically to registered voters.[23] The result was an overwhelming victory for all fourteen propositions. The largest number of voters ever to participate in a bond issue, more than 83,000, supported the propositions in almost every section of town. At the Petroleum Club, where Jonsson and council members listened to vote returns, Councilwoman Sibyl Hamilton dramatically kissed him on his bald head. "If that turns out to grow, you'll make a fortune," he said.[24]

⌒

A major part of the bond program designated $12.6 million for improvements and expansion at Fair Park, which was owned and operated jointly by the City of Dallas and the State Fair of Texas. The improvements included $2.6 million for renovations of Fair Park's Cotton Bowl.

The Dallas Cowboys football team, en route to becoming "America's Team," played in the Cotton Bowl as its home field. Attendance was skyrocketing. But in direct contrast to the team's sophisticated image, the Cotton Bowl was outmoded. Restrooms and concession stands were inadequate, dressing rooms lacked air-conditioning for the visiting team, spectator seating on wooden benches was tight and uncomfortable, and press accommodations were declared "hopeless" by the Football Writers of America. The surrounding neighborhood was a deteriorating, high-crime area where many fans had to park their cars while attending games.

In November 1965, Dallas Cowboys' owner, Clint Murchison Jr., began to press for a new stadium in downtown Dallas. He sent Jonsson a letter showing a projected cost of $8.5 million to $10 million for a facility with covered seats. A poll showed that citizens would approve a bond issue for such a stadium by a 3–1 margin.[25] Murchison argued that a downtown stadium had advantages that could never accrue to Fair Park. Major transportation arteries already existed. New parking spaces for some 5,000 to 6,000 automobiles would be available on weekdays for downtown workers. The stadium could generate additional revenue from conventions or special events. It would draw people into downtown Dallas on weekends and remove some thirty acres of unattractive railroad switching yards. Polls indicated that by a 4–1 margin those who had attended Cotton Bowl games preferred a stadium away from Fair Park. The project, Murchison believed, would pay for itself.[26]

Jonsson was not persuaded, and the ensuing struggle would come to be viewed as a personal dual between these two men. George Schrader said years later that this impression was incorrect. Jonsson, he said, busy with the airport and the upcoming Crossroads bond election, believed the decision belonged to the city's nearly autonomous park board and the State Fair of Texas board of directors, presided over by his friend Robert B. Cullum. Jonsson, though, recognized as the ultimate authority on all civic matters, inevitably was drawn into the controversy.[27]

He did not want a downtown stadium. Neither did I.M. Pei nor the urban planners Vincent Ponte and Warren Travers, who had been hired by the City of Dallas to help with downtown planning. "I got a unanimous answer from them," Jonsson later said. "If you put the stadium downtown, you'll hate it so much, you'll tear it down in ten years for what it does to your traffic and because it's dead space only used once a week."[28]

Cullum, recognizing the obvious inadequacies of the Cotton Bowl, announced in April 1966 that State Fair directors would study the possibility of building an entirely new 81,000-seat Cotton Bowl inside an expanded Fair Park rather than merely improving the present stadium. That fall they considered two additional possibilities: rebuilding the Cotton Bowl for $17 million or remodeling it for $3 million. Cullum favored a new stadium, as did Orville Cartwright, president of the Dallas Chamber of Commerce, who said Dallas needed a gigantic "image correction program," in which a "brand new, splendidly designed, well-appointed Cotton Bowl" would be one of the first steps.[29]

Murchison was not persuaded, and he held a trump card. For just under $1 million, he had purchased a ninety-acre site in Irving, immediately west of Dallas, at a strategic location with excellent highway access. He could build a stadium there with the participation of the City of Irving. It would be, he said, "the finest football stadium to date in the world." Uniquely, the playing field would be open to the elements, but all seats would be covered.[30]

In March 1967, the Cowboys' owner appeared before the city council with a prepared handout. "At issue here is not the issue of a stadium—which certainly should have been started several years ago—but a much more important issue, that concerning the progress of our city," he said. Jonsson had a question: "If you take the Cowboys out of Fair Park, what are you suggesting we put there instead?" Murchison had a quick response: "How about an electronics plant?"[31]

In Jonsson's papers is an unattributed note to city manager McDonald: "Clint is beginning to sound irresponsible—even to Cowboy fans. . . .We can't squander thirty-two acres of our precious central core on a football field to be played on 10 times a year. . . . The site itself will cost about $8,000,000.[32]

There was, indeed, the matter of affordability. Jonsson said that "every morning" he received letters from widows who were living on less than $125 a month and who could not pay more taxes on their small cottages without losing them. "I must think of these people, along with those who want a football stadium or an opera house."[33]

The *Dallas Morning News* sportswriter Sam Blair wrote that the mayor's civic leadership was drastically deficient in sports apprecia-

tion: "Let's face it: He simply isn't a sports fan. Or, far more disturbing, he isn't aware of how valuable sports can be to his city."[34] Other
sportswriters jumped into the fray. Blackie Sherrod of the *Dallas Times
Herald* accused Jonsson of giving Murchison the runaround: "A new
stadium is EVERYBODY's business—the city, the Chamber, the butcher
and baker, and, yes, even the mayor's."[35]

A weekly newspaper, the *Oak Cliff Tribune*, urged Murchison to run
against Jonsson for mayor in the approaching April 4 city election. The
editorial was reprinted by two other suburban newspapers and read on
a radio station. Murchison sent a note to Jonsson: "I think you will be
happy to learn that . . . I intend to vote for the entire CCA slate."[36]

Murchison said a downtown stadium could be built for $11 million
on a thirty-five-acre site west of Memorial Auditorium, which would
cost another $11 million to buy. Revenues from rental fees, concessions,
and weekday parking fees would retire a bond issue. In effect, he argued,
the stadium would be free.[37]

Jonsson remained firm. He took special exception to Murchison's
plan to build a stadium seating only 55,000—the Cotton Bowl seated
75,000. Thousands of faithful fans would be unable to attend games.
"I sincerely call upon Mr. Murchison to reconsider his proposal," Jonsson said.[38]

The 1967 Crossroads bond program already guaranteed improve-
ments for the Cotton Bowl: theater-type seats, an improved press box,
and air-conditioning for the visitors' locker room. Murchison remained
adamant. "An overwhelming majority of the people of Dallas do not
want a stadium at Fair Park at any price," he said. "The best thing you
could build at Fair Park is a moat."[39]

Jonsson's mailbox overflowed with letters from fans who were
shocked at the possibility of losing the Cowboys to Irving. To someone who accused Jonsson of not being a football fan, he responded: "I
know of no basis, except erroneous rumor, that would lead you to the
understanding that I do not like football; the reverse is, in fact, the case.
I am anxious, as soon as it is possible to afford it for the city. . . . However, I believe that there are other things more essential to the ongoing
progress of the community in the immediate future." Jonsson might
have mentioned, but did not, that he was a director of the Cotton Bowl
Athletic Association.[40]

"I am a pretty rabid sports fan," he told the *Dallas Morning News*
sports columnist Roy Edwards. Although many sportswriters had

criticized him severely, he pointed out that not one of them had ever called him. "It's a funny thing," he said. "Nobody noticed how bad the Cotton Bowl was until the Astrodome was built."[41] That comment drew Murchison's sharp retort. "Dear Erik: I noted in the morning paper your comment that until the Astrodome was built, everyone thought the Cotton Bowl was pretty good. Of course, until the transistor was developed, people thought the vacuum tube was pretty good. Sincerely, Clint."[42]

On August 28, 1967, the Cowboys played the Green Bay Packers in a preseason game at the Cotton Bowl before more than 75,000 fans. Afterward, as fans walked to their cars into the surrounding high-crime neighborhoods, people's worst fears were realized. Hoodlums assaulted or robbed more than a dozen fans. One man was shot and his wife severely beaten; another man was stabbed almost to death. A father and son were struck by sticks and clubs and robbed. Bold page-one headlines told of the assaults. (A year later, for the same preseason game against the Packers, the Dallas Police Department assigned more than 240 officers to the area to prevent a repeat of the mayhem.)[43]

The violence and the ensuing publicity made Murchison's decision easier. He announced that he would build in Irving a modern, space-age football field with a semienclosed roof. Luxury suites would encircle the top of the stadium. The team would play in the Cotton Bowl until the new Irving stadium was ready. And no, he said, the team would not change its name to the Irving Cowboys.

Beginning in 1971, the Dallas Cowboys started playing in what would become one of the most familiar sports arenas in the nation, Texas Stadium. The Cowboys organization would be recognized as the nation's most successful and valuable sports franchise. The Cotton Bowl, although enhanced with $2.6 million in improvements, would lose the Cowboys and eventually the SMU football team's home games. It would continue to host the annual Texas-Oklahoma football game and, for the next years, the New Year's Day Cotton Bowl classic. But its luster was gone.

Murchison wryly described his experiences in pushing for a downtown stadium. "I exposed the plan to civic leaders. Great, they said. Merchants liked it; hotel operators liked it; restaurateurs liked it; convention promoters liked it; the president of the Dallas Citizens Council liked it so much he even proposed expanding the concept; both newspapers loved it. Erik Jonsson hated it." Jonsson's verdict, Murchison said, came "as sure and swift as a Turk's scimitar" after a final two-hour luncheon with him and State Fair of Texas president Cullum. Jonsson told him there was no stadium in his plans in the foreseeable future. "And thus," Murchison said, "was born Texas Stadium."[44]

Texas Stadium and its open roof became a familiar American icon, but nearly four decades later the Cowboys, under the ownership of Jerry Jones, resisting a call to return to Dallas, moved in 2009 to a futuristic new stadium in Arlington. Texas Stadium was demolished.

↩

The mastoid operation that Jonsson underwent as a four-year-old boy caused a slight loss of hearing that worsened as he grew older. He sometimes used a hearing aid. In his council chambers chair, a small amplifier attached discreetly to the top of his chair helped him. A careful observer might have noticed that the mayor often leaned his head, positioning himself closer to the amplifier.[45]

The mayor's concern about hearing problems prompted his involvement with the local Pilot School for the Deaf. Sometime in the late 1950s, while chairman of its advisory council, he suggested to Nelle Johnston that she consider volunteer work there. Johnston followed through, found it satisfying, and wrote a twenty-page prospectus describing the need for improvements to the school. With her boss's support and his financial contributions, she led a drive to establish a more comprehensive institution to address the loss of hearing and associated communications issues. The result was that in 1964 the Pilot School for the Deaf and the Dallas Speech and Hearing Center were merged and renamed the Callier Hearing and Speech Center. Johnston became its president, and Jonsson assumed a position on the board of directors.

In December 1966, groundbreaking ceremonies were held for a $3.5 million, 5.5-acre facility adjacent to the University of Texas Southwestern Medical School.[46] The opinion was "widely held," Jonsson said, that Callier was "the most complete institution in the world" for dealing with communications disorders.[47] Vice President Spiro T. Agnew dedicated the building on October 9, 1969. That evening, Jonsson sat at the head table at a $100-a-plate fund-raising dinner for Agnew, an event attended by dignitaries including Congressman George H. W. Bush and the comedian Bob Hope.

Nelle Johnston would serve for many years as president of Callier, with Jonsson continuing as a board member. His interest in hearing problems would always be keen, especially his support for the invention of an artificial ear.[48] (In 1975 the Callier Center merged with the University of Texas at Dallas.)

↝

Midway through Jonsson's years as mayor, it was obvious that he could not please everyone. Controversies surrounding the new city hall and, especially, the football stadium; his alleged lack of feeling for the ordinary citizen; and charges that he was dictatorial made that clear. Yet, overall, his popularity was probably higher than that of any mayor in Dallas's history, a fact punctuated by his reelection in 1967 without opposition. Jonsson's presence offered comfort. He was seen as firm but genial, a father figure, a general presiding over lieutenants. His commanding nature, his insistence on addressing future needs, his reluctance to engage in meaningless debate, and his lack of interest in political or pecuniary gain won him the confidence and thanks of a large majority of citizens. They saw his willingness to take on difficult tasks when he could have rested easily on his wealth. Even the Dallas Charter League declined to get involved in the April 4, 1967, municipal election. Voters elected the entire slate of CCA-endorsed candidates.

The *Dallas Times Herald* believed that Jonsson deserved election by acclamation. In his three years, the newspaper noted, Dallas had made "fantastic progress." Indeed, despite the shadow of the assassination, the city had continued to boom economically. In the first nine months of 1964, it experienced a 14 percent increase in business activity compared with the same period in 1963.[49]

The public's chance to interact with the mayor came primarily at Monday-afternoon city council sessions. In these sessions, usually tedious but occasionally volatile, Jonsson presided calmly, politely recognizing council members when they had something to say but urging them to move along when matters dragged on, charming the press with witty informalities, and listening patiently as citizens levied wide-ranging complaints that sometimes made little sense. He concealed as best he could his frustrations, but during intense moments his hands sometimes would break out in what appeared to be hives, and he scratched them constantly.

So busy was the mayor that, except for board meetings, he had little time for Texas Instruments. He also had little time for home life as he moved from meeting to meeting and appointment to appointment. Besides his hectic schedule as mayor, there were many other commitments—the airport, Republic National Bank, Braniff Airways, the

Graduate Research Center of the Southwest, Goals for Dallas, the Dallas Citizens Council, and speeches to civic groups, service clubs, business organizations, and schools and colleges,

In late 1965, the City of Dallas traded in his 1955 Cadillac for a new one. At Jonsson's request, it was black.[50] The advantage of having a driver and car was simple—he could be dropped off and picked up at the door of appointments. Frequently, Jonsson's driver would greet him at his house early in the morning, carry him from one meeting or another through the day, and deposit him at home late in the afternoon.

Jonsson wasted little time on his wardrobe, choosing inevitably a dark gray suit, white shirt, and subdued necktie. For evening meetings when there was no time to go home, he usually would have an extra fresh white shirt. One day, councilwoman Anita Martinez took up a collection and presented him with a blue blazer. He cheerfully donned it to applause, but it was the last time he was seen wearing it.[51]

Erik and Margaret now lived alone. They had two telephone lines, one listed number and the other unlisted. People called at all hours with complaints, demands, or queries. They complained about barking dogs, power failures, garbage pickups, and water bills. Margaret tried to take all the late-night calls because her husband inevitably was exhausted from his busy work schedule of about seventy hours a week. One day, as she attempted to drive away from home, a woman blocked her path and refused to leave unless she would talk to her. Margaret pulled back closer to the house, locked her car doors, and waited until the woman finally left. When a neighbor's dog was poisoned, Dallas police assigned an unmarked car to watch the Jonsson's house; it was feared the dog had been silenced so that burglars could strike.[52]

Ordinary citizens sent countless letters with requests that should have gone to the city manager's office or to a specific department. Jonsson frequently acknowledged them in return letters, then forwarded the queries or complaints to the city manager, city attorney, or public utilities supervisor on an official City of Dallas memorandum.[53] Some requests were impossible to handle. A high school student, assigned to debate liquor by the drink, wrote: "If it is at all possible, would you please send me both pro and con sides of this issue by Tuesday of next week?"[54] An official for one of the largest cemeteries in town, having read that one of the first things Jonsson did on arriving in Dallas was to buy cemetery lots, called to ask whether he would write a promotional

letter for him. Nelle Johnston summed up the request in an accompanying note: "You won't believe this one," she wrote.[55]

She appended the same astonishment on an envelope containing a
1966 Christmas card addressed simply to "Mayor & People, City Hall,
Dallas, Texas." The card had a photograph of Elvis Presley, in black
trousers and a red jacket, with the printed notation, "Seasons Greet-
ings[,] Elvis and the Colonel[,] 1966."[56]

One continuing concern at city hall was Dallas's rising crime rate.
Despite the assassination, the city enjoyed a reputation for being a
clean-cut place full of churchgoers. Yet the city had one of the highest
crime rates in the nation in major categories such as murder, robbery,
aggravated assault, and burglary.[57] The battle against crime was a constant struggle. Unlike efforts to construct a new city hall and a new airport, work done by Jonsson and the council in addressing crime could
not result in a lasting, tangible monument. Nor would their work on
such vital issues as traffic, pollution, housing, and zoning create results
that would be readily visible to the average citizen.

In the minds of many, the social ills that Jonsson saw as a major cause
of crime extended to the movie industry, where sex, profanity, and violence were major ingredients in a growing number of films. A national
rating system did not exist, and Councilman Joe H. Golman proposed
a local board to review movies and to designate them as suitable for
families or strictly for adults. Some 250 aroused citizens overflowed the
council chambers in February 1965 to debate the issue, presenting Jonsson with perhaps his toughest assignment in maintaining order.

PTA officers, ministers, and members of the new Citizens Committee for Decent Movies spoke fervently in favor of the ordinance.
"Whoredom and harlotry," a Baptist minister said in describing con-
temporary films. Dallas Cowboys football coach Tom Landry argued
that "the time has come to take a stand." Such an ordinance would violate the First Amendment and be the "first form of thought control"
charged an attorney representing the drive-in theater industry.[58]

It was not a cause in which the mayor cared to take a leading role,
but he received a heavy volume of mail on the subject. Editorials and
letters to the editor appeared in the newspapers. Almost all who wrote
favored a strong ordinance prohibiting young people from seeing
adult-classified movies.

The adoption of Dallas's own movie classification board, coming before a national rating system was put in place, was approved. It prohibited anyone under eighteen from seeing movies classified as "adult."[59] When the ordinance was challenged in the federal courts, Judge Sarah T. Hughes found that provisions permitting the confiscation of projection equipment and the revocation of licenses of offending theaters were too broad. The ordinance was rewritten to satisfy her complaints. When challenged again, it wound its way to the U.S. Supreme Court, where it was overturned as too vague. The film industry, under attack elsewhere, began classifying its films with ratings such as G (general), PG (parental guidance), R (restricted), and X (adults only). Thus began the national rating system that today is so familiar.[60]

Another emotional issue was whether to add fluoride to the Dallas water supply. Across the nation, the question had sparked arguments, with opponents alleging "poisoning," forced mass medication, and corrosion of water pipes. Some even suggested it was part of a communist plot. Proponents pointed to the health benefits of fluoride, particularly in the prevention of dental decay.

A public hearing on the matter, called by Jonsson in August 1965, revealed the depth of feelings. More than a hundred persons registered to speak. As the four-hour session began, Jonsson, anticipating unusual histrionics, laid down a precise set of ground rules and pointed to a police officer, who was present to maintain proper discipline.[61]

After the council approved fluoridation, opponents mounted a successful petition drive to force a city referendum. (A related petition drive, unsuccessful, sought to remove Jonsson and five other council members from office because of their pro-fluoride votes.) In the January 1966 referendum, Dallas voters confirmed fluoridation of the water supply by a 3–1 margin. It was said to be the first time that voters in a city of more than 500,000 people had approved a fluoridation referendum.[62]

Gun control was not an issue that normally confronted a mayor in a council-manager form of government, but in June 1968, when Robert F. Kennedy was assassinated, that question was raised in Dallas. As mayor of the city where Kennedy's brother had been shot and killed, Jonsson was awakened by a call from a reporter at three thirty in the morning to get his opinion on gun control. Yes, Jonsson said, he believed some control of arms was very much in order.[63]

Walking a Tightrope

As mandated by Texas Instruments' policy, Eugene McDermott retired in 1964 at sixty-five. Two years later, Cecil Green reached the same milestone. In April 1966, Erik Jonsson, approaching sixty-five, presided for the last time over the annual shareholders' meeting. TI stock had reached an all-time high in February: 195¾. Shareholders approved a two-for-one stock split and an increase in dividend payments. Jonsson took the title of honorary chairman and continued, as did McDermott and Green, to serve on the board. Haggerty became chairman and announced a ten-year sales goal for 1976 that was staggering—$3 billion. Mark Shepherd became president.[1]

Jonsson continued to work as mayor from his TI office until the fall of 1967, when he leased offices high in the new Republic Bank Tower in downtown Dallas. Nelle Johnston moved downtown with him to coordinate a staff of three secretaries, all on Jonsson's personal payroll. Only a few people—the city manager, the city attorney, Robert B. Cullum, Bryghte Godbold, and a few more—could expect Johnston to put their calls through to the mayor without first being quizzed about their purpose. Each day she prepared a daily schedule for her boss with notations on what he could expect at his destination. She made summaries of telephone calls. She helped write many of his speeches. Her power as gatekeeper equaled or bettered that of almost any city official. The city secretary, Harold G. Shank, advised his staff to refer calls for the mayor directly to Johnston. Her influence is suggested in the schedule she prepared for her boss for August 28, 1967: "I have set up date with Judge [county judge W. L.] Sterrett for lunch on Friday; I talked to [councilman] Jack Moser this morning and asked him to try to get with you after the Council meeting on Monday; that if this failed we would get you together next Friday morning by phone or in person for discussion ... See Earl Cullum's ltr [letter] and proposed news release. Wouldn't it be more forceful to make announcement during Council meeting and discuss with newsmen afterwards?"[2]

Johnston, a former librarian, had begun at Texas Instruments in 1947 when the new Lemmon Avenue building attracted her. She lived nearby with her parents. One day she simply walked in and asked for a job. Now she worked exclusively for "Mr. J.," as she often called him, with the title of executive secretary.[3]

$\backsim$

As the turbulent decade of the 1960s neared its end, Dallas had escaped the upheavals experienced in many cities as disadvantaged and resentful African Americans shocked the nation. As racial tensions heightened, Jonsson and others feared that an unforeseen incident might touch off an outbreak of violence in Dallas.

African Americans constituted about 30 percent of Dallas's population. Leaders in the black community had worked with some success to remove racial barriers in voting, employment, and education since the 1930s, seeking not to antagonize the city's white leadership. Some major advancements were made through an unofficial but powerful biracial committee in 1961 that worked to desegregate major institutions and to prepare the way for peaceful integration of the public schools. But progress was slow, and activists unaffiliated with traditional African American organizations were taking center stage.

Dallas's public schools remained almost entirely segregated, although a federal court order in 1961 had mandated a plan in which one grade at a time, beginning with the first, was to be integrated. Dallas's first black state legislator, Joseph Lockridge, elected in 1966, died in an airplane crash two years later and was succeeded by a black minister, the Reverend Zan W. Holmes Jr. The city had only a handful of black police officers and no black firefighters. No African American would serve on the Dallas school board until 1967, when Emmett Conrad was elected. Except for those holding menial jobs, African American employees at city hall or the courthouse were rare.

Jonsson did not share the segregationist inclinations of so many native Texans. Neither, though, was he a crusader for civil rights. Having overcome obstacles himself, he believed that anyone who worked hard and led a principled life could achieve a satisfactory degree of prosperity and happiness.

Overt racial discrimination was not practiced at Texas Instruments. But neither had the company actively sought to recruit or promote minorities. A Conference Board study of black employment in America, released in 1966, quoted Jonsson's response to an observation that a black engineer would be lonely in Dallas. "No more lonesome than a Brooklyn Swede in Dallas some thirty years ago," he had said.[4]

From his first days in office, Jonsson and other city, county, and school officials faced increasingly aggressive demands for desegregation. By 1964, the Congress of Racial Equality (CORE) had a local representative in Dallas pushing hard. His demands, national events, and the Civil Rights Act of 1964 prompted the local NAACP and the Negro Chamber of Commerce to lobby aggressively for change. A Committee for Racial Harmony, composed largely of well-known black leaders, submitted to Jonsson in July 1964 a proposal for improved schooling and enhanced job opportunities. Jonsson promised to "give thorough study to all of the recommendations."[5] But the recommendations were shunted aside and soon disappeared. Still, Jonsson felt comfortable in believing at the end of 1965 that "we have maintained very good relationships and wide-open communications between our races."[6]

꙳

When Roy Wilkins, the NAACP's executive director, flew to Dallas in February 1966 to attend a rally in his honor, Jonsson greeted him at the airport and won compliments from the black community. Wilkins said the entire nation was talking about how Dallas had managed to avoid "sharp outbursts of racial tensions." Even so, he said, certain things needed to be done. Dallas banks, he said, were apparently afraid that Negroes could not count past twenty, since they were not hiring them as bank tellers.[7]

A black SMU student called Jonsson's office to ask his opinion on civil disobedience. Jonsson gave him this statement: "Civil disobedience implies disregard for the duly constituted laws of this land and since I believe that lawlessness leads to anarchy, I disagree completely that civil disobedience is an appropriate way to bring about social reform. Reasonable men working together to understand each other's needs and to assist toward mutual achievements can make deeper inroads on needed social reforms."[8]

As rioting spread across the nation after Martin Luther King Jr.'s assassination, Dallas officials made contingency plans. Police quietly investigated persons, black or white, who advocated rapid desegregation and who criticized the slow responses of Dallas institutions. They sent confidential reports to Jonsson and other officials.[9]

Complaints by African Americans about harsh treatment by police officers became frequent and potentially violent. Several tense situations threatened to lead to uncontrolled outbreaks of violence, especially the vigorous and prolonged picketing of a small chain of South Dallas grocery stores. Protestors alleged that the stores offered inferior products and that they should be owned by African Americans. The demonstrations led to the conviction of the two protest leaders for destruction of private property. Both were convicted and given fifteen-year prison sentences.[10]

City council meetings, more and more, became a forum for airing grievances, often delivered as not-so-veiled threats. Goals for Dallas conferees addressed racial discrimination only vaguely, citing a need to "form a human resource council to identify and recommend solutions to community problems involved in the individual's adjustments to urban living." Town hall meetings seconded that goal by recommending that a city ordinance establish a human relations commission.[11]

Jonsson faced strong pressure to accomplish this goal. The fact that it was a Goals for Dallas recommendation did not persuade him. The goals, he said, were not his personal ones, and he was not bound to support every one of them. He feared that a commission would serve as a forum for irresponsible criticism of the police. He especially did not want a human relations commission with subpoena power.[12]

The mayor appeared on an ABC television program, *One Nation: Indivisible*, and boasted that Texas Instruments had hired 4,100 Negroes and was constantly seeking talent regardless of race, creed, or color. A letter writer wondered whether he knew about the Negro engineer employed by TI who was having difficulty securing housing in the nearby North Dallas area because of his race. Jonsson, alarmed, sent a copy of her letter to TI's personnel department, asking naively whether this could be true.

Indeed, it was true. The personnel director, Marvin Berkeley, reported that the engineer finally had been referred to the black real estate agent who was the "safety valve" for handling black employees. That agent identified an area in North Dallas where some 60–70 percent of the residents were black, and the engineer found a home there.[13]

Finally, Jonsson called on James W. Aston of Republic National Bank to negotiate with the leading proponent of the human relations commission, an attorney named Sid Stahl. The result was creation of the Greater Dallas Community Relations Commission, a voluntary body without subpoena power, funded by United Way. Tom Unis, an establishment attorney in whom Jonsson had confidence, became the first president; Stahl agreed to be vice president.[14]

～

Meanwhile, an issue surfaced that for the first time personally involved Jonsson in an explosive situation. It sprang from the city's condemnation of African American residences in a fifty-acre area between Fitzhugh and Pennsylvania Streets in order to gain additional parking space for Fair Park. An underlying reason, stated in a 1966 report, "Redevelopment Program for the State Fair of Texas," declared that removal of the houses was necessary because the area "did not project the image of prosperous, progressive and pleasant Dallas."[15]

Proceedings to purchase 308 parcels of land were initiated in August 1968. Homeowners, many of them elderly, complained that the "fair market value" offered—75 cents a square foot—would not allow them to buy comparable housing elsewhere. Additionally, they were displeased at being uprooted from their neighborhood for a project that seemed unnecessary.

Many white Dallas residents empathized with them. Finally, the city raised the offer from 75 cents to a dollar a square foot. These new offers were termed "still grossly unfair."[16] Ralph Abernathy of the Southern Christian Leadership Conference sent a telegram to Jonsson and the city council, blaming them for failing to show "the least amount of humaneness." He demanded a halt to the condemnation procedures.[17] Abernathy sent a young full-time field representative to Dallas, the Reverend Peter Johnson, who began pulling together a coalition of aggressive new groups.[18]

Johnson eventually issued an ultimatum that pulled the reluctant mayor directly into the situation. On the very next day, Johnson said, unless the mayor agreed to personally examine the homeowners' plight, a large group of protestors would block the nationally televised New Year's Day parade preceding the Cotton Bowl game. Confronted with this possible embarrassment on national television, Jonsson agreed. As a final gesture, he agreed to share his car in the parade with J. B. Jackson Jr., one of the activists who earlier had threatened to picket city hall.[19]

For his conciliatory action, Jonsson received a flood of congratulatory letters. By now, the city already had acquired about two-thirds of the properties, but further acquisitions were halted until Jonsson could report his conclusions.[20]

By mid-February, Jonsson was ready to give his report, but the homeowners now wanted him to meet with their own consultants so that their differing evaluations could provide a basis for compromise.[21] Jonsson reluctantly agreed. They met at the downtown public library, where the consultant, with homeowners in attendance, presented a fifty-four-page study indicating that the properties were worth four times the amount the city was paying. These differences, Jonsson said, were "so broad that there was no need to go much further."[22] Tensions heightened in the following days. Jonsson was declared a "paper mayor," accused of leaking one-sided information to the press, and charged with rejecting the consultant's recommendations because he belonged to an ethnic minority group.[23]

Jonsson agreed to another meeting. Homeowners and their representatives insisted that it be held at the branch library in South Dallas, a location Jonsson opposed because he expected that a hostile crowd there would exert "extraordinary pressures." He was under the impression that they agreed, however, to return to the downtown public library for the meeting.[24]

Two days before the meeting, Jonsson was advised that the homeowners would be at the South Dallas branch library.[25] Jonsson said he "long ago" had reserved the downtown library conference room, and his busy schedule made it imperative that they meet there.[26] Jonsson and his own citizens' committee—five civic leaders—arrived at the downtown public library at the appointed hour. The homeowners' group went to the South Dallas branch library.[27] After waiting an hour and fifteen minutes, Jonsson and his committee went home.

Representatives of the homeowners immediately called a press conference and charged Jonsson with "playing plantation politics."[28] Peter Johnson of the SCLC said he was "outraged, disgusted and fully disappointed in the Honorable Mayor's immoral, unethical, and undemocratic handling." Jonsson's behavior proved beyond a shadow of a doubt that, according to his ethics, "nickels and dimes are worth more than flesh and blood." The mayor, he said, left him no alternative but "to declare Dallas in a 'Moral State of Emergency.'" Johnson said he would request national help to remedy the situation. The talking had stopped, he said; "the war has begun." He was personally canceling all previous engagements to concentrate on it.[29] J. B. Jackson Jr. said the mayor "had lied to him and broken faith." Battle plans were being laid, Jackson said, for a legal, economic, and social attack on "discriminatory institutions of the city."[30]

Jonsson responded that homeowners were being manipulated by "an outsider from Atlanta" (Peter Johnson) who had personally attacked him and impugned the motives of the council.[31] That evening the city council met privately in emergency session in the city attorney's office. "I think we have gone as far as reasonable human beings can be expected to go," Jonsson said. They agreed to resume condemnation proceedings.[32]

The executive director of the Greater Dallas Council of Churches, the Reverend Louis A. Saunders, wrote candidly to Jonsson. There was a growing suspicion among the Fair Park homeowners, and among minorities in general, he said, that the "goodwill" of the larger Dallas community is "good" only when it served the "will" of the power structure: "There seems to be communication gaps and the feeling is that the source of this gap is the mayor's office."[33]

Jonsson, taken aback, said he had been expected to conform to standards not met by the other side. He simply wanted to talk directly to the homeowners, not their firebrand agents.[34] Three days later, he sent a letter to each homeowner asking for that sort of meeting at the downtown Lone Star Gas Company auditorium: "I still seek to report to you with the hope that in mutual respect and dignity we can resolve this situation with the greatest possible equity to *all* who are involved. As one human being to another, let me express the simple hope that you will agree to meet with me." He enclosed an RSVP card with each letter.[35] Expecting individual responses, Jonsson instead received a single telegram signed "Fair Park Property Owners." They agreed to meet, but still wanted him to see their own experts.[36]

By this time, the city had acquired 217 of 277 parcels at a cost of more than $2.3 million. One hundred and eighty-eight of those had been purchased through direct negotiations; twenty-nine through eminent-domain proceedings.[37]

More than fifty homeowners came to Jonsson's closed-door meeting. In a thoughtful presentation, he stressed his belief in the "dignity and value of the human being—rich or poor, black or white." Human beings such as himself, he said, are "fallible, subject to mistakes, misunderstandings." He admitted that he now suspected that city officials had treated the homeowners "in a thoughtless, perhaps even abrupt, unkind manner." For this he apologized.[38] But, he said, he could find no basis for a figure of $4 a square foot. If the properties had been worth that much, the owners would have been taxed at that rate.[39]

He showed slides depicting some of the homes, citing the prices the homeowners had paid for them and the larger amounts they now were being offered. He showed exterior and interior views of affordable housing in other parts of town that was available for amounts less than or equal to those being offered the homeowners.[40] He showed pictures of houses whose owners had already accepted the city's offers, and then pictures of their new houses purchased elsewhere for less than they had been paid for their previous ones.

Jonsson's script, thirty-eight pages long and illustrated with slides, brimming with precise detail and personal comments, appeared to be heartfelt. But it fell mostly on deaf ears. The homeowners demanded again that he meet with their own consultants. He reluctantly agreed to do so if they could come within a week. "The only thing I'm obligated to do is to listen to their so-called experts," he said afterward. "And I'm not making any commitment other than to listen." Asked whether he would have any future meetings with the homeowners, he replied, "I'm through with that."[41] Later, when asked to extend the imposed one-week deadline, he consulted with city attorney Bickley and followed his advice to decline. Further delays would interfere with ongoing condemnation proceedings.[42]

In November 1970, a civil action was filed against Jonsson and the City of Dallas to halt condemnation proceedings. A federal judge dismissed the case less than two months later.[43] In late 1971, Mike Wallace and a CBS-TV 60 Minutes crew came to Dallas and reported on the trouble. Acquisition of the remaining properties quietly moved forward, but was not completed until after Jonsson left office in 1971. One of the longest, potentially explosive episodes in Dallas history slowly reached a conclusion that pleased neither side.

The Fair Park dispute represented a critical moment in race relations in Dallas at a time when racial unrest in America was at its highest. As mayor and a wealthy white leader of the city's establishment, Jonsson found himself an easy target for accusations of racism. Afterward, the old ways of handling racial problems no longer would apply. Arising was a new generation of militant black leaders—future city council members Elsie Faye Heggins and Albert Lipscomb, transit board member J. B. Jackson Jr., the Reverend Peter Johnson (who remained in Dallas) and others—who refused to permit previous and more compliant African American leaders to negotiate on their behalf.

Erik Jonsson had never encountered such issues at TI, nor had his mayoral predecessors at city hall. During his last years in office, he sat patiently as increasingly strident African American leaders vented their frustrations and made demands that he and others on the council could not satisfy. Councilman Wes Wise, who would succeed Jonsson as mayor, wondered how one accustomed to chairing board meetings at TI could tolerate this for more than five seconds. Jonsson told him: "Wes, it's a lot better to let them get all of that off their chests in the council chambers then in the streets of Dallas."[44]

⤸

Jonsson's GOP connections were known. He continued to make financial contributions to the party. In 1966, when he gave $6,000 to the national party—a large amount at the time—he was one of only three Texans who contributed more than $5,000.[45] As a nonpartisan mayor, though, he refrained from involvement in local Republican politics. Requests for advice routinely came his way from Republican legislative candidates, but he inevitably declined, citing his nonpartisan position.[46]

He sometimes agreed to help national GOP candidates in less direct ways. In the summer of 1967, he sat at the head table for a well-publicized $100-a-plate dinner honoring Texas senator John Tower.[47] A few months later, he attended a luncheon at which California's governor, Ronald Reagan, spoke. He presided over the GOP's 1967 fund-raising effort at the Petroleum Club in Dallas. In that single event, he visited with two Republican congressmen who later would be presidents of the United States—Gerald Ford and George H. W. Bush.[48]

Such activities, as well as Jonsson's success as mayor, inevitably brought up discussion about his being a GOP candidate for statewide or national office. His possible candidacy as a gubernatorial nominee began to be speculated about in November 1967.[49]

In December, the New York Times reported that Republican insiders favored two candidates to replace incumbent governor John Connally, who would not run for reelection. Their first choice was George H. W. Bush, a newly elected U.S. congressman from Houston. The other was Mayor Erik Jonsson of Dallas. Bush, just elected to his first term in Congress, said he was inclined to stay there.[50]

That left Jonsson. A quick telephone poll indicated that he would be a formidable candidate against the possible Democratic nominee, U.S. senator Ralph W. Yarborough, who had a longtime itch to become governor. Of one hundred respondents, fifty-three favored Jonsson; twenty-nine, Yarborough; and eighteen, neither.[51] Party officials asked Jonsson, now sixty-six, to consider the race. He appreciated challenges; he enjoyed big stages; he knew he would not lack financial support; and the Republican Party wanted him. Party leaders believed that his presence on the ballot would benefit Republican state-legislative and congressional candidates.[52]

But Jonsson had projects in Dallas that would be "difficult to leave." He would have to "think very hard about something like this."[53] The filing deadline for primaries on February 5 was less than two weeks away. He was going to Houston the next day for a TI meeting, and he announced that he would decide afterward.

Meanwhile, 235 enthusiastic telegrams, many of them from Republican officials throughout the state, urged him to run. "The people of our state would reward your campaign efforts with a smashing victory at the polls in November," said Senator John Tower.[54] Richard Nixon, now an attorney in private practice and preparing for his own presidential race, called Jonsson twice while he was in Houston. He missed other calls that day, too, including those from Congressman Gerald Ford and H. L. Hunt.[55]

Back in Dallas, Jonsson said he would not be a candidate. For the past four years, he said, he had spent almost all his time and energy studying the problems of American cities in general and those of Dallas in particular. Now was not the time to leave that commitment. Cities were the "front line" in solving the problems of the day, and that was where he wanted to be.[56]

On that day, a Dallas County poll pitted Jonsson against Eugene M. Locke, the likely Democratic nominee for governor. Jonsson was favored, 71–29 percent. But he had decided; he would not run.[57] It was Preston E. Smith, the conservative Democratic lieutenant governor from West Texas, who would be elected governor. (Ten years later, William P. Clements Jr. become the state's first Republican governor in modern history.)

In the race for the presidency, Richard Nixon defeated Hubert Humphrey, giving Jonsson a friend in the White House. Their relationship dated to 1958, when Jonsson chaired the Economic Mobilization Conference. News surfaced that Nixon was considering Jonsson for several posts—secretary of commerce, secretary of health, education and welfare, or perhaps another cabinet position. The position he was most highly considered for, according to the Jonsson confidant George Schrader, was secretary of transportation.[58]

Charles G. Cullum, Jonsson's closest city council ally, knew that Jonsson was being "strongly considered" for a position in the new administration. As the spring 1969 city election approached, Jonsson asked Cullum to run for mayor if he went to Washington. Cullum agreed to do so if that eventuality occurred.[59] But a direct offer to Jonsson never came. As he noted, it would have been "exceedingly difficult" for him to serve in Washington, and he likely expressed this reluctance to the White House. An important reason was Margaret Jonsson's health, which recently had not been good.[60]

There was one high-profile, full-time position in Texas, though, that was attractive to Jonsson. James E. Webb, NASA's chief administrator, retired in 1968, and his successor awaited Nixon's appointment. Four days after Webb's retirement, *Apollo 7* orbited the earth. Plans were under way for the first landing on the moon. Jonsson, with his experience at TI, his engineering background, his involvement with high-security defense contracts, his success as mayor of a large city, and his record as a contributor to the Republican Party, had all the qualifications to succeed Webb, an attorney and Washington insider before his NASA appointment. A high authority representing Nixon advised Jonsson of the possibility. Jonsson believed he could not decline such an offer, nor did he want to. "When the president comes to you, you don't turn him down," he told George Schrader. Jonsson told Bryghte Godbold, staff director for Goals for Dallas, to pack his bags—he wanted him to move to Houston with him.[61]

But there was no announcement. Margaret Jonsson, still chafing over her husband's prolonged stay in the mayor's office, wanted no part of a move to Houston. How much should she be asked to endure?[62] For years she had sacrificed for her husband. Her health now had declined. She was through with sacrificing, and her husband understood that.[63] Jonsson finally sent word that he did not want to be considered. On March 21, 1969, Thomas O. Paine shed his "acting" prefix, and upon Nixon's nomination and Senate approval, he became administrator for NASA.

In the early spring of 1969 Jonsson faced another quandary. Should he run for a third term? Election would be a certainty. He had held the office for five years, more than fulfilling his obligation. The CCA had a long-standing tradition of two-term limitations—four years—for its officeholders. But there had been exceptions for mayors. Woodall Rodgers and Robert L. Thornton both had served four terms. There was growing sentiment, however, that if the two-term exception were made for Jonsson, other council members, some of whom coveted a third term, would deserve the same.

Jonsson's public references to "next year" and projects still in the mill made it seem likely that, whatever his wife's feelings, he would run. "Jonsson's dream of excellence is so urgent that he sometimes leaves his fellow civic leaders a little breathless," the *Dallas Times Herald* columnist Bert Holmes wrote. "He dares to dream big dreams." He had sometimes been impatient with city hall's ways, but as mayor he had looked at Dallas as a whole, for glue to unify it, and he had become a serious student of cities—reading, talking, inspecting, conferring with planners, professors, and officials of other cities and with federal officers. Who could replace such a man?[64]

Even Pleasant Grove's gadfly, Max Goldblatt, urged him to run for a third term. So much of the work he had done for Goals for Dallas and for the D/FW Airport might be lost if a "self-seeking" individual replaced him, Goldblatt said. Maurice Carlson, founder of the Dallas Charter League, which had opposed the CCA for years, also urged enthusiastic support for Jonsson.[65]

Jonsson had a demand of his own. He had feuded with incumbent CCA councilman Jesse Price of Pleasant Grove, and if the CCA endorsed Price again, he said he would not seek reelection, bringing criticism that he was seeking veto power over the CCA slate. He denied this, confirming only that he would not run on a ticket that had "weak spots."[66] When the CCA slate was announced in February 1969, Price's Place 7 was left blank. Price announced that he would campaign as an independent.

Jonsson's only opponent for the April 1, 1969, election was an unfunded independent candidate. Jonsson led the CCA ticket with 33,683 votes; his opponent, Herbert G. Green Jr., had 8,930. An independent candidate with strong name recognition, the former television newsman Wes Wise, easily defeated Henry Stuart, the CCA incumbent for Place 5, by a vote of 26,955 to 14,946. Price, as an independent, defeated Goldblatt in a runoff. He and Jonsson picked up where they had left off, butting heads on many issues at city hall.[67]

⌒

As a conservative, Jonsson had shared widespread sentiment in Dallas for the city to shun federal subsidies and address its own problems. His years as mayor, however, coincided with the advent of new and aggressive federal programs in President Lyndon Johnson's War on Poverty. Richard M. Nixon's ascendancy to the presidency did not change that, and indeed enhanced Jonsson's connections with Washington.

Urban problems simply could not be ignored, Jonsson knew, warning that U.S. cities would risk "another Watts" if they neglected areas where poverty and hunger existed. He at first had believed the city should address these problems without federal aid, but in 1967 he said that "if a slum is bad enough, I don't believe very many people will object to [federal] urban renewal." Six months later, Jonsson and the city council applied to the U.S. Department of Housing and Urban Development for $11.2 million in federal funds to assist South Dallas homeowners with home repairs. The mayor also signed a letter asking HUD to pay for two-thirds of the cost of a $1.5 million multiuse service center in South Dallas.[68]

Jonsson refused to go along with conservatives who sought to dismantle an agency of the War on Poverty, the Dallas Legal Services Project. Many viewed it as a hotbed of radicalism after its attorneys filed a series of class-action suits. Dallas county judge W. L. (Lew) Sterrett and others launched a fierce, headline-making campaign against the agency. Sterrett wanted the county government and the City of Dallas to withdraw sponsorship and to fire the chairman of the local War on Poverty effort, the SMU law school dean, Charles O. Galvin. Jonsson refused, and he met with the principal parties at his home. Afterward, he made the mistake of telling a *Times Herald* reporter that he had held the meeting "to let the judge blow off steam." Sterrett, a longtime courthouse figure with close ties to the business establishment, was incensed. He added Jonsson to his enemies' list. Sterrett won heavy community support for his position, but Jonsson remained firm, and the Legal Services Project continued.[69]

When Republican leaders in Congress sought in 1967 to trim the budget for the Office of Economic Opportunity, Jonsson was one of twenty-one big-city mayors who sent a telegram urging restraint.[70] A front-page headline in the *Dallas Times Herald* summed up his position: "Jonsson Likes U.S. Money." He was now so convinced of the necessity of federal-city partnerships that he thought Dallas might need a lobbyist in Washington. Since Nixon was in the White House, Jonsson was traveling frequently to Washington. "I got cooperation in the last administration when I began to look for it. Now, I get more. You have to look for it," he said. He especially was interested in federal financing for a mass transit system, noting that San Francisco had built its system with 90 percent federal financing. As for the old feeling that federal bureaucracy was always meddling in local operations and creating endless red tape, Jonsson now saw it as federal cooperation rather than federal interference.[71]

In 1967, Jonsson suggested that the city consider subsidizing bus route extensions to link indigent families with welfare agencies. In 1969 he emphasized that an efficient public transportation system could not be achieved solely by a city, a region, or a state. It required federal participation because mayors and council members were too busy fighting fires, dealing with crime, responding to citizens, handling mountains of correspondence, performing ceremonial duties, and giving speeches.[72]

Jonsson's growing insights into urban affairs were especially evident to new councilman Wes Wise. Wise, an independent, watched him with admiration. He noted that Jonsson was at his best in briefings preceding formal council meetings; he often initiated philosophical discussions on urban affairs and government, displaying knowledge that he had gained through his experience and curiosity. "I considered myself fortunate to be given this unusual preparation to possibly be mayor some day myself," Wise said years later. And indeed, Wise succeeded Jonsson as mayor.[73]

Shortly after leaving the mayor's office in 1971, Jonsson accepted appointment as cochairman of the Texas Citizens Committee for Revenue Sharing. The committee was affiliated with a national bipartisan lobbying group that generated support for legislation that sent federal money to local governments for such things as public safety, environmental protection, public transportation, and youth recreation programs.[74]

In a telegram to House Ways and Means Committee members, Jonsson said that seven years as mayor had convinced him that revenue sharing was "without qualification" the only practical way the nation's cities could meet their increasing demands for services.[75] He sent letters to mayors throughout Texas to garner support, and he sponsored a luncheon at which the chairman of the Congressional Task Force on Revenue Sharing explained the program to a room filled with about a hundred local officials and distinguished citizens.[76]

Jonsson's basic conservatism continued to be reflected in his opposition to labor unions. He opposed them at the municipal level because "their ability to strike and their predilection to do so when they feel it necessary" was not acceptable where matters of firefighting, policing, and health were concerned. Nor were there any unions at Texas Instruments. He believed that a direct relationship between management and employees produced greater benefits.[77]

City of Excellence

Erik Jonsson's critics said he hobnobbed only with the wealthy and prominent, and that the only time the average citizen could see him was while he presided at city council meetings. His old nickname, "Swede," might have helped. Recognizing that perceptions of aloofness might be a problem when he became mayor, he had sent word to the press that he preferred being identified as "Erik Jonsson," not "J. Erik Jonsson." In his 1969 reelection campaign, he said he wanted to meet more citizens, but it was impossible. His schedule was unbelievably full, and regardless of his desires, Nelle Johnston protected her boss from intrusions.[1]

Besides his duties as mayor, his responsibilities as chairman of the airport board in many ways duplicated those at city hall—attending board meetings and committee meetings, handling correspondence, serving as liaison with airport administrator Tom Sullivan, and giving press interviews. He had obligations as a TI board member, just as he did at Republic National Bank and Equitable Life Assurance. Goals for Dallas was an ongoing concern. His duties as chairman of the board at the Lamplighter School expanded in 1968 after he announced plans for a new $1.5 million building. Speeches across the continent, and frequent visits to New York City and Washington, D.C., were part of his schedule. He and Margaret tried to spend a month each summer at Lake Tahoe for their "annual rest."[2]

⌒

The unusual duties that came Jonsson's way were sometimes surprising. In March 1966, Prince Philip (husband of Queen Elizabeth II) visited Dallas as a guest of Braniff Airways. Jonsson was cohost with Braniff's Harding Lawrence. The prince toured Braniff's Love Field facilities, attended a luncheon at Brook Hollow Golf Club (Jonsson's favorite), and then held a press conference. A Braniff official advised reporters and cameramen that the prince would not answer "controversial, argumentative or political questions." Then he appeared, and after an initial awkwardness, dialogue flowed when he responded to a query about the usefulness of royalty in modern society. Royalty, he said, brings youthfulness—his wife was twenty-six when she ascended to the throne. "I doubt seriously if you would all be here for some 70-year-old president of a European country wondering what color underwear he wore," the prince said.[3]

That broke the ice. A reporter from a men's fashion publication assured the prince that he *would* like to know the color of his underwear. "Well, I wouldn't," the Prince retorted. The reporter continued, "Sir, do you wear polka dot underwear?" "Let's keep that under wraps, shall we?" the prince replied to great laughter. Then came a series of other frivolous questions and answers—how the prince felt about long hair for men and the like—that kept both the press and the royal visitor in high spirits.[4]

Jonsson was alarmed. He construed the lighthearted exchange to indicate a lack of respect for the prince. After this royal figure departed, Jonsson reprimanded the reporters for failing to treat him courteously. "I have never heard such unintelligent questions anywhere," the mayor said.[5] Learning of this, the British consul general in Dallas, C. J. Simpson, disagreed completely: "The Prince thought it was great fun—he obviously enjoyed it." A correspondent for the *Sunday Times* of London shared that view: "It was by far the best press conference the Prince has had during his trip."[6]

The notion that Jonsson selflessly gave so much time to the city he loved inspired some young Dallas entrepreneurs. About thirty of them—many destined to become important themselves in the city's affairs—formed a group in 1970 called the Dallas Leadership Council. With some trepidation, they invited Jonsson to speak at their first official meeting. Wanting to be as light a burden as possible on him, the chairman's letter asked Jonsson whether he could spend "about ten minutes" outlining how they might help Dallas.[7]

Jonsson accepted, but he shocked them when he appeared: "I'm insulted. I work my heart out for the city of Dallas and you want me to talk about it for ten minutes. Ten minutes? If you have any interest

at all meet me at the Petroleum Club a week from Saturday at 8 o'clock
in the morning and be prepared to stay the day and we will talk about
the problems of the City of Dallas. Thank you very much." Then he
walked out.[8]

The chastened young men showed up the next Saturday, beginning
a series of meetings with him. Important relationships formed. One
member of the group, an automobile dealer named Carl Sewell, later
served a term as chairman of the Goals for Dallas program. (Jonsson
told Sewell about his own experiences in the auto business: "I was kind
of a failure at what you're doing.")[9] Others in the group included Ray L.
Hunt, son of the oilman H. L. Hunt, who became one of the city's most
influential developers and head of the oil company his father founded;
Tom Luce, cofounder of what became one of the city's most prestigious
law firms, Hughes & Luce; and Tom Dunning, who became president of
the Dallas Citizens Council.

Jonsson tackled three unfinished projects during his final two years
in office: the city hall, the airport, and Goals for Dallas.

The 1967 Crossroads bond program included $42.4 million for the
city hall, $7.4 million less than what was needed. Pei's architectural
fee of $3.1 million raised eyebrows. A *Times Herald* editorial cartoon
showed the city hall as a pinball machine with costs bouncing ever
higher.[10] Thirteen of twenty-eight city department heads now were
located outside the present municipal building. "Drab rooms, cut-up
offices, desks jammed together and a lack of privacy are characteristic
of our headquarters facilities today," Scott McDonald said.[11]

But opposition to a new city hall nonetheless increased. Former
councilmen Joe Geary and William E. Cothrum both wanted voters
to take another look. Cothrum, who had butted heads with Jonsson
over the Cotton Bowl by siding with Clint Murchison, said a "credibility
gap" had arisen and that voters should be given another opportunity to
express themselves. John Stemmons also wanted the project resubmit-
ted to voters for confirmation.[12]

Jonsson found himself more and more alone, even on the city council. But he had no intention of resubmitting the issue to voters. Funds to
handle cost overruns could be developed by other means, he thought.[13]

Some of Jonsson's longtime supporters were turning against the
building. As the *Dallas Times Herald* reported in a page-one headline, "'Downtown' Sends City Hall the Word: Trim Spending." Jonsson

might face more than just a revolt of the common taxpayer, the story reported. There were indications that "wealthy, influential Dallas civic leaders" were headed for a showdown with Jonsson over the soaring costs. County commissioner Jim Tyson charged that city's officials were more interesting in building a "$40 million monument to themselves" than in solving the crime problems.[14]

As complaints grew louder, Jonsson redoubled his defense of Pei's building as a "symbol of the kind of dynamic, fast-moving, fast-growing, solid city we are." A design pleasing everyone, he said, would lack innovation. He deemed the plaza especially important because an excess of asphalt was endangering the heart of Dallas.[15]

At a dinner briefing for the city council in March 1970, Pei, representatives of the associated architects Harper & Kemp, Jonsson, and city manager Scott McDonald made a presentation about the building's potential benefits. "Each city has a turning point in history," Pei said, and this was such a time for Dallas. The building's forward-leaning design, he explained, was intended to indicate friendliness and an invitation to step inside. While the cost was higher than that of a conventional office building, every space was "custom-made" for municipal operations. "You can move right in," Pei said.[16]

Finally, excluding the $10 million in land costs, the low bid was $52.2 million, $5 million more than anticipated. Pei and the associated architects went back to the drawing board to design a "hollow shell" building with two-thirds of the interior incomplete. One of the three underground parking levels was omitted. Five weeks later, the council voted to ask for new bids on this scaled-down version.[17]

Criticism continued, though. Geary now complained that the new plan did not match what voters thought they were getting in the original bond program. Jonsson could not hide his irritation. When a man who identified himself as president of United Taxpayers Inc. appeared before the council to demand a new design, Jonsson questioned him about the size and background of his organization. Finally, Jonsson asked to see a copy of the organization's charter, which, of course, was not available.[18]

When new bids for four alternate plans with varying degrees of completeness were opened in September 1970, the low bidder once again was Robert E. McKee, Inc. This time the bids ranged from $23.1 million for a building with no interior furnishing to $27.7 million.[19]

At this point Jonsson unexpectedly asked the council to postpone the project indefinitely. His decision, he said, was based on economics, an uncertain business future, and the fact that the incomplete building would not fulfill original objectives. "I certainly had no desire to run over the people of Dallas and their wishes in any way," he said. Surprised council members complimented the mayor. Both newspapers editorially hailed his decision.[20]

Pei was disappointed. He said his firm had entered the project when Goals for Dallas was being initiated, a time of great expectations. "They wanted Dallas to be something special," Pei said. "We came in under that atmosphere. Since then, there has been this great change."[21] Tom Sullivan, director of the D/FW Airport, sent a note to Jonsson: "I was truly proud of you as I watched you on TV last night. . . . It must have been most difficult to reach such a decision, and it took a big man to make it!"[22] A few citizens declared postponement a mistake. More, though, cheered the halt and urged that the plans be dropped entirely. Nelle Johnston carefully tagged the numerous letters with a "for" or "against" notation.[23]

The drama was not over. One week later, the chairman of the Dallas Board of Realtors reported to the city council that his board had voted 19–1 in favor of the project. His comments sparked a discussion. Jonsson acknowledged that he "would be delighted if a groundswell of opinion would say 'go ahead and build it.'" Two days later, the Dallas chapter of the American Institute of Architects and the Home and Apartment Builders of Metropolitan Dallas also called for construction without undue delay. Council members began discussing another bond issue or a referendum.[24] Further incentive came from the Dallas chapter of the Associated General Contractors of America, whose president estimated that a five-year delay could virtually double the cost to $49.6 million.[25]

Some cynics saw Jonsson's secret hand behind this spurt of interest, but he insisted that he no longer was active in the matter.[26] Behind the scenes, though, he had been working to revive the project. According to the mayor pro tem, Jack McKinney, Jonsson hinted to him that if he took the lead in resurrecting the project, he would be in a good position to be the city's next mayor. McKinney took the bait. Jonsson also approached John Schoellkopf, a rising young civic leader who had just left an executive position with the *Dallas Times Herald*, and told him that he anticipated holding a new municipal bond election to cover the deficit for the building. He asked Schoellkopf to take the lead in promoting it. Schoellkopf, who lived across the street from the mayor, hesitated. He wanted to think about it. His hesitancy visibly angered Jonsson, and Schoellkopf quickly agreed to head such a campaign.[27]

At McKinney's request, the council voted to hold such an election in November. Voters would be asked for approval to sell the needed bonds to complete a finished building.[28] City manager McDonald calculated that the amount needed would be approximately $9.6 million, an amount so high that it dismayed many council members. Nevertheless, they authorized city attorney Bickley to prepare the documents for a bond election on November 24, 1970.[29]

McKinney was out of town when McDonald made his presentation, and he was shocked to learn of the amount. "I bought a paper and almost fell into the ocean," he said, adding that if the figure truly were around $10 million, he wanted to withdraw his motion for the bond election. Other councilmen were tight-lipped, but at least five of them were thought to have second thoughts about the election.[30]

The success of such an election required the support of the Dallas Citizens Council, which typically funded expensive campaigns to win voter approval on such matters. Jonsson called the DCC's executive committee into private session and asked for its support. Schoellkopf and Bickley accompanied him. Jonsson always found kindred spirits among these civic-minded men. Many of them were his closest friends. His request, though, prompted a spirited debate. Committee members were deadlocked, 7–7, and the motion to support the election failed. Schoellkopf saw the mayor in tears. "If the people who are the backbone of this town won't support this project, I don't know who will," he said.[31]

McKinney, as he had indicated, withdrew his motion for a bond election, and the city council supported him.[32] The project Jonsson had envisioned and nurtured since his early days as mayor seemed moribund. Nearly $25 million in authorized bonds were unissued. Architectural blueprints for which the city had paid $3.1 million seemed wasted.

Yet, incredibly, three months later, the situation again changed. McKinney offered and won council approval for a resolution directing the city manager to review the project's status. Jonsson, with less than three months remaining as mayor, was elated, but he would have to wait until his term was over for the city manager's report.[33]

↬

In the summer of 1970, Goals for Dallas entered its third stage—

achieving the goals. Jonsson wanted the support of as many citizens as possible, and after five years approximately 100,000 citizens had participated. Many goals were under way or already had been achieved: public school kindergartens, expanded use of public school buildings, a pretrial release system, expansion of family planning services, a human relations commission, a plan for the downtown area, and numerous public buildings. In July 1970, Jonsson estimated that progress was being made on almost 90 percent of the goals.[34]

To celebrate, some 1,800 volunteer workers were guests for "Dinner with Bob Hope" at the Apparel Mart. Jonsson personally escorted the comedian to the event in his city limousine. In the type of arrangement that so frequently irritated Margaret, her husband asked city manager McDonald to give her a ride. At the televised event, the famous comedian told the audience that Goals for Dallas had inspired the rest of the country.[35]

A number of cities now had similar programs. Jonsson visited some of them. Albuquerque honored him as the "father of municipal goals programs." In Lubbock, he drew a standing ovation at the Chamber of Commerce's annual banquet.[36] San Jose, California; Abilene, Texas; Lansing, Michigan; College Park, Maryland; and Wichita, Kansas, were among other cities that instituted goals programs.

An invitation came from President Nixon for Jonsson to discuss an "Institute for National Objectives," to be modeled after Goals for Dallas. The distraction of Watergate, however, ended this possibility.[37]

The greatest recognition for Goals for Dallas came in the 1970 All-America City competition sponsored by the National Municipal League and *Look* magazine. The award brought prestige and publicity that was largely without parallel. In July 1970, Jonsson signed his name to a five-page entry for Dallas, the linchpin of which was the Goals program. In early 1971 came the news that Dallas was the largest of eleven winners of the All-American City competition for 1970 and the only winner to be saluted in a two-page profile. The city, at last, seemed to be out from under the dark cloud that had been hanging over it since 1963.

Look's story, appearing on March 23, 1971, highlighted the Goals program and its creator, Mayor Erik Jonsson, "a transplant from the Northeast." The largest photograph, extending across two pages, showed two police officers in a storefront office, listening intently to a black man telling of problems with his landlord. Another photograph depicted a nurse in a neighborhood health center helping a young black child. A third portrayed a small black boy enjoying a free school lunch that was helping him become "a better scholar."[38]

Both daily newspapers published special sections on the award. The week of April 12–18 was officially proclaimed All-America City Week, observed by churches with "special sermons, music or prayers." Civic clubs hosted speakers from the Goals for Dallas Speakers Bureau. The Dallas Symphony gave a celebratory "dollar concert." At midweek a huge civic luncheon attended by Goals workers, citizens, and public officials was held, where a representative of the National Municipal League presented the award to Jonsson.[39]

Official All-America flags were displayed at city hall and other public buildings; new shoulder patches with the All-America emblem were provided to uniformed city employees; and a wide range of other promotional activities were undertaken. The city council passed a resolution congratulating the mayor "for his foresightedness and outstanding leadership."[40]

With each passing year, Jonsson found it more difficult to control council meetings. The growing militancy of African American leaders who showed him disdain was taking a heavy toll. One of the most persistent, Albert Lipscomb, now appeared at each Monday's city council meeting as a watchdog for signs of racism. Bearded, beaded, and wearing his hair in an Afro, he was to many a frightening figure as he roared his disapproval or spoke from the podium. Occasionally, when he resisted the mayor's efforts to silence him, police escorted him from the council chamber. (In 1984, Lipscomb would be elected to the city council.)[41]

Even Jonsson's fellow CCA city council members were less accommodating. They had followed him only reluctantly, if at all, on the new city hall. Its rejection by the DCC, many of whom were his best friends, had been terribly disappointing. Now in his last term, Jonsson later acknowledged that it had been time to "get out of there" and he was ready.[42]

The *Dallas Times Herald*, sensing his frustration, urged readers to thank him for his work: "He needs to know that his many 18-hour days of public service have borne much fruit. He needs to know that his dedication to his job and his community have made him one of the most respected mayors of the nation. . . . He is an honest, keenly intelligent man who loves his city. What he doesn't get is a kind word now and then from those who could say: 'Mayor, you are one great guy and we thank you.'"[43] Letters and notes of heartfelt appreciation quickly filled his mailbox. Deeply touched, he thanked each writer. "The friendship of Dallas people is the richest reward one could have" was a phrase he used in many of his written responses.[44]

The DCC honored him at its December 1970 annual meeting, where former governor John Connally called him a leader of "wisdom, vision and courage" who endured the slings and arrows of those who always direct them at those holding public office. Robert B. Cullum, master of ceremonies, presented Jonsson with a pair of platinum cufflinks for his service as mayor.[45]

⌐

In November 1969, an announcement was made that Jonsson was acquiring one of the city's major radio-broadcasting entities, the news-oriented KRLD-AM and KRLD-FM. He told George Schrader that he had been dissatisfied with the quality of news coverage, and that owning the station, generally the top-rated one in town, would be the realization of his thwarted ambition when the Columbia School of Journalism declined to admit him. He was buying the station in behalf of his family, although none of the three children expressed any enthusiasm for the idea.[46]

The sale was completed for $6.75 million two months after Jonsson left the mayor's office. He had decided to take no role in the station's operations, but he held nonvoting debentures. Besides his three children, KRLD Corporation would have just two other stockholders, his TI friends C. J. Thomsen and Robert W. Olson.[47]

KRLD, founded in 1926, was one of the city's oldest stations. Its 50,000 watts of power on the AM frequency meant that it reached an average radius of 150 miles during daylight hours and the entire Southwest in the evening. Despite excellent ratings, the station was not a significant moneymaker. During the Jonssons' ownership, that would change, especially after the station acquired the rights to broadcast the Dallas Cowboys' football games. In early 1978, the three Jonsson children, who by then had bought out Thomsen and Olson, sold the radio station's AM and FM entities to different owners at twice the amount paid for them.[48] Philip, who had taken offices adjacent to his father's in the Republic Bank Tower during these years, moved on to other long-lasting broadcasting interests outside Dallas.

⌐

The dynamics of Dallas were changing; the old guard was under attack; the antiestablishment mood was gaining ground. But Jonsson believed that business-minded leadership was needed more than ever. He wanted his successor as mayor to have good business experience. Charles G. Cullum especially suited him. It had been two years since Cullum had completed his second term on the council. He had been the mayor's closest ally. Following Jonsson's request, Cullum earlier had been ready to run for the office if Jonsson took a government job in Washington. Now, with Jonsson's support, he was ready.[49]

With Jonsson's approval and as a gesture to the changing times, the CCA anointed John Schoellkopf as its president, a realization that the association had to appeal to younger voters. Schoellkopf's important assignment was to identify a slate of council candidates. He would propose Cullum as the mayoral candidate. Following traditional CCA practice, Schoellkopf worked behind the scenes to ensure support for Cullum from the two biggest banks. First National Bank's Robert H. Stewart III, who had opposed the new city hall, surprised him. He told Schoellkopf that his directors and officers had had a "belly full" of Erik Jonsson because he had been belittling First National's civic contributions as compared with Republic's. First National would support any number of candidates for mayor, Stewart said, but not Cullum, who, like Jonsson, was a Republic Bank man.[50]

Taken aback, Schoellkopf called on Aston at Republic Bank. Aston, also surprised at the reaction, observed that the banks always had worked together, and it was important that they not now became embroiled in a fight over Cullum. Consequently, Cullum would not do.[51] To Schoellkopf fell the chore of telling Cullum that he would not get the CCA nomination. Finally, a compromise candidate from the Oak Cliff section, Avery Mays, the owner of a construction firm with a record of civic involvement, was anointed as the CCA candidate.

Wes Wise, the popular independent city councilman and former television sportscaster, announced early for the position as independent. Jonsson discouraged him, citing his lack of business experience. Wise aptly replied: "Does this mean no lawyer, no accountant, no journalist can ever be mayor of the City of Dallas?" The activist Albert Lipscomb also filed, becoming the city's first African American mayoral candidate. Four other minor candidates, including a television chef, ran for the office. It was the most hotly contested race in years.[52]

Jonsson, surprisingly, refused to endorse Mays, preferring to appear to be not involved. Yet he obviously favored him as the CCA candidate. Voters, he hoped, would not make decisions "on one or two shallow characteristics" such as "a pretty face with naught behind it."[53] Mays enjoyed the CCA's financial backing and endorsement by both daily newspapers, factors that inevitably brought automatic election. Wise, young, handsome, and energetic, had far greater name recognition and a flair for communicating. Both major candidates endorsed the new city hall and promised to get it built. Both promised full support for Dallas/Fort Worth Regional Airport. Wise emphasized his ability to relate to all people in Dallas. He carried an empty chair to his campaign appearances to dramatize Mays's reluctance to debate him. Mays touted his civic and business experience. In the April election, Mays, as expected, earned more votes than anyone, but not enough to avoid a runoff with Wise.

In the runoff, Wise won a smashing victory, 57,776 to 39,947, becoming the first non-CCA mayor in three decades. Jesse Price, shorn of his CCA backing and now an independent, also won reelection, but CCA candidates captured all other seats. "We just got licked," Jonsson said.[54] Wise's victory signaled important attitude changes in Dallas. As second-term winner Garry Weber, a CCA man himself, explained, voters were "sick" of having CCA candidates "crammed" down their throats. A new era had arrived, a fact acknowledged by a CCA-commissioned study that concluded an increasing number of residents were simply outside the business community's domain.[55]

At the first council meeting after the election, as Wise prepared to take his regular place at the end of the horseshoe-shaped table, he was startled to see the mayor approaching him, half running, with his big hand extended. "Congratulations," Jonsson told him. "You did it and you did it clean."[56]

The initial furor against the new city hall was spent. Early in his term of office, Wise said he kept hearing from other mayors who asked him when that great new city hall was going to be built. Further cost-saving adjustments were made, and in May 1972, with Jonsson sitting in the chambers as a spectator, new bids were opened. Robert E. McKee, Inc., again was low bidder, this time at $30.1 million for the building alone, less than anticipated.[57]

The project went forward. In August 1972, Jonsson, Pei, and Wise donned hard hats and broke ground together. Pei complimented both men: "With Mayor Jonsson you have a dream. Now with Mayor Wise

you are about to realize that dream." It was an occasion, he said, to celebrate the wisdom of the people who had elected Jonsson and Wise and
the councils with which they served. "It was Wes Wise who finally got
the contracts signed," Jonsson acknowledged.[58]

Four years later, as the uncompleted project took recognizable shape,
the *New York Times* architectural critic Ada Louise Huxtable wrote a
glowing review. Although "style," she wrote, was a word one hesitated
to use in Dallas, the new city hall—or officially the Municipal Administration Center (Pei called it the MAC)—would be "one of the most
important public buildings in the country." It was a "decisive architectural image-maker" for which Dallas "should feel nothing but pride."[59]

For Jonsson, the building almost literally represented Dallas.
"It's strong, and the people of Dallas are strong people. Concrete is
simple, and they are simple people—in the best sense of the word,
plain people."[60]

The completed building opened in 1978, having cost a total of more
than $70 million. Jonsson (approaching his seventy-seventh birthday),
Pei, and Wise were joined for the ceremony by new mayor Robert Folsom, former city manager McDonald, and the present city manager,
George Schrader. Pei, always eager to credit Jonsson, wrote to him afterward: "There would be no building without your unflagging support."[61]

Jonsson told Pei later that one of the highest compliments he had
heard was that employees came early and stayed late. With the completion of this stunning building that forever would be identified with
them, their friendship grew even closer.[62]

A Busy "Retirement"

Aweek before leaving office, Erik Jonsson, nearly seventy, told Ot Hampton, a *Dallas Times Herald* reporter, that he now would pursue his youthful dream of becoming a writer.[1] His first book would deal with local government and how to improve it. Next would be his memoir.[2]

He hoped, Margaret's health permitting, to travel with her. Perhaps he would do some gardening. He would maintain offices at the Republic National Bank Tower with Nelle Johnston and additional secretarial help. He would boost Dallas, but not become a "Monday morning quarterback."[3]

If the "retired" mayor and industrialist really thought he was going to become a writer, he miscalculated. His published writing would be confined to an introduction to a coffee-table book about Dallas.[4] By choice he continued as chairman of the boards of both the Dallas/Fort Worth International Airport and Goals for Dallas. He still had responsibilities at Texas Instruments. He accepted speaking engagements. His service on a number of boards required travel. There was no lessening of his involvement with institutions across the country. His correspondence was unrelenting. Leaving the mayor's office signaled his supposed availability to old friends, recent acquaintances, and strangers, who felt freer than ever to approach him.[5] He tried to be resolute in refusing additional commitments, promising this not only to himself but also "more importantly to my lady," a term he sometimes substituted for "Mama."[6]

A week after her husband left the mayor's office, Margaret became temporarily bedridden. Precisely what ailed her was uncertain. In

November, she was hospitalized for at least two weeks. Jonsson began declining almost all evening engagements so he could be with her.[7]

In November 1972, he finally relinquished leadership of Goals for Dallas. Of more than a hundred specific goals, 27 percent had been achieved and substantial progress made in another 43 percent. His financial commitment was larger than most knew. Most of the $1.3 million spent had come from his pocketbook. The program would continue until 1992.[8]

Certain invitations could not be declined. The National Business Hall of Fame installed him in 1975 in Chicago as one of only four living inductees, joining past giants such as Henry Ford, John D. Rockefeller, J. Pierpont Morgan, Alfred P. Sloan, Andrew Carnegie, George Eastman, and Thomas A. Edison. *Fortune* magazine hailed him for proving that a new company could best "such giants as General Electric and RCA for leadership of the transistor market."[9]

↫

Some political involvements could not be resisted. He and Margaret went to former governor John Connally's ranch at Floresville, Texas, for a gala affair honoring President Nixon and his wife. A *New York Times Magazine* photograph showed the Jonssons at the serving line with the Nixons and Connally.[10]

Not long afterward, Jonsson agreed to chair Nixon's 1972 reelection campaign in Texas. He predicted an easy Nixon victory because the Democrats were "so badly split" and front-runner George McGovern was "pretty far left."[11] That was about as severe as he wanted to get in his comments. His dislike for the rough-and-tumble aspects of politics likely brought the appointment of William P. Clements Jr. as his cochairman. Clements was a newcomer to politics, but he was plainspoken and effective. After Nixon's victory, Clements was appointed deputy secretary of defense. Later, he would become the first Republican governor of Texas since Reconstruction.[12]

Jonsson concentrated on raising money. Under his leadership, gross proceeds in Texas for the series of "Salute to the President" dinners in November 1971 reached $222,209. In the following September, twenty-three "Texas Victory" dinners at $1,000 a plate added about $100,000 to the Nixon campaign chest.[13]

Although the Watergate break-in already had occurred, Nixon thus far had escaped implication. Jonsson was irate when his own name appeared briefly. His name was a minor part of the story in Washington, but it made headlines for one day in Dallas. His supposed link came when the *Washington Star* reported that Jonsson's name was on a secret list of four Texans whose contributions by check had wound up in the bank account of one of the men involved in the break-in. This allegation, Jonsson charged, was "completely irresponsible, and probably libelous," for although he had made sizeable contributions to the Republican Party, they had been done through transfers of stock (worth $25,746.75) and not by checks. His name disappeared as quickly as it had surfaced.[14]

&

On January 31, 1972, Jonsson's fourth two-year appointment to the Dallas/Fort Worth Airport board would end. Yielding his chairmanship would offer his schedule great relief. But with the airport's dedication approaching, he was in no mood for such a change, although he had been chairman longer than anticipated. Fort Worth had understood that the chair would be rotated regularly between the cities, but at the end of Jonsson's first term, he had provided such strong leadership that Fort Worth's representatives preferred not to upset the progress. Thus, Jonsson continued as chairman into his second, third, and fourth terms. Now he wanted a fifth term. Wes Wise, the new mayor, reappointed him to the board, and board members unanimously reelected him to his fifth consecutive term as chairman.[15]

As the September 20–23, 1973, dedication approached, Jonsson's personal schedule was as "vicious" as he had ever known it to be. He found time to send an invitation to his old buddy Malcolm Bedell in New Jersey. Bedell wrote back: "This may be the most valuable of your many contributions to the region." He wanted him to "stop off for a mug of moonshine" whenever in the area. If he would let him know, he would "fire up the still."[16]

&

The four-day dedication likely was unmatched in aviation history. Former governor Connally was the "commissioner general." Dignitaries, diplomats, public officials, airport executives, journalists, business leaders, entertainers (Doc Severinsen, Willie Nelson, and Peter Nero among them), military parachute and flying teams, pilots of antique airplanes, and trick aerialists were prominent. Nixon sent White House counselor Anne Armstrong, a Texan, as his substitute. The Concorde SST, which had never before landed on North American soil, flew in.[17]

A Friday-evening party attracted about 7,500 people, far more than the anticipated 5,500. The traffic jam caused both Connally and Jonsson, the hosts, to be late. Parking was a nightmare. Some guests waited afterward for four hours for attendants to retrieve their automobiles.[18]

The airfield's enormous size impressed everyone. It was three times as big as New York's Kennedy, twice the size of Chicago's O'Hare, and six times as big as Los Angeles International. It was twenty times as big as Love Field and twice the size of any airport ever built. A *Washington Post* reporter noted that it would barely fit inside the District of Columbia. One visitor quipped that birds at the north end could fly to the south end for the winter.[19]

On January 14, 1974, the airport opened—a year behind schedule because of problems with the automated system for moving passengers, baggage, and mail.[20] Love Field yielded its position as the world's tenth-busiest airport to D/FW, which within three years would be the nation's fourth busiest. Two runways and four terminals handled more than 800 flights a day. Ample space was available for expansion. D/FW Airport had its own zip code, and it was believed to be the first airport with its own telephone exchange.[21]

By 2013, D/FW was generating more than $16 billion a year for the North Texas economy, or more than a million dollars every hour, with some sixty million passengers passing through annually. Direct flights throughout North America and the world inspired the relocation of so many big companies to the area that it eventually boasted being home to the nation's third-largest number of Fortune 500 companies.[22]

Upon completion of his term in early 1975, Jonsson left the board. When board members in 1984 observed the airport's tenth anniversary, they declared Jonsson to be "the man most responsible" for making it a reality and created the annual J. Erik Jonsson Aviation Award for the person making unusually significant contributions to aviation.[23]

↜

Dallas was on a high horse. The airport was thriving; city hall was under construction; a new central library was planned. Skyscrapers seemed to pop up every month. The outlandish television soap opera *Dallas* glamorized the city.

Political dynamics at city hall continued to change, and in Jonsson's opinion, for the worse. He continued to believe that election of council members by citywide vote was best. The *Dallas Morning News* columnist Carolyn Barta chided him for his "Father knows best" attitude. He was, Barta said, a part of that core of dedicated business and civic leaders who liked to make decisions and then "spoon-feed" them to the average citizen.[24]

The CCA declined to field a mayoral candidate against Wise in 1973, and the former newsman won his second term. CCA candidates still dominated the council, but many of them acted as independents. John Schoellkopf had broadened the organization's slate of candidates to include not just conservative businessmen but liberals and minorities.

In January 1975, U.S. district judge Eldon Mahon struck down Jonsson's favored at-large system because it gave undue power to white-dominated groups "such as the Citizens Charter Association." In response, the city council devised an 8–3 plan in which eight members would be elected from single-member districts and three, including the mayor, by citywide vote. Candidates in single-member districts now could win by gaining only the support of their districts.[25]

Jonsson joined Schoellkopf in seeking a high-profile CCA candidate to prevent Wise from winning a third term. Jonsson's criteria were record of service, feelings about the city, capability for the job, and electability.[26] But no candidates surfaced. Jonsson's friend and Republic Bank associate James W. Aston declined to run. So did Robert Folsom, a developer and former SMU football hero who bemoaned that the CCA had "lost touch with the people." Louis Weber Jr., president of the Dallas Bar Association, also demurred. "If people are indifferent and politicians mediocre," Jonsson said, "we will do what cities have done in the past—live on the short-range goals and neglect the long-range ones." Schoellkopf lamented that "the establishment, as it once was, is dead, and we can't put it together again." Finally, Schoellkopf entered the race himself—against Jonsson's wishes.[27] Wise won a third term. In years to come, conservative businessmen would routinely be elected mayor, but they, along with other council members, would be independents. Jonsson was the last CCA mayor. Schoellkopf's successor as CCA president, Dave Braden, announced in 1976 that the CCA probably would never again make political endorsements.[28]

Jonsson, disappointed, believed that business leadership had to reassert itself. Dissolution of the CCA, he believed, would introduce political partisanship at city hall. In single-member council districts, politicians rather than civic leaders would take over. The day of the enlightened, civic-minded citizen who ran for office out of a sense of public duty rather than for personal gain, he felt certain, was threatened.[29]

With these thoughts, Jonsson sent letters to twenty-six business-men in February 1977, inviting them to a Petroleum Club luncheon to discuss the matter. Fourteen sent their regrets. The meeting was held, but it merited only a brief newspaper notice.[30] No more such meetings took place.

Jonsson also wanted to modify the council-manager plan by giving the mayor "a little more power" to compensate for the independent power base of those elected from single-member districts. For instance, the mayor might be given veto power that could be overridden by a majority (or two-thirds or three-fourths) vote.[31] (Twenty-four years later, in 2005, Dallas voters twice rejected charter changes to strengthen the mayor's powers.)

What concerned Jonsson in 1981 was the tendency in a single-member-district system for council members to engage in mutual back-scratching: "Very often this leads to the support of projects that are not as sound as they might be in exchange for support of a councilman's own pet projects."[32] (By 2009 this had become an acknowledged prob-lem, identified as one of the reasons for the greatest scandal in Dallas municipal history. The mayor pro tem, Don Hill, was convicted in a federal court for bribery and sentenced to thirty years in prison. The head of the city plan commission and thirteen others, including devel-opers, also were found guilty or pleaded guilty.)

⌒

By the end of the 1980s, downtown Dallas had a huge amount of empty office space as businesses, department stores, and movie the-aters departed for the suburbs. William Whyte declared in 1988 that the American city that had done the most to kill off its streets was Dallas. One gathered, he wrote, that the proponents of its tunnel and skybridge system would be delighted if pedestrians could be eliminated from the streets altogether.[33] In fact, that is exactly what Jonsson and city plan-ners Vincent Ponte and Warren Travers had had in mind—keeping the streets free for traffic and placing pedestrians in the underground tun-nels and on skybridges.

Dallas's downtown public library, built in 1955, had obvious inade-quacies—no parking, overcrowded shelves, limited research space, and other problems. Goals for Dallas stressed the need for library improve-ments, and in their 1967 city hall presentation, Jonsson, Pei, and city planners proposed a new central library.

In 1972, the city council approved the tract directly north of the new city hall as its site. Fisher and Spillman Architects were hired, surely pleasing Jonsson, for Pat Y. Spillman had written the Goals for Dallas essay "The Design of the City."[34] The architects designed a ten-story structure with 600,000 square feet and the capacity to hold 2.3 million volumes. Featuring an inverted center portion and bold lines, it was a perfect counterpart to the new city hall across the street. Of course, there was not enough money for its estimated cost of $37 million—$44 million after furniture, equipment, and professional fees were added. A bond issue supplemented by federal funds left a shortfall of about $10 million.[35]

Jonsson told city manager George Schrader that he would raise the money himself, and he did. Often in tandem with the library's director, Lillian Bradshaw, he began calling on foundations and affluent Dallas citizens, and with about half of the goal collected, groundbreaking ceremonies were held in December 1977. Across the street, municipal workers were moving into the long-delayed city hall. Jonsson said he would be unable to wait that long for the library.[36]

By the time the fund-raising effort ended, Jonsson had collected more than $13 million (including $2 million from himself) in private contributions, $3 million more than the original goal. In April 1982, the Dallas Central Library opened with a week of special programs, exhibits, and activities. Bradshaw, who had had a long and distinguished career as the library's first female director, sent a heartfelt letter to Jonsson: "We would not have had our fine new Central Library without the forethought, the help, and the guidance you gave us." Jonsson responded, saying that of all his undertakings, the library may well have the greatest influence on the lives of others.[37]

Dallas entrepreneur Ross Perot, a friend but not an especially close associate, saw a need to correct what he considered to be an oversight. Despite Jonsson's contributions to Dallas, no building bore his name. Perot worked behind the scenes to change the name of D/FW International Airport to Jonsson (even winning the assent of Fort Worth leaders), but Jonsson had absolutely refused. Perot, still working without publicity, shifted his efforts to the library. In August 1986, city council members changed its name to the J. Erik Jonsson Central Library.[38]

Thanking the council for that honor, the eighty-four-year-old Jonsson choked back tears. "Now you've hit me where I live," he said. Not forgotten was the fact that eleven of the city's eighteen branch libraries had been opened during his tenure as mayor. Mayor A. Starke Taylor

Jr. declared the library a "lasting monument" to Jonsson. "Erik Jonsson will always be mayor," he said. "The rest of us have just kind of been substitutes."[39]

⤿

Probably no institution appreciated Erik Jonsson more than Rensselaer Polytechnic, whose trustees declared in 1990 that "never before in the history of Rensselaer" had an individual made a greater impact on RPI than Jonsson. Through December 1979, he and Margaret had given $10.1 million to the institution, and more was to follow. He had served as an RPI trustee for thirty-five years.[40]

Jonsson's devotion to Skidmore College included seventeen years as a member of its board of visitors, including a term as chairman. Skidmore celebrated his ninetieth birthday on the campus with a huge party featuring Texas-style barbecue and country music. David Porter, the college's president, said that without Jonsson, Skidmore "would be a profoundly different place."[41]

His contributions to the University of Texas System were recognized in December 1977 with the Santa Rita Award, the system's highest honor.[42] His role in creating the University of Texas at Dallas was widely known, but fewer knew of his deeds for the Southwestern Medical School at the University of Texas Southwestern Medical Center. There, he and Margaret had endowed two chairs, one in medicine in honor of his friend and physician Paul J. Thomas, and another in surgery; provided an unrestricted endowment fund; contributed generously to school programs; and given funds to landscape the campus.[43]

⤿

But surely the most significant contribution occurred after two of the medical school's most accomplished physician-researchers, Michael Brown and Joseph Goldstein, were being enticed to join the University of California, San Francisco medical school as directors of a new research institute to be funded with an endowment of approximately $25 million. Charles C. Sprague, Southwestern's president, could not match this lucrative offer, but he and Dr. Donald Seldin, chairman of the internal medicine department, were absolutely convinced that retaining these scientists was critical to Southwestern's future success. Sprague went to Jonsson for help. Jonsson guaranteed whatever was needed to keep the two. He immediately pledged $200,000 and prevailed upon a handful of other philanthropists for additional money.[44]

Jonsson called Brown and Goldstein to come see him in his top-floor office at the Republic Bank Tower ("As close to God as you could get in Dallas in 1977," Brown later recalled). He led them to his floor-to-ceiling windows on three sides and pointed with pride to the institutions in the distance that he had played an important part in building—D/FW Airport, the new city hall, the new downtown library, and others. Then he made his pitch: "Boys, I understand you have a lucrative offer in San Francisco. First of all, you should never consider living in California. It's a terrible place to live, especially if you are raising children." From there he continued his arguments for Dallas and the benefits of staying at Southwestern. He took a small piece of paper and wrote a number on it. "The leaders of Dallas will never let your research fail for lack of money. If you need money for any purpose whatsoever—be it a salary for an associate or an expensive piece of equipment, or anything else. Here is my home telephone number. If you need money for any specific purpose whatsoever, please call this number. A check will be on your desk the next morning."[45]

"As we left Erik's office we were literally on cloud nine," Brown later recalled. The most powerful man in Dallas had promised that we would never lack resources for our science. What could possibly be more reliable than that?" The two physician-researchers rejected the offer in San Francisco and stayed in Dallas.[46]

In 1985, Brown and Goldstein, the "Gold Dust Twins," won the most prestigious award of all, the Nobel Prize in Medicine. Their research on cholesterol metabolism directly made possible the development of what often are called one of the wonder drug groups of the twentieth century—the statins. The Nobel Prize brought worldwide attention not only to Brown and Goldstein, but also to the medical school and to Dallas as a center of medical research. It was the first time the Nobel Prize had been awarded to any individual doing research in Texas. By 2013, five Nobel Prizes had been awarded to faculty members for work done at the UT Southwestern Medical Center.[47]

On Jonsson's eightieth birthday party the two scientists sent their benefactor a congratulatory telegram:

To Erik:
Who has a city at his feet,
New plans up his sleeve,
And a pair of Nobel Laureates in his back pocket.
Happy birthday.[48]

∽

When, in 1982, Jonsson addressed the graduating class at the University of Texas at Dallas, he returned to the theme of research and development. "We shall face a critical shortage of scientists and engineers in many fields—*at least for the next decade*," he said. "We must address this issue quickly, for the hour grows late." In the 1950s, he said, some 80 percent of all technological innovations were marketed first by Americans, but now that figure was less than 50 percent. Spending for research and development was in a ten-year slump.[49]

Especially disappointing to him was UTD's failure to establish an engineering school. Jonsson believed that this lapse violated a gentleman's agreement. For reasons that were political as well as practical, it had not been achieved. For one thing, the nearby University of Texas at Arlington already had an engineering school. As an established part of the UT system, it had priority for engineering resources. Dallas civic leaders and SMU officials worried about the impact of a nearby tax-supported engineering program with much lower tuition. SMU had a powerful ally—William P. Clements Jr., governor of Texas from 1979 and 1983 and an ardent Mustang supporter. Approval for an engineering school at UTD had to be given by the University of Texas System's board of regents, who were appointed by the governor and not immune to political pressures.

More than ever, Jonsson believed that Dallas and the area needed more engineers to compete with other high-tech centers. A principal reason for UTD's failure to create an engineering school thus far, he declared, was Governor Clements, "a fellow that wants to see SMU have all the engineering students." Since Clements would be leaving the governor's mansion in 1983, Jonsson was optimistic about future prospects.[50]

The value of land and buildings given to the UT System by the TI founders' Excellence in Education Foundation was no small matter. The original 1969 gift was worth an estimated $50 million by 1985; the 1975 gift of 500 acres was believed now to have a potential value of approximately $200 million.[51]

UTD officials estimated that it would cost $61 million to establish an engineering school. Of this amount, $24.5 million would have to be privately raised. To do so, the Excellence for Education Foundation, which Jonsson chaired, pledged further significant gifts ($3.5 million in 1987 and 1988 alone). Dallas mayor A. Starke Taylor Jr. organized a task force that declared—once again—that the creation of high-technology jobs was vital for the area and that it supported a school of engineering and computer science at UTD.[52]

Finally, in 1986, UTD established the Erik Jonsson School of Engineering and Computer Science. In 1988, ground was broken for a $20 million building. The first doctorate in electrical engineering was awarded in August 1991. In 1992, when Jonsson was ninety-one, a dedication was held for a state-of-the-art, three-story, 150,000-square-foot building for high-tech studies in electronics manufacturing, microelectronics, telecommunications, and computer science.[53]

The Cecil and Ida Green Center for the Study of Science and Society was dedicated at the same time. Both Green and Jonsson gave closing remarks at the dedications. Scheduled for five minutes, Jonsson spoke for fifteen. "You were the hit of the party!" the vice president for university affairs wrote to him, thanking him for his "thought-provoking and touching remarks." Jonsson had quoted the concluding line from "Ulysses," his favorite childhood poem, written by Alfred, Lord Tennyson. It had been Jonsson's personal credo: "to strive, to seek, to find, and not to yield."[54]

By 2013, the Erik Jonsson School of Engineering and Computer Science had more than 4,000 graduate and undergraduate students and 168 full-time faculty members. It offered PhD degrees in eight programs. Overall undergraduate and graduate enrollment at UTD was more than 21,000. Major campus buildings bore the founders' names; the Founders Building commemorated all three of them. Lifelike busts of the trio were on permanent display on the campus.

The Excellence in Education Foundation, through which Jonsson, McDermott, and Green had provided tens of millions of dollars to the cause of higher education, completed its original goal in 1991 when its remaining assets were distributed. These final gifts included $30 million to the UT Southwestern Medical Center.[55] Ross Perot, who attended the press conference, asserted that Jonsson, Green, and McDermott had changed the world through their foundation. The donors were memorialized through the Erik Jonsson Center for Research in Molecular, Genetics and Human Disease, the Cecil H. Green Distinguished Chair in Cellular and Molecular Biology, and the Eugene McDermott Distinguished Chair in Molecular Genetics.[56]

From their first days of giving, Erik and Margaret Jonsson were interested in medical philanthropy. In 1970 they donated 7,500 shares of Texas Instruments, valued at $1 million, to Baylor University Medical Center's drive for a new building. The $12 million, seven-story structure was named the Erik and Margaret Jonsson Medical and Surgical Hospital.[57]

In the mid-1970s, Jonsson headed a $5 million capital campaign for a new hospital in southwestern Dallas County. The successful campaign included a sizeable gift from the Jonssons, and the $11 million Charlton Methodist Hospital was named for Margaret Ellen Jonsson Charlton, who presided over the ribbon cutting. Margaret Ellen, the first woman elected to the board of First National Bank in Dallas, was now the mother of three children, Laura Katherine, Emily Elizabeth, and Erik Allen.[58]

In California, Kenneth Jonsson, president in 1974–75 of the California Institute for Cancer Research, chaired its $10 million fund-raising effort for the UCLA Cancer Center.[59] The Jonsson family foundation gave a $1 million incentive donation. The University of California board of regents named the completed facility the Jonsson Cancer Center.[60]

Erik Jonsson's philanthropic involvements had no geographic limitations. Buildings, fellowships, and endowed chairs bore his name at a remarkable number of institutions. For fifteen years, from 1962 to 1977, he was on Tulane University's board of visitors, including a stint as chairman. In 1981, Tulane honored him with a doctor of science degree, and in 1988 the university dedicated the Erik and Margaret Jonsson Commons and Learning Center for the School of Engineering.[61]

At Harvard University, Jonsson served six years on the visiting committee for the Graduate School of Business Administration; he established a fellowship to support business students; and in 1989 he made an unrestricted $15,000 gift to the medical school.[62]

Besides his friendship with Stanford University's president, J. E. Wallace Sterling, Jonsson's interest in that institution was whetted by the fact that his grandson and namesake, Erik, and his granddaughter Laura (Margaret's children) were students there. They no doubt spent time in the Jonsson Library of Government Documents.[63]

Making commencement addresses and receiving honorary degrees was routine. Rensselaer Polytechnic, the University of Texas at Dallas, Skidmore College, Carnegie-Mellon, Austin College, Southern Methodist University, the University of Dallas, the University of Arkansas, Oklahoma Christian College, Hobart and William Smith Colleges, Arlington State College (now the University of Texas at Arlington), and

Polytechnic University in Brooklyn were among those where he spoke. Eleven of those institutions awarded him honorary doctorates.

From 1966 to 1977 he was a trustee at Austin College in Sherman, Texas, where in 1970 he gave the convocation speech. He chaired the college's $30 million fund-raising "Campaign for the 70s," the most important financial undertaking since the institution's founding in 1849.[64]

Another institution favored by the Jonssons as well as by other TI executives, particularly Haggerty, was the University of Dallas, a Catholic institution in suburban Irving. Jonsson served on its board of trustees, and in 1966 he, Cecil H. Green, Eugene McDermott, and former U.S. senator William Blakley were presented papal honors because of their contributions. In 1968 the university awarded Jonsson an honorary doctor of civil laws degree.[65]

Jonsson's beneficence included especially Dallas's private school, Lamplighter, which offered a progressive learning experience for students in preschool through the fourth grade. As chairman of the board, Jonsson arranged the long-term lease of twelve acres on a corner of the expansive Hockaday School property (which he had been largely responsible for acquiring); hired his friend O'Neil Ford to design a new facility, which included a barn and barnyard where children cared for animals; and kicked off a $1.5 million fund-raising drive by giving $500,000.[66] He was chairman of the board from 1967 through 1984.[67]

Jonsson's relations with Southern Methodist University grew warmer as the university made progress in its engineering program. After Jonsson made a financial commitment to the upgraded program in 1970, SMU president Willis M. Tate recalled fondly the days of their dream for engineering education and the way in which Jonsson had lifted SMU's sights to plan for the best. "After some false starts and disappointments we are now on schedule.... You certainly must feel a warm glow, knowing that it was your original gift and dream that has made this accomplishment possible," Tate wrote to him. Jonsson served on SMU's Foundation for Science and Engineering until 1979. In 1997 the university created the J. Erik Jonsson Ethics Award presented to individuals who epitomized his spirit of moral leadership and public virtue.[68]

On August 24, 1973, an era ended when Eugene McDermott died of prostate cancer at the age of seventy-four. McDermott's insatiable curiosity had led him to many endeavors, many of them far removed from the scientific background he had used when he teamed up with J. C. Karcher to found Geophysical Service, Inc. His most intense interests combined science with engineering. Moneymaking had become incidental.

He was no less generous than Jonsson and Green with his wealth, channeling most of his gifts through his McDermott Foundation. In 2010, his Eugene McDermott Foundation, managed by his widow, Margaret, and their daughter Mary McDermott Cook, had assets of approximately $110 million.

In the year of McDermott's death, TI had forty plants in seven countries. Jack Kilby's integrated circuit had made it possible for a single chip of silicon less than one-fifth of an inch square to contain all the necessary elements for a computer. The microchip was being used in microwave ovens, dishwashers, telephones, vending machines, electronic games, and many other industrial and consumer products.[69]

In 1972, TI introduced the world's first scientific calculator capable of performing trigonometric and hyperbolic functions. It was small enough to hold in the palm. Five years later, TI offered another startling consumer product, Speak & Spell, which utilized the first single-chip speech synthesizer and introduced the world of actual speech to toys.

In 1976, after thirty years at TI, Haggerty retired as chairman of the board, and Cecil Green retired as honorary director and founder-director at the mandatory retirement age of seventy-five.[70] The next year Jonsson, too, turned seventy-five, and he relinquished his role as honorary chairman and founder-director. He owned about 825,000 TI shares valued at slightly under $100 each.[71]

In the early fall of 1980, Haggerty was diagnosed with a fast-spreading malignancy. The man who, in Jonsson's words, was "the best thing that ever happened to our company," died on October 1, 1980, at the age of sixty-six.[72] He had been replaced earlier as chairman by Mark Shepherd Jr.

By 1980, net revenue at TI had reached $4.1 billion. The company had nearly 90,000 employees worldwide. Just ahead, though, was a speed bump that alienated Jonsson and some former executives. The problem developed from a new retail product, a home computer that initially was well received. By the end of 1982, the TI-99/4 was the nation's most popular home computer, with 35 percent of the market share. But fierce competition forced a series of price cuts, and by mid-1983, TI was selling its computers below cost. In October 1983, TI withdrew from the home computer field. The company was said to have lost $660 million in its home-computer experience. From 1980 to 1984, the value of a share of TI fell from $150 to $75.[73]

Jonsson and Green, no longer on the board, viewed these developments with alarm. Longtime officers C. J. Thomsen, S. T. Harris, and Bryan F. Smith, still on the board, were concerned, too. (Smith even wrote a book-length manuscript about the episode, entitled, "When the Storm Slept," but withdrew it before publication because of concern for the privacy of the people involved and the company's well-being.) Philip Jonsson recalled confrontational sessions between his father and Shepherd in his Republic Bank Tower offices. Finally, Shepherd informed Jonsson that Thomsen, Harris, Smith, and John Walker would be removed as directors.[74]

Jonsson was irate because his protégés had been targeted. (In the end, only Smith and Walker were removed.) He sold virtually all his TI stock. His daughter, Margaret Ellen, and son Philip believed that he sold it all, but upon his death in 1994 he held 3,000 shares, a far cry from the 825,000 shares he once held.[75]

⌒

Feeling nostalgic, Jonsson asked Malcolm Bedell in 1974 to find for him a number of his favorite phonograph records from earlier days— DeWolf Hopper's version of "Casey at the Bat"; Ted Lewis's renditions of "Frankie & Johnny," "Somebody Stole My Gal," and "Some of These Days"; Fats Waller's "Basin Street Blues"; and recordings by Fritz Kreisler and Jascha Heifetz.[76]

He continued to go to his Republic Bank Tower office, where Nelle Johnston and other secretaries worked in his behalf. But his days were shorter, beginning generally at about ten and including lunch at the Petroleum Club, a few games of gin rummy, and then perhaps two more hours in the office.[77]

By the late 1970s and early 1980s, health problems plagued both Erik and Margaret. In 1978, Margaret fell and broke five ribs. In April 1979, she was hospitalized for a month. At about the same time, Jonsson experienced food poisoning. Six months later he was in the hospital because of an evident viral inflammation of the lining around the heart. Then came yet another round of food poisoning for both of them—"bad oysters apparently," Jonsson said. In December 1979, he told O'Neil Ford that he was experiencing vertigo, and two months later he was still suffering from its effects.[78]

Yet despite such problems, as late as 1979 Erik and Margaret lived alone. Margaret continued to prepare all meals. Their only domestic help, a housekeeper, arrived at nine and departed at three each day.[79]

But Margaret's health continued to spiral downward. In December 1981 her gall bladder was removed. In March 1982 she was back in the hospital after a fall at the house prompted by a fainting spell. Doctors installed a pacemaker in hopes that the fainting would end. She spent nearly six weeks in the hospital, and when she came home, her husband hired practical nurses to be with her around the clock. More than ever, Jonsson felt obliged to be close to "Mama."[80]

In the fall of 1983, Margaret spent another forty-eight days in the hospital following her third surgery in less than a year.[81] Along with her many other problems, she was suffering from a form of Parkinson's disease.

At the age of eighty-one, three weeks before her sixty-first wedding anniversary, Margaret Elizabeth Fonde Jonsson died. Services were held at the Jonssons' church, Highland Park United Methodist Church, with the senior associate, the Reverend Kenneth M. Dickson, presiding.[82] "If I hear Erik correctly," Dickson said in his eulogy, "Margaret was the 'Chief Executive Officer' of understanding, nurture, and companionship in that most important corporation to which any of us will ever belong: the family. She capitalized her family with *character*."[83]

Forty-three years earlier, Jonsson had called the family together to tell them about the possibility of purchasing GSI with his associates. He asked for and gained their permission, for there would be sacrifices. Jonsson had been right. His wife especially had suffered, undergoing emotional stress and even a sense of abandonment as her husband toiled long hours. She had borne her burden stoically but faithfully. The children had missed hours of companionship with their father, and so had the grandchildren.

Three months after Margaret's death, Jonsson enrolled in a fitness program at Dr. Kenneth Cooper's Aerobics Center. The center featured him, smiling and wearing a white "muscle shirt," on the cover of its publication.[84]

His children and grandchildren urged him to travel again, and he did. The previous July he had gone alone to Sweden to accept an award as Swedish American of the year of 1983, honored at a dinner with speeches by U.S. chief justice Warren Burger and the U.S. ambassador to Sweden. The king of Sweden sent a congratulatory telegram.[85]

He returned to Sweden in 1984, accompanied by Dr. Paul Thomas, his physician, and his wife Marge. After five days in Stockholm, the three boarded the *Royal Viking Sea* in Copenhagen for a fourteen-day cruise of the Nordic fjords.[86] Returning to Dallas for a few days, Jonsson next was off to his favorite retreat, Lake Tahoe, for the rest of the summer.[87]

In December 1984, he underwent prostate surgery, recuperating slowly at Margaret Ellen's home. He returned to the hospital at the end of February 1985, and spent four days in the cardiac care unit, suffering from fibrillation. Nelle Johnston regularly visited him and kept him advised of the correspondence that continued to arrive. When he was discharged, his doctor told him he had a "perfect cardiogram and blood pressure like a teenager's."[88]

At the end of 1985 he moved from his house on Shadywood into a high-rise apartment building, the Warrington, on Turtle Creek Boulevard. "You are starting a new life," his son Philip wrote to him.[89] Three blocks away, Cecil and Ida Green lived at the more famous 3525 Turtle Creek, where Greer Garson and her oilman husband, Buddy Fogelson, had the penthouse.

In his mideighties, gaunt and frail from weight loss, Jonsson knew he now looked old, but he made the best of it. When the Dallas Council on World Affairs gave him an award in 1987, he told the audience how much fun it had been when he tried to convince a young lady that he was 104 years old.[90]

The correspondence handled by Nelle Johnston and several secretaries ranged widely; it came from longtime friends and associates such as Malcolm Bedell and Cecil Green and from more recent ones such as I. M. Pei and several university presidents. It included, significantly, matters related to his philanthropy. A constant flow of letters and telephone calls came from others whom he did not know. His responses often brought further replies. The cycle seemed never-ending.

Many afternoons Jonsson left his office to descend to the street-level Merrill Lynch brokerage office, where Dick Davis handled his investments, heavy in bonds and blue chips. The two sometimes would sit for an hour or two, chatting casually about the stock market and life in general.[91]

He enjoyed hearing from his grandchildren. All of them seemed genuinely proud of his accomplishments. Suzanne, Philip's daughter in Massachusetts, advised him: "Just make sure you spend all this time

being happy. . . . You have fulfilled (many times over) all your responsibilities and can now just enjoy yourself."[92]

⤶

In the late 1980s, Jonsson met a woman from Summit, New Jersey, who became a special interest. In his daughter's judgment, he was
"very smitten" with her. She was a development officer at a university, a
young divorcée probably in her thirties; Jonsson was in his late eighties.
She visited the family compound at Lake Tahoe several times, staying
as long as a week. Ken had fun calling her "Mom" even though she was
a couple of decades younger than he. Her letters and postcards to Jonsson closed with "love" and *xxx* and *ooo*. Jonsson visited her on several
occasions, and she thanked him especially for the "experience, wisdom
and counsel" he imparted to her son. Jonsson wanted to marry her, and
although they obviously enjoyed time together, she refused because of
their age difference. They remained friends, though.[93]

⤶

An unforgettable honor came in the fall of 1990 when some 125 business, civic, and academic leaders gathered at the Mansion on Turtle
Creek hotel to honor Jonsson for his "extraordinary leadership for Dallas." Someone like Erik Jonsson, proclaimed Peter O'Donnell Jr., comes
along only once in two hundred years. A framed letter of appreciation
came from President George H. W. Bush ("you have been a real inspiration to me").[94]

⤶

Many who saw Nelle Johnston's devotion to her boss suspected that
it reflected deeper personal feelings. She had merged her life with his
to such a degree that she knew far more about his activities than even
Margaret and other family members. Some speculated that after Margaret's death, Nelle held hopes for marriage.

Jonsson's children became alarmed that at this stage of his life
Nelle was exerting so much influence on their father. Her domain had
expanded beyond office hours. She even escorted him to family gather-
ings and sometimes announced when it was time for him to leave. She
hired and fired his household help; she exerted some authority over
his investments. Jonsson realized, along with his children, that she was
overstepping her authority, but he was reluctant to curtail her after her
years of dedicated service.

Finally, he agreed with his children that the situation had to change.

Nelle, who was approaching seventy, would be offered retirement. The children would manage their father's affairs. They would close the downtown office for one closer to his apartment.[95]

Nelle was not ready to retire; she did not want to close the downtown office. Jonsson offered her a handsome settlement and a compensatory luxury cruise for her and a friend. She spurned the offer, and the long and fruitful relationship between the two ended unhappily. Jonsson moved his office that summer to a building at 5600 West Lovers Lane in North Dallas. Margaret Ellen assumed authority over his affairs, maintaining secretarial help. But Jonsson stopped going to that office, too.[96]

Nelle Johnston never got over her anger. She did not attend Jonsson's funeral.

With his leisure time, Jonsson tried to maintain a limited social schedule. He was driving his own car. Finally, Margaret Ellen's second husband, Robert D. Rogers (she and George Charlton had divorced), told his father-in-law that his driving was "scaring his children to death." Jonsson agreed to have a driver. Occasionally, he had lunch with his friends, especially at Brook Hollow Country Club, enjoying a single Bloody Mary rather than his longtime favorite, Scotch. For a while, Margaret Ellen arranged for former card-playing friends to visit him, but the magic had worn off. Jonsson inevitably spent more time alone, reading and watching television.[97]

After he suffered a few falls, Margaret Ellen hired help to be with her father twenty-four hours a day and to prepare his meals. When he complained about the food, he renewed his membership in the nearby Dallas Country Club so he could eat there, paying a $30,000 membership fee. Jonsson had a single meal there, was displeased, and resumed eating in his apartment. His children laughed afterwards—the single meal had cost $30,000.[98]

↤

With his memories overflowing, Jonsson submitted to numerous oral history interviews. The Sixth Floor Museum, which had taken over the old Texas School Book Depository from which Oswald shot Kennedy, was one of several institutions to record his recollections. His interviewers at the Sixth Floor Museum were Wes Wise, who had covered the assassination as a journalist (as well as succeeding Jonsson as mayor), and Bob Porter, formerly of the *Dallas Times Herald*. The Dallas Public Library also interviewed him for its oral history collections.

His recollections of Dallas/Fort Worth International Airport were taken in two interviews when he was ninety-two.[99]

Honors occasionally still came. In 1988, the Greater Dallas Chamber of Commerce established the J. Erik Jonsson Award for the private citizen who best followed Jonsson's example in "leading others to greatness for the public good." The chamber noted that Jonsson was the only person to have served as chairman of both the Chamber of Commerce and the Dallas Citizens Council, not to mention as mayor.[100]

Aging establishment leaders, calling themselves the "Old Guard," occasionally met with him for lunch. When, in 1992, Jonsson responded to Trammell Crow's invitation to the Old Guard's next meeting, he said he never knew until the morning of an appointment whether he would be able to make it. "If I don't show up," he said, "you will know that I am not feeling very well." Penciled in later at the bottom of a copy of this letter was a note from a secretary who assisted him with his occasional letters: "Mr. J could not attend. Woke up 2/24 a.m. not feeling well—upset stomach & dizzy spell."[101]

Old Guard members commissioned a noted sculptor, Edgar Barvo Bárcenes, to create a life-size bronze statue of him. The city's Cultural Affairs Commission placed the large statue in the main lobby of city hall. Dedicated on December 14, 1994, with Jonsson present, it depicted him moving forward with his coat tossed over his shoulder. He looked at the statue with his mouth agape in feigned disbelief.[102]

Carl Sewell, the automobile dealer with whom he had formed a close friendship, found a retired Dallas police officer to take Jonsson on occasional outings. The former mayor, who had for so many years enjoyed being the center of attention, had become, in Sewell's words, "lonely, very lonely."[103]

Sometimes a spark came through letters from old friends and associates such as Cecil and Ida Green. William R. Guffey sent him a "letter" that Jonsson had written to Guffey's father in 1950. It was a vertical sheet of paper containing only long columns of indecipherable Chinese lettering, prefaced with Jonsson's handwritten greeting, "Dear Roy," and closed with "Sincerely, Erik."[104]

On the rare occasions when Jonsson ventured out, his appearance was surprising to those who remembered him as a domineering figure. Now he was thin faced and gaunt, his neck swallowed up in a shirt collar that looked too big.

In July 1994, Jonsson, approaching his ninety-third birthday, signed his last will, bequeathing most of his personal effects to his three children and his financial assets to the Jonsson Foundation. The three thousand shares of Texas Instruments he had retained were overshadowed by larger amounts of other blue-chip stocks. Other than his children, no individuals were named as beneficiaries.[105]

In the mid-1990s, a series of small strokes left him bedridden. Communication became impossible. In August 1995 he contracted pneumonia, and on Friday, September 1, five days before his ninety-fourth birthday, he died at his Turtle Creek Boulevard apartment.[106]

His death surprised many who assumed he was already dead. "Erik Jonsson is and always will be the standard by which Dallas mayors will be judged," said Dallas mayor Ron Kirk, the first African American to hold that office. Margaret McDermott perhaps had the most telling remark—her late husband, Eugene, had believed that the luckiest thing that had ever happened to him was to meet Erik Jonsson.[107]

At Hillcrest Memorial Park, his coffin was placed next to that of his wife. A public service was held at the Highland Park United Methodist Church. The Reverend Kenneth M. Dickson, who also had presided over Margaret's funeral, officiated. The sanctuary overflowed, and some mourners returned home because they could find no parking for blocks around. At the service, a number of friends recalled memories. Ray L. Hunt and Jerry Junkins (of Texas Instruments) read from Psalms. Peter O'Donnell Jr. and Dr. Kern Wildenthal paid tribute, as did Margaret Ellen's husband, Robert D. Rogers. The schoolchildren of Lamplighter sang. The order of service bore Jonsson's words: "We must dream no small dreams. We must envision great, ambitious, difficult goals. Yet our objectives must be within our reach."[108]

One of the speakers, Al Lipscomb, the former militant who recently had completed three terms as a councilman, praised him, as he had been doing for some years. The Reverend Peter Johnson, who had taken the leadership against Jonsson in the Fair Park homeowner controversy, recalled working with Jonsson to improve conditions for minorities and the poor. Jonsson's grandson Erik Charlton put it this way: "He was tough to the bone, always outspoken, and doggedly committed to his friends and his community."[109]

Particularly remembered were Erik Jonsson's civic contributions—the airport, the new city hall, the Goals for Dallas program, and the new library. These encomiums just as well could have centered on his role in transforming a relatively small oil exploration company into the pioneering electronics colossus Texas Instruments. Or they might have emphasized his philanthropy and work in education—the University of Texas at Dallas, Rensselaer Polytechnic Institute, Skidmore College, Lamplighter, Hockaday, and so many others.

Years before, Jonsson had sent African violets to the attorney John N. Jackson to thank him for a civic deed. Jackson replied how incongruous it was for him to have sent such an appreciation to someone so deeply in Jonsson's debt for so many things. "Knowing you and observing you as you proceed from one incredible undertaking to the rest, in infinite succession, always accomplishing the impossible with grace, has been one of the truly great experiences of my life," Jackson wrote. "I hope you know how profoundly I appreciate all that you have done."[110] It was a private message, but one that would have been endorsed by so many others throughout Dallas and the nation.

On the day Jonsson was put to rest, Ross Perot placed a full-page memorial to him in the *Dallas Morning News*: "So long, Erik, and thanks for everything."[111]

The expansive and imaginative life of John Erik Jonsson brought into sharp focus the extraordinary and revolutionary technological changes of his century. His journey from delivery boy, dishwasher, stamp dealer, motorcycle salesman, auto mechanic, magazine salesman, munitions factory worker, and car salesman to industrialist, mayor, visionary ,and philanthropist resembled and often was likened to a Horatio Alger story. But Jonsson's life was played on a bigger canvas, and it was true.

Notes

CHAPTER 1: A BOY IN BROOKLYN

1. "A Conversation with Mayor Erik Jonsson," transcript of a television interview conducted Apr. 26, 1971, by WFAA-TV, Dallas, file 2, box 114, J. Erik Jonsson Papers, DeGolyer Library, Southern Methodist University, Dallas. The following abbreviations are used in citations hereafter: JEJ for John Erik Jonsson, and Jonsson Papers for J. Erik Jonsson Papers, DeGolyer Library.

2. R. R. L'Hommedieu, "The Wage Earner's Automobile," *Overland Monthly*, Jan. 1913, 101, 102.

3. [Buzz Selby], "Personal Recollections and Sayings of J. Erik Jonsson," 18, May 10, 1979, typescript by Texas Instruments, file 2, box 114, Jonsson Papers (hereafter cited as "Personal Recollections"); U.S. Census, 1900, roll 1048, book 1, 83; "Erik Jonsson's Life: Transcription of Interviews between Erik Jonsson and Holland McCombs," 1959, file 2, box 114, Jonsson Papers (hereafter cited as McCombs interview). A microfilm copy of the "Index to Passenger Lists of Vessels Arriving at Philadelphia, 1800–1900," prepared by the National Archives, does not list his name.

4. "Conversation with Mayor Jonsson," 2; "Personal Recollections," 19.

5. The document is in the private papers of Margaret Jonsson Rogers, J. Erik Jonsson's daughter. The following abbreviations are used in citations hereafter: MJR for Margaret Jonsson Rogers, and MJR Papers for the Margaret Jonsson Rogers Papers, Dallas.

6. "Personal Recollections," 21; Ellen Palmquist to John Palmquist, Oct. 28, 1880, MJR Papers.

7. U.S. Census, 1900, roll 1048, book 1, 83. The name "Ellen Charlotte Palmquist" does not appear in the "Index of Passengers Arriving in Boston, 1848–1891," prepared by the National Archives.

8. Erik Jonsson's own captions (hereafter cited as Jonsson captions) accompanying a collection of early family photographs, MJR Papers; Robert A. Wilson, "Erik Jonsson: American Visionary," 4, typescript, file 1, box 114, Jonsson Papers.

9. Typescript of conversation between JEJ and Alice Hallis Fortner, July 15, 1993, MJR Papers; hereafter cited as Jonsson and Fortner Conversation. Fortner knew Jonsson and his family when they lived in Montrose, New Jersey.

10. "Personal Recollections," 20.

11. The marriage certificate is in the MJR Papers.

12. U.S. Census, 1900; Wilson, "Erik Jonsson," 2; Jonsson captions, MJR Papers.

13. Untitled speech to the Southwest Metal Conference, Nov. 1955, Richard Tuck Papers. Tuck is a former Texas Instruments electrical engineer who conducted extensive research on JEJ's life. He accumulated many relevant documents and interviewed JEJ's relatives, business associates, and friends. Tuck very graciously gave his carefully organized materials to the author.

14. U.S. Census, 1910, roll 975, book 2, 155b. Years later, Erik Jonsson's daughter, Margaret Ellen Rogers, recalled a vague impression that a death may have occurred, although she could not confirm it. A three-year-old child, Howard C. Jonsson, parents unknown, of Kings County, died Apr. 18, 1899, Death Certificate 6570 (1899), Kings County, New York, Death Index, 1862–1948, online database.

15. JEJ, interview by Larry Secrest, Sept. 12, 1970, 1, 2. Secrest conducted a later interview with

JEJ on Nov. 28, 1970, and interviews with Cecil H. Green (June 17, 1970) and Eugene McDermott (along with Gary Hoffman, Apr. 9, 1971), which are in the same document. Both JEJ interviews occurred in Jonsson's downtown Dallas office in the Republic Bank Building; they are cited hereafter as Secrest interview, with the appropriate date. A note at the bottom of each page states that they were "copied from the collections in the Center for American History, the University of Texas at Austin," although they are not listed today among the center's oral histories and are not known there to exist. The document containing all the interviews is in the MJR Papers.

16. McCombs interview, 1.
17. Ibid.
18. Secrest interviews, Nov. 28, 1970, 2, and Sept. 12, 1970, 7.
19. McCombs interview, 3; Jonsson captions.
20. McCombs interview, 7.
21. Ibid.; Lana Henderson, "Erik Jonsson: Dreamer, Builder," *Dallas Times Herald,* Nov. 24, 1974.
22. Wilson, "Erik Jonsson."
23. Secrest interview, Sept. 12, 1970, 4.
24. McCombs interview, 6.
25. "Personal Recollections," 24.
26. "Conversation with Mayor Jonsson," 13.
27. JEJ, interview by Mike Hazel, Nov. 18, 1993, 18, Dallas (hereafter cited as Hazel interview); Joe Dealey Jr., "Interview with J. Erik Jonsson," Dec. 13, 1993, 1, file 3, box 118, Jonsson Papers.
28. McCombs interview, 2–3.
29. Ibid.
30. Ibid.
31. Secrest interview, Sept. 12, 1970; McCombs interview, 8. MJR has a photograph of Erik with his bicycle; see Jonsson captions.
32. "Conversation with Mayor Jonsson," 4–5; McCombs interview, 8–9.
33. Jonsson captions.
34. The report cards are in file 22, box 115, Jonsson Papers.
35. Jonsson captions; Dealey interview, 6–7; Wilson, "Erik Jonsson," 3.
36. "Personal Recollections," 19; McCombs interview, 8.
37. "Personal Recollections," 30.
38. Ibid., 27–30; McCombs interview, 2.
39. Jonsson captions.
40. Secrest interview, Nov. 28, 1970, 15.
41. McCombs interview, 4.
42. Secrest interview, Sept. 12, 1970, 7.

CHAPTER 2: BECOMING A WORKAHOLIC

1. George Rodrigue, "Erik Jonsson Saw Future, Helped Bring It to Dallas," *Dallas Morning News,* Dec. 27, 1983; Henderson, "Jonsson: Dreamer, Builder."
2. Dealey interview, 3.
3. Secrest interview, Nov. 28, 1970, 5.
4. Jonsson captions.
5. Ibid.; Secrest interview, Sept. 12, 1970, 9.
6. Jonsson captions; Secrest interview, Sept. 12, 1970, 9,
7. Jonsson captions.
8. Rodrigue, "Erik Jonsson Saw Future."
9. Wilson, "Erik Jonsson," 4; Secrest interview, Sept. 12, 1970, 9; Rodrigue, "Erik Jonsson Saw Future."
10. Dealey interview, 6.
11. Report cards in file 22, box 115, Jonsson Papers.
12. H. M. Dutch to Mr. and Mrs. John Jonsson, Dec. 16, 1915, file 21, box 115, Jonsson Papers.
13. H. M. Dutch to Mr. and Mrs. John Jonsson, May 14, 1917, in ibid.

14. He wrote his first short story, "An Alarming," in March 1914. Many of his stories are in file 23, box 115, Jonsson Papers.

15. Quoted in William G. Smith, "Erik Jonsson: TI's Founder Began by Minding Dad's Store," *Texas Business*, June 1980, 33.

16. The note is inserted in the May 1917 issue of the *Bulletin*, file 20, box 115, Jonsson Papers.

17. Secrest interview, Sept. 12, 1970, 9; Jonsson captions.

18. Secrest interview, Sept. 12, 1970, 9.

19. The issue is dated Dec. 1916; it is in file 20, box 115, Jonsson Papers. JEJ's comments are from Secrest interview, Nov. 28, 1970, 16.

20. DeGolyer's life is portrayed by Lon Tinkle in *Mr. De: A Biography of Everette Lee DeGolyer* (Boston: Little, Brown, 1970). His achievements are summarized in the *New Handbook of Texas History* (Austin: Texas State Historical Association, 1996), 2:563–64.

21. Secrest interview, Nov. 28, 1970, 9–10; Holland McCombs, "The Tall Story of Texas Instruments" [1960], 18, unpublished paper, file 3, box 183, Holland McCombs Papers, University of Tennessee at Martin (hereafter cited as McCombs Papers); Jonsson and Fortner Conversation, 8.

22. JEJ, typescript for remarks at Southwest Research Institute, San Antonio, Nov. 27, 1972, 4, and "Speeches for an Occasion, Major Address—Erik Jonsson," Southwest Research Institute, [9], file 32, box 1, Jonsson Papers.

23. Smith, "Jonsson: TI's Founder," 33; McCombs, "Tall Story of Texas Instruments," 18; JEJ, "Address by J. E. Jonsson, Junior Achievement Futures Unlimited Banquet," May 15, 1957, file 27, box 6, Jonsson Papers.

24. T. C. Closthin to Mr. and Mrs. Johnson [*sic*], Oct. 4, 1915, file 5, box 119, Jonsson Papers.

25. Pay envelope, Apr. 8, 1916, in file 23, box 115, Jonsson Papers; "Interview with a Goal Setter," *At Rensselaer*, Summer 1985, 25.

26. Secrest interview, Sept. 12, 1970, 11.

27. Jonsson and Fortner Conversation, 8.

28. Secrest interview, Sept. 12, 1970, 10.

29. Ibid., 11.

30. Henderson, "Jonsson: Dreamer, Builder"; JEJ in conversation with Philip R. Jonsson and Steve W. Jonsson, June 16, 1978, transcript courtesy of Steve W. Jonsson.

31. JEJ, "Jonsson's First Days at RPI," autobiographical tape recording, n.d. [probably late 1970s], file 184, box 166, Jonsson Papers; Secrest interview, Nov. 28, 1970, 17; "Conversation with Mayor Jonsson," 7. The tape recording is part of a series, evidently made on a dictation machine, undated and unidentified, perhaps reflecting a series of sessions in 1959 with Holland McCombs. A partial transcript of the interviews, entitled "Erik Jonsson's Life," appears in file 2, box 114, Jonsson Papers; the recordings themselves are in box 166.

32. Secrest interview, Nov. 28, 1970, 17.

33. Ibid.

34. The scholarship certificate is in file 1, box 100, Jonsson Papers. See also Jonsson captions; "Erik Jonsson—Millions from Microminiatures," *Rensselaer Review*, Winter 1964, 8, file 12, box 100, Jonsson Papers.

35. Secrest interview, Sept. 12, 1970, 16; Jonsson captions, 24.

36. Secrest interview, Sept. 12, 1970, 12.

37. Report cards are in file 22, box 115, Jonsson Papers.

38. Rickets to H. M. Dutch, June 25, 1918, file 21, box 115, Jonsson Papers.

39. Jonsson and Fortner Conversation, 1; "John Svenson Dies on Ship Enroute Home," *Montclair (NJ) Times*, Sept. 9, 1954, file 8, box 48, Jonsson Papers.

40. JEJ, "Jonsson's First Days at RPI."

41. *The Rensselaer Hand Book, 1920–21*, file 2, box 116, Jonsson Papers.

42. JEJ, "Jonsson's First Days at RPI."

43. Ibid.

44. JEJ to parents, Sept. 12 and 21, 1918, file 6, box 119, Jonsson Papers.

45. Secrest interview, Sept. 12, 1970, 13; JEJ to parents, Oct. 2, 1918, file 6, box 119, Jonsson Papers.

46. JEJ to parents, Sept. 12 and Oct. 2, 1918; JEJ, "Jonsson's First Days at RPI."

47. Secrest interview, Sept. 12, 1970, 12.

48. JEJ to parents, Sept. 26, 1918, file 6, box 119, Jonsson Papers.

49. JEJ to parents, Oct. 2, 1918.

50. JEJ to parents, Oct. 11, 1918, file 6, box 119, Jonsson Papers.

51. Ibid.

52. Undated letter marked "Up North," file 6, and undated letter in envelope postmarked Mar. 19, 1919, file 7, box 119, Jonsson Papers; JEJ conversation with Philip and Steve Jonsson, [2].

53. JEJ to father, Mar. 15, [1919], file 7; JEJ to parents, Apr. 17, 1919, file 7; undated letters, file 6, box 119, Jonsson Papers.

54. JEJ to parents, Jan. 5, 1919, file 7, box 119, Jonsson Papers.

55. JEJ conversation with Philip and Steve Jonsson, [3].

56. Jonsson captions; Secrest interview, Sept. 12, 1970, 17.

57. Secrest interview, Sept. 12, 1970, 17.

58. Ibid., 3–4.

59. Ibid.

60. Secrest interview, Nov. 28, 1970, 4.

61. JEJ to parents, Oct. 26, 1919, file 7; Nov. [unreadable date in postmark], 1919, file 8; Dec. 8, 1919, file 7, box 119, Jonsson Papers.

62. JEJ to parents, n.d., file 10, box 119, Jonsson Papers.

63. "Motorcycle Club," Feb. 8, 1920, newspaper clipping attached to undated letter to parents, envelope postmarked Mar. 29, 1920, file 8, box 119, Jonsson Papers.

64. JEJ to parents, June 7, 1920, in ibid.

65. JEJ to parents, Apr. 11 and Feb. 4, 1920, in ibid.

66. JEJ to parents, Apr. 11, May 8, May 10, and June 7, 1920, in ibid.; JEJ to parents, n.d., file 7, box 119, Jonsson Papers.

67. JEJ to parents, July 26, 1920, file 8, box 119, Jonsson Papers.

68. Ibid.

69. Secrest interview, Nov. 28, 1970, 4.

70. Jonsson captions; JEJ, "College Years," tape recording, file 187, box 166, Jonsson Papers.

71. JEJ to parents, Feb. 4, 1920, file 8, box 119, Jonsson Papers.

72. JEJ, "Fraternity Life and ALCOA," tape recording, file 186, box 166, Jonsson Papers.

73. JEJ to parents, Oct. 12, 1919, file 7, box 119, Jonsson Papers; JEJ, "Fraternity Life and ALCOA."

74. Ibid.; JEJ to parents, Nov. 9, 1920, MJR Papers; JEJ, "Jonsson on Rensselaer," tape recording, file 185, box 166, Jonsson Papers.

75. JEJ to parents, n.d., MJR Papers.

76. JEJ, "Mr. President, Ladies and Gentlemen of the Southwest Metal Conference and Those of You Who Managed to Slip in without a Ticket," undated speech, MJR Papers.

77. The diary is in file 24, box 115, Jonsson Papers.

78. JEJ, "Jonsson on Rensselaer."

79. JEJ to parents, Feb. 27, 1921, file 9, box 119, Jonsson Papers; Secrest interview, Sept 12, 1970, 1.

80. JEJ, "College Years."

81. Secrest interview, Sept. 12, 1970, 3; JEJ, "College Years"; JEJ to "Ma," n.d., file 10, box 119, Jonsson Papers.

82. *Annual Record of the Tau Omega Fraternity* (Troy, N.Y.: Rensselaer Polytechnic Institute, 1920), [19]; JEJ to parents, Feb. 4 and 19, 1920, and undated letter, all in file 8, box 119, Jonsson Papers.

83. JEJ to parents, Sept. 20, 1920, and Nov. 10, 1919, in ibid.

84. Dealey interview, 4–5; JEJ to parents, July 26, 1920, file 8, box 119, Jonsson Papers.

85. JEJ to parents, Oct. 20, 1918, file 6, box 119, Jonsson Papers; Secrest interview, Sept. 12, 1970, 14; JEJ to parents, n.d. [1920], file 8, box 119, Jonsson Papers.

86. Smith, "Jonsson: TI's Founder," 33.

87. Ibid.; JEJ to parents, n.d., file 25, box 115, Jonsson Papers; "Ninety-Sixth Annual Commencement, Reading of Theses of the Graduating Class of 1922," file 2, box 116, Jonsson Papers.

88. Secrest interview, Sept. 12, 1970, 6.

89. JEJ to parents, n.d., file 25, box 115, Jonsson Papers; Rensselaer graduation program, 1922, MJR Papers.

90. Commencement program, MJR Papers; JEJ, "Address by J. E. Jonsson, President, Texas Instruments, Inc., at the Annual Meeting—June 7, 1957—National Society of Professional Engineers," file 35, box 116, Jonsson Papers.

91. JEJ, "Jonsson on Rensselaer."

92. "The Board of Trustees at Rensselaer Polytechnic institute Pays Tribute to J. Erik Jonsson, '22, October 26, 1990," file 23, box 111, Jonsson Papers.

Chapter 3: Lessons in Business

1. Secrest interview, Nov. 28, 1970, 7.

2. Ibid., 7–8.

3. Ibid.; JEJ to his parents (from the Aluminum Club), [July 1922], file 25, box, 115, Jonsson Papers; JEJ, "Fraternity Life and ALCOA."

4. JEJ, "Fraternity Life and ALCOA."

5. Ibid.

6. Secrest interview, Sept. 12, 1970, 16. In this interview, Jonsson erroneously recalled that the sale of the store took place "about the time" he was a senior in high school. Letters to his parents in 1919 confirm a later date, however; see the letter dated Apr. 17, 1919, in which Erik offers to try to find a buyer in Troy—file 7, box 119, Jonsson Papers.

7. JEJ to his parents, n.d. [July 1922], from New Kensington, Pennsylvania, postmarked Aug. 4, 1922, file 25, box 115, Jonsson Papers; Jonsson and Fortner Conversation, 2.

8. JEJ to his parents, Aug. 4, 1922.

9. Secrest interview, Nov. 28, 1970, 11–12; JEJ, "Alcoa and Married Life," tape recording, file 188, box 166, Jonsson Papers.

10. Secrest interview, Nov. 28, 1970, 11, 13–14; Hazel interview, 17.

11. JEJ to "Diz & Rosie," July 27, 1922, file 25, box 115, Jonsson Papers.

12. JEJ to his mother, Nov. 13, 1922, in ibid.

13. Lana Henderson, "Flowers Blossom in Her Steps," *Dallas Times Herald*, Oct. 22, 1972.

14. Secrest interview, Nov. 28, 1970, 16; *Aluminum Bulletin*, Sept. 1920, 5, copy in file 23, box 119, Jonsson Papers. Jonsson carefully preserved the *Aluminum Bulletin* bearing Margaret's picture. Jonsson first bought a secondhand Ford and later a secondhand Buick Roadster; see "Conversation with Mayor Jonsson," 9; JEJ, "Alcoa and Married Life."

15. Secrest interview, Nov. 28, 1970, 16; JEJ, "Alcoa and Married Life."

16. Secrest interview, Nov. 28, 1970, 16; Jonsson and Fortner Conversation, 3; "Conversation with Mayor Jonsson," 10; MJR told of her grandmother riding on the horse (interview by the author, Oct. 14, 2003, Dallas).

17. JEJ, "Alcoa and Married Life."

18. Ibid.

19. Secrest interview, Nov. 28, 1970, 16; marriage license, MJR Papers; "A Conversation with Mayor Erik Jonsson," 10; JEJ, "Alcoa and Married Life." While the marriage license states that the Reverend W. R. Dawson presided over the wedding, a hand-painted announcement on felt, "Our Wedding Day," states that J. Erik Jonsson and Margaret Fonde were married at 5 p.m. at Minister House by Matthew Dixon; the announcement is article 84, Wedding Announcement, box 151X, Jonsson Papers.

20. JEJ, "Alcoa and Married Life."

21. Warranty deed, June 6, 1923, and Jonsson to Mobile County Tax Collector, Dec. 28, 1925, both in file 37, box 120, Jonsson Papers.

22. "Mrs. Jonsson Dies in Texas," *Marysville (TN) Daily Times*, Jan. 17, 1984; e-mail from Ellen Fonde to MJR, May 26, 2001, both in MJR Papers; Henderson, "Flowers Blossom in Her Steps"; Secrest interview, Nov. 28, 1970, 5; JEJ, "Alcoa and Married Life."

23. Mary C. Gray to Margaret Jonsson, Oct. 24, 1927, file 12, box 120, Jonsson Papers.

24. "Ma and Pa" Jonsson to Margaret and Erik, Apr. 22, 1923, in ibid.

25. Secrest interview, 16–17.

26. JEJ, "The Fabrication of Aluminum: Present Practice," file 4, box 116, Jonsson Papers. Jonsson's description is in Smith, "Jonsson: TI's Founder," 33.

27. McCombs, "Tall Story of Texas Instruments."

28. Secrest interview, Nov. 28, 1970, 1.

29. JEJ to C. C. Finch, Nov. 25, 1924, file 27, box 115, Jonsson Papers.

30. Secrest interview, Nov. 28, 1970, 17.

31. Smith, "Jonsson: TI's Founder," 34.

32. Henderson, "Flowers Blossom in Her Steps"; JEJ, "Alcoa," tape recording, file 190, box 66, Jonsson Papers.

33. Secrest interview, Nov. 28, 1970, 1–2; Smith, "Jonsson: TI's Founder," 33.

34. Dealey interview, 5.

35. Secrest interview, Nov. 28, 1970, 2.

36. Ibid., 3.

37. Ibid.; Smith, "Jonsson: TI's Founder," 34. The "friend and another fellow" are not identified. But a friend who signed his name only as "John" sent Jonsson a letter on Aug. 15, 1928, on Alcoa stationery from the Edgewater plant, asking when he might expect payment of the loan of $500 he had given him; file 29, box 117, Jonsson Papers.

38. Corporate Records of Bergen Oakland Company, Dumont, New Jersey, June 8, 1926, and Certificate of Incorporation, May 26, 1926, file 1, box 121, Jonsson Papers.

39. Dumont Motor Car Co., Corporation Income Tax Return for Calendar Year 1926, file 4, box 117, Jonsson Papers; Corporate Records of Bergen Oakland Co., Aug. 4, 1926, file 1, box 121, Jonsson Papers; Secrest interview, Nov. 28, 1970, 3.

40. Corporate Records of Bergen Oakland Company, May 16, 1927, file 1, box 121, Jonsson Papers.

41. L. C. Covell, district manager, to Jochim-Jonsson, Jan. 6, 1927, file 34, box 117, Jonsson Papers; Ed Cray, Chrome Colossus: General Motors and Its Times (New York: McGraw-Hill, 1980), 248; president of Jochim-Jonsson [unsigned] to Oakland Motor Car Co., Jan. 22, 1927, file 31, box 117, Jonsson Papers; Secrest interview, Nov. 28, 1970, 3.

42. Unsigned letter to Miss G. Grasse, Apr. 19, 1927, file 34, box 117, Jonsson Papers.

43. Wilson, "Erik Jonsson," 7; Reis Realty Co. to JEJ, Oct. 30, 1926, and statement of payment due, Oct. 28, 1926, file 6, box 116, Jonsson Papers.

44. Secrest interview, Nov. 28, 1970, 3; Robert B. McKee to JEJ, June 1, 1927, file 33, box 121, Jonsson Papers; Henderson, "Jonsson: Dreamer, Builder"; R. E. Powell to JEJ, June 6, 1927, file 33, box 121, Jonsson Papers.

45. Unsigned letter to Mr. Armstrong, Oct. 22, 1927, file 16, box 121, Jonsson Papers.

46. L. C. Covell to Jochim-Johnson [sic], Apr. 16, 1927, file 34, box 117, Jonsson Papers.

47. Sales summary, Aug. 15, 1927; WODA sales document, n.d.; letter from WODA, Aug. 18, 1927, all in file 32, box 117, Jonsson Papers.

48. JEJ to Mr. Reiser, Aug. 11, 1927; E. C. Shephard, asst. treasurer, to Dumont Motor Car Co., Aug. 17, 1927; J. T. Larking to Dumont Motor Car Co., Dec. 16, 1927; H. Dolch, manager, U.S. Mercantile Collection Agency, to Jonsson, Jochim, Inc., Sept. 13, 1927; Leland F. Ferry to Dumont Motor Car Co., Aug. 23, 1927; Dumont Motor Car Co. to Seufert & Elmore, Aug. 27, 1927, all in file 16, box 121, Jonsson Papers; S. S. Bliss to Dumont Motor Car Co., June 20, 1929, file 30, box 117, Jonsson Papers.

49. Mary C. Gray to Margaret Jonsson, Oct. 24, 1927, file 34, box 117, Jonsson Papers.

50. Memorandum for Use of "Owner" When Policy Is Held by Mortgagee, Jan. 10, 1928, file 6, box 117, Jonsson Papers; Agreement for Extension of Mortgage, Feb. 8, 1928, file 5, in ibid.

51. JEJ to L. C. Covell, Aug. 29, 1927, file 32, box 117, Jonsson Papers; Secrest interview, Nov. 28, 1970, 3.

52. Secrest interview, Nov. 28, 1970, 4.

53. Fidelity Union Title and Mortgage Guaranty Co. to JEJ, Jan. 11, 15, 1929; Howard D. Crane to JEJ, Jan. 4, 1929, both in file 30, box 117, Jonsson Papers.

54. H. A. Cornell, credit manager, to Dumont Motor Car Co., Jan. 8, 1929; Dumont to Dunlop, Feb. 20, 1929; R. B. Mann of Dunlop to Dumont, Feb. 21, 1929; JEJ to Mr. Godfrey, Jan. 15, 1929;

Dumont to Brighton Auto Supply Co., Jan. 23, 1929; J. J. Matthews to Dumont Motor Car Co., Feb. 7, 1929; all in file 30, box 117, Jonsson Papers; *Bergen Evening Record* to Dumont Motor Car Co., Mar. 4, 1929; JEJ to Oakland Motor Car Co., May 20, 1929, both in file 17, box 121, Jonsson Papers.

55. JEJ to Robbie, Jan. 16, 1929, file 17, box 121, Jonsson Papers; JEJ to John, Apr. 3, 1929, file 30, box 117, Jonsson Papers.

56. Secrest interview, Nov. 28, 1970, 5.

57. Ibid.; insurance loan documents, especially those dated Dec. 28, 1929, are in file 8, box 120, Jonsson Papers; R. H. Snyder, GMAC, to "Eric Johnson," Sept. 29, 1932, file 2, box 122, Jonsson Papers.

58. H. C. Fonde to JEJ, Nov. 14, 1929, file 10, box 117, Jonsson Papers.

59. Undated, unsigned letter, translated from Swedish and addressed to Lilly Erickson, MJR Papers.

60. Mortuary record of Ellen C. Jonsson, Van Tassel & Roy; Van Tassel & Roy to JEJ, Nov. 1 and Dec. 15, 1930, all in file 10, box 120, Jonsson Papers; Van Tassel & Roy to JEJ, Nov. 10, 1931; Palmer Convalescent Home to JEJ, May 2, 1931, both in file 1, box 122, JEJ.

CHAPTER 4: A CALCULATED RISK

1. Warehouse receipt, Oct. 4, 1924, file 9, box 117, JEJ; Philip Jonsson, interview by the author, Dec. 1, 2003, Dallas.

2. Jonsson and Fortner Conversation, 10–11; MJR, interview by the author, Oct. 14, 2003, Dallas; Philip Jonsson, interview by Richard Tuck, July 19, 2002, Dallas.

3. Secrest interview, Nov. 28, 1970, 6.

4. "Commission Analysis," Dec. 19, 1929–Jan. 31, 1930, file 5, box 120, Jonsson Papers; Secrest interview, Nov. 28, 1970, 6.

5. Henderson, "Jonsson: Dreamer, Builder"; Secrest interview, Nov. 28, 1970, 7–9.

6. McCombs interview, 1.

7. Secrest interview, Nov. 28, 1970, 10–11; McCombs interview, 3.

8. McCombs interview, 3–4. In his manuscript for a history of the company, McCombs writes that DeGolyer retained 51 percent interest rather than 50 percent. Most accounts list 50 percent, but there seems to be a good chance that 51 percent is correct; see McCombs, "Tall Story of Texas Instruments," 11.

9. The preceding information is found in the following sources: Eugene McDermott, interview by Larry Secrest and Gary Hoffman, Apr. 9, 1971, 1, 2, 5, MJR Papers; Cecil H. Green, "Dr. John Clarence Karcher (1894–1978): Father of the Reflection Seismograph," draft of an article for *Geophysics: The Journal of the Society of Exploration Geophysicists*, June 1979, file 6, box 8, Jonsson Papers; McCombs, "Tall Story of Texas Instruments," 4–5; Eugene McDermott, interview by Holland McCombs, Aug. 5, 1959, 3, file 21, box 80, McCombs Papers. An excellent source for this information is the first chapter of an unpublished history of Texas Instruments that was started in 1976 by Patrick Haggerty upon his retirement and completed in 1985 by Kenneth Martin of History Associates, Inc. This 773-page manuscript is in box 95, Jonsson Papers (cited hereafter as TI unpublished history).

10. McCombs, "Tall Story of Texas Instruments," 11.

11. There are two contradictory versions of the job offer. JEJ stated that McDermott first suggested him for the job ("Conversation with Mayor Jonsson," 13). But McCombs describes Karcher as having suggested JEJ, at which point McDermott thought it might be unfair to ask him to leave Alcoa ("Tall Story of Texas Instruments," 15). Both telegrams are in file 27, box 116, Jonsson Papers.

12. Secrest interview, Nov. 28, 1970, 13; Holland McCombs, "Founding Phase," unpublished paper, 14, file 1, box 182, McCombs Papers; Henderson, "Jonsson: Dreamer, Builder."

13. "Conversation with Mayor Jonsson," 12; Secrest interview, Nov. 28, 1970, 11.

14. Secrest interview, Nov. 28, 1970, 13; TI unpublished history, 13; Henderson, "Jonsson: Builder, Dreamer"; E. J. McLaughlin to JEJ, July 15, 1932, file 10, box 115, Jonsson Papers.

15. JEJ believed he began work on July 15, 1930 (Secrest interview, Nov. 28, 1970, 13); for the quotation, see Karcher to "Eric Johnson," July 26, 1930, file 27, box 116, Jonsson Papers.

16. "Conversation with Mayor Jonsson," 14–15.

17. Secrest interview, Nov. 28, 1970, 14.

18. Ibid.

19. Dolores Proubasta, "Erik Jonsson," *Geophysics: The Leading Edge of Exploration*, June 1986, 20. "It wasn't a laboratory at all, it was just a shop for putting instruments together that were contracted for in four or five different shops so nobody knew what we were doing," Jonsson said in comments for the Strategic Planning Conference, Mar. 1977, MJR Papers.

20. JEJ, interview by Wes Wise with Bob Porter, June 30, 1992, Oral History Collection, Sixth Floor Museum at Dealey Plaza, 3–4 (hereafter cited as JEJ, Sixth Floor Museum oral history); Jonsson and Fortner Conversation, 7.

21. TI unpublished history, 14–15; William Cunningham "Bill" Edwards, interview by Holland McCombs, Aug. 4, 1959, 1, file 14, box 180, McCombs Papers.

22. Theodore Barrington, "A Tribute to Cecil Green," *Leading Edge*, Apr. 2004, 330.

23. Ibid.; Robert R. Shrock, *Cecil and Ida Green: Philanthropists Extraordinary* (Cambridge, Mass.: MIT Press, 1989), 36, 41, 52.

24. Cecil Green, interview by Larry Secrest, June 17, 1970, 1–15, Dolph Briscoe Center for American History, University of Texas at Austin; "Erik Jonsson's Tribute to Cecil Green," Nov. 6, 1978, file 2, box 114, Jonsson Papers; Mark Seal, "Cecil and Ida Green," *Dallas Morning News*, Dec. 25, 1983, file 12, box 112, Jonsson Papers; Shrock, *Cecil and Ida Green*, 81, 98.

25. Cecil Green, interviewed for the video . . . *And Not to Yield*, produced by Texas Instruments for the University of Texas at Dallas, 1989.

26. Al Altwegg, "Erik Jonsson Describes How He Became Employee of GSI," *Dallas Morning News*, Jan. 17, 1967; Proubasta, "Erik Jonsson," 20.

27. Henderson, "Jonsson: Dreamer, Builder."

28. Wilson, "Erik Jonsson," 8; correspondence between JEJ and manufacturers detailing the new parts, file 5, box 170, Jonsson Papers.

29. McCombs, "Tall Story of Texas Instruments," 13.

30. C. J. (Tommy) Thomsen to author, n.d. [2004].

31. Philip Jonsson interview, Dec. 1, 2003.

32. Simon P. Northrup to JEJ, Dec. 17, 1930, file 12, box 120, Jonsson Papers; the hospital bill is in file 10 in ibid.

33. JEJ to Stewart McFarlane, Feb. 17, 1931, file 18, box 116, Jonsson Papers.

34. H. C. Fonde to JEJ, May 19, 1931, file 10, box 116, Jonsson Papers; copy of the bankruptcy notice and attorneys' notification (dated Aug. 10, 1932) to JEJ of his discharge from bankruptcy on Aug. 1, 1932, file 2, box 122, Jonsson Papers; undated "Schedule" concerning bankruptcy, MJR Papers.

35. Secrest interview, Nov. 28, 1970, 6.

36. H. C. Fonde to Margaret Jonsson, Dec. 3, 1931, and Feb. 20, 1932, file 10, box 116, Jonsson Papers.

37. Jonsson to Polly Moran, *Newark Ledger*, Sept. 21, 1931, file 10, box 116, Jonsson Papers.

38. "The Tall Story Club," file 14, box 100, Jonsson Papers.

39. Hiram C. Fonde v. Margaret E. Jonsson and John E. Jonsson, May 5, 1933, file 2, box 122, Jonsson Papers; printed notice of bankruptcy, file 16, box 120, Jonsson Papers.

40. Philip Jonsson interview, Dec. 1, 2003. The camp that Philip Jonsson attended was Camp Waganaki in East Waterford, Maine. An invoice is in file 1, box 122, Jonsson Papers.

41. Mrs. Hiram Fonde to Margaret Jonsson, Feb. 13, 1936, file 4, box 119, Jonsson Papers.

42. "Sixty-three Discoveries of Pools on Gulf Coast Are Credited to the Use of Geophysics," *Oil and Gas Journal*, Oct. 5, 1933, 10–11, 34; GSI advertisement, *Oil and Gas Journal*, Dec. 28, 1933, 148.

43. Secrest interview, Nov. 28, 1970, 15.

44. Ibid.; TI unpublished history, 21.

45. McCombs interview, 11.

46. Ibid.

47. Quoted in Al Altwegg, "Erik in Love with Dallas," *Dallas Morning News*, Jan. 18, 1967; McCombs, "Tall Story of Texas Instruments," 22.

48. Al Altwegg, "Jonsson Recalls How He Went to Work for Company," *Dallas Morning News*,

Jan. 16, 1967; Philip Jonsson, interview by Richard Tuck, Aug. 14, 2002, Dallas; Philip Jonsson interview by author, Dec. 1, 2003, Dallas.

49. Cecil and Ida Green, diary entries, Dec. 25 and 31, 1934, and Jan. 1, 1935, Cecil H. and Ida Green Papers, Special Collections, University of Texas at Dallas (hereafter cited as Green Papers).

50. Cecil and Ida Green, diary entries, Mar. 30, Apr. 22, May 7, Nov. 4, Dec. 14, and Dec. 31, 1935, Green Papers.

51. John Peter Jonsson to Margaret and Erik Jonsson, n.d. [1934]; John Peter Jonsson to JEJ, July 9, 1935; both in file 1, box 119, Jonsson Papers.

52. TI unpublished history, 23; Holland McCombs's notes for a history of Texas Instruments, 15, file 1, box 182, McCombs Papers.

53. Henderson, "Erik Jonsson: Dreamer, Builder."

54. Ibid.

55. Altwegg, "Erik in Love with Dallas."

56. TI unpublished history, 24; Mary Ann Murphy, "History of the Semiconductor Industry," *Circuit News*, Apr. 15, 1979, photocopy in MJR Papers.

57. Philip Jonsson interview, Dec. 1, 2003.

58. JEJ, interview by Mavis Bryant, May 30, 1972, "What I Would Do If I Were 20 Today," MJR Papers (hereafter cited as Erik Jonsson and Mavis Bryant interview).

59. TI unpublished history, 25.

60. J. C. Karcher to JEJ, Feb. 26, 1935, file 27, box 116, Jonsson Papers; Secrest interview, Nov. 28, 1970, 1.

61. JEJ to Van Tassell, Apr. 22, 1935, file 2, box 122, Jonsson Papers.

62. "General Release," June 20, 1940, in ibid.; MJR, interview by the author, Oct. 14, 2003, Dallas.

63. Philip Jonsson interview, Dec. 1, 2003; "Tiny Tot Parade" program, Nov. 22, 1935, file 3, box 120, Jonsson Papers.

64. Philip Jonsson interview, Dec. 1, 2003; Dorothy Barton to Margaret Jonsson, Jan. 5, 1935, file 4, box 119, Jonsson Papers.

65. TI unpublished history, 26.

66. Henderson, "Jonsson: Dreamer, Builder."

67. Harris Cox to JEJ, May 20, 1937, file 5, box 170, Jonsson Papers.

68. G. H. Westby, Society of Petroleum Geophysicists, to JEJ, Dec. 2, 1935, file 5, box 170, Jonsson Papers.

69. The picture accompanies an article, "Tanner Elected President Dallas Purchasing Agents Association," *Southwestern Purchaser*, May 1937, 21, file 13, box 120, Jonsson Papers.

70. "Brockway's Visit to Texas Associations Stirs Increased Interest in N.A.P.A.; Eric [*sic*] Jonsson Elected President Dallas Association," *Southwestern Purchaser*, Apr. 1938, 10, in ibid.

71. Typewritten notes for undated speech, file 26, box 116, Jonsson Papers.

72. Program for Southwestern Sales Managers Anniversary Conference, Apr. 19–20, 1940, Fort Worth, file 13, box 100, Jonsson Papers.

73. "Among Ourselves," *Southwestern Purchaser*, Aug. 1938, 12, file 13, box 120, Jonsson Papers; JEJ to John Svenson, Feb. 4, 1939, file 10, box 116, Jonsson Papers.

CHAPTER 5: ANOTHER TURNING POINT

1. TI unpublished history, 34.

2. Ibid., 35.

3. McDermott interview by McCombs, 6.

4. "Did Trucks Ever Lick a Tougher Assignment," file 18, box 116, Jonsson Papers.

5. Contract dated Apr. 1, 1936, file 39, box 120, Jonsson Papers; TI unpublished history, 27.

6. "True and correct copy of bill of sale," Dec. 29, 1938, file 39, box 120, Jonsson Papers.

7. TI unpublished history, 29; Jonsson's salary is on the Treasury Department's Form 1099 for 1940, file 26, box 116, Jonsson Papers.

8. Philip Jonsson interview, Dec. 1, 2003. The sales slip for the piano is in file 19, box 119, Jonsson Papers.

9. Kenneth Jonsson, telephone interview by Richard Tuck, Sept. 6, 2002, transcript held by

author; Philip Jonsson interview, Dec. 1, 2003. The photograph in the *Dallas Morning News* appeared on Apr. 18, 1940, and is in file 28, box 100, Jonsson Papers.

10. Philip Jonsson interview, Dec. 1, 2003.

11. Ibid.

12. Ibid.

13. Kenneth Jonsson to his family, various dates, file 3, box 119, Jonsson Papers.

14. Kenneth Jonsson interview, Sept. 6, 2002.

15. George Renner to John P. Jonsson, Aug. 23, Aug. 25, and Sept. 30, 1939, MJR Papers.

16. John Svenson to JEJ, Jan. 2, 1939, and JEJ to Svenson, Feb. 4, 1939, file 10, box 116, Jonsson Papers; Fortner interview, 1.

17. John Peter Jonsson's obituary, *Dallas Morning News*, Sept. 28, 1942. His State of Texas death notice was no. 39533; see Secrest interview, Nov. 28, 1970, 1.

18. Henderson, "Jonsson: Dreamer, Builder."

19. Cecil Green interview, 1–15; "Erik Jonsson's Tribute to Cecil Green"; Seal, "Cecil and Ida Green"; Shrock, *Cecil and Ida Green*, 81, 98; TI unpublished history, 36.

20. Cecil and Ida Green, diary entry, June 12, 1941, Green Papers.

21. TI unpublished history, 36–38. News of Stanolind's purchase of Coronado appeared some three weeks before the completion of the purchase of GSI by JEJ, McDermott, Green, and Peacock; see "Stanolind Oil Buys Coronado," *New York Times*, Nov. 13, 1941.

22. TI unpublished history, 37. There are minor differences in the details of how the four principals were selected to buy GSI. JEJ said in an interview with Al Altwegg of the *Dallas Morning News* that when he reached McDermott in California, McDermott was the one who suggested that Green be one of the principals ("Chance to Buy GSI Came," *Dallas Morning News*, Jan. 19, 1967).

23. Henderson, "Jonsson: Dreamer, Builder"; TI unpublished history, 37.

24. Cecil and Ida Green diary entries, June 14 and 17, Aug. 27, 29, 30, and 31, 1941, Green Papers.

25. Ibid., Oct. 12 and 16, 1941.

26. TI unpublished history, 35, 37; Proubasta, "Biography: Erik Jonsson."

27. "Geophysical Service Capital Stock Purchased," *Oil Weekly*, Nov. 17, 1941, 80, file 19, box 116, Jonsson Papers.

28. Cecil Green diary entries, Oct. 24 and 27, Nov. 4, 5, 6, 7, 8, and 10, 1941, Green Papers.

29. Ibid., Nov. 4 and 5, 1941.

30. *Dallas Times Herald*, Nov. 10, 1941; Green diary entry, Nov. 10, 1941.

31. Herbert Robertson, *The ABCs of De: A Primer on Everette Lee DeGolyer, Sr.: 1886–1956* (Dallas: Red Horse Press, 2002), 19; "Stanolind Oil Buys Coronado," *New York Times*, Nov. 13, 1941; Henderson, "Jonsson: Dreamer, Builder"; "Conversation with Mayor Erik Jonsson," 16–17. Jonsson's son Philip had a "strong impression" that his father first went to First National Bank for a loan, but was turned down. Only then, he believes, did his father go to Florence at First National (Philip Jonsson interview, Dec. 1, 2003).

32. Agreement dated Dec. 5, 1941, and "An Announcement," file 39, box 120, Jonsson Papers; TI unpublished history, 37; "Geophysical Service Capital Stock Purchased," *Oil Weekly*, Nov. 17, 1941, file 19, box 116, Jonsson Papers. On several occasions JEJ gave descriptions of the purchase of GSI that differ in some respects from the one given here. He did not mention that negotiations had gone on throughout the summer of 1941. In JEJ's recollection, Karcher called him in November to alert him to the possibility of buying GSI and gave him just ten days to arrange it. Jonsson said he had difficulty in locating McDermott, Peacock, and Green in order to give them this news, and he signed the loan documents himself for all four men on Saturday, Dec. 6, 1941, the last day before the deadline. Green's diary entries say the documents were signed a day earlier, on Dec. 5, 1941, the same date appearing on the documents, and that all four principals were there in person. For JEJ's recollections, see TI unpublished history, 37; Al Altwegg, "Chance to Buy GSI Came," *Dallas Morning News*, Jan. 19, 1967; Henderson, "Jonsson: Dreamer, Builder."

33. Green diary entry, Dec. 6, 1941, Green Papers.

34. Henderson, "Jonsson: Dreamer, Builder."

35. Agreement dated Dec. 5, 1941, file 39, box 120, Jonsson Papers.

36. Altwegg, "Chance to Buy GSI Came."

37. Proubasta, "Biography: Erik Jonsson."

38. Cecil Green diary entry, Dec. 29, 1941, Green Papers.

39. Ibid., May 3, 4, 6, and 7, 1942.

40. Ibid., May 7, 10, and 14, June 13, and July 14, 18, 1942.

41. Ibid., July 18, 1942.

42. Cecil Green interview, 17.

43. Cecil and Ida Green diary entry, May 13, 1942, Green Papers; "Conversation with Mayor Jonsson," 19; McCombs interview, 9.

44. Proubasta, "Biography: Erik Jonsson"; McDermott interview by McCombs, [2].

45. TI unpublished history, 44.

46. Ibid., 45, 47.

47. "GSI Knows the Score Because GSI Makes the Machines that Keep the Score," *Southwestern Purchaser*, July 1945, reprinted in *Southwest Business*, July 1971, 17.

48. E. J. Toomey, interview by Holland McCombs, Aug. 12, 1959, 2, file 27, box 180, McCombs Papers.

49. Ibid.; McCombs, "Tall Story of Texas Instruments," 23.

50. Samuel Eliot Morison, *History of United States Naval Operations: The Atlantic Battle Won, May 1943–May 1945* (Boston: Little, Brown, 1964), 94–95.

51. TI unpublished history, 40.

52. "Jonsson Had Successor Ready," *Dallas Morning News*, Jan. 20, 1967.

53. TI unpublished history, 45.

54. Ibid., 42.

55. Quoted in ibid., 41.

56. Ibid., 47; JEJ, "Opening Remarks, 25th Anniversary Observance[,] Transistor Radio and Silicon Transistor," file 43, box 116, Jonsson Papers; McCombs, "Tall Story of Texas Instruments," 32.

57. Patrick Haggerty, interview by Holland McCombs, [c. 1959], file 16, box 180, McCombs Papers; "Jonsson Had Successor Ready."

58. Quoted in TI unpublished history, 46.

59. Philip Jonsson interviews, Dec. 1, 2003, Aug. 14, 2002, and Sept. 26, 2002. Philip Jonsson's letters to his parents detail his experiences during these wartime years; they are in file 2, box 119, Jonsson Papers.

60. Form 1099 for JEJ, 1942, file 19, and Form 1040 for JEJ, 1943, file 20, box 119, Jonsson Papers.

61. Receipts and documents listing these organizations and donations are found in files 19 and 20, box 119, Jonsson Papers. Philip refers to his father as the "big exec" in an undated letter to him [c. 1943] in file 2, box 119, Jonsson Papers.

62. McCombs interview, section entitled "The Knights of the Round Table, Take 12."

63. "Ye Editor Gossips: Dallas, Texas," *Excalibur*, Mar.–Apr. 1943, 11, file 1, box 104, Jonsson Papers.

64. "Convention Personalities," *Excalibur*, Aug.–Sept. 1948, 8, file 1, box 104, Jonsson Papers.

65. Smith, "Jonsson: TI's Founder," 36.

CHAPTER 6: FORESEEING THE FUTURE

1. "Conversation with Mayor Jonsson," 18–19.

2. Proubasta, "Erik Jonsson," 22–23; "History of Innovation," Texas Instruments website, accessed May 28, 2002, http://www.ti.com/corp/docs/company/history/interactivetimeline.shtml.

3. Erik Jonsson and Mavis Bryant interview.

4. Haggerty interview.

5. McCombs, "Tall Story of Texas Instruments," 33.

6. Ibid., 35; Haggerty interview, [22].

7. Haggerty interview, [18].

8. McCombs, "Tall Story of Texas Instruments," 32.

9. Haggerty to JEJ, n.d. [stamped "Received Oct. 29, 1946"], file 19, box 116, Jonsson Papers; Robert W. Olson, interview by Holland McCombs, Aug. 7, 1959, 2, file 22, box 180, McCombs Papers.

10. Haggerty to JEJ, n.d. [stamped "Received Oct. 29, 1946"], file 19, box 116, Jonsson Papers; Haggerty interview, [23].

11. TI unpublished history, 54.

12. JEJ, "Opening Remarks"; "GSI Private Payroll, July 1947," file 19, box 116, Jonsson Papers; "Jonsson Had Successor Ready."

13. Robert W. Olson, interview by Holland McCombs, Aug. 7, 1959, [1], file 22, box 180, McCombs Papers.

14. JEJ, "Opening Remarks"; JEJ, untitled and undated notes [1959], file 1, box 117, Jonsson Papers; McCombs, "Tall Story of Texas Instruments," 33.

15. JEJ, "Opening Remarks"; W. J. Hebard, Marquette University, "To Whom It May Concern," Mar. 6, 1942 (reference letter for Haggerty's proposed commission in the military), file 19, box 116, Jonsson Papers.

16. TI unpublished history, 46.

17. Ibid., 57; McCombs, "Tall Story of Texas Instruments," 38; Haggerty interview, [25].

18. TI unpublished history, 57; McCombs, "Tall Story of Texas Instruments," 39; Haggerty interview, [24].

19. JEJ related this information to Carl Sewell; see Sewell, interview by the author, June 20, 2004, Dallas. This was confirmed by C. J. (Tommy) Thomsen in an interview with the author, June 11, 2004, Dallas.

20. Haggerty interview, [24]; "Industrial Plant," *Architectural Forum* (reprint), Aug. 1949, file 19, box 112, Jonsson Papers.

21. E. J. Toomey, interview by Holland McCombs, Aug. 12, 1959, [3], file 27, box 180, McCombs Papers.

22. C. J. Thomsen, interview by Holland McCombs, n.d. [c. 1959], [1, 5], file 26, box 180, McCombs Papers; Thomsen interview, June 11, 2004.

23. W. F. "Wally" Joyce, interview by Holland McCombs, Aug. 7, 1959, [5], file 18, box 180, McCombs Papers.

24. S. T. Harris, interview by Holland McCombs, Aug. 6, 1959, [3], file 17, box 180, McCombs Papers; McCombs, "Tall Story of Texas Instruments," 58.

25. Joyce interview, 6–8; McCombs, "Tall Story of Texas Instruments," 37.

26. McCombs, "Tall Story of Texas Instruments," 50.

27. TI unpublished history, 58.

28. Ibid., 66.

29. Ibid.

30. Ibid., 69.

31. Ibid., 74.

32. Ibid., 69, 72.

33. McCombs, "Tall Story of Texas Instruments," 36, 40.

34. Ibid.

35. Ibid., 43, 70; TI unpublished history, 71; Proubasta, "Erik Jonsson," 23; P. E. Haggerty, *Management Philosophies and Practices of Texas Instruments, Incorporated* (Dallas: Texas Instruments, 1965), 17.

36. TI unpublished history, 73; Harris interview.

37. General Instruments, announcement, n.d., file 19, box 112, Jonsson Papers; "General Instruments, Inc., Dallas, Texas, Aug. 11, 1951," typewritten summary of the company, file 20, box 116, Jonsson Papers.

38. McCombs, "Tall Story of Texas Instruments," 50.

39. Ibid., 51.

40. TI unpublished history, 74.

41. Ibid.

42. Michael Riordan and Lillian Hoddeson, *Crystal Fire: The Birth of the Information Age* (New York: Norton, 1997), 8.

43. "Tubeless Radios," *Science Digest*, Sept. 1948, 93–94.

44. "The Time Machine: 1947," *American Heritage*, Dec. 1997, 97.

45. "Tubeless Radios," 93–94; "The Tiny Transistor," *Newsweek*, Sept. 6, 1941, 44.

46. McCombs, "Tall Story of Texas Instruments," 59. A TI employee named Earl Thomas said he brought the transistor's potential to Eugene McDermott's attention. McDermott was enthusiastic about the idea and was the "pusher" for exploring it as a TI project; see "Interview with Earl Thomas, July 13, 1996," conducted by John Daniels and Alvin C. Clement, University of North Texas Oral History Collection, no. 1130, 28–33, 42.

47. Haggerty quoted in TI unpublished history, 84.

48. Ibid.; Bryan F. Smith with Jim Henderson, "When the Storm Sleeps: The Hard Fall of Texas Instruments and the Case for Boardroom Independence," 23. This unpublished manuscript, completed in 1995, was provided to the author by Smith.

49. Quoted in McCombs, "Tall Story of Texas Instruments," 59–60.

50. Quoted in TI unpublished history, 86.

51. McCombs, "Tall Story of Texas Instruments, 60.

52. Quoted in ibid.

53. Dunlap's recollection quoted in TI unpublished history, 87.

54. Riordan and Hoddeson, *Crystal Fire,* 196–97.

55. McCombs, unpublished biographical profile of Shepherd, Dec. 5, 1961, file 24, box 180, McCombs Papers.

56. McCombs, "Tall Story of Texas Instruments," 41–42; TI unpublished history, 60.

57. TI unpublished history, 90–91.

58. Smith, "When the Storm Sleeps," 21.

59. "List of Stockholders," Oct. 2, 1952, and "List of Stockholders," Nov. 17, 1952, file 20, box 116, Jonsson Papers; Smith, "When the Storm Sleeps," 24.

60. TI unpublished history, 90; Bryan F. Smith, telephone interview with the author, Apr. 12, 2004. Peacock died on Aug. 17, 1985, in Dallas.

61. JEJ to V. Y. Rejebian, Feb. 16, 1948, file 2, box 48; John D. O'Brien, Brentano's, to JEJ, Feb. 11, 1949, file 3, box 48, Jonsson Papers.

62. James M. Moroney to JEJ, Apr. 28, 1948, file 2, box 48, Jonsson Papers.

63. "Personal History Statement," May 3, 1948, file 1, box 114; JEJ to Paul Hotchkiss, Mar. 11, 1949, file 3, box 48; George Waverly Briggs to JEJ, Jan. 4, 1949, file 3, box 48, all in Jonsson Papers.

64. JEJ, untitled summary of luncheon meeting with Manning Gurian, dated Nov. 7, 1947, and JEJ to Manning Gurian, Nov. 15, 1947, both in file 11, box 116, Jonsson Papers; JEJ to Philip Jonsson, Nov. 5, 1948, file 2, box 48, Jonsson Papers.

65. "Ice Parade of 1950," program, file 4, box 103, Jonsson Papers; John M. Haymes to Mrs. J. E. Jonsson, Aug. 16, 1951, file 5, box 48, Jonsson Papers; Secrest interview, Nov. 28,1970, 10–12.

66. Scholdan later perished with eighteen members of the U.S. World Figure Skating Team in an airplane crash near Brussels in 1961.

67. Kenneth Jonsson, telephone interview by Richard Tuck, Aug. 28, 2002, and Sept. 13, 2002.

68. Philip Jonsson interview, Sept. 26, 2002.

69. Information from the caption for a photograph of Margaret Jonsson in *Dallas Morning News,* Dec. 1, 1944, file 10, box 107, Jonsson Papers.

70. These included decisions to build competence in solid-state physics, institutionalize TI's approach to geophysics, expand engineering and manufacturing capabilities internationally, broaden the customer base, become less dependent on military procurement, establish the vertical integration of products, and diversify company capabilities; see Haggerty, *Management Philosophies,* 45–46.

71. TI unpublished history, 81; C. J. Thomsen, interview by the author, June 9, 2004, Dallas.

Chapter 7: A New Day

1. John McDonald, "The Men Who Made TI," *Fortune,* Nov. 1961, 116.

2. TI unpublished history, 89.

3. Smith, "When the Storm Sleeps," 19.

4. These reports for 1951 and 1952 were shown to the author by C. J. Thomsen, June 11, 2004; TI unpublished history, 94.

5. TI unpublished history, 95.

6. Ibid.; Smith, "When the Storm Sleeps," 24–25; Bryan F. Smith, interview by the author, Feb. 22, 2005, Dallas.

7. Agreement signed Dec. 31, 1945, between N. E. Wink, first party, and Eugene McDermott and JEJ, second parties; Sol Goodell to JEJ and McDermott, Aug. 6, 1947, both in file 16, box 116, Jonsson Papers.

8. McCombs, "Tall Story of Texas Instruments," 54; TI unpublished history, 109; "Addresses by the Presidents of Texas Instruments Incorporated and Houston Technical Laboratories," Oct. 26, 1956, file 23, box 116, Jonsson Papers.

9. TI unpublished history, 99–101; untitled *Business Week* clipping, Apr. 17, 1954, file 14, box 100, Jonsson Papers; Smith, "When the Storm Sleeps," 26.

10. TI unpublished history, 98–99.

11. Ibid., 103–5; Thomsen interview, June 11, 2004.

12. TI unpublished history, 104.

13. Ibid., 105–6; McCombs, "Tall Story of Texas Instruments," 57; McDonald, "Men Who Made TI," 218.

14. TI unpublished history, 105–6; Bryan F. Smith, interview by the author, May 20, 2004, Dallas.

15. Bryan F. Smith, interview by the author, Sept. 8, 2004, Dallas.

16. Bryan F. Smith, interview by the author, May 27, 2005, Dallas.

17. McCombs's notes on profile of Shepherd, Dec. 5, 1961, file 24, box 180, McCombs Papers; "History of the Semiconductor Industry: The Birth of Texas Instruments," *Circuit News*, Apr. 15, 1979, MJR Papers.

18. McCombs's notes on profile of Shepherd; "History of the Semiconductor Industry"; TI unpublished history, 125, 126, 131; "Miniature Became Huge," *Dallas Morning News*, May 13, 2005.

19. TI unpublished history, 125.

20. Francis Bello, "The Year of the Transistor," *Fortune*, Mar. 1953, 129.

21. Thomsen interview, June 11, 2004; TI unpublished history, 127–28.

22. A reprint of the advertisement with an accompanying letter from JEJ to shareholders is in file 4, box 133X, Jonsson Papers.

23. Gordon Teal, interview by Holland McCombs, n.d., [1–5], file 25, box 180, McCombs Papers; McDonald, "Men Who Made TI," 121; Bryan F. Smith, interview by the author, Apr. 20, 2005, Dallas.

24. Riordan and Hoddeson, *Crystal Fire*, 197.

25. Teal interview, [6–7]; TI unpublished history, 123.

26. Teal interview, [12]; TI unpublished history, 135–36.

27. TI unpublished history, 137.

28. Teal interview, [10].

29. TI unpublished history, 137–38; Teal interview, [10–11].

30. "Silicon Transistors Now in Production," advertisement appearing in June 1954 in *Electronics, Instruments, and Automation, Telell-Tech*, and *Proceedings of I.R.E*; copy in file 17, box 93, Jonsson Papers.

31. John McDonald, "The Men Who Made T.I.," *Fortune*, Nov. 1961, 116. The second part by the same author, "Where Texas Instruments Goes from Here," appeared in Dec. 1961.

32. "History of the Semiconductor Industry," 4.

33. TI unpublished history, 140–41; "Newcomer's Growth," *Time*, Apr. 8, 1957, 79–81; McCombs, "Tall Story of Texas Instruments," 57; Annual Report 1957, Texas Instruments, 7, 9, file 17, box 94, Jonsson Papers.

34. TI unpublished history, 158.

35. Ibid., 141; Haggerty, *Management Philosophies*, 53.

36. Riordan and Hoddeson, *Crystal Fire*, 211.

37. TI unpublished history, 145.

38. Michael F. Wolff, "The Secret Six-Month Project," *IEEE Spectrum*, Dec. 1985, 64–69; Riordan and Hoddeson, *Crystal Fire*, 211.

39. Wolff, "Secret Six-Month Project."

40. Ibid.; "President's Letter," Annual Report 1954, Texas Instruments, file 17, box 94, Jonsson Papers.

41. Riordan and Hoddeson, *Crystal Fire*, 212–13.

42. TI unpublished history, 157–58.

43. Ibid., 155–56; Riordan and Hoddeson, *Crystal Fire*, 7.

44. TI unpublished history, 159.

45. President's Letter, Annual Report 1954, TI.

46. Thomas J. Watson Jr. and Peter Petre, *Father, Son & Co.: My Life at IBM and Beyond* (New York: Bantam, 1990), 296–97.

47. TI unpublished history, 192–93.

48. Watson and Petre, *Father, Son & Co.*, 297.

49. TI unpublished history, 160.

50. Ibid., 160–63; Riordan and Hoddeson, *Crystal Fire*, 7.

51. TI unpublished history, 204–210; McCombs, "Tall Story of Texas Instruments," 72.

52. "Stage of Growth—1955," typewritten sheet, file 35, box 6, Jonsson Papers.

53. A. D. Bestebreurtje to JEJ, Mar. 15, 1955, file 22, box 116, Jonsson Papers.

54. Quoted in TI unpublished history, 164.

55. Ibid., 167–68.

56. "Research Packed with Ph.D.s," *Business Week*, Dec. 22, 1956, 56–58, 63–64.

57. JEJ, "The Story of Texas Instruments, Incorporated," a talk before the New York Society of Security Analysts, Dec. 13, 1956, file 27, box 95, Jonsson Papers.

58. Notice of Annual and Special Meeting of Stockholders, Mar. 21, 1955, file 20, box 94, Jonsson Papers; McDonald, "Men Who Made TI," 116.

59. Joe Cunningham, "Jonsson of Texas' Transworld 'TexIns,'" *Texas Parade*, Mar. 1958, 42–46, file 1, box 112, Jonsson Papers.

60. McCombs, "Tall Story of Texas Instruments," 82.

61. Carl M. Franklin to JEJ, May 16, 1963, file 11, box 102, Jonsson Papers.

62. Speech list, 1953–68, file 2, box 1, Jonsson Papers.

63. "Problem Solving Clinic," *Management Methods*, Dec. 1957, 71, file 8, box 100, Jonsson Papers.

64. Ibid.

65. C. J. Thomsen, interview by Richard Tuck, Aug. 23, 2002, Dallas; "Personal Recollections"; program for AMA General Management Conference, Jan. 24, 27, 1955, file 8, box 100, Jonsson Papers.

66. JEJ, "Controls for Growth," in *Controls and Techniques for Better Management*, General Management Series 176 (New York: American Management Association, 1955), 15–23, file 35, box 6, Jonsson Papers.

67. "Jonsson Elected Vice President," undated and unidentified newspaper clipping, file 8, box 100, Jonsson Papers.

68. Economic Mobilization Conference program, May 19–20, 1958, and dinner program, May 20, 1958, file 8, box 100, Jonsson Papers; "Forecasting a Turn for the Better," *Business Week*, May 24, 1958, file 9, box 100, Jonsson Papers.

69. Sam B. Lyons, "A Summit Meeting of Business," *Finance*, June 15, 1958, 30, file 9, box 100, Jonsson Papers.

CHAPTER 8: AGENT OF CHANGE

1. Haggerty interview, [23].

2. Smith interviews, Apr. 12 and May 20, 2004.

3. "A Plant with an Upstairs Basement," *Architectural Forum*, Sept. 1958, 132–34.

4. Smith interview, Sept. 8, 2004.

5. "Jack St. Clair Kilby: The Chip That Jack Built," Texas Instruments, http://www.ti.com/corp/docs/kilbyctr/jackbuilt.shtml; "Jack S. Kilby: Biographical," Nobelprize.org, http://www.nobelprize.org/nobel_prizes/physics/laureates/2000/kilby-bio.html; Texas Instruments, Annual Report 1959, 11.

6. Another inventor, Robert Noyce, of Fairchild Semiconductor, achieved a similar breakthrough and applied for a patent six months after Kilby. In 1967, the Board of Patent Interferences

ruled that Kilby's patent covered Noyce's method. Fairchild won an appeal in 1969 from the U.S. Court of Customs and Patent Appeals. The two companies eventually decided to cross-license their technologies. Kilby and Noyce are considered coinventors of the integrated circuit.

7. Mary Bellis, "The History of the Integrated Circuit aka Microchip: Jack Kilby and Robert Noyce," About.com, http://inventors.about.com/od/istartinventions/a/intergrated_circuit.htm.

8. "Jack St. Clair Kilby"; "Jack S. Kilby: Biographical"; Mary Bellis, "History of the Integrated Circuit.

9. JEJ, "1957, Dallas Chamber of Commerce" (a summary of events), file 4, box 100, Jonsson Papers.

10. "Jonsson Kicks Off Match," *Dallas Morning News*, Dec. 10, 1957, in ibid.

11. "Erik Jonsson Named Leading '58 Salesman," *Dallas Morning News*, Jan. 31, 1959, file 15, box 100, Jonsson Papers; "The Greater Dallas Chamber of Commerce J. Erik Jonsson Award," typescript document, Sept. 1, 1988, file 20, box 102, Jonsson Papers.

12. Clardy McCullar, "Jonsson: Work and Daring," *Dallas Morning News*, Feb. 23, 1958, file 14, box 120, Jonsson Papers.

13. JEJ to Orville Cartwright, Sept. 11, 1961, file 13, box 48, Jonsson Papers.

14. The anecdote was related to the author by several persons, including Ross Perot and Hunt's daughter, Caroline Rose Hunt.

15. McCullar, "Jonsson: Work and Daring"; JEJ to C. B. Lambert, Dec. 4, 1958, file 8, box 48, Jonsson Papers.

16. MJR, interview by the author, May 14, 2004, Dallas.

17. Henry J. Kaiser Jr. to Erik and Margaret Jonsson, May 19, June 8, and June 24, 1960, file 28, box 100, Jonsson Papers; JEJ to Henry J. Kaiser Jr., Aug. 24, 1960, and JEJ to Herbert Barchoff, Aug. 17, 1960, both in file 10, box 48, Jonsson Papers.

18. MJR interview, May 14, 2004; Betty Carper, "Dallas Woman's Club Head Inspires Members," *Dallas Times Herald*, June 8, 1961, file 10, box 107, Jonsson Papers.

19. "Personal Recollections"; Lisa Palmquist Olson to JEJ, Nov. 11, 1954, file 12, box 116, Jonsson Papers.

20. Lisa Palmquist Olson to JEJ, Nov. 11, 1954.

21. Charles M. Bedell to JEJ, Jan. 23 and Mar. 5, 1958, MJR Papers.

22. C. J. Thomsen, interview by the author, June 22, 2004, Dallas.

23. "Presentation to Dallas Classroom Teachers Association, December 5, 1960," file 24, box 5, Jonsson Papers.

24. Cecil Green to R. M. Kimball, Dec. 1957, file 8, box 48, Jonsson Papers.

25. Material related to Hockaday and Jonsson's tenure as chairman are in file 23, box 100, Jonsson Papers; "Dallas' Man of the Year," *Sunday*, magazine supplement to the *Dallas Times Herald*, Dec. 30, 1962, file 16, box 100, Jonsson Papers.

26. "Dedication, The Hockaday School," Oct. 21, 1962, file 23, box 100, Jonsson Papers.

27. "Graduate Education in the Southwest," *Journal of the Graduate Research Center*, Mar. 29, 1961, 85, file 29, box 100, Jonsson Papers.

28. "Engineer of the Intellect: John Erik Jonsson," *Saturday Review*, June 3, 1961, 46; "SRC: Bold New Plan for a Bright New Day," *Dallas Morning News*, Feb. 24, 1963; both in file 30, box 100, Jonsson Papers.

29. "SMU Research and Computer Centers Mark Progressive Bond," *Dallas*, Nov. 1957, 21; "Graduate Research Center A-building," *Dallas Morning News*, undated clipping, file 29, box 100, Jonsson Papers.

30. "Univac Goes to Work," *Dallas Morning News*, Nov. 16, 1957, file 29, box 100, Jonsson Papers; "Research Unit Draws Top Scientists to Area," *Dallas Times Herald*, Nov. 28, 1961.

31. The Univac message is attached to a news story describing the event: "Military Controls for Missiles Asked," *Dallas Times Herald*, Nov. 15, 1957.

32. "Research Center Plans Building," *Dallas Morning News*, Mar. 22, 1959.

33. "$750,000 Gift Boosts SMU Science Center," *Dallas Times Herald*, Mar. 22, 1959; "Research Center Chief Predicts Revolution in Graduate Education," *Dallas Times Herald*, Dec. 4, 1960.

34. "Distinguished Scientist Comes to GRC," *SMU Mustang*, Feb. 1961, n.p., file 29, box 100, Jonsson Papers.

35. McElvaney's introduction of Jonsson is in file 25, box 5, Jonsson Papers.

36. "Contribution Agreement," Feb. 18, 1961; "Agreement with Respect to Public Solicitation for Contributions," Feb. 18, 1961; both in MJR Papers.

37. L. V. Berkner, "Graduate Education in the Southwest," *Journal of the Graduate Research Center*, May 1961, 117, file 29, box 100, Jonsson Papers.

38. Berkner, foreword to "Graduate Education in the Southwest," [v], in ibid.

39. "Engineer of the Intellect," 46–47.

40. "Fine Arts Project Given Significant Support," *SMU Mustang*, Feb. 1961, 12, file 29, box 100, Jonsson Papers; Willis M. Tate to JEJ, May 27, 1960, file 12, box 48, Jonsson Papers; "Historic McFarlin Rededicated," *SMU Mustang*, Jan.–Feb. 1962, file 30, box 100, Jonsson Papers; "McFarlin Auditorium," *Sunday* (magazine supplement to the *Dallas Times Herald*), Nov. 19 [1961], file 10, box 5, Jonsson Papers.

41. "Scientific Library at SMU Dedicated," *Dallas Morning News*, Nov. 4, 1961; "Service of Dedication, Science Information Center of Southern Methodist University"; both in file 30, box 100, Jonsson Papers.

42. "Toward a Plan for the Development of the Graduate School of Southern Methodist University: Part I—Advanced Studies of Engineering, Mathematics, and Natural Science, 1960–1961," May 30, 1961, file 40, box 93, Jonsson Papers.

43. Willis M. Tate to JEJ, June 26, 1961, file 40, box 93, Jonsson Papers.

44. "Ex-Mayor Is Determined to Create Engineering School," *Dallas Times Herald*, June 5, 1983.

45. "The Master Plan of Southern Methodist University, 1963–1969," Southern Methodist University, 67, 9.

46. "Can It Make the Leap to Greatness?," *D Magazine*, Dec. 1986, 111, file 5, box 90, Jonsson Papers.

47. Quoted in Peter O'Donnell Jr., interview by the author, Sept. 26, 2005, Dallas.

48. "Research Hub Due," *Dallas Times Herald*, Sept. 23, 1962.

49. "Research Building Opens," *Dallas Morning News*, Oct. 30, 1964; Tommy Ayres, "Brainpower Plant," *Dallas Times Herald*, Feb. 25, 1968. The word "quasar" was used in a *New York Times* article (Dec. 21, 1964) on the symposium; cited in . . . *And Not to Yield* (1989), a TI video prepared for UTD.

50. C. Arthur Booth, "Lloyd Viel Berkner: A Man of Distinction," unpublished paper, May 1978, iii, file 31, box 105, Jonsson Papers.

51. Program for SMU's forty-ninth annual convocation, commencement exercises, and conferring of degrees, June 1, 1964, file 30, box 100, Jonsson Papers.

52. Willis M. Tate to JEJ, Aug. 2, 1964, file 4, box 170, Jonsson Papers.

53. Ibid.

54. "Brainpower Plant."

55. TI unpublished history, 323–24.

56. "EEF Intends to Give 500 Acres to UT-Dallas," *Advance*, Mar. 20, 1975, file 20, box 90, Jonsson Papers.

57. "Four Delegates Attend Congress Held This Summer in Houston," *Delta Mu News*, Oct. 1958, file 27, box 100; J. D. McKelvy to JEJ, June 22, 1948, file 2, box 48; program for "Class of 1922 Thirtieth Reunion," June 6 and 7, 1952, file 6, box 48; all in Jonsson Papers.

58. Program, "Rensselaer Polytechnic Institute, One Hundred Fifty-Third Commencement," June 5, 1959, file 12, box 100, Jonsson Papers.

59. "RPI Benefactor Subject of Article in Magazine," undated newspaper clipping, file 12, box 100, Jonsson Papers; Livingston W. Houston to JEJ, Dec. 17, 1959, file 27, box 100, Jonsson Papers; *Margaret and Erik Jonsson and RPI: Partners in Progress*, booklet, Apr. 1980, MJR Papers.

60. "RPI Benefactor"; "Tour Guide, Jonsson & Rowland Laboratories of the Science Center," file 12, box 100, Jonsson Papers; "College Honors Erik Jonsson," *Dallas Morning News*, June 15, 1963; *Margaret and Erik Jonsson and RPI*.

61. Program, "The Board of Trustees of Rensselaer Polytechnic Institute pays tribute to J. Erik Jonsson '22 October 26, 1990," F23, B111, Jonsson Papers.

62. Val H. Wilson to JEJ, Oct. 10, 1957; JEJ to Wilson, Oct. 17, 1957; both in file 8, box 15, Jonsson Papers.

63. Norma MacRury, dean, to Mr. And Mrs. Jonsson, Oct. 23, 1957; Val H. Wilson to JEJ, Dec. 10, 1957, and Jan. 22, 1958; all in ibid.

64. JEJ to Val H. Wilson, Jan. 27, 1958, in ibid.

65. Val H. Wilson to JEJ, June 25 and Sept. 24, 1959, in ibid.

66. Val H. Wilson to JEJ, June 15 and July 21, 1960, in ibid.

67. Skidmore College booklet entitled *The New Skidmore Campus*, [1962]; "Skidmore College Head Lauds Johnson [*sic*] for Gift," Jan. 16, 1961; both in file 25, box 100, Jonsson Papers.

68. O'Neil Ford to JEJ, Nov. 12, 1979, file 10, box 8, Jonsson Papers.

69. Val H. Wilson to JEJ, Aug. 20, Sept. 23, and Oct. 25, 1960, file 8, box 15; "Texan Gives Skidmore Woodlawn Park," *Saratogian*, Oct. 22, 1960, clipping in file 25, box 100; all in Jonsson Papers.

70. Val H. Wilson to trustees, Sept. 13, 1960, file 8, box 15, Jonsson Papers.

71. George Davis's handwritten note to JEJ on letter to trustees of Skidmore, Oct. 27, 1960, in ibid.

72. Mrs. George E. Ladd Jr. to JEJ, n.d., in ibid.

73. JEJ to Val H. Wilson, Nov. 7, 1960, in ibid.

74. "Investment in the Future," *Albany Times Union*, Mar. 5, 1963, file 25, box 100, Jonsson Papers.

75. "Ex-Dallas Mayor Honored at Skidmore Ceremonies," *Albany Knickerbocker News, Union-Star*, May 1, 1972, file 9, box 15, Jonsson Papers.

76. Mrs. Everett Case to JEJ, May 12, 1980; JEJ to Mrs. Everett Case, May 19, 1980; both in file 9, box 15; James E. McCabe to William A. Sharkey, Nov. 24, 1976, file 35, box 105; all in Jonsson Papers.

77. JEJ to Tommy Sparrow, Aug. 19, 1960, and Sept. 6, 1961; Nelle Johnston to Sparrow, Jan. 29, 1962, all in MJR Papers.

CHAPTER 9: CENTER STAGE AT A NATIONAL TRAGEDY

1. Martin S. Buehler, MD, to JEJ, Aug. 8, 1961, file 11, box 102, Jonsson Papers.

2. "Linz Award Presented to Jonsson," *Dallas Morning News*, Feb. 24, 1961.

3. "United Fund Tops Goal," *Dallas Times Herald*, undated clipping; "Jonsson Named to United Fund Advisory Unit," *Dallas Times Herald*, Oct. 24, 1961; John D. Miller to JEJ, June 7, 1978; brochure entitled "Step Into the Future," 1989; all in file 11, box 105, Jonsson Papers.

4. Herbert Gambrell to JEJ, Apr. 16, 1960; JEJ to Gambrell, Feb. 9, 1962, file 19, box 102, Jonsson Papers.

5. MJR interview, Oct. 14, 2003.

6. "Meet the New First Lady of Dallas," *Dallas Times Herald*, Feb. 9, 1964.

7. The photograph with caption is in a clipping in file 10, box 107, Jonsson Papers. It appears to be from the *Dallas Morning News*, although a *Dallas Times Herald* dateline, May 2, 1961, is attached to it.

8. "Sen. Blakley Sells Stock in Braniff," *Dallas Morning News*, May 20, 1961; untitled news release, May 19, [1961], file 1, box 102, Jonsson Papers; "Blakley Sells Interest in Braniff," *Dallas Times Herald*, May 19, 1961.

9. "Braniff Names Erik Jonsson to Board Post," *Dallas Times Herald*, Aug. 7, 1961; "Firm to Assume Braniff Control," *Dallas Morning News*, July 8, 1964.

10. Richard Curry, "Perspective," *Dallas Times Herald*, Dec. 5, 1965.

11. William Manchester, *The Death of a President: November 20–November 25, 1963* (New York: Harper and Row, 1967), 21.

12. Jonsson's personal calendar for 1963 lists the Citizens Council meeting at 12:15 p.m., Oct. 1, 1963, file 4, box 114, Jonsson Papers.

13. Manchester, *Death of a President*, 22; Darwin Payne, *Big D: Triumph and Troubles of an American Supercity in the 20th Century* (Dallas: Three Forks Press, 2000), 358–59; Mike Quinn, "JFK Parley by Connally Requested," *Dallas Morning News*, Oct. 1, 1963; "J. Erik Jonsson," Oral History Collection, Sixth Floor Museum at Dealey Plaza, interview 1, conducted by Wes Wise and Bob Porter, June 30, 1992, 10 (hereafter cited as JEJ, Sixth Floor Museum oral history).

14. Payne, *Big D*, 358–59.

15. "Birch Leader Says He Doubts Ike Red," *Dallas Morning News*, Oct. 30, 1963.

16. J. Erik Jonsson, interview by Alan Mason, Mayor's Oral History Program of East Texas State University and the Dallas Public Library, June 26, 1980, 2, file 1, box 1, Jonsson Papers; "The Unspoken Speech of John F. Kennedy at Dallas, November 22, 1963," privately printed for Stanley Marcus, 1964, file 11, box 91, Jonsson Papers.

17. JEJ, Sixth Floor Museum oral history, 10; "Mr. Jonsson's 36 ticket list—plus JEJ's 2 guest tickets equals 38," typewritten sheet, MJR Papers. In his undelivered address, President Kennedy acknowledged in his first sentence his pleasure at being invited to a special meeting of the Dallas Citizens Council; see "Unspoken Speech."

18. Manchester, *Death of a President*, 24; JEJ, Sixth Floor Museum oral history, 10.

19. JEJ, Sixth Floor Museum oral history, 10–11.

20. Margaret Jonsson, untitled, undated handwritten memoir, MJR Papers.

21. Quoted in Theodore C. Sorenson, *Kennedy* (New York: Harper and Row, 1965), 750.

22. JEJ, Sixth Floor Museum oral history, 14.

23. Jonsson's comments were recorded by KDFW-TV, and the videotape is in the KDFW-TV Collection, Sixth Floor Museum at Dealey Plaza.

24. Ibid.

25. JEJ, Sixth Floor Museum oral history, 14.

26. Ibid.; *Dallas Morning News*, Nov. 23, 1963; "Twenty Years Later," from a special section in the *Dallas Morning News*, Nov. 20, 1983; JEJ, Sixth Floor Museum oral history, 14.

27. JEJ, Sixth Floor Museum oral history, 14.

28. The rough draft of the statement is on an untitled typewritten sheet on Dallas Market Center letterhead; a more polished version is on a typewritten page entitled "A Statement from the Dallas Citizens Council, the Dallas Assembly and the Science Research Center"; both are in the MJR Papers.

29. JEJ to Mrs. John F. Kennedy, telegram, Nov. 22, 1963, MJR Papers.

30. "Statement from the Dallas Citizens Council."

31. JEJ, handwritten notes chronicling key events of the weekend of Nov. 22–24, 1963, MJR Papers.

32. JEJ, Sixth Floor Museum oral history, 16.

33. Ibid., 15–16; JEJ, events of Nov. 22–24, 1963.

34. JEJ, Sixth Floor Museum oral history, 16.

35. Ibid., 14; Margaret Jonsson, handwritten memoir.

36. JEJ, Sixth Floor Museum oral history, 16–17.

37. Ibid., 17.

38. Ibid., 18.

39. Ibid., 19.

40. Robert S. Altger, Pacific Palisades, California, to Cabell, Nov. 24, 1963, file 1, box 11, MSS 16, Earle Cabell Papers, DeGolyer Library, Southern Methodist University.

41. All quoted in Payne, *Big D*, 366–67.

42. JEJ, Sixth Floor Museum oral history, 19.

43. Ibid., 19–20.

44. Ibid., 1; "MEMO, November 26, 1963, To Mr. Jonsson, Record of Calls," typewritten sheet, MJR Papers.

45. "Dallas & World Opinion: So Much To Do," *PR Reporter*, Dec. 9, 1963, MJR Papers.

46. O'Neil Ford to JEJ, [Nov. 25, 1963], file 11, box 91, Jonsson Papers.

47. "Minutes of the First Meeting of the John F. Kennedy Citizens Memorial Committee," typewritten, Dec. 3, 1963, MJR Papers; "Joint Statement of County Judge Lew Sterrett[,] Mayor Earle Cabell," Dec. 2, 1963, file 16, box 11, MSS 16, Earle Cabell Papers.

48. JEJ, Sixth Floor Museum oral history, 20.

49. Second page of undated memo from SGP [Sid G. Pietzsch], file 21, box 6, Earle Cabell Papers.

50. JEJ, Sixth Floor Museum oral history, 20.

51. "Jonsson Agrees to Become Mayor If Cabell Resigns," *Dallas Morning News*, Jan. 15, 1964.

52. JEJ, Sixth Floor Museum oral history, 21.

53. Ibid.

54. Peyton Davis, "Sunday Q&A," *Dallas Times Herald*, Sunday magazine, Nov. 14, 1976, 17.

55. "Conversation with Mayor Jonsson," 21–22.

56. "Jonsson Agrees to Become Mayor."

57. "Mayor Post To Jonsson?," *Dallas Times Herald*, Jan. 15, 1964.

58. "Jonsson Selection Irks Pair," *Dallas Times Herald*, Jan. 15, 1964.

59. Jim McDade to Jonsson, Jan. 17, 1964; Jonsson to McDade, Jan. 21, 1964, file 11, box 14, Jonsson Papers.

60. Melville M. Mercer to JEJ, Jan. 17, 1964; typescript of program, "Congressman Alger Reports to the People: 'Dallas' Golden Decade,'"; both in file 20, box 69, Jonsson Papers.

61. Quoted in Payne, *Big D*, 368; Elizabeth Blessing, oral history interview by Gerald Saxon, Apr. 28, 1981, tape 172, side 2 of 4, Dallas Public Library; Francis Raffetto, "Jonsson Takes Office as Cabell Steps Down to Run for Congress," *Dallas Morning News*, Feb. 4, 1964.

62. Quoted in Warren Leslie, *Dallas Public and Private: Aspects of an American City* (New York: Grossman, 1964), 67–68.

63. "Mr. Mayor: One Coming . . . ," *Dallas Times Herald*, Feb. 5, 1964.

64. Dick Hitt, "News in the Names," *Dallas Times Herald*, Feb. 6, 1964.

65. JEJ's full text is reprinted in "New Mayor's 'Convictions,'" *Dallas Morning News*, Feb. 8, 1964; "Understanding Problems Forte of Dallas Mayor," *Dallas Times Herald*,, Feb. 9, 1964.

66. "New Mayor's 'Convictions.'"

67. Cecil H. Green to Mr. and Mrs. J. E. Jonsson, Feb. 7, 1964; R. L. Thornton to JEJ, Feb. 7, 1964; both in file 15, box 11, Jonsson Papers.

68. Edwin O. Cartwright to JEJ, Feb. 4, 1963, file 16, box 11, Jonsson Papers.

69. JEJ to W. M. Holland, Feb. 11, 1964, file 15, box 11, Jonsson Papers.

CHAPTER 10: IN THE PUBLIC ARENA

1. Nelle Johnston to Martha Riggs, Feb. 15, 1965, file 12, box 17, Jonsson Papers.

2. "Nelle Johnston: An Oral History Interview," conducted by Alan Mason, Aug. 28, 1980, East Texas State University and Dallas Public Library, 4.

3. Richard Austin Smith, "How Business Failed Dallas," *Fortune*, July 1964, 157–63, 211–14, 216.

4. Stanley Marcus to JEJ, Mar. 26, 1964, file 15, box 69, Jonsson Papers.

5. "Understanding Problems of Dallas Mayor," *Dallas Times Herald*, Feb. 9, 1964.

6. JEJ, Sixth Floor Museum oral history, 21.

7. "Eric [*sic*] Jonsson Interview," n.d., by LC, file 17, box 88, Jonsson Papers.

8. "New Mayor Gets Test under Fire," *Dallas Times Herald*, Feb. 11, 1964.

9. "A Father, a Brother, a Son," *Dallas Morning News*, Feb. 17, 1964.

10. "Jonsson's Talk Draws Praise from Carlson" and "Facing Our City's Future" (editorial), *Dallas Times Herald*, Apr. 2, 1964; "City Seeks Way to Lighten Heavy Load of Zoning Cases," *Dallas Times Herald*, Mar. 15, 1964; "Jonsson Sees Future Need for Flexibility," *Dallas Times Herald*, Apr. 1, 1964; all in file 7, box 60, Jonsson Papers.

11. "Jonsson Reviews First Three Months," *Dallas Morning News*, May 3, 1964.

12. Ibid.; Nelle Johnston to *New York Times* Circulation Dept., Mar. 2, 1964, file 18, box 48, Jonsson Papers. JEJ listed his subscriptions on a survey sheet in ibid.

13. Documents related to the tour are in file 6, box 21, and file 14, box 60, Jonsson Papers. The list of luncheon guests is attached to a letter from Andrew DeShong to Ray E. Hubbard, Apr. 22, 1964, file 6, box 21, Jonsson Papers.

14. Andy DeShong to JEJ, May 12, 1964, file 6, box 21, Jonsson Papers.

15. Charles G. Cullum, interview by the author, June 17, 2004, Dallas.

16. Garland Cullum, "Red Carpet Out for Dallas Group," *Dallas Times Herald*, May 27, 1964. The author, the wife of Charles Cullum, was a part-time columnist for the newspaper.

17. "Dallas Group Visits Sweden," *Dallas Morning News*, undated clipping, file 14, box 60, Jonsson Papers; Charles G. Cullum, telephone interview by the author, June 24, 2003.

18. Colin McFadyean to S. T. Harris, Apr. 22 and 28, 1964, file 6, box 21, Jonsson Papers.

19. "'Violent Image' of Dallas Found Abroad by Mayor," Associated Press, in *Dallas Times Herald*, May 26, 1964.

20. "London Letter," *Guardian*, May 27, 1964, file 14, box 60, Jonsson Papers.

21. Keith Deves, "So We Are All Wrong about Big D," *Daily Herald (UK)*, May 27, 1964; "A Dallas Defender: Its Mayor Abroad," Reuters, in *New York Post*, May 27, 1964; both in file 14, box 60, Jonsson Papers.

22. "Swedish Planning Impresses Jonsson," *Dallas Morning News*, May 30, 1964; "Parks Impress Mayor on Trip," *Dallas Times Herald*, May 31, 1964.

23. Cullum interview, June 17, 2004.

24. "Mayor Asks Recognition of City's Weaknesses," *Dallas Morning News*, June 5, 1964, file 9, box 60, Jonsson Papers.

25. JEJ, Sixth Floor Museum oral history, 4. In the basement connecting these two buildings, Jack Ruby shot and killed Lee Harvey Oswald.

26. Ibid.

27. "Eric Jonsson Interview," 2; JEJ, Sixth Floor Museum oral history, 5.

28. "Eric Jonsson Interview," 3.

29. "Mayor for Move," *Dallas Morning News*, May 27, 1964.

30. "Mayor Urges Grander Plan for City Hall," *Dallas Times Herald*, Sept. 3, 1964; "City Expansion Group Given Mission Outline," *Dallas Morning News*, Sept. 3, 1964; "Work Units Formed For City Hall Study," *Dallas Morning News*, Sept. 24, 1964; "Group Readies Site Report on City Hall," *Dallas Times Herald*; all in file 13, box 60, Jonsson Papers.

31. John N. Jackson to JEJ, Dec. 12, 1964, with attachment entitled "City Hall Site Committee Memorandum of Sites Considered"; "Sites Recommended for New City Hall," *Dallas Morning News*, Dec. 12, 1964.

32. Committee memo to John N. Jackson, Jan. 26, 1965, file 2, box 18, Jonsson Papers; Thomsen interview, June 22, 2004.

33. "City Dreamers Seeing Reruns," *Dallas Times Herald*, Apr. 30, 1967.

34. The quotation is from a talk given to the Rotary Club of Dallas in 1931, reprinted as "Prophecy," *Dallas*, Feb. 1956.

35. Darwin Payne and Kathy Fitzpatrick, *From Prairie to Planes: How Dallas and Fort Worth Overcame Politics and Personalities to Build One of the World's Biggest and Busiest Airports* (Dallas: Three Forks, 1999), 19–20.

36. Ibid., 71, 98.

37. Willard Barr (mayor of Fort Worth, 1965–67), interview, audiotape, Nov. 22, 1993, DFW Airport Public Affairs Department.

38. Payne and Fitzpatrick, *From Prairie to Planes*, 98–99.

39. "Airport Decision Appeal Requested," *Dallas Times Herald*, Apr. 9, 1964; "Fort Worth Cites Urgency, Plans Appeal to Full CAB," *Dallas Morning News*, Apr. 10, 1964.

40. "Dallas Feels Love Field Position Remains Sound," *Dallas Times Herald*, June 14, 1964; "Dallas Officials Will Search for Arrangements on Airport," *Dallas Morning News*, Oct. 1, 1964.

41. "Airport Proposal Rejected," *Dallas Times Herald*, Sept. 15, 1964.

42. Payne and Fitzpatrick, *From Prairie to Planes*, 101.

43. "Officials Search for Arrangements"; "Mayor Sees Joint Airport in 70s," *Dallas Times Herald*, Oct. 1, 1964.

44. "Mayor Sees Joint Airport"; Hazel interview, 3–4.

45. "C of C Panel Agrees to Back Love Field," *Dallas Morning News*, Oct. 3, 1964.

46. "Dallas, Ft. Worth Open Area Airport Sessions," *Dallas Times Herald*, Oct. 20, 1964.

47. "Cooperation in Airport Talks Noted," *Dallas Morning News*, Nov. 3, 1964.

48. Bayard Friedman (May 15, 1998) and J. Lee Johnson III (May 6, 1998), interviews by Darwin Payne and Kathy Fitzpatrick, as cited in Payne and Fitzpatrick, *From Prairie to Planes*, 102; Dealey interview, 9.

49. "Dallas, Fort Worth Leaders Agree to Push for Joint Airport Authority," *Dallas Times Herald*, Jan. 6, 1965.

50. "Airport Amity Step Draws CAB Praise," *Dallas Times Herald*, Jan. 7, 1965.

51. "J. E. Jonsson and Goals for Dallas," paper prepared at Harvard University, 1985, no author, [2], courtesy of Steve Jonsson.

52. JEJ, Sixth Floor Museum oral history, 3.

53. Al Hester, "Mayor Urges Expert Help in Long-Range Planning," *Dallas Times Herald*, Nov. 11, 1964; "Detailed Planning Urged by Jonsson," *Dallas Morning News*, Nov. 12, 1964.

54. The editorial, "City of Excellence," and the cartoon, "Blueprint for the Future," are in the *Dallas Morning News*, Nov. 13, 1964; "Jonsson and Goals for Dallas," [2].

55. "Planning Program For City Unveiled," *Dallas Times Herald*, Dec. 2, 1964; "Jonsson Expands on Goals Project," *Dallas Morning News*, Dec. 3, 1964.

56. "Jonsson Expands on Goals Project"; Hester, "Mayor Urges Expert Help."

57. JEJ, Sixth Floor Museum oral history, 3.

58. "Mayor's Race Discussed by Jonsson," *Dallas Times Herald*, Dec. 25, 1964.

59. "Jonsson Plans Race for Mayor," *Dallas Morning News*, Dec. 25, 1964.

60. Henry Stowers, sports column, *Dallas Morning News*, June 30, 1970.

CHAPTER 11: MASTER OF CITY HALL, MAKER OF THE AIRPORT

1. "Tough Campaign Promised by CCA," *Dallas Times Herald*, Jan. 15, 1965, file 19, box 60, Jonsson Papers.

2. "CCA Head Vows 'Same Government,'" *Dallas Morning News*, Jan. 16, 1965, in ibid.

3. "Mrs. Blessing Will Run For Mayor's Post," *Dallas Morning News*, Feb. 21, 1965.

4. Untitled, undated typewritten statement, file 18, box 70, Jonsson Papers.

5. "Dallas Mayor at Meeting," *Dallas Times Herald*, Feb. 17, 1965; TI, untitled news release, Feb. 17, 1965; both in file 12, box 17, Jonsson Papers.

6. "Jonsson Sees 'Queen' Bid; Mrs. Blessing Hits Secrecy," *Dallas Morning News*, Mar. 25, 1965.

7. Cullum interview, June 24, 2003; W. J. Durham to JEJ, Mar. 30, 1965, and "Is Dallas in Bad Shape?," *Pleasant Grove Shopping News*, Mar. 24, 1965, both in file 12, box 17, Jonsson Papers; "Dear Fellow Citizen," letter, n.d., and numerous campaign speeches, files 6 and 7, box 17, Jonsson Papers.

8. Speech entitled "Mayor Warns City of Spoils System Danger," n.d., file 7, box 17, Jonsson Papers.

9. P. E. Haggerty to McDermott, Mar. 22, 1965, file 11, box 17, Jonsson Papers; "Expenses Listed by Candidates," *Dallas Times Herald*, Apr. 19, 1965.

10. "Campaign Methods Hit; Blessing Reveals Offer," *Dallas Morning News*, Apr. 3, 1965.

11. "CCA Chief Lashes at Mrs. Blessing, Cites Debt Suits," *Dallas Morning News*, Apr. 2, 1965.

12. "Campaign Methods Hit."

13. "Letter From Elizabeth Blessing," *Dallas Morning News*, Apr. 6, 1965.

14. "Election Margin Near 3–1" and "Loser Issues Statement of Concession," *Dallas Times Herald*, Apr. 7, 1963.

15. "Expenses Listed by Candidates."

16. Front-page photograph, *Dallas Times Herald*, Apr. 7, 1965; "Jonsson Acts to Carry Out His Pledges, *Dallas Morning News*, Apr. 7, 1965; Cullum interview, June 24, 2003.

17. "Closer Check on Spending Due," *Dallas Times Herald*, May 4, 1965, file 5, box 106, Jonsson Papers.

18. News release for the *Dallas Times Herald* entitled "Re: Love Field," Mar. 22, 1965; untitled, undated news release, file 7, and "Report of the Dallas Representatives of the Joint Committee of Dallas and Fort Worth, Texas[,] to Investigate Regional Airport Location," Mar. 6, 1965, submitted to Dallas City Council, file 8; both in box 17, Jonsson Papers.

19. "Report of the Dallas Representatives."

20. "2 Mayors Differ on Airport 'Pact,'" *Dallas Times Herald*, Mar. 24, 1965, file 8, box 17, Jonsson Papers.

21. United States of America Civil Aeronautics Board, Dallas–Fort Worth Regional Airport Investigation, Docket 13959, Order No. E-22028, Apr. 13, 1965, file 17, box 41, Jonsson Papers.

22. Carl Harris, "Cities' Accord Call for 1971 Airport Target," *Dallas Morning News*, May 30, 1965.

23. R. M. Stovall (mayor of Fort Worth, 1969–75, and member of the airport's board of directors), interview, Nov. 23, 1993, DFW Airport Public Affairs Department.

24. *Dallas Times Herald*, Sept. 26, 1965, as cited in Payne and Fitzpatrick, *From Prairie to Planes*, 107.

25. Payne and Fitzpatrick, *From Prairie to Planes*, 108.

26. JEJ, Sixth Floor Museum oral history, 10.

27. J. Lee Johnson III, interview, Jan. 13, 1994, DFW Airport Public Affairs Department; Payne and Fitzpatrick, *From Prairie to Planes*, 108–10.

28. Payne and Fitzpatrick, *From Prairie to Planes*, 111.

29. Citizens Information Committee, North Central Texas Airport Authority, news release, n.d. [1967], file 8, box 41, Jonsson Papers.

30. "Plan of Financing," Apr. 25, 1967, Confidential, file 11, box 41, Jonsson Papers; Payne and Fitzpatrick, *From Prairie to Planes*, 112–13.

31. Daily appointment schedules, file 10, box 12, Jonsson Papers.

32. Payne and Fitzpatrick, *From Prairie to Planes*, 114; "Telephone Message Monday & Tuesday," file 11, box 41, Jonsson Papers.

33. "Defeat Stuns Civic Chiefs; Labor Claims Vote Credit," *Dallas Times Herald*, June 8, 1967, file 7, box 38, Jonsson Papers; Payne and Fitzpatrick, *From Prairie to Planes*, 115.

34. H. C. Miles, letter to the editor, *Dallas Times Herald*, undated clipping, file 20, box 80, Jonsson Papers.

35. "Defeat Stuns Civic Chiefs."

36. "Airport Law Prevents 'Dallas Domination,'" *Dallas Morning News*, June 11, 1967, file 7, box 38, Jonsson Papers; Payne and Fitzpatrick, *From Prairie to Planes*, 114.

37. Report of the Dallas–Fort Worth Regional Airport Special Meeting, Apr. 12, 1968, DFW Airport Public Affairs Department.

38. Payne and Fitzpatrick, *From Prairie to Planes*, 116.

39. Dealey interview, 13.

40. George Schrader, interview by the author, Jan. 20, 2005, Dallas; Payne and Fitzpatrick, *From Prairie to Planes*, 137.

41. Payne and Fitzpatrick, *From Prairie to Planes*, 126–28; Hazel interview, 25.

42. Wilson, "Erik Jonsson," 24; contract signed by Sullivan and Jonsson, Feb. 22, 1968, file 18, box 43, Jonsson Papers; Stovall interview.

43. "Crull Resigns as City Manager," *Dallas Times Herald*, June 6, 1966, file 23, box 106, Jonsson Papers.

44. Andrew DeShong to JEJ, Jan. 27, 1965, file 15, box 114, Jonsson Papers; Cullum interview, June 24, 2003; W. Scott McDonald, interview by the author, Aug. 5, 2004, Dallas.

45. Ibid.

46. Cullum interview, June 24, 2003; William E. Cothrum, telephone interview by the author, Aug. 5, 2004; "Crull Resigns as City Manager"; Francis Raffetto, "Crull Leaves Post with Record Admired by Many City Professionals," *Dallas Morning News*, June 7, 1966; "City Loses Valued Manager," *Dallas Times Herald*, June 7, 1966, last three in file 23, box 106, Jonsson Papers. In an undated interview, JEJ years later downplayed his own role in Crull's resignation (page 7, file 17, box 88, Jonsson Papers). There are obvious errors in his account, and I have accepted the versions offered by then–council members Charles Cullum and William Cothrum.

47. "McDonald's 'Big Week' Becomes Even Bigger," *Dallas Times Herald*, June 7, 1966.

48. "Scott McDonald: An Oral History Interview," conducted by Alan Mason, July 7, 1980, 3–4, East Texas State University and Dallas Public Library.

49. "George Schrader: An Oral History Interview," conducted by Gerald Saxon, May 14, 1981, 30–31, East Texas State University and Dallas Public Library; Schrader interview, Jan. 20, 2005.

50. "City Atty. Kucera Retiring," *Dallas Times Herald*, May 16, 1965; "Bickley Go-Gettum Alex," *Dallas Times Herald*, Apr. 4, 1971, file 5, box 106, Jonsson Papers.

51. Schrader interview, Jan. 20, 2005.

52. Payne and Fitzpatrick, *From Prairie to Planes*, 137; Charles W. Ferguson to JEJ, Aug. 10, 1973, file 17, box 40; Thomas M. Sullivan to JEJ, Jan. 27, 1969, file 3, box 43, Jonsson Papers.

53. Payne and Fitzpatrick, *From Prairie to Planes*, 122, 128–30.

54. Prokosch to JEJ, Aug. 16, 1968; JEJ to Prokosch, Sept. 4, 1968, file 20, box 43, Jonsson Papers.

55. *Fort Worth Star-Telegram*, Sept. 28, 1968, as quoted in Payne and Fitzpatrick, *From Prairie to Planes*, 129.

56. Bill Rives, "Views," *Denton Record-Chronicle*, Dec. 15, 1968, as quoted in Payne and Fitzpatrick, *From Prairie to Planes*, 134.

57. Letters on this subject are in file 7, box 43, Jonsson Papers; Ross Perot, telephone interview by the author, July 15, 2005.

58. Payne and Fitzpatrick, *From Prairie to Planes*, 140, 144–45.

59. Ibid., 149–51.

60. Stovall interview.

CHAPTER 12: GOALS, THE COWBOYS, AND I. M. PEI

1. "New Program Challenging, Jonsson Says," *Dallas Times Herald*, Dec. 5, 1965; "Concept of Future Dallas Born in Planning Session," *Dallas Times Herald*, Dec. 4, 1965; "Panel Proposes 'Dallas Goals,'" *Dallas Morning News*, Dec. 4, 1965.

2. "Panel Proposes 'Dallas Goals.'"

3. "Goals for Dallas Fund Drive Set," *Dallas Times Herald*, Feb. 23, 1966; acknowledgments, *Goals for Dallas* (Dallas: Goals for Dallas, 1966), xiii.

4. "Writers Begin Essays on City," *Dallas Morning News*, Mar. 2, 1966.

5. *Goals for Dallas*, 36, 43, 54, 47, 217, 219, 235.

6. "Jonsson and Goals for Dallas," [8–9].

7. Christopher Berrisford, oral history interview, 1983, St. Mark's Archives, as related to the author by Bill Simon. Berrisford served as headmaster from 1963 to 1969.

8. Bradshaw related the story after JEJ's death; see "Ex-Mayor J. Erik Jonsson dies at 93," *Dallas Morning News*, Sept. 2, 1995.

9. "Jonsson and Goals for Dallas," [9].

10. Ibid.

11. "City Goals Ideas Put before Public," *Dallas Times Herald*, June 20, 1968; Frank Langston, "The Government of the City," *Goals for Dallas*, 36.

12. "Jonsson and Goals for Dallas," [10–11].

13. "City Goals Ideas Put before Public."

14. JEJ, preface to *Goals for Dallas*, x; Larry Howell, "For an Ever-Renewing Greatness," *Dallas Morning News*, Dec. 9, 1967, file 1, box 54, Jonsson Papers.

15. "Goals for Dallas: Historical Funding Statement," June 30, 1975, file 17, box 86, Jonsson Papers.

16. "I. M. Pei: An Oral History Interview: Henry Moore's *The Dallas Piece*," conducted by Bonnie A. Lovell, Aug. 1, 2002, 29, Dallas Public Library.

17. Ibid., 30.

18. Ibid., 23.

19. Ibid., 27–28, Dallas Public Library; Carter Wiseman, *I. M. Pei: A Profile in American Architecture* (New York: Abrams, 1990), 126.

20. Wiseman, *I. M. Pei*, 124; Lee Cullum interview with Erik Jonsson, n.d., file 17, box 88, Jonsson Papers; Pei interview, 23–24.

21. "Dallas Gets First Peek at Plans for New City Hall," *Dallas Times Herald*, Apr. 27, 1967.

22. "Dallas at the Crossroads" campaign brochures, file 7, box 80, Jonsson Papers.

23. "'Hard Sell' Bond Drive Winds Up," *Dallas Times Herald*, Aug. 6, 1967; typescript, "Dallas at the Crossroads," file 9, box 80; Jonsson Papers.

24. Maryln Schwartz, "Returns Helped Appetites," *Dallas Morning News*, Aug. 9, 1967, file 12, box 80, Jonsson Papers.

25. Clint Murchison Jr. to JEJ, Nov. 5, 1965, file 15, box 24, Jonsson Papers.

26. "Considerations Concerning Construction of a 55,000 Seat Stadium and Park Complex in Downtown Dallas," n.d., file 15, box 24, Jonsson Papers.

27. Schrader interview, Jan. 20, 2005.

28. Carolyn Barta, "Jonsson's City Hall Stand Likened to Town Stadium," *Dallas Morning News*, Oct. 10, 1970.

29. "Plans Hailed for Fair Park Facelift," *Dallas Times Herald*, Apr. 20, 1966; "Facelifting at the Fairgrounds," *Dallas Times Herald*, Nov. 20, 1966; "President of State Fair Favors New Cotton Bowl," *Dallas Morning News*, Dec. 8, 1966; "New Cotton Bowl Urged," *Dallas Morning News*, Dec. 7, 1966; all in file 11, box 24, Jonsson Papers; JEJ to Clint Murchison Jr., Jan. 20, 1967, file 4, box 21, Jonsson Papers.

30. Gary Cartwright, "Clint Tosses Stadium Pass," *Dallas Morning News*, Jan. 29, 1967.

31. Untitled, undated statement [Mar. 1967], file 15, box 24, Jonsson Papers; Jane Wolfe, *The Murchisons* (New York: St. Martin's, 1989), 303.

32. Unsigned note to Scott McDonald, Mar. 17, 1967, file 15, box 24, Jonsson Papers.

33. "Airport, Stadium, Opera?," *Dallas Morning News*, Feb. 26, 1967.

34. Sam Blair, "The Rally's Overdue," Feb. 3, 1967; Blair, "Some Laugh, Some Don't," Feb. 5, 1967, *Dallas Morning News*.

35. Blackie Sherrod, "Stretched to Breaking Point," *Dallas Times Herald*, Jan. 30, 1967.

36. "Murchion [sic] Not in Race," *Dallas Times Herald*, Feb. 8, 1967, file 11, box 24, Jonsson Papers; Clint Murchison to JEJ, Mar. 13, 1967; JEJ to Murchison, Mar. 25, 1967, file 13, ibid.

37. Steve Perkins, "Murchison Offers 'Free' Bowl Plan," *Dallas Times Herald*, Apr. 4, 1967.

38. "A Proposed Statement Concerning the Cotton Bowl," n.d., file 11, box 24, Jonsson Papers; "Mayor Indicates Council to Be Asked to Compare Stadium Ideas," *Dallas Morning News*, Apr. 6, 1967.

39. Wolfe, *The Murchisons*, 302.

40. JEJ to Jack H. Sealy, Jan. 16, 1968, file 11, box 24, Jonsson Papers.

41. Roy Edwards, "The Mayor's View," *Dallas Morning News*, July 3, 1967.

42. Clint Murchison Jr. to JEJ, July 3, 1967, file 12, box 24, Jonsson Papers.

43. "Task Force Will Guard Cotton Bowl," *Dallas Morning News*, Aug. 24, 1968.

44. "Clint's Corner," *Cowboys Insiders Newsletter*, Oct. 9, 1970, as quoted in Barta, "Jonsson's City Hall Stand."

45. Schrader interview, Jan. 20, 2005.

46. "Speech Center Hailed at Site Ceremonies," *Dallas Morning News*, Dec. 10, 1966; "Nelle Johnston: An Oral History Interview," conducted by Alan Mason, Aug. 28, 1980, East Texas State University and Dallas Public Library, 1983.

47. JEJ to Robert H. Finch, Mar. 31, 1969; "Draft, Fact Sheet, Callier Hearing and Speech Center"; both in file 27, box 2, Jonsson Papers.

48. Schrader interview, Jan. 20, 2005.

49. "The Man for Mayor," *Dallas Times Herald*, Jan. 18, 1967; Payne, *Big D*, 371.

50. "City Buys Mayor Limousine," *Dallas Morning News*, Oct. 19, 1965.

51. Wes Wise to the author, Nov. 8, 2005.

52. Erik Jonsson, interview by his grandson Steve Jonsson, Lake Tahoe, California, July 21, 1978, courtesy of Steve Jonsson; "Weather Vane," *Dallas Morning News*, Nov. 24, 1968.

53. Files containing these communications are in the Jonsson Papers.

54. Susan Crice to JEJ, Apr. 19, 1967; JEJ to Susan Crice, Apr. 27, 1967; both in file 6, box 54, Jonsson Papers.

55. NJ [Nelle Johnston] to JEJ, memorandum, [1967], file 7, box 54, Jonsson Papers.

56. The card is in file 16, box 23, Jonsson Papers.

57. Jonsson Advocates Dallas 'War on Crime,'" *Dallas Morning News*, Mar. 23, 1965.

58. "Council Calls for Citizens Study of Film Ban," *Dallas Morning News*, Feb. 16, 1965; "Special Panel to Probe Issue of Movie Law," *Dallas Times Herald*, Feb. 16, 1965.

59. Draft of ordinance, file 26, box 66, Jonsson Papers.

60. Darwin Payne, *Indomitable Sarah: The Life of Judge Sarah T. Hughes* (Dallas: SMU Press, 2004), 292.

61. "Fluoride Hearing Today," *Dallas Times Herald*, Aug. 2, 1965; "Fluoride Issue Pondered after Tame 4-Hour Debate," *Dallas Morning News*, Aug. 3, 1965.

62. "Dallas Voters Okay Fluoridation 3–1," *Dallas Times Herald*, Jan. 30, 1966.

63. JEJ to Tom Anthony, June 12, 1968, file 13, box 55, Jonsson Papers.

CHAPTER 13: WALKING A TIGHTROPE

1. TI unpublished history, 441; Annual Report 1964, TI, file 18, box 94, Jonsson Papers.

2. Calendar, Aug. 28, 1967, file 12, box 10; JEJ to Pam Cassella, Apr. 25, 1969, file 15, box 56; Harold G. Shank memo, Aug. 1, 1969, file 7, box 57; all in Jonsson Papers.

3. Johnston interview, 4.

4. TI unpublished history, 422.

5. W.J. Durham to JEJ, July 30, 1964; JEJ to Durham, Aug. 3, 1964; file 3, box 22, Jonsson Papers.

6. JEJ to Larry Worrall, Dec. 10, 1965, file 1, box 22, Jonsson Papers.

7. "Wilkins Lauds Dallas Racial Progress," *Dallas Morning News*, Feb. 17, 1966.

8. JEJ to Nelle Johnston, note, Aug. 2, 1967, file 16, box 21, Jonsson Papers.

9. Payne, *Big D*, 393; "The City of Dallas, Texas: The Administration of Justice during a Civil Disorder," a document with attachments in possession of the author; Philip Wilson, president, Dallas Bar Association, to JEJ, Mar. 22, 1968, file 3, box 56, Jonsson Papers.

10. "SNCC Leaders Given 10 Years," *Dallas Morning News*, Aug. 24, 1968; Payne, *Big D*, 394.

11. *Goals for Dallas*, 5; *Proposals for Achieving the Goals* (Dallas: Goals for Dallas, 1969), 3.

12. "League Endorses Rights Panel Bid," *Dallas Times Herald*, n.d.; Mrs. Laurence Perrine to JEJ, Apr. 3, 1967; petition to JEJ, Dec. 16, 1966; JEJ to Douglas Jackson, June 5, 1967; all in file 15, box 21, Jonsson Papers; "Creation of Human Relations Commission Seen," *Dallas Morning News*, Mar. 10, 1967; "Human Relations Commission Stands in Doubt," *Dallas Morning News*, June 23, 1968.

13. Mrs. Barry Korman to JEJ, May 26, 1968; JEJ to Marvin Berkeley, memorandum, June 10, 1968; Bob Smith to Berkeley, June 28, 1968; all in file 11, box 21, Jonsson Papers.

14. Sid Stahl, telephone interview by the author, Sept. 3, 2004; "Community Council Plans Panel on Human Relations," n.d., file 11, box 21, Jonsson Papers.

15. Elizabeth Durham Davies, "Fair Park Expansion: A Case Study of Political Bias and Protest in Urban Politics" (MA thesis, North Texas State University, 1974), 15.

16. Typewritten document entitled "Position of Fair Park Block Partnership," file 3, box 21, Jonsson Papers; "Blacks Reject City Offer," *Dallas Morning News*, n.d., file 2, ibid.

17. Ralph David Abernathy to JEJ, telegram, Nov. 14, 1969, file 1, ibid.

18. "Minority Coalescence in Dallas," *Life Lines*, Dec. 26, 1969, file 2, ibid.

19. "Mayor to Look into Fair Park Issue," *Dallas Morning News*, [Jan. 1970], file 1, ibid.

20. These letters are in file 1, box 21, Jonsson Papers, along with [JEJ] to J. B. Jackson, Jan. 27, 1970.

21. Dorothy Joiner and J. B. Jackson to JEJ, telegram, Feb. 11, 1969, file 5, ibid.; JEJ, speech to Fair Park homeowners, n.d. [May 28, 1970], file 13, box 20, Jonsson Papers; Dorothy Joiner and J. B. Jackson to JEJ, telegram, Feb. 6, 1970, file 1, box 21, Jonsson Papers.

22. "Fair Park Homeowners, Jonsson Reach Standoff," *Dallas Morning News*, May 15, 1970, file 1, box 21, Jonsson Papers; "Official Action of the City Council, City of Dallas," meeting of May 18, 1970, ibid.

23. JEJ, speech to Fair Park Homeowners.

24. "Official Action of City Council, Dallas," May 18, 1970; "Jonsson Gives Up on Negotiating," *Dallas Morning News*, May 15, 1970.

25. W. R. Farmer to JEJ, May 12, 1970, file 5, box 21, Jonsson Papers.

26. JEJ to W. R. Farmer, May 12, 1970; W. R. Farmer to JEJ, May 13, 1970; both in file 5, box 21, Jonsson Papers.

27. They were C.A. Tatum, chairman, Dallas Power & Light; the Reverend Thomas H. Shipp, president, Dallas Urban League; Thomas C. Unis, president, Dallas Community Relations Commission; Peter Bernays, chairman, Dallas Real Estate Board; and Julius Schepps, vice president, Dallas Park Board.

28. "Fair Park Homeowners, Jonsson Reach Standoff"; JEJ to Jackson, telegram, May 14, 1970, file 3, box 21, Jonsson Papers.

29. "Jonsson Gives Up on Negotiating"; Peter Johnson, press statement, "Morality vs. Desperation," file 14, box 20, Jonsson Papers.

30. Statement, "Fair Park Residents to Battle City," n.d., file 14, box 20, Jonsson Papers.

31. "Jonsson Gives Up on Negotiating."

32. Ibid.

33. The Reverend Louis A. Saunders to JEJ, with attachments, May 14, 1970, file 13, box 20, Jonsson Papers.

34. "Official Action of City Council, Dallas," May 18, 1970.

35. JEJ to Brown, May 21, 1970, file 14, box 20, Jonsson Papers.

36. Fair Park Property Owners to JEJ, telegram, May 26, 1970, ibid.

37. W. S. McDonald to JEJ, May 25, 1970, file 13, box 20, Jonsson Papers.

38. JEJ, speech to Fair Park homeowners.

39. Ibid.

40. Ibid.

41. "Jonsson to Listen to Block 'Experts,'" *Dallas Times Herald*, May 29, 1970.

42. JEJ, untitled talk, June 8, 1970, file 13, box 20, Jonsson Papers.

43. Fred and Dorothy Joiner et al. vs. City of Dallas, Texas, et al., Civil Action No. Ca-3-4322-A,; "Judge Dismisses Fair Park Action," *Dallas Morning News*, Jan. 12, 1971.

44. Wes Wise to the author, Nov. 7, 2005.

45. "Dallasites' Gifts Listed in Top 171," *Dallas Times Herald*, Aug. 16, 1967.

46. JEJ to John K. Paden, June 9, 1967, file 4, box 54, Jonsson Papers.

47. Peter O'Donnell Jr. to JEJ, July 3, 1967, with attachments, file 6, box 74, Jonsson Papers; "Percy Urges GOP to Broaden Base," *Dallas Times Herald*, June 24, 1967.

48. C. Langhorne Washburn to JEJ, Nov. 7, 1967; Fred J. Agnich to Sam Wyly, Nov. 7, 1967; both in file 2, box 74, Jonsson Papers.

49. "Jonsson Plays It Cool," *Dallas Times Herald*, Jan. 23, 1968.

50. Martin Waldron, "Local Victories Spur Texas G.O.P.," *New York Times*, Dec. 17, 1967, file 7, box 92, Jonsson Papers.

51. "A telephone poll taken December 7, 1957," file 10, box 92, Jonsson Papers.

52. "Jonsson Weighing Governor's Race," *Dallas Morning News*, Jan. 23, 1968; "Jonsson's Word Awaited on Gubernatorial Race," *Dallas Times Herald*, Jan. 22, 1968; "Jonsson Dims GOP's Hopes by Saying 'No,'" *Dallas Morning News*, Jan. 25, 1968.

53. "Jonsson Weighing Governor's Race"; "Jonsson's Word Awaited."

54. John G. Tower to JEJ, telegram, Jan. 23, 1968, file 1, box 31, Jonsson Papers.

55. JEJ's response to Nixon, Feb. 5, 1968, a list of telephone calls, and many other communications on the subject are in file 6, box 11, Jonsson Papers; letters related to JEJ's candidacy for governor are in file 1, box 31, Jonsson Papers.

56. "Statement by Mayor Erik Jonsson," Jan. 24, 1968, Dallas, Texas, file 11, box 17, Jonsson Papers; "Jonsson Turns Down Bid to Seek Governor's Seat," *Dallas Times Herald*, Jan. 24, 1968; "Jonsson Dims GOP's Hopes."

57. Untitled poll results in file 1, box 31, Jonsson Papers.

58. "Nixon Considering Jonsson, Price," *Dallas Morning News*, Dec. 10, 1968; Schrader interview, Jan. 20, 2005.

59. Cullum interview, June 24, 2003.

60. Mr. and Mrs. Harry Joseph Morris to JEJ, Dec. 31, 1968; JEJ to Mr. and Mrs. Harry Joseph Morris, Jan. 8, 1969; both in file 13, box 10, Jonsson Papers.

61. Wilson, "Erik Jonsson," 35; Bryghte Godbold, interview by the author, Aug. 4, 2003, Dallas.

62. Wilson, "Erik Jonsson," 35; Godbold interview, Aug. 4, 2003; Kenneth Alan Jonsson, telephone interview by Richard Tuck, Sept. 13, 2002.

63. MJR, interview, May 14, 2004; "$10,000 Is Given Children's Home," *Maryville-Alcoa Daily Times*, Oct. 24, 1966, file 10, box 107, Jonsson Papers.

64. "Names Bandied for Races," *Dallas Morning News*, Jan. 15, 1969; Bert Holmes, "Jonsson Moves on Wide Front in Pursuit of City Excellence," *Dallas Times Herald*, Feb. 6, 1969.

65. Max Goldblatt to JEJ, Feb. 10, 1969, file 12, box 19, Jonsson Papers; "2nd Term Urged for Jonsson," *Dallas Morning News*, Feb. 11, 1969.

66. "Mayor 'Available' If . . . Jonsson Due to Ask Veto Power to Run," *Dallas Morning News*, Feb. 4, 1969; "Jonsson Awaiting CCA Nomination," *Dallas Morning News*, Feb. 5, 1969.

67. "It's CCA, Wes Wise and Runoff," *Dallas Times Herald*, Apr. 2, 1969; "Jonsson Leads CCA to Another Victory," *Dallas Morning News*, Apr. 2, 1969; "Jonsson Captures Biggest Percentage," *Dallas Morning News*, Apr. 3, 1969.

68. "Slum Areas Cause Risk, Mayor Tells Architects," *Dallas Morning News*, Nov. 5, 1966; "Dallas Slum Post Goes to Flaxman," *Dallas Times Herald*, Feb. 7, 1966; "U.S. Aid Unwanted In Anti-Slum Drive," *Dallas Times Herald*, Feb. 11, 1966; "Mayor Says Go Slow on Slum Help," *Dallas Morning News*, Dec. 2, 1966; "City Asks U.S. Funds," *Dallas Times Herald*, June 6, 1967.

69. "Judge Sterrett Calls Galvin 'Mayor's Boy'" and "Galvin Receives Jonsson Backing," *Dallas Morning News*, Feb. 17, 1966; "Sterrett Says Mayor Told Confidence in Galvin Lacking," *Dallas Times Herald*, Feb. 16, 1970; all in file 15, box 107, Jonsson Papers.

70. "Cut His, Not Mine," *Dallas Morning News*, Oct. 16, 1967.

71. "Jonsson Likes U.S. Money," *Dallas Times Herald*, Oct. 26, 1969.

72. "Mayor Suggests Buses for Indigent," *Dallas Morning News*, Feb. 25, 1967; "Presentation by Mayor Erik Jonsson[,] Urban Transportation Intergovernmental Relations Panel, Fourth International Conference on Transportation, March 12, 1969," file 6, box 3, Jonsson Papers.

73. Wes Wise to author, Nov. 7, 2005.

74. JEJ to Alex Bickley, May 15, 1971, file 5, box 24, Jonsson Papers.

75. JEJ to Ways and Means Committee chairman Wilbur Mills and committee members Omar Burleson and John J. Duncan, May 24, 1971, file 5, box 24, Jonsson Papers.

76. Correspondence concerning the luncheon is in file 8, box 24, Jonsson Papers.

77. JEJ to Brenda J. Shepard, Apr. 8, 1968, file 1, box 58, Jonsson Papers.

CHAPTER 14: CITY OF EXCELLENCE

1. Nelle Johnston to JEJ, memorandum, Mar. 16, 1970, file 5, box 58, Jonsson Papers.

2. JEJ to Mrs. G.R. Marck, July 30, 1970, file 13, box 58, Jonsson Papers.

3. Jim Lehrer, "About Princes and Polka Dots," *Dallas Times Herald*, Mar. 13, 1966; "Prince Finds Straight Men," *Dallas Morning News*, Mar. 13, 1966.

4. Ibid.

5. "Officials Raise Eyebrows over 'Unprincely' Questions, *Dallas Times Herald*, Mar. 13, 1966.

6. Ibid.

7. Tom G. Hodges to JEJ, June 12, 1970, file 9, box 20, Jonsson Papers.

8. Carl Sewell, interview by the author, June 20, 2004

9. Ibid.

10. "Jonsson Appears Winner," *Dallas Morning News*, June 1, 1969; "Parking Shortage Due for City Hall," Apr. 16, 1968, *Dallas Morning News*; Bob Taylor, editorial cartoon, *Dallas Times Herald*, Apr. 30, 1969.

11. "Council Gets Sales Pitch on New City Hall," *Dallas Morning News*, Mar. 8, 1970.

12. "Geary Raps City Hall Cost," *Dallas Times Herald*, May 4, 1969; "Geary Questions City Hall Project," *Dallas Morning News*, May 6, 1969; "City Hall Too Much?" *Dallas Times Herald*, May 18, 1969; JEJ to Joseph W. Geary, June 24, 1969, file 1, box 57, Jonsson Papers; "City Hall Raps All Premature, Jonsson Says," *Dallas Morning News*, Sept. 22, 1969; "'Downtown' Sends City Hall the Word: Trim Spending," *Dallas Times Herald*, Sept. 21, 1969.

13. "'Downtown' Sends City Hall the Word."

14. Ibid.; "City Hall Controversy Still Simmers," *Dallas Times Herald*, May 25, 1969.

15. "New City Hall Termed 'Symbol,'" *Dallas Times Herald*, May 28, 1969; "Jonsson Opposes City Hall Addition," *Dallas Morning News*, May 28, 1969.

16. "Council Gets Sales Pitch on New City Hall," *Dallas Morning News*, Mar. 8, 1970; "New City Hall Vote Possible," *Dallas Times Herald*, Mar. 5, 1970.

17. "Council Votes to Take Bids On 'Hollow Shell' City Hall," *Dallas Times Herald*, May 26, 1970.

18. Ibid.

19. "City Hall Bids Near to Estimate," *Dallas Times Herald,* Sept. 18, 1970.

20. "City Hall Plans Shelved," *Dallas Times Herald*, Sept. 21, 1970; "Mayor Proposes Delay in Plans for City Hall," *Dallas Morning News*, Sept. 22, 1970; "Council Members Seem to Give Mayor

Support," *Dallas Morning News*, Sept. 22, 1970; "A Wise Deferment," *Dallas Morning News*, Sept. 23, 1970; "Delay of New City Hall," Sept. 23, 1970, *Dallas Times Herald*.

21. "Plans for City Hall Feared Dead," *Dallas Morning News*, Sept. 26, 1930.

22. Thomas M. Sullivan to JEJ, Sept. 22, 1970, file 25, box 85, Jonsson Papers.

23. These letters are in ibid.

24. "Realtors Revive City Hall Interest," *Dallas Times Herald*, Sept. 29, 1970; "Architects, Builders Extend Backing for City Hall Plan," *Dallas Times Herald*, Sept. 30, 1970; "City Hall May Be on Ballot," *Dallas Morning News*, Sept. 30, 1970; "New City Hall Plans Still in Limbo," *Dallas Times Herald*, Oct. 6, 1970.

25. R. Sandy Hallman to Dallas City Council, Oct. 3, 1970, with attachment, "Report to Dallas City Council on the Proposed City Hall Building," file 25, box 85, Jonsson Papers; "Future Costs for City Hall Would Go Up," *Dallas Morning News*, Oct. 7, 1970.

26. "Mayor's City Hall Position Called 'Charade' by Fielding," *Dallas Times Herald*, Oct. 2, 1970; "Vote on City Hall Mulled," *Dallas Times Herald*, Oct. 11, 1970.

27. John Schoellkopf, interview by the author, Aug. 15, 2003, Dallas.

28. "City Hall Bond Vote Shaping," *Dallas Times Herald*, Oct. 12, 1970; "City Hall Via Bond Election," *Dallas Morning News*, Oct. 13, 1970.

29. "City Mulls $11 Million Bond Vote," *Dallas Times Herald*, Oct. 20, 1970.

30. "McKinney Balks at New Bond Hike," *Dallas Times Herald*, Oct. 30, 1970; "City Hall May Be Delayed," *Dallas Morning News*, Nov. 1, 1970.

31. Schoellkopf interview.

32. Ibid.; "McKinney Plans Move To Kill City Hall Vote," *Dallas Times Herald*, Nov. 1, 1970; "City Hall Election Junked by Council," *Dallas Times Herald*, Nov. 3, 1970; "City Hall Project Killed," *Dallas Morning News*, Nov. 3, 1970.

33. "New City Hall Revived," *Dallas Morning News*, Feb. 9, 1971; "Pei Design Gains Boost," *Dallas Morning News*, Feb. 11, 1971.

34. Preface, *Goals for Dallas*, x–xi.

35. "Goals Workers Get Hope, Pep," *Dallas Times Herald*, June 10, 1970; "Phase Closed Out in Goals for Dallas," *Dallas Morning News*, June 10, 1970; staff memorandum to B. D. Godbold, n.d., file 33, box 109, Jonsson Papers.

36. "Dallas Mayor Cites Goals Program Value," *Albuquerque Journal*, Mar. 1, 1969; "Dramatic 'Goals for '70s' Cited," *Lubbock Avalanche Journal*, Oct. 29, 1969; both in file 45, box 106, Jonsson Papers.

37. Kenneth R. Cole Jr. to JEJ, Jan. 20, 1972; JEJ to Cole, Jan. 25, 1972; file 13, box 9, Jonsson Papers. JEJ gave his views on these programs in "Goals for Dallas," *Nation's Cities*, Nov. 1970; the article also appeared in Sept. 1972 in *Civil Engineering–ASCE* under the same title. Both the reprint and the article are in file 28, box 109, Jonsson Papers.

38. "All America Cities 1970," *Look*, Mar. 23, 1971, 72–74, and two following pages marked "M."

39. News releases, programs, and other documents concerning the celebration are in file 6, box 63, Jonsson Papers.

40. Resolution dated Mar. 8, 1971, ibid.

41. "City Council Watchdogs," *Dallas Times Herald*, undated clipping [Dec. 1970].

42. JEJ, Sixth Floor Museum oral history, 8.

43. "Thanks to Mayor Jonsson," *Dallas Times Herald*, Oct. 18, 1970.

44. The letters and JEJ's responses are in file 21, box 58, Jonsson Papers.

45. "Connally Says Mayor 'No Dreamer,'" *Dallas Morning News*, undated clipping [Dec. 1970], file 2, box 59, Jonsson Papers.

46. "Mayor Would Buy KRLD," *Dallas Times Herald*, Nov. 25, 1969; Philip Jonsson, interview by the author, Feb. 3, 2005, Dallas; "Jonsson Family Acquires KRLD Radio Properties," *Dallas Times Herald*, July 1, 1970.

47. "Jonsson Family Acquires KRLD."

48. Philip Jonsson interview, Feb. 3, 2005.

49. "Cullum Receives Backing," *Dallas Times Herald*, July 9, 1970.

50. Schoellkopf interview.

51. Ibid.

52. Payne, *Big D*, 404–5.

53. "Jonsson Won't Tell Choice for Mayor," *Dallas Times Herald*, Apr. 16, 1971.

54. "Mays Offers to Help Wise," *Dallas Morning News*, Apr. 21, 1971.

55. The study was conducted by the firm of Louis, Bowles & Grace; see Payne, *Big D*, 407.

56. Wes Wise to author, Nov. 7, 2005.

57. "Optimism on City Hall," *Dallas Morning News*, May 10, 1972.

58. "Dignitaries Turn Earth for City Hall," *Dallas Morning News*, Aug. 15, 1972; Wes Wise to author, Nov. 7, 2005.

59. Ada Louise Huxtable, "'One of Our Most Important Public Buildings,'" *New York Times*, Nov. 28, 1976, file 1, box 86, Jonsson Papers.

60. Ibid.

61. I. M. Pei to JEJ, Mar. 17, 1978, file 1, box 86, Jonsson Papers.

62. JEJ to I. M. Pei, Mar. 22, 1978, in ibid.

Chapter 15: A Busy "Retirement"

1. Nelle Johnston to JEJ, note, Apr. 21, 1971, file 2, box 10, Jonsson Papers.

2. Ot Hampton, "Jonsson to Turn Talents to Writing," *Dallas Times Herald*, Apr. 25, 1971, file 9, box 107, Jonsson Papers. JEJ earlier had confided his intentions to write books to Alan L. Bean; see Alan L. Bean to JEJ, Apr. 21, 1971, file 2, box 10, Jonsson Papers.

3. Ibid.

4. His introduction is in Evelyn Oppenheimer and Bill Porterfield, *The Book of Dallas* (New York: Doubleday, 1977).

5. Appointment and Event Log, 1971, file 1, box 10, Jonsson Papers.

6. JEJ to Phil Clegg, May 15, 1971; JEJ to Paul M. Herzog, May 17, 1971; both in file 3, box 10, Jonsson Papers.

7. Nelle Johnston to JEJ, note, May 10, 1971, file 3; JEJ to Mike Echols, July 12, 1971, and JEJ to Dan Herrin, Aug. 9, 1971, file 4; JEJ to E. I. Jones, Nov. 18, 1971, file 6; all in box 10, Jonsson Papers.

8. "Jonsson Wants Others to Take Over Goals," *Dallas Morning News*, Nov. 8, 1972.

9. Max Ways, "A Hall of Fame for Business Leadership," *Fortune*, Jan. 1975, 64–73; Jonsson's citation is on 72.

10. Undated photograph in the *New York Times Magazine*, attached to JEJ to Harold B. Gores, Nov. 23, 1979, file 10, box 8, Jonsson Papers.

11. "Erik Jonsson Heads Nixon Campaign," *Dallas Times Herald*, June 19, 1972; "Jonsson Sees It All Nixon," *Dallas Times Herald*, Nov. 5, 1972.

12. Richard M. Nixon to JEJ and William P. Clements Jr., telegram, Nov. 8, 1972, file 9, box 92, Jonsson Papers.

13. Peter O'Donnell Jr. to JEJ, Dec. 24, 1971, file 6, box 14, Jonsson Papers; "Mayor, Five Oilmen Listed as Nixon Contributors," *Dallas Morning News*, Sept. 21, 1968.

14. "Jonsson Denies Allegation," *Dallas Morning News*, Sept. 10, 1972; "Jonsson Denies Link to Bugging," *Dallas Times Herald*, Sept. 10, 1972.

15. Payne and Fitzpatrick, *From Prairie to Planes*, 152–53; Bayard Friedman, interview by Darwin Payne and Kathy Fitzpatrick, May 15, 1998, Fort Worth; Schrader interview, Jan. 20, 2005.

16. JEJ to Lester J. Strother, May 15, 1973, file 18, box 40, Jonsson Papers; JEJ to C. Malcolm Bedell, Aug. 13, 1973, and Bedell to JEJ, Sept. 3, 1973, file 11, box 9, Jonsson Papers.

17. Payne and Fitzpatrick, *From Prairie to Planes*, 162; JEJ to John Connally, Dec. 4, 1972, file 5, box 41, Jonsson Papers.

18. "Largest Airport Dedicated," *Washington Post*, Sept. 23, 1973, file 5, box 41, Jonsson Papers; Payne and Fitzpatrick, *From Prairie to Planes*, 165–66.

19. Payne and Fitzpatrick, *From Prairie to Planes*, 160.

20. JEJ to Paul Thayer, June 13, 1970, and Oct. 30, 1973, file 16, box 40, Jonsson Papers.

21. Payne and Fitzpatrick, *From Prairie to Planes*, 160, 180, 184.

22. Ibid.

23. Payne, *Big D,* 474–76; Payne and Fitzpatrick, *From Prairie to Planes,* 237.

24. Carolyn Barta, "Does Father Really Know Best?," *Dallas Morning News,* Nov. 13, 1972.

25. Payne, *Big D,* 411.

26. "Jonsson Seeks Mayor Candidate," *Dallas Times Herald,* Nov. 24, 1974.

27. Robert W. Decherd, "Looking to Future Thanksgivings," *Dallas Morning News,* Nov. 28, 1974; Payne, *Big D,* 410–11; Schoellkopf interview.

28. Payne, *Big D,* 414.

29. Ibid., 415.

30. JEJ to Joe D. Denton, Feb. 11, 1977, and to others on attached list, file 8, box 7, Jonsson Papers; "Jonsson Asks Firms to Form Political Action Groups," *Dallas Morning News,* Feb. 27, 1977.

31. Erik Jonsson II, interview by Gerald Saxon, May 29, 1981, 38–46, Dallas Mayors Oral History and Records Project, East Texas State University and Dallas Public Library.

32. Ibid.

33. William Whyte, *City: Rediscovering the Center* (1988), as cited in Payne, *Big D,* 443. In 2005, Dallas mayor Laura Miller called the tunnels the "worst urban planning decision that Dallas has ever made"; quoted in "Rethinking Skyways and Tunnels," *New York Times,* Aug. 3, 2005.

34. Michael V. Hazel, *The Dallas Public Library: Celebrating a Century of Service, 1901–2001* (Denton: University of North Texas Press, 2001), 160.

35. Ibid., 156–60, 165–66.

36. Ibid., 167; "Personal Recollections"; Hazel, *Dallas Public Library,* 167–68.

37. Lillian M. Bradshaw to JEJ, May 7, 1982; JEJ to Bradshaw, May 12, 1982; both in file 12, box 103, Jonsson Papers.

38. Perot interview; "City to Rename Main Library for Ex-Mayor Erik Jonsson," *Dallas Morning News,* Aug. 28, 1986, file 12, box 103, Jonsson Papers; program for "J. Erik Jonsson Central Library, Dallas Public Library," 1986, courtesy of Steve Jonsson.

39. "Ceremony Honors Ex-Mayor," *Dallas Morning News,* Oct. 21, 1986, file 12, box 103, Jonsson Papers.

40. Program, "The Board of Trustees of Rensselaer Polytechnic Institute Pays Tribute to J. Erik Jonsson '22, October 26, 1990," file 23, box 111; memorial to JEJ by the board of trustees passed on Sept. 30, 1965, file 24, box 113; JEJ to Mrs. Ernestine Gilbreth Carey, Sept. 29, 1978, file 4, box 8; all in Jonsson Papers. *Margaret and Erik Jonsson and RPI: Partners in Progress* (Apr. 1980), a booklet published by RPI, lists the donations to the institution up to that point; copy in MJR Papers.

41. "Skidmore Celebrates Jonsson's 90th Birthday," *Saratogian,* Sept. 7, 1991, file 18, box 90; "Man Who Led Move of Campus Receives Thanks," *New York Times,* Sept. 15, 1991, file 8, box 115; both in Jonsson Papers.

42. "Remarks by Dr. Charles A. LeMaistre, Santa Rita Award, December 15, 1977," file 25, box 1, Jonsson Papers.

43. "Santa Rita Releases," n.d., file 10, box 7, Jonsson Papers.

44. Wilson, "Erik Jonsson," 45; Peter O'Donnell, telephone interview by the author, June 14, 2004; Charles C. Sprague, MD, to JEJ, Oct. 27, 1977, file 13, box 7, Jonsson Papers; Dr. Daniel W. Foster to the author, e-mail, Jan. 27, 2005; Kern Wildenthal, MD, PhD, "Remarks at the Memorial Service of Erik Jonsson," Sept. 5, 1995, file 1, box 114, Jonsson Papers.

45. Michael Brown, interview by the author, Nov. 6, 2013, Dallas; Brown to the author, e-mail, Nov. 7, 2013.

46. Brown interview.

47. In 2003, Brown and Goldstein won the $500,000 Albany Medical Center Prize in Medicine and Biomedical Health for their post-Nobel research done on cholesterol buildup.

48. JEJ to Dr. Paul MacDonald, Sept. 29, 1981, file 8, box 13; "Joe, Mike, and Alice" to JEJ, telegram, Sept. 9, 1986, file 15, box 114; both in Jonsson Papers.

49. JEJ, script for UTD commencement address, May 22, 1982, file 16, box 88, Jonsson Papers.

50. "Ex-Mayor Is Determined to Create Engineering School," *Dallas Times Herald,* June 5, 1983.

51. Sol Goodell to JEJ, Jan. 31, 1985, file 2, box 86, Jonsson Papers.

52. Ibid.; Kent Black to JEJ, May 16, 1985; Robert H. Rutford to JEJ, June 16, 1987, file 2, box 86, Jonsson Papers.

53. "Remarks, Dedication of the UT-Dallas Engineering Building," Oct. 8, 1992, in ibid.

54. Scherry F. Johnson to JEJ, Oct. 9, 1992, in ibid.

55. "Medical Center Plans Expansion," *Dallas Morning News*, Dec. 5, 1991.

56. "Out of the Barracks," *Dallas Morning News*, Dec. 5, 1991, file 18, box 90, Jonsson Papers.

57. *Dedication of the Erik and Margaret Jonsson Medical and Surgical Hospital*, brochure, Sept. 2, 1970, file 18; "Baylor Opens a New Hospital," *Dallas Times Herald*, Sept. 6, 1970, file 18; news release, "Erik and Margaret Jonsson . . . Add Dimension to City and Invest in Community Health," file 20; all in box 101, Jonsson Papers.

58. *Opening Ceremony: Margaret Jonsson Charlton Methodist Hospital, Sunday, December 7, 1975*, brochure, file 7; Glenn Scott to Mr. and Mrs. J. Erik Jonsson, Dec. 9, 1975, file 6; "Methodists Seek Funds to Build Branch Hospital," *Oak Cliff Tribune*, Mar. 1, 1972, file 6; all in box 104, Jonsson Papers.

59. Philip R. Jonsson to Jonsson Foundation trustees, memorandum, June 5, 1975, and attachment, "UCLA's Cancer Center," file 9, box 105, Jonsson Papers.

60. "A Brief History of the Jonsson Comprehensive Cancer Center (JCCC)," appearing in the program for Gala 90: Sunday in the Park, Feb. 4, 1990, file 9, box 105; Sherman M. Mellinkoff, MD, to Philip R. Jonsson, Aug. 18, 1976, file 13, box 90; Kenneth I. Shine to Kenneth A. Jonsson, Dec. 1, 1989, file 5, box 82; all in Jonsson Papers.

61. *Tulane University, the Board of Visitors, 1962*, pamphlet, file 11, box 90, Jonsson Papers; "Tulane Honors John Erik Jonsson," printed citation, and undated program for dedication of the Erik and Margaret Commons and Learning Center, May 6, 1988, file 12, box 90, Jonsson Papers.

62. JEJ to William K. Stone, Dec. 15, 1989, file 12, box 89, Jonsson Papers.

63. "Texas Instrument President First Speaker of Year," *Harbus News*, Sept. 25, 1959, file 39, box 5; "Jonsson Library of Government Documents, 1988–1989 Annual Report," file 9, box 90; both in Jonsson Papers.

64. Letters describing the Margaret Jonsson Plaza from President John D. Moseley to Mrs. Jonsson are in file 22, box 88, Jonsson Papers.

65. Robert F. Sasseen to JEJ, Oct. 21, 1982, file 14, box 90, Jonsson Papers.

66. "Private School Facility Planned at $1.5 Million," *Dallas Times Herald*, Feb. 19, 1968; "The Lamplighter School," *Texas Monthly*, Sept. 1974, 74–75; promotional piece entitled "The Lamplighter School $1,500,000 Development Fund," July 1968; all in file 22, box 89, Jonsson Papers; "Jonssons Help Dedicate 'New' Lamplighter School, *Dallas Morning News*, Mar. 19, 1972.

67. JEJ to Mr. and Mrs. Herbert W. Smith, Sept. 29, 1978, file 4, box 8, Jonsson Papers; "Private School Facility Planned"; "Lamplighter School"; "Lamplighter School $1,500,000 Development Fund."

68. Tate to JEJ, Oct. 1, 1970, file 6, box 31; James E. Brooks to JEJ, May 5, 1975, file 3, box 9; JEJ to James H. Zumberge, Mar. 7, 1979, file 7, box 8; all in Jonsson Papers.

69. Texas Instruments, "50 Years of Innovation: The History of Texas Instruments—A Story of People and Their Ideas," June 1980, file 4, and "The Semiconductor Becomes a New Marketing Force," *Business Week*, Aug. 24, 1974, 34–35, 39, file 3; both in box 112, Jonsson Papers.

70. JEJ, "Texas Instruments—Metroplex Growth Company," typescript of an article written in 1976 for the *Southwest Metroplex Newsletter*, file 5, box 7, Jonsson Papers.

71. Richard West, "The Texas Monthly Reporter," *Texas Monthly*, Feb. 1977, 53.

72. "Former TI Chairman Pat Haggerty, 66, Dies," *Dallas Morning News*, Oct. 2, 1980.

73. First Quarter and Stockholders Meeting Report, 1984, TI, 2.

74. Smith, "When the Storm Sleeps," 148–49; Philip Jonsson, interview by the author, Jan. 20, 2005, Dallas.

75. MJR, interview by the author, Dec. 30, 2004, Dallas; Philip Jonsson interview, Jan. 20, 2005.

76. Malcolm Bedell to JEJ, Aug. 20, 1974, file 21, box 114, Jonsson Papers.

77. Charles M. Bedell to JEJ, May 13, 1978, file 2, box 8; JEJ to Donald H. McAllister, Oct. 15, 1975, file 5, box 9; JEJ to R. Palmer Baker Jr., Sept. 27, 1978, file 4, box 8; JEJ to Mr. and Mrs. Cecil Green, Oct. 26, 1977, file 12, box 7; all in Jonsson Papers.

78. JEJ to Dr. B. C. Halley Jr., Sept. 11, 1979, file 8; JEJ to Philip A. Fisher, June 18, 1979, file 9; JEJ to O'Neil Ford, Dec. 10, 1979, file 10; all in box 8, Jonsson Papers.

79. JEJ to Mrs. Dorothy Burt, Dec. 27, 1979, file 10, box 8, Jonsson Papers.

80. JEJ to Mr. and Mrs. Harold Gores, Jan. 3, 1982, file 14; JEJ to George Low, Mar. 22, 1982, file 10; JEJ to Coy Eklund, July 16, 1982, file 11; all in box 13, Jonsson Papers.

81. JEJ to H. M. Rozendaal, Nov. 30, 1983, file 14, box 13, Jonsson Papers.

82. "Margaret Jonsson, Philanthropist, Dies," *Dallas Morning News*, Jan. 17, 1984.

83. Dickson's message, given on Jan. 18, 1984, is in the MJR Papers.

84. "TI Founder & Mayor Erik Jonsson Enjoying Old Age, Walking at 83," *Aerobics*, Oct. 1984, 1–2, 8, file 17, box 13, Jonsson Papers; "Nutritional Recommendation for John E. Jonsson, April 4, 1984," file 2, box 115, Jonsson Papers.

85. "The Swedish-American-of-the-Year Celebration for the Year 1983," *Vasa Star*, Jan. 1984, 10, file 31, box 104; JEJ to Harold Gores, n.d. [1983], file 14, box 13; both in Jonsson Papers.

86. JEJ to the Hon. Franklin S. Forsberg and Mrs. Forsberg, Stockholm, Apr. 23, 1984, file 16, box 13, Jonsson Papers.

87. JEJ to Mr. and Mrs. Michael Jonsson, May 15, 1984, file 16, box 13, Jonsson Papers.

88. Nelle Johnston to Graham Allison, Jan. 4, 1985, file 15, box 114; JEJ to Mr. and Mrs. Robert Moschell, Mar. 12, 1985, file 13, box 13; both in Jonsson Papers.

89. JEJ to his three children, Sept. 30, 1985, file 13, box 13; Philip Jonsson to JEJ, Sept. 6, 1985, file 19, box 114; both in Jonsson Papers.

90. "Former Dallas Mayor Jonsson Given Award for Life of Service," *Dallas Morning News*, June 17, 1987.

91. Dick Davis, telephone interview by the author, Jan. 31, 2005.

92. Suzanne Jonsson to JEJ, Sept. 29, 1985, file 19, box 114, Jonsson Papers.

93. Martha to JEJ, Feb. 20, 1988, July 5, Aug. 14, and Nov. 4 1989, file 9, box 114, Jonsson Papers; MJR interview, Dec. 30, 2004.

94. JEJ to Decherd, Meyerson, O'Donnell, Sept. 17, 1990; "City Leaders Honor Jonsson," *Dallas Morning News*, Sept. 15, 1990; "Jonsson's Vision," *Dallas Morning News*, Sept. 18, 1990; all in file 31, box 103, Jonsson Papers.

95. MJR, interview by the author, Oct. 26, 2005.

96. Schrader interview, Jan. 20, 2005; MJR interview, Dec. 30, 2004.

97. MJR interview, Dec. 30, 2004.

98. Ibid.

99. JEJ, Sixth Floor Museum oral history; "J. Erik Jonsson," Oral History Collection, Sixth Floor Museum at Dealey Plaza, interview 2, conducted by Wes Wise and Bob Porter, Aug. 17, 1992; J. Erik Jonsson, interview by Alan Mason, Mayor's Oral History Program of East Texas State University and the Dallas Public Library, June 26, 1980, 2, file 1, box 1, Jonsson Papers; D/FW Airport interviews with JEJ conducted by Mike Hazel on Nov. 18, 1993, and by Joe Dealey on Dec. 13, 1993, both in file 3, box 114, Jonsson Papers.

100. "The Greater Dallas Chamber of Commerce J. Erik Jonsson Award," announcement, Sept. 1, 1988, file 20, box 102, Jonsson Papers.

101. JEJ to Trammell Crow, Feb. 7, 1992, file 8, box 109, Jonsson Papers.

102. Bill Cooper to members of the Old Guard, Aug. 3, 1994, in ibid.; front-page photograph, *Dallas Morning News*, Dec. 15, 1994.

103. Sewell interview.

104. William R. Guffey to JEJ, Mar. 10, 1995, with the "letter" from JEJ to Roy Guffey, postmarked Sept. 28, 1950, file 22, box 114, Jonsson Papers.

105. John E. Jonsson, Case No. 95-03345-P3, Probate Court No. 3, Dallas County, Texas.

106. Bruce Tomaso, "Ex-Mayor J. Erik Jonsson Dies at 93," *Dallas Morning News*, Sept. 2, 1995.

107. Ibid.

108. "A Service of Celebration and Remembrance for J. Erik Jonsson," Steve Jonsson Papers, Little Rock, Arkansas.

109. "Memorial Service Set for J. Erik Jonsson," *Dallas Morning News*, Sept. 4, 1994; "Ex-Mayor Jonsson Mourned," *Dallas Morning News*, Sept. 6, 1995.

110. John N. Jackson to JEJ, Dec. 3, 1977, file 13, box 7, Jonsson Papers.

111. "Erik, 1901–1995," advertisement, *Dallas Morning News*, Sept. 5, 1991.

Bibliography

Archival Sources

J. Erik Jonsson Collection, A98.2191, DeGolyer Library, Southern Methodist University, Dallas, Texas; cited as Jonsson Papers.

    The rich variety of documents in this collection, filling 170 large boxes, represents Jonsson's lifelong habit of preserving correspondence, memorandums, speeches, telephone logs, newspaper and magazine clippings, invitations, birthday cards, and such. They relate to all aspects of his life—personal, business, political, civic, educational, and philanthropic. The collection includes a large number of photographs, videos, tape recordings, certificates, plaques, and artifacts. All these items are described in a 363-page finding guide prepared by the library staff.

Bruce Alger Papers, Texas and Dallas History, J. Erik Jonsson Central Public Library, Dallas.

Earle Cabell Papers, DeGolyer Special Collections, Southern Methodist University.

D/FW Airport Public Affairs Department records.

Cecil H. and Ida Green Papers, Special Collections, University of Texas at Dallas.

Holland McCombs Papers, University of Tennessee at Martin.

Margaret Jonsson Rogers Papers, privately held; cited as MJR Papers.

Steve Jonsson Papers, privately held.

Published Works

Advance. "EEF Intends to Give 500 Acres to UT-Dallas." Mar. 20, 1975.

Aerobics. "TI Founder & Mayor Erik Jonsson Enjoying Old Age, Walking at 83." Oct. 1984.

Aluminum by Alcoa. Alcoa, 1969.

American Heritage. "The Time Machine: 1947." Dec. 1997.

The Annual Record of the Tau Omega Fraternity. Troy, N.Y.: Rensselaer Polytechnic Institute, 1920.

Architectural Forum. "Industrial Plant." Aug. 1949.

———. "A Plant with an Upstairs Basement." Sept. 1958.

At Rensselaer. "Interview with a Goal Setter." Summer 1985.

Baker, Ray Palmer. *A Chapter in American Education: Rensselaer Polytechnic Institute, 1824–1924.* New York: Scribner's Sons, 1964.

Barrington, Theodore. "A Tribute to Cecil Green." *Leading Edge,* Apr. 2004.

Bello, Francis. "The Year of the Transistor." *Fortune,* Mar. 1953.

Berkner, L. V. "Graduate Education in the Southwest." *Journal of the Graduate Research Center,* May 1961.

———. "Renaissance in the Southwest." *Saturday Review,* June 3, 1961.

Brown, Robert U. "Shop Talk at Thirty." *Editor and Publisher,* Nov. 29, 1969.

Business Week. "For Company Presidents, More—Not Less—'Outside' Activity." Aug. 23, 1958.
————. "Forecasting a Turn for the Better." May 24, 1958.
————. "Research Packed with Ph.D.s." Dec. 22, 1956.
Cray, Ed. *Chrome Colossus: General Motors and Its Times.* New York: McGraw-Hill, 1980.
Cunningham, Joe. "Jonsson of Texas' Transworld 'TexIns.'" *Texas Parade,* Mar. 1958.
Dallas. "Chamber Members Elect Seven New Directors." Dec. 1954.
————. "Science Research Center Dedication." Dec. 1964.
————. "SMU Research and Computer Centers Mark Progressive Bond." Nov. 1957.
Delta Mu News. "Four Delegates Attend Congress Held This Summer in Houston." Oct. 1958.
Excalibur. "Convention Personalities," Aug.–Sept. 1948.
————. "Touche!" Dec. 1947–Jan. 1948.
————. "Ye Editor Gossips: Dallas, Texas." Mar.–Apr. 1943.
Fairbanks, Robert B. *For the City as a Whole: Planning, Politics, and the Public Interest in Dallas, Texas, 1900–1965.* Columbus: Ohio State Univ. Press, 1998.
Goals for Dallas. Dallas: Goals for Dallas, 1966.
Goals for Dallas: Achieving the Goals. Dallas: Goals for Dallas, 1970.
Green, Cecil H. "Dr. John Clarence Karcher (1894–1978): Father of the Reflection Seismograph." *Geophysics: The Journal of the Society of Exploration Geophysicists,* June 1979.
Grimes, Johnnie Marie. *Willis M. Tate: Views and Interviews.* Dallas: SMU Press, 1978.
Haggerty, P. E. *Management Philosophies and Practices of Texas Instruments, Incorporated.* Dallas: Texas Instruments, 1965.
Harris, William B. "The Electronic Business." *Fortune,* June 1957.
Hazel, Michael V. *The Dallas Public Library: Celebrating a Century of Service, 1901–2001.* Denton: Univ. of North Texas Press, 2001.
Janson, Florence Edith. *The Background of Swedish Immigration, 1840–1930.* Chicago: Univ. of Chicago Press, 1931.
Jonsson, Erik. "Controls for Growth." In *Controls and Techniques for Better Management.* General Management Series 176. New York: American Management Association, 1955.
————. "Goals for Dallas." *Nation's Cities,* Nov. 1970.
Journal of the Graduate Research Center. "Graduate Education in the Southwest." Mar. 29, 1961.
L'Hommedieu, R. R. "The Wage Earner's Automobile." *Overland Monthly,* Jan. 1913.
Life Lines. "Minority Coalescence in Dallas." Dec. 26, 1969.
Look. "All-America Cities 1970." Mar. 23, 1971.
Lyons, Sam B. "A Summit Meeting of Business." *Finance,* June 15, 1958.
Management Methods. "Problem Solving Clinic." Dec. 1957.
Manchester, William. *The Death of a President: November 20–November 25, 1963.* New York: Harper and Row, 1967.
McDonald, John. "The Men Who Made T.I." *Fortune,* Nov. 1961.
————. "Where Texas Instruments Goes from Here." *Fortune,* Dec. 1961.
Morison, Samuel Eliot. *History of United States Naval Operations.* Vol. 10, *The Atlantic Battle Won, May 1943–May 1945.* Boston: Little, Brown, 1964.
Murphy, Mary Ann. "History of the Semiconductor Industry: The Birth of Texas Instruments." *Circuit News,* Apr. 15, 1979.
The New Handbook of Texas. Edited by Ron Tyler. 6 vols. Austin: Texas State Historical Association, 1996.
Newsweek. "The Tiny Transistor." Sept. 6, 1941.
Oil and Gas Journal. "Sixty-Three Discoveries of Pools on Gulf Coast Are Credited to the Use of Geophysics." Oct. 5, 1933.
Oil Weekly. "Geophysical Service Capital Stock Purchased." Nov. 17, 1941.
Oppenheimer, Evelyn, and Bill Porterfield. *The Book of Dallas.* New York: Doubleday, 1977.
Payne, Darwin. *Big D: Triumph and Troubles of an American Supercity in the 20th Century.* Dallas: Three Forks, 2000.
————. *Indomitable Sarah: The Life of Judge Sarah T. Hughes.* Dallas: SMU Press, 2004.

————, and Kathy Fitzpatrick. *From Prairie to Planes: How Dallas and Fort Worth Overcame Politics and Personalities to Build One of the World's Biggest and Busiest Airports.* Dallas: Three Forks, 1999.

PR Reporter. "Dallas & World Opinion: So Much To Do." Dec. 9, 1963.

Proposals for Achieving the Goals. Dallas: Goals for Dallas, 1969.

Proubasta, Dolores. "Erik Jonsson." *Geophysics: The Leading Edge of Exploration,* June 1986.

Rensselaer Review. "Erik Jonsson—Millions from Microminiatures." Winter 1964.

Riordan, Michael, and Lillian Hoddeson. *Crystal Fire: The Birth of the Information Age.* New York: Norton, 1997.

Robertson, Herbert. *The ABCs of De: A Primer on Everette Lee DeGolyer, Sr., 1886–1956.* Dallas: Red Horse, 2002.

Rubenstein, James M. *Making and Selling Cars: Innovation and Change in the U.S. Automotive Industry.* Baltimore: Johns Hopkins Univ. Press, 2001.

Saturday Review. "Engineer of the Intellect: John Erik Jonsson." June 3, 1961.

Science Digest. "Tubeless Radios." Sept. 1948.

Sheldon, William H. *Atlas of Men: A Guide for Somatotyping the Adult Male of All Ages.* New York: Harper and Bros., 1954.

Shrock, Robert R. *Cecil and Ida Green: Philanthropists Extraordinary.* Cambridge, Mass.: MIT Press, 1989.

Smith, Richard Austin. "How Business Failed Dallas." *Fortune,* July 1964.

Smith, William G. "Erik Jonsson: TI's Founder Began by Minding Dad's Store." *Texas Business,* June 1980.

SMU Mustang. "Ceremony Commemorates Science Information Center." Nov.–Dec. 1960.

————. "Distinguished Scientist Comes to GRC." Feb. 1961.

————. "Fine Arts Project Given Significant Support." Feb. 1961.

————. "Historic McFarlin Rededicated." Jan.–Feb. 1962.

Sorenson, Theodore C. *Kennedy.* New York: Harper and Row, 1965.

Southwestern Purchaser. "Among Ourselves." Aug. 1938.

————. "Eric Jonsson Elected President Dallas Association." Apr. 1938.

————. "Tanner Elected President Dallas Purchasing Agents Association." May 1937.

Thometz, Carol Estes. *The Decision-Makers: The Power Structure of Dallas.* Dallas: Southern Methodist Univ. Press, 1963.

Time. "Newcomer's Growth." Apr. 8, 1957.

Tinkle, Lon. *Mr. De: A Biography of Everette Lee DeGolyer.* Boston: Little, Brown, 1970.

Watson, Thomas J., Jr., and Peter Petre. *Father, Son & Co.: My Life at IBM and Beyond.* New York: Bantam, 1990.

Ways, Max. "A Hall of Fame for Business Leadership." *Fortune,* Jan. 1975.

West, Richard. "The Texas Monthly Reporter." *Texas Monthly,* Feb. 1977.

Wiseman, Carter. *I. M. Pei: A Profile in American Architecture.* New York: Abrams, 1990.

Wolfe, Jane. *The Murchisons: The Rise and Fall of a Texas Dynasty.* New York: St. Martin's, 1989.

UNPUBLISHED WORKS

"J. E. Jonsson and Goals for Dallas." Paper prepared at Harvard University, 1985. Steve Jonsson Papers.

Jonsson, J. E. "The Fabrication of Aluminum: Present Practice." File 4, box 116, Jonsson Papers.

[Martin, Kenneth R.] Untitled history of Texas Instruments prepared by History Associates, Inc., 1982–85. Commissioned by Texas Instruments. Files 1–19, box 95, Jonsson Papers.

McCombs, Holland. "The Tall Story of Texas Instruments," [1960]. McCombs Papers.

Smith, Bryan F., with Jim Henderson. "When the Storm Sleeps: The Hard Fall of Texas Instruments and the Case for Boardroom Independence," 1995.

Wilson, Robert A. "Erik Jonsson: American Visionary." File 1, box 114, Jonsson Papers.

INTERVIEWS CONDUCTED BY THE AUTHOR

Charlton, George. June 23, 2004, Dallas.
Cothrum, William E. Telephone interview, Aug. 5, 2004.
Cullum, Charles G. June 17, 2004, Dallas.
Davis, Dick. Telephone interview, Jan. 31, 2005.
Friedman, Bayard. May 15, 1998, Fort Worth.
Godbold, Bryghte. July 2004.
Haberecht, Rolf. May 24, 2005, Dallas.
Johnson, J. Lee, III. May 6, 1998, Fort Worth.
Jonsson, Philip R. Dec. 1, 2003, and Jan. 20, 2005, both in Dallas.
McDonald, W. Scott. Aug. 2004, Dallas.
O'Donnell, Peter, Jr. June 14, 2004, Dallas.
Perot, H. Ross. Telephone interview, July 15, 2005.
Rogers, Margaret Jonsson. Mar. 3, 2004; Oct. 14, 2003; May 14, 2004; Dec. 30, 2004; and Oct. 26, 2005, all in Dallas.
Schoellkopf, John. Aug. 15, 2003, Dallas.
Schrader, George. Jan. 20, 2005, Dallas.
Sewell, Carl. June 20, 2004, Dallas.
Smith, Bryan F. Apr. 12, 2004; May 20,2004; Sept. 8, 2005; Feb. 22, 2005; and May 27, 2005, all in Dallas.
Stahl, Sid. Telephone interview, Sept. 3, 2004.
Thomsen, C. J. (Tommy). June 22, 2004, Dallas.

INTERVIEWS CONDUCTED BY OTHERS

Green, Cecil. Interview by Larry Secrest, June 17, 1970. Dolph Briscoe Center for American History, University of Texas at Austin.
Johnson, J. Lee, III. Interview by D/FW Airport Public Affairs Department, Jan. 13, 1994.
Johnston, Nelle. Interview by Alan Mason, Aug. 28, 1980. Transcribed in 1983. East Texas State University and Dallas Public Library.
Jonsson, J. Erik. Interview by Mavis Bryant, May 30, 1972. MJR Papers.
———. Interview by L.C., n.d.
———. Interview by Joe Dealey Jr., Dec. 13, 1993.
———. Interview by Alice Hallis Fortner, July 15, 1993.
———. Interview by Michael V. Hazel, Nov. 18, 1993.
———. Interview by Philip R. Jonsson and Steve W. Jonsson, July 21, 1978.
———. Interview by Alan Mason, June 26, 1980. Mayor's Oral History Program, East Texas State University and the Dallas Public Library.
———. Interview by Jim Mitchell. Broadcast on WFAA-TV, Apr. 26, 1971. Transcript published by WFAA-TV as "A Conversation with Mayor Erik Jonsson."
———. Interviews by Gerald Saxon, June 26, 1980, and May 29, 1981. Mayor's Oral History Program, East Texas State University and the Dallas Public Library.
———. Interviews by Larry Secrest, Sept. 12 and Nov. 28, 1970. Dolph Briscoe Center for American History, University of Texas at Austin.
———. Interview by Buzz Selby, May 10, 1979. Typescript printed by Texas Instruments under the title "Personal Recollections and Sayings of J. Erik Jonsson."
———. Interviews by Wes Wise and Bob Porter, June 30, 1992, Aug. 17, 1992, and Nov. 10, 1992. Oral History Collection, Sixth Floor Museum at Dealey Plaza, Dallas.
Jonsson, Kenneth Alan. Interviews by Richard Tuck, Aug. 28, Sept. 6, and Sept. 13, 2002.
Jonsson, Philip. Interviews by Richard Tuck, Sept. 2, 2002, and July 19, 2003, both in Dallas.
McCombs, Holland. As a Dallas correspondent for Time-Life, McCombs's interviews with key Texas Instruments officials became the basis for *Fortune*'s two-part series in November and December 1961. The interviews are in the Holland McCombs Papers, University of Tennessee

at Martin. His interviewees included William C. Edwards, Pat Haggerty, W. T. Harris, J. Erik
Jonsson, W. F. Joyce, Eugene McDermott, Robert W. Olson, Mark Shepherd, C. J. Thomsen,
Gordon Teal, and E. J. Toomey.

McDermott, Eugene. Interview by Larry Secrest and Gary Hoffman Apr. 9, 1971. Dolph Briscoe
Center for American History, University of Texas at Austin.

McDonald, W. Scott. Interview by Alan Mason, July 7, 1980. East Texas State University and the
Dallas Public Library.

Pei, I. M. Interview by Bonnie A. Lovell, Aug. 1, 2002. Henry Moore's *The Dallas Piece* Oral History Project, Dallas Public Library.

Schrader, George. Interview by Gerald Saxon, May 14, 1981. East Texas State University and the
Dallas Public Library.

Stovall, R. M. Interview by D/FW Airport Public Affairs Department, Nov. 23, 1993.

Thomsen, C. J. Interview by Richard Tuck, Aug. 23, 2002.

RECORDINGS

J. Erik Jonsson made a series of autobiographical recordings, probably in the late 1970s; they are
in box 166, Jonsson Papers. There is no interviewer, and the recordings are without docu-
mentation. They appear under a number of titles, including "Jonsson's First Days at RPI,"
"Fraternity Life and ALCOA," and "Alcoa and Married Life."

Index

Intercontinental Rubber Co., 83–84
International Geophysical Year, 106
Irving, Texas, 165, 166, 167

Jackson, Albert, 117
Jackson, J.B., Jr., 177, 178–79, 180
Jackson, John N., 221
Jochim, John A., 32–33
Jochim-Jonsson, Inc., 33
Johansen (cigar store employee), 7–8
John Birch Society, 118
Johnson, Gifford K., 110
Johnson, J. Lee, III, 141, 142, 150, 153, 156
Johnson, Lady Bird, 120
Johnson, Lyndon B., 109, 120, 147, 185
Johnson, Peter, 177, 178–79, 180, 220
Johnson, Philip, 126
Johnson, Tom L., 131
Johnston, Nelle, 122, 133, 168–69, 171, 173, 174,
    192, 200, 214, 216, 217–18
Jones, Jerry, 168
Jones, Margo, 79
Jones, Morton, 87
Jonsson, Anne (Kenneth Alan Jonsson's
    daughter), 102
Jonsson Cancer Center, 211
Jonsson, Christina Ann (Philip Jonsson's
    daughter), 102
Jonsson, Eileen Margaret (Petie) (Philip
    Jonsson's daughter), 102
Jonsson, Ellen Carlotta Palmquist (JEJ's
    mother), 30, 103
        early life, 2–3
        work in family cigar shop, 4, 10–11
        trips to Staten Island, 6–7
        stressing culture, education for her son,
            5, 13
        her illnesses, 13, 28, 34–35, 36–37
Jonsson, Emily (Margaret Ellen Jonsson's
    daughter), 113
Jonsson, Erik (Kenneth Alan Jonsson's son),
    102
Jonsson, Erik, School of Engineering and
    Computer Science, 210
Jonsson, Erik, Center for Research in
    Molecular Genetics and Human Disease,
    210
Jonsson, Erik and Margaret, Commons and
    Learning Center, 211
Jonsson, Erik and Margaret, Medical and
    Surgical Hospital, 211
Jonsson Foundation, 220
Jonsson, J. Erik Aviation Award, 203
Jonsson, J. Erik Award (for private citizen), 219

Jonsson, J. Erik Award for Voluntarism, 114
Jonsson, J. Erik Ethics Award, 212
Jonsson, John Erik:
    his childhood in Brooklyn, 1–9
    his father and his influence, 3–6, 7–8, 11,
        12
    his mother and her influence, 2–6
    his adolescence in New Jersey, 10–17
    his insistence on continuing his
        education, 11–13
    his college days at Rensselaer, 16–26
    as a Rensselaer alumnus, 26, 67, 71,
        110–111, 112, 207, 211, 221
    his part–time jobs, 13–15, 18–22, 23–24,
        31–32, 221
    and writing as a career goal, 12–13, 16,
        200
    his motorcycle dealership, 20–22
    his courtship and marriage, 29–30
    his employment at Alcoa, 27–31, 33,
        38–39, 41–42
    and building and selling radios, 31–32
    his auto dealership, 32–36
    his financial problems and bankruptcy,
        34–38, 45–47
    his work at Geophysical Service, Inc.,
        (GSI) in Newark, 39–47
    his work at GSI in Dallas, 47–52, 54–55
    and negotiating for GSI ownership with
        three partners, 58–62
    and gaining war-time government
        contracts for GSI, 62–64
    his domestic life in New Jersey, 31–32, 33,
        36, 41, 42, 45–46
    and births of his children, 31, 45, 52–53
    and residences in New Jersey and Dallas,
        31, 33, 35, 36, 45, 47, 56, 102,115–16, 216,
        220
    his domestic life in Dallas, 47–51, 52–53,
        56–57, 66, 78–79, 101–103, 115, 170, 183,
        200, 214, 215, 216, 217–18
    contrasts New Jersey and Dallas, 42, 48,
        49, 133
    and family conference about his business
        goals, 66, 215
    his early relationship with Pat Haggerty,
        62, 64, 67–74
    and establishing a manufacturing unit,
        68–69, 70
    and naming of Texas Instruments, 74–75
    his leadership role at Texas Instruments,
        74–75, 76, 81–85, 94–96, 97, 100, 103–
        104, 143, 173, 201, 213–14
    his handling of financial affairs, 71–72, 81,